The Flight of the Mind

The Flight
of the Mind

*Virginia Woolf's Art
and Manic-Depressive Illness*

THOMAS C. CARAMAGNO

University of California Press

Berkeley   Los Angeles   Oxford

University of California Press
Berkeley and Los Angeles, California

University of California Press, Ltd.
Oxford, England

© 1992 by
The Regents of the University of California

Printed in the United States of America
9   8   7   6   5   4   3   2   1

The paper used in this publication meets the minimum requirements of
American National Standard for Information Sciences—Permanence of
Paper for Printed Library Materials, ANSI Z39.48–1984. ∞

Library of Congress Cataloging-in-Publication Data

Caramagno, Thomas C.
    The flight of the mind : Virginia Woolf's art and manic-depressive
illness / Thomas C. Caramagno.
        p.   cm.
    Includes bibliographical references and index.
    ISBN 0-520-07280-4 (cloth : alk. paper)
    1. Woolf, Virginia, 1882–1941—Criticism and interpretation.
2. Woolf, Virginia, 1882–1941—Biography—Health. 3. Novelists,
English—20th century—Biography—Health. 4. Manic-depressive
psychoses—Patients—Biography. 5. Literature and mental illness.
I. Title.
PR6045.O72Z566   1992
823'.912—dc20
[B]   91-38836
                                                                    CIP

This book is dedicated to my wife and colleague
Dr. Susan Laura Wing
and to the memory of my father
Joseph Caramagno
(1915–1991)

I am not the one you think I was
Rather, yonder you have
With your pens given me another being
And another breath with your life. . .

You have praised the image of
Your very own idea
And being yours, it well deserves
Your very own applause.

—Sor Juana Ines De La Cruz
(Mexico, 1651–95;
trans. Amanda Powell)

But suicides have a special language.
Like carpenters they want to know *which* tools.
They never ask *why build.*

—Anne Sexton, "Wanting to Die"

Contents

List of Figures and Illustrations xi

Introduction 1

1. "I Owned to Great Egotism":
   The Neurotic Model in Woolf Criticism 6

2. "Never Was Anyone So Tossed Up & Down
   by the Body As I Am":
   The Symptoms of Manic-Depressive Illness 33

3. "But What Is the Meaning of 'Explained' It?"
   Countertransference and Modernism 75

4. "In Casting Accounts, Never Forget to Begin with
   the State of the Body":
   Genetics and the Stephen Family Line 97

5. "How Completely He Satisfied Her Is Proved
   by the Collapse":
   Emblematic Events in Family History 114

6. "How Immense Must Be the Force of Life":
   The Art of Autobiography and Woolf's Bipolar Theory
   of Being 134

7. "A Novel Devoted to Influenza":
   Reading without Resolution in *The Voyage Out* 156

8. "Does Anybody Know Mr. Flanders?"
   Bipolar Cognition and Syncretistic Vision in *Jacob's Room* 185

9. "The Sane & the Insane, Side by Side":
   The Object-Relations of Self-Management in *Mrs. Dalloway* 210

10. "It Is Finished":
    Ambivalence Resolved, Self Restored in *To the Lighthouse* 244

11. "I Do Not Know Altogether Who I Am":
    The Plurality of Intrasubjective Life in *The Waves* 270

Epilogue: Science and Subjectivity   296

Afterword, by Dr. Kay Redfield Jamison   303

Appendix: Virginia Woolf's Mood Swing Chart (1895–1941)   307

Notes   313

Works Cited   335

Index   349

Figures and Illustrations

Figures

Figure 1. Peak occurrence of suicide by month   61
Figure 2. Stephen family affective disorders   100

Illustrations

(following p. 118)
Leslie Stephen
Harriet ("Minny") Thackeray
Julia Duckworth
Anne Thackeray
Virginia Stephen
Virginia Woolf

Introduction

In this interdisciplinary study of Virginia Woolf I reexamine her madness and her fiction in the light of recent discoveries about the biological basis of manic-depressive illness—findings allied with drug therapies that today help nearly one million American manic-depressives to live happier, more productive lives. In the real world of the clinic, the use of lithium, anti-depressants, and antipsychotics has revolutionized psychiatric care for bipolar disorder and produced remissions in cases that thirty years ago would have been considered hopeless. In the rarefied atmosphere of academia, however, many psychoanalytically inclined literary critics cling to the outmoded, simplistic Freudian model of this disorder as a neurotic conflict that the patient is, either consciously or unconsciously, unwilling to resolve.

By integrating neuroscience, psychobiography, and literary theory, I challenge these critics' often disparaging evaluations of Woolf's life and art and argue against the arbitrary and subjective practice of reading all symptoms or texts as neurotic disguises supposedly obscuring a causative origin. Freud was a great pioneer in the study of the human psyche, but he himself, given today's knowledge about the brain, would have moved on, incorporating his most enduring insights with ongoing research in neuroscience. We literary scholars can no longer afford to remain comfortably ignorant of the mechanisms of the brain or to pretend that, in any particular biographical case (and especially that one in which we have invested so much of our self-esteem and academic destiny), biology did not affect the mind. As academics, we are in the business of proving our mastery over our material and ourselves; perhaps that is why we are ungenerous toward those artists who show less control. But when we unthinkingly blame the victim for his or her illness, we simplify our work by ignoring the mind/brain nexus from which everything most human about literature arises. Neuroscience at the least teaches literature to soften its focus on the infantile, the cowardly, and the regressive in its subjects.

1

The science/literature model I use silences, not Woolf's own voice, but the voices of those Freudians who pontificate upon matters that cross the line between brain and mind without first investigating where the line is drawn or what it might mean for their conclusions. The biological realities of manic-depressive illness limit the critic's freedom to tie events in Woolf's life to symptoms that seem metaphorically similar. Biology lifts from Woolf's shoulders the derogatory weight of responsibility for her illness. It allows us to see that her fiction was not necessarily produced by hypothetical unconscious conflicts, her supposed flight from sex, or her morbid preoccupation with death—all the favorite Freudian themes which, not coincidentally, sustain sexist assumptions about the nature of the creative woman. I argue that Woolf's novels were produced by a sane, responsive, insightful woman—hardly a surprise, since, like "normal" individuals, most bipolars are thoughtful, deliberate, perceptive, and responsible when they are not ill.[1] Manic-depressive illness is *periodic*; it comes and goes, and when it is gone, individuals are not sick or insane (unlike neurotics, whose unconscious conflicts seep into and determine even "normal" behavior). By remembering this, we can hear what Woolf wants to say, or remember, or feel, without thinking it must somehow be implicated in a twisted desire to remain ill.

But can a neurobiography be written to present the psychological consequences of genetic makeup, or biological dysfunction, infection, or injury, and still hold meaning for literary readers? Must ego find only its own glittering image interesting? The biological base upon which modern psychiatric theory builds has much to teach us. Subjectivity seems so self-evident to us that we do not stop to consider how much our perceptual apparatus mediates reality and limits introspection. Neuroscience tells us some very disturbing things about how complicated and problematic it is to ascribe meaning to events. Its warnings are worth hearing. I do not mean to argue that mind (or free will or subjectivity or character) is a negligible by-product of a series of chemical and electrical switches. On the contrary, a complex and creative mind seems to be the primary purpose of neurological structure, but because this is so, studying the mind requires a much more detailed knowledge of the brain than the literary psychobiographer has heretofore thought necessary.

Virginia Woolf's symptoms fulfill the manic-depressive paradigm. Taking this premise as my basis, I apply contemporary psychiatric theory to our knowledge of her life. This approach alters our reading of Woolf, explains the therapeutic value of her bold experiments in fiction, and points to the source of her profound insights into subject-object transactions and the pitfalls of literary interpretation. Chapter 1 places Woolf's disorder in a historical context, explicating the changes that have occurred since Woolf's time in biological and psychological models for the illness and demonstrating how outmoded attitudes have infected biographical approaches to Woolf. Chapters 2 and 4 present current knowledge about manic-depressive illness (also known as bipolar affective disorder)—its genetic transmission, symptoms, and cognitive distortions—both in general terms and in relation to Virginia Woolf. Chapter 3 discusses the implications of biology for psychoanalytic criticism, the function of bipolar cognitive style in creativity, and reader-response theory. In Chapters 5 and 6 I argue that Woolf learned important object-relations lessons from her psychotic breakdowns and from her family's related symptoms; she used this knowledge creatively in her theories about fiction, mental functioning, and self-structure. Studies of her life and work by psychoanalytically inclined literary critics have often resulted in a reduction of the surface multiplicity of her fiction. In the service of a psychological model that is no longer relevant to her illness, they have attempted to impose coherence upon what seems deliberate incoherence or disjointedness. I contend that her work is not a neurotic evasion or a loss of control, but an intelligent and sensitive exploration of certain components of her mood swings that undermines our traditional approach to reading a text and invites us to question how we construct meaning from a text.

Chapters 7 through 11 deal with the epistemological difficulties of interpretation. Through analyses of five of Woolf's novels, I attempt to show how these difficulties are intimately bound up with Woolf's manic-depressive illness, with an inner world that oscillated unpredictably between moments when the self seemed magically enhanced and empowered, imposing meaning and value indiscriminately on the outside world, and other moments when the emptiness and badness of the world lay revealed, corrupting (or corrupted by) the sickening self. Woolf's inconstant perceptual relationships with objects and self became one of the models by which she shaped and understood ambiguous and disturbing fictions. Her novels dramatize her struggle to read her perceptions correctly and to establish a bipolar sense of identity. Her understanding of her disorder, though fundamentally based on her personal experience of symptoms, was also influenced by her parents' maladaptive responses to loss and by her own childhood traumas, not as "Freudian" cause but as a source for cognitive model building. Woolf's lifelong quest for a "moment of being" aimed not only to resolve issues of subjective and objective knowledge but also to reconcile the conflicting psychological patterns rife in her family that resembled elements of manic-depressive illness. In assuming the role of mediator between fictionalized representatives of her family and of her seemingly bifurcated self, Woolf discovered the power and self-confidence that insight and creativity bring to the artist. By imagining and mastering psychic fragmentation in fiction, she restored form and value to her self. Today's research into interhemispheric processing suggests that the same benefits may be achieved by readers who respond to a text by successfully entertaining other selves and various reading strategies in order to explore and enjoy the brain's potential for multiple domains of consciousness.

I wish to take this opportunity to express my gratitude to certain members of the English department at the University of California, Los Angeles, for their guidance and support during the early stages of this project: Gwin J. Kolb, Jr., Barbara L. Packer, Michael Cohen, Fran Horn, Robert Kinsman, Susan D. Brienza, Romey T. Keys, Geraldine Moyle, Kathy Spencer, Ross Shideler, and John Espey. Help on general issues in psychiatry and on autism derived from conversations with Drs. Michael McGuire and Susan Smalley at UCLA's Neuropsychiatric Institute. I am personally most beholden to my mentor and dissertation director, Albert D. Hutter. His sharp questioning and exploration of new and rich areas of psychoanalytic criticism provided me with a model of academic writing that was both scholarly and exciting. My thanks go also to Kay Redfield Jamison, former director of the UCLA Affective Disorders Clinic and now associate professor in the department of psychiatry at Johns Hopkins University, and to Dr. William Cody, chief of psychiatry at Kaiser Hospital in Honolulu, for sharing their expertise in manic-depressive illness.

I thank my former colleagues in the department of English at the University of Hawaii, particularly George Simson, editor of *Biography,* Cristina Bacchilega, Arnie Edelstein, Elton Fukumoto, Robert Martin (now at Oxford), Joseph Kau, Alan Leander MacGregor, James Caron, Barbara Gottfried (now at Bentley), Val Wayne, and Stephen Canham for their interest and encouragement. Thanks also go to the industrious members of the department's Second Critical Theory Group, especially Marc Manganaro (now at Rutgers), Russell Durst (now at Ohio State), and Anne Simpson (now at California State University at Pomona).

Considerable research support for this project came from Harvard University in several forms: the award of a very timely 1989–1990 Andrew W. Mellon postdoctoral fellowship in the humanities; use of their extensive libraries (Widener for literary materials, the Houghton for unpublished letters, and Countway, the Harvard Medical School Library, for psychiatric holdings); and the criticism and encouragement of the director of the Mellon Program, Richard Hunt, the chairman of the English department, Robert Kiely, Susan Lewis, and Kathryne V. Lindberg. Support also came from a National Endowment for the Humanities summer stipend in 1988 for travel abroad to examine Leonard Woolf's diaries in the Monk's House Papers collection at the University of Sussex Library (special thanks go to Helen Bickerstaff, assistant librarian in manuscripts). Along the way I received insight and guidance from members of G.A.P. (Group for the Application of Psychology) and the Institute for the Psychological Study of the Arts at the University of Florida, Gainesville, particularly from its director, Norman N. Holland, and its associate director, Andrew Gordon, who provided several opportunities for me to present my research both in Europe and in America. Critical help also came from Alex Zwerdling of the University of California at Berkeley; David Willbern of the State University of New York at Buffalo; Jane Marcus at the City College of New York; Janice Rossen and Carol Hanbery MacKay at the University of Texas at Austin; Robert Silhou of the Université de Paris VII; Antal Bokay of the Janus Pannonius University in Pecs, Hungary; and Phyllis Franklin and the five members of the MLA's William Riley Parker Prize Selection Committee, Thomas W. Best, Stephen Booth, Mary Ann Caws, David J. DeLaura, and Blanche H. Gelfant. I particularly want to thank the students of my Woolf seminars, both at the University of Hawaii and at Harvard, for their lively discussions and open affection for Woolf.

I am most grateful to my parents, Joseph and Elizabeth Caramagno, my aunt, Jean Selden, and Catherine Lord, for their love of learning and respect for truth. Without them, this book would never have been written.

Finally, I thank my wife, Susan, for all her help and her love.

University of Nebraska
Lincoln

1 "I owned to great egotism"

The Neurotic Model in Woolf Criticism

And I haven't said anything very much, or given you any notion
of the terrific high waves, and the infernal deep gulfs, on which I
mount and toss in a few days.

(*Letters* 3: 237)

In her biography, diaries, and letters Virginia Woolf left ample evidence
to convince psychiatric specialists that she suffered from a "classical case
of manic-depressive illness."[1] Literary-psychoanalytic studies of her life
and art, however, have shied away from the biological implications of
such a diagnosis. They have focused instead on her childhood traumas,
explaining her mental breakdowns as neurotic, guilt-driven responses to
the untimely death of her mother, the patriarchy of her father, and the
sexual abuse inflicted by her half-brothers. Virginia's nephew Quentin Bell,
for instance, regards his aunt's symptoms as manifestations of a profound
longing for virginity tied to morbid guilt and repressed sexuality. Others
conclude that Woolf did not grow beyond her preoedipal attachment to
her mother, so that her lifelong sense of loss and her desperate fear of adult
sexuality alternately produced novels and madness instead of full womanhood, or that Woolf might have been driven mad by a "profound but
unconscious guilt" inspired by oedipal jealousy and an unacknowledged
wish that her mother would die. Some, conversely, claim that Woolf's
fiction functioned as a defense mechanism against grieving, against confronting unresolved feelings of guilt, defilement, anger, and loss. Given
Woolf's suicide, one critic worries that her much-touted "moments of
being" may not have been epiphanies at all but dark dissolutions of the
self, flirtations with death disclosing a misguided desire to escape her
individuality, her very self.[2]

Most recently, three book-length psychobiographies have consoli-
dated these arguments. In *Virginia Woolf and the "Lust of Creation": A*

Psychoanalytic Exploration, Shirley Panken portrays Woolf as "self-destructive, masochistic," "deeply guilt-ridden" because of her early closeness to her father, humiliated by her sexual inhibitions, and victimized by a "passive aggression [that] masks oral rage." For Panken, even Woolf's physical symptoms must be seen as psychosomatic, a "channeling of her guilt, grief, and anger."[3]

Alma H. Bond, in *Who Killed Virginia Woolf? A Psychobiography,* acknowledges that "manic-depression has an inherited, probably metabolic substructure," but then inexplicably dismisses the implications this admission has for psychology and hunts instead for oedipal and preoedipal origins of Woolf's symptoms: a mother's ambivalence, a child's masochistic wish to surrender to an idealized mother, a daughter's envy of the father's penis. Because psychoanalysis privileges mentation over metabolism, Bond concludes that Woolf "chose" to become manic or depressive as a way of avoiding growing up, and because psychoanalysis gives early events etiological priority over later, Bond resorts to an unsupported speculation that Woolf's lifelong sense of failure and self-hatred "probably" resulted from her mother's having "devalued" her daughter's feces. Working backward, Bond uses adult breakdowns to prove the existence of childhood trauma, which is then cited as the cause of psychosis. At a critical juncture, having found numerous psychological similarities between family members (which should have prompted her to grant due importance to genetic inheritance in mood disorder), she contorts logic by arguing: "As a result, although father and daughter in a genetic sense resembled each other uncannily, it seems unnecessary to postulate a biochemical factor as the major 'cause' of Virginia Woolf's manic-depressive illness."[4]

Finally, Louise DeSalvo, in *Virginia Woolf: The Impact of Childhood Sexual Abuse on Her Life and Work,* follows the old formula of explaining complex mental states in terms of simple trauma because of a metaphorical similarity between the two. DeSalvo argues that, since Woolf was sexually abused as a child and since victims of childhood abuse often develop symptoms of depression as adults, we may therefore conclude that her "madness" was not really insanity but only expressed a logical reaction to victimization. But DeSalvo's theory cannot account for full-blown mania, for the cyclic and often seasonal form of bipolar breakdowns, or for their severity (to DeSalvo, psychotic behavior is merely amplified anger), because she does not venture beyond a narrow theoretical context: the reactive depressions of incest victims. Certainly, victims of childhood abuse do suffer depressions, and DeSalvo forcefully presents their pain and argues eloquently for our understanding. But she oversimplifies etiology, for she fails to discriminate between different types of depression: (1) those depressions which result from psychological conflicts (e.g., those created by the trauma of sexual abuse), (2) those which are inherited genetically and/or physiological in origin (such as manic-depressive illness), and (3) those in which both psychological and physiological causes interact. DeSalvo dismisses "inherent madness" as an "archaic" notion and so frees herself from the task of reading recent biological research. Unwilling to consider an imposed mood disorder, she looks instead for explanations of why Woolf would want to die, and incest serves as a reasonable cause. We lack specifics about Woolf's victimization: Was it rape or unwelcome caresses? Was it frequent or rare? Was it long-term or short? The evidence is scarce and ambiguous. So DeSalvo uses the severity of Woolf's adult depressions as proof that her childhood abuse must have been rape, quite frequent, and chronic. The problem here is that inherited biochemical depression can be very severe without any preceding childhood trauma. Suicidal impulses cannot, by themselves, serve as a reliable indicator of the significance of early or late trauma, because despondency results from various conditions, some merely biochemical. And when severe depression alternates with mania in a family with a history of inherited mood disorders, unconscious conflict resulting from trauma is the least likely origin. DeSalvo's rubric for judging mental states fails to differentiate between the despair of a molested daughter and the despair of a manic-depressive. It ignores the inconvenient complexity of mind-brain interaction.[5]

Psychobiographers ignore psychobiology, in part because they are afraid of having to undertake a whole new program of self-education—reading dense biological texts, digesting unfamiliar jargon, and, perhaps worst of all, poring over psychiatric journals for late-breaking developments (nearly 1,200 reports on manic-depressive illness appear each year worldwide in medical journals). Psychoanalytic literature evolves more slowly, is frequently taught in graduate school, and has often been adapted to literary study. It also fortifies common cultural stereotypes about artists. Underlying Freudian thinking is the unspoken (and even unconscious) assumption that Virginia Woolf became a great artist *because* she was a neurotic, that her books are filled with references to death and strange desires for a depersonalized union with the cosmos because, like all neurotics, she was afraid to live fully. Books were her lonely refuge, plaintive elegies sung by a confined, poignant Lady of Shalott, half mad, half magical, more beautiful dead than alive, especially for critics. Once neuroticized, Woolf becomes the target for all sorts of accusations. Picturing her as "a damaged thing, a spoilt, wingless bird," one writer has made the sexist accusation that Virginia "would take refuge in nervous stress" to escape her marital problems.[6] Critics point to her suicide as proof of a lifelong morbidity, some even arguing that Woolf unconsciously chose drowning in the "boundaryless waters" of the Ouse to symbolize her repressed wish to merge with her dead mother.[7] Biographers value continuity in the inconvenient anarchy of an artist's life, and so they tend to view Woolf's death almost as if it were a work of art itself and her novels elaborate drafts of a suicide note.

Why should psychoanalytic criticism be so morbid? Freud's ideas about art were closely tied to the Romantic tradition, which stressed the irrational, unconscious, and reputedly insane states of mind that artistic inspiration can induce. But Freud the scientist was a thoroughgoing materialist who sought to reduce mental operations to drives and defenses. However mysterious he found the appeal of art, Freud focused his analytic attention on instinctual demands and infantile traumas, viewing art more as a fearful evasion than as a joyous exercise of skill and perception[8]—an attitude that led one ardent devotee, Frederick Crews, to express serious misgivings about the psychoanalytic method itself:

> Indeed, because the regressiveness of art is necessarily more apparent to the analytic eye than its integrative and adaptive aspects are, psychoanalytic interpretation risks drawing excessively pathological conclusions. When this risk is put together with the uncertainties plaguing metapsychology itself, one can see why Freudian criticism is always problematic and often inept.[9]

Since Crews made his denunciation, a few revisionists have begun to offer intriguing approaches to patients and/or texts in nonreductive ways. But, with the exception of feminist psychoanalytic criticism, little new light has fallen on Woolf studies, which still cherish what Crews aptly calls "the anaesthetic security" of the old Freudian bias toward the model of the neurotic artist.[10] In inexpert hands this paradigm invites misdiagnosis, because it reinforces the biographer's wish to explain mentality through events, which are, of course, the staple of life histories. Neurosis readily provides coherence for biographical data, but in past Woolf criticism it has often been a reductionist order that points backward, emphasizing the infantile and evasive in art rather than the adult and adaptive. Inevitably, the critic plays the role of the adult and casts the artist as the sick child.

This was certainly not the way Woolf's friends felt about her, as Rosamond Lehmann remembers:

> She had her share of griefs and bore them with courage and unselfishness. It is important to say this in view of the distasteful myths which have risen around her death: the conception of her as a morbid invalid, one who "couldn't face life", and put an end to it out of hysterical self-pity. No. She lived under the shadow of the fear of madness; but her sanity was exquisite.[11]

And Clive Bell objected to the tendency of biographical postmortems to depict Woolf as "the gloomy malcontent": "Let me say once and for all that she was about the gayest human being I have known and one of the most lovable."[12] But psychobiographers find well-adjusted subjects dull material and find irresistible the great Freudian temptation of explaining even Woolf's happy periods as the result of a defensive repression of those shameful horrors that were unleashed suddenly during her breakdowns.

The problem of pathology is compounded by Woolf's own misdiagnosis, which was affected by both her experience of the disorder and the alternative explanations available to her. In her letters she sometimes fell into a description of her illness in terms of the prevalent model of her time—the neurotic artist. When Walter Lamb confronted Woolf with "dreadful stories" of bad behavior, she quickly confessed guilt as well as madness: Lamb "was puzzled by parts of my character. He said I made things into webs, & might turn fiercely upon him for his faults. I owned to great egoism & absorption & vanity & all my vices," the same self-accusation she made to Leonard during their courtship.[13] In a letter to Vita Sackville-West, she again blamed herself for suffering mood swings:

> And I haven't said anything very much, or given you any notion of the terrific high waves, and the infernal deep gulfs, on which I mount and toss in a few days. . . . . And I'm half ashamed, now I try to write it, to see what pigmy egotisms are at the root of it, with me anyhow—
> (*Letters* 3: 237)

Manic-depressives typically confuse mood swings with egotism, because the initial (and usually mild) symptoms often mimic egotistic behavior; patients may become overly concerned with themselves (e.g., exhibit hypochondria), draw attention to themselves through boisterous behavior, or misinterpret events solely in relation to themselves (e.g., experience feelings of persecution). Such an impression was evidently shared by some of the specialists of the time: in 1931 a psychologist, Helge Lundholm of Duke University, argued that egotism was an *integral* component of manic-depressive illness and that it was a *precursor,* marking the loss of psychic inhibition and an increased vulnerability to a major breakdown—just as Woolf herself thought.

And Woolf had a much nearer "nervous" model on which to base her diagnosis: the style and even the content of her self-analyses resemble the self-descriptions of her "hypochondriacal" and "egotistical" father, Leslie Stephen, with whom she identified not only as a writer but as the source of her disorder:

> But—oh damn these medical details!—this influenza has a special poison for what is called the nervous system; and mine being a second hand one, used by my father and his father to dictate dispatches and write books with—how I wish they had hunted and fished instead!—I have to treat it like a pampered pug dog, and lie still directly my head aches. (*Letters* 4: 144–45)

In Leslie's "violent rages and despairs" (*Letters* 4: 353), his feelings of failure and his self-abasements alternating with excitement and satisfaction, Virginia saw milder forms of her own symptoms and could have reasoned that the cause of both was "an egoism proper to all Stephens" (*Diary* 1: 221). Manic-depressive children do tend to over-identify with any close family member, and particularly a parent, who they think also has the disorder.[14] The old family doctor, George Savage (1842–1921), reinforced the neurotic-genius model in Virginia's mind by diagnosing her illness as "neurasthenia," the same label he had earlier put on Leslie's complaints. Although Virginia experienced much more severe manias and depressions than her father had, Leslie's nervous breakdowns from 1888 to 1891 were accompanied by "fits of the horrors" and "hideous morbid fancies" of despair and death—feelings his daughter certainly could have recognized.[15]

Ascertaining just what Woolf did think of her illness is complicated by her doctor's inconsistent explanations of nervous disorders. Neurasthenia ("nerve weakness") was a Victorian euphemism that covered a variety of vaguely recognizable symptoms, just as the term *neurosis* lumped together various disorders for much of this century (today, in psychiatry, neurosis is considered an outmoded category, no longer listed in the statistical manual of the American Psychiatric Association as the basis for establishing a diagnosis).[16] Certainly the theory of neurasthenia was thoroughly materialistic. The essential elements of the Silas Weir Mitchell (1829–1914) rest cure that Savage prescribed for Woolf's breakdowns were extended sleep and "deliberate overfeeding to stabilize the irregular brain cells supposedly responsible for the illness."[17] Later nineteenth-century neurologists such as Savage were "deeply antagonistic, not merely to psychological *explanations* of insanity, but to any sustained or systematic attention to mental therapeutics."[18] Savage himself believed that patients who came from "neurotic stock," especially those families that produced geniuses or ambitious intellectuals (an apt description of the Stephen family), were more likely to go out of their minds periodically for purely biological reasons. He was particularly convinced that patients who experienced auditory hallucinations (Virginia heard birds speaking Greek and King Edward shouting obscenities in the garden bushes) had inherited their madness. Because he believed in the somatic basis of insanity, Savage saw a connection between mental breakdowns and physical stress, especially that caused by influenza, fatigue, fever, alcoholism, and irregular temperature,[19] an association both Leonard and Virginia discussed:

> If Virginia lived a quiet, vegetative life, eating well, going to bed early,
> and not tiring herself mentally or physically, she remained perfectly
> well. But if she tired herself in any way, if she was subjected to any
> severe physical, mental, or emotional strain, symptoms at once
> appeared which in the ordinary person are negligible and transient,
> but with her were serious danger signals. The first symptoms were
> a peculiar "headache" low down at the back of the head, insomnia,
> and a tendency for the thoughts to race. If she went to bed and lay
> doing nothing in a darkened room, drinking large quantities of milk
> and eating well, the symptoms would slowly disappear and in a week
> or ten days she would be well again. (L. Woolf, *Beginning Again* 76)

> I pass from hot to cold in an instant, without any reason; except that I
> believe sheer physical effort and exhaustion influence me. (*Letters* 1: 496)

> I had the flu again—but a slight attack, and I feel none the worse and
> in my view the whole thing is merely a mix up of influenza with my
> own remarkable nervous system, which, as everybody tells me, can't be
> beaten for extreme eccentricity, but works all right in the long run.
> (*Letters* 2: 560)

> My soul diminished, alas, as the evening wore on; & the contraction
> is almost physically depression. I reflect though that I'm the sink of

50 million pneumonia germs with a temperature well below normal.
And so these contractions are largely physical, I've no doubt. (*Diary* 2: 236)

Significantly, recent medical research suggests that influenza, fevers, and
a variety of other infections and physically stressful disorders may indeed
be associated with the timing of manic-depressive episodes, and even in
1921 Emil Kraepelin reported that headaches were "extraordinarily
frequent" among his patients.[20] Manic-depressive illness, perhaps more
than any other psychiatric disorder, exemplifies the close connection
between brain and mind. It is

> a kind of biological rhythm. Episodes of mania and depression remit
> and relapse spontaneously, and recur in a quasi-periodic manner. Also,
> the occurrence and severity of affective symptoms [a person's emotional
> coloring and responsivity toward the world] sometimes seem to be strongly
> influenced by normal biological rhythms. For example, the classical
> feature of diurnal variation in mood in endogenous [biochemical]
> depression suggests that some daily physiological rhythm aggravates or
> mitigates the depressive process. The association of exacerbations of
> affective symptoms with phases of the menstrual cycle and seasons of
> the year has been repeatedly observed by physicians treating individual
> patients and by epidemiologists surveying populations of patients. In
> recent years experimental evidence has accumulated that shows that
> rhythms in the body, especially the daily sleep-wake cycle, may be cen-
> trally involved in the processes responsible for depression and mania.[21]

Moreover, depressive symptoms can manifest themselves *as* physical
disorders: that is, the depression can express itself in bodily disturbances,
hypochondria, and other psychosomatic illnesses before its distinctive
psychological effects become noticeable:[22]

> The initial complaint of depressed patients is quite often likely to be
> some common physical complaint rather than one of sadness, hopeless-
> ness, or a feeling of failure. Some of the manifestations, such as fatigue,
> headache, insomnia, and gastrointestinal disturbances are similar to
> those produced by anxiety; others are more distinctive, such as anorexia
> and weight loss, bad taste in the mouth, chronic pain, loss of interest,
> inactivity, reduced sexual desire, and a general feeling of despondency.
> It can be appreciated readily that anxiety-depression can mimic many
> diseases or disorders.[23]

Such symptoms would indeed seem like precursors to a breakdown, to
many other doctors and patients as well as to Savage and Woolf. Woolf's

mood swings often did coincide with headaches, toothaches, influenza, and fatigue.

We cannot dismiss the further possibility (as yet inconclusively researched) that depression itself affects immune-system function, rendering its victims more susceptible to infection, which might then exacerbate the mood disorder.[24] Panken's statement that Woolf's physical symptoms were "unconsciously resorted to in hope of restoring or appeasing her mother" or were an "attention-getting" device to regain her father's love is therefore most likely wrong. Panken assumes that Woolf's incomplete mourning for her dead mother and a neurotic "channeling of her grief, guilt, and anger" produced the somatic disturbances of her manic-depressive breakdowns, but a disease with such potent metabolic changes may very well affect bodily health and mental functioning without involving self-destructive wishes.[25] So, too, biology should dissuade us of Louise DeSalvo's speculation that Woolf feared becoming sick because she had once been molested by Gerald Duckworth while recovering from whooping cough.[26] Much more than simple association is at work here.

Despite his arguments for biology and heredity, however, Savage also had "psychological" opinions of mental illness, though they are hardly more than the products of personal bias and culturally prescribed Victorian stereotype. He believed, for instance, that spoiled children were likely to develop unsound minds and that too much education was mentally harmful for the lower classes and for intelligent young women rebelling against their natural roles as wives and mothers.[27] But, what was perhaps worse, in his published essays Savage explained some kinds of mental disorders as a "defect" in "moral character," and he expressed irritation at what he perceived to be his patients' self-indulgence in their illnesses (especially when they did not get well under his care)—a reaction he may have picked up from Silas Weir Mitchell himself, who believed that "yielding too easily to the expression of all and any emotion" was a predisposing cause of nervous disorders. Both physicians advocated "order, control, and self-restraint" as a cure for mental illness, an attitude not uncommon among Victorian doctors.[28] Savage should have had little difficulty in convincing Woolf that her excessive emotionalism fit the moral-weakness bill, especially since her own father, Leslie, adopted Savage's line when he referred to the mental difficulties of his first daughter, Laura, as a moral deficiency caused by "willful perversity," an obstinate waywardness he thought he could cure by imposing "a stronger will and greater self-discipline."[29] Consequently, in the first year of their marriage, Leonard found he had to reassure Virginia that an episode of depression was merely "illness & nothing moral" (L. Woolf, *Letters* 191). Virginia had learned early on to attribute her symptoms to family genes and yet to blame herself for losing control of her emotions, as she does in the following diary entry and three apologetic letters, two to Violet Dickinson and the third to her sister Vanessa:

> —a little more self control on my part, & we might have had a boy of 12, a girl of 10: This always [m]akes me wretched in the early hours. So I said, I am spoiling what I have. . . . No doubt, this is a rationalisation of a state which is not really of that nature. Probably I am very lucky. (*Diary* 3: 107)

> I know I have behaved very lazily and selfishly, and not cheerfully as Ozzy [Dickinson] would have me. I feel numb and dumb, and unable to lay hands on any words. (*Letters* 1: 279)

> When I hear of your worries and wishes—I dont know if a pen is as fatal to you as it is to me—I feel positively fraudulent—like one who gets sympathy on false pretenses. (*Letters* 1: 280)

> Oh my beloved creature, how little use I am in the world! Selfish, vain, egoistical, and incompetent. Will you think out a training to make me less selfish? It is pathetic to see Adrian developing virtues, as my faults grow. (*Letters* 1: 411)

Psychoanalytic critics have only detected the obvious without questioning its context when they see her as both perversely resistant to self-insight and riddled with unconscious guilt—convenient signposts of neurosis.[30]

Savage's dualistic attitude was typical of many Victorian doctors. The nineteenth century developed these two parallel lines of psychiatric thought, each having its vogue for several decades: either insanity was so biologically based that it was not intelligible at all (and so patients were warned not to think about their "ill" experiences), or madness resulted from a weak character and immoral decisions voluntarily made.[31] Symptoms of madness, therefore, were either meaningless epiphenomena of underlying morbid states or representations of one's sinful nature. Patients could feel either disconnected from their own illness or ashamed for failing to control themselves. Woolf, at times, felt both.

As a woman, Woolf faced an additional challenge. Her illness and her femaleness both threatened her with a profound sense of powerlessness and depersonalization. In her own family her mother Julia and her half-sister Stella had shown her what it was like to be sacrificed to the

Victorian god of feminine decorum. She instinctively rebelled against what she called "non-being," that selfless emptiness enforced by a sexist society—and by her depressions. But open rebellion was risky. Under the Lunacy Act of 1890, 70 percent of Britain's mentally ill were certified and committed by 1900, most often for suicide attempts, leading one scholar to conclude:

> If Virginia Woolf had been certified and admitted to an asylum in the hopeless condition in which we find her in 1912, it is possible she could have been lost on the back wards and even her private physicians would not have been able to legally obtain her release.[32]

Only as long as Woolf cooperated with what was essentially an unacknowledged parody of Victorian stereotypes about femininity could she remain safe from institutionalization.[33]

It was a ticklish situation. Both her feminism and her manic-depressive experiences urged Woolf to further exploration of the mind, but overt self-assertion or preoccupation with symptoms was viewed either as self-indulgence or as evidence of madness. Savage, like Mitchell, evaluated his patients' progress in terms of their submission to his conservative view of reality: the patient was told to relinquish control to the doctor, to follow directions without question. Because Savage identified sanity with social conformity, he denigrated the value of self and brushed aside the patient's experience of her illness.[34] After Woolf's "summer madness" in 1904, which included an unsuccessful suicide attempt (she threw herself out of a second-story window), Savage pronounced her "cured" by January and had no better advice for Virginia than that she should disregard what had happened:

> I am discharged cured! Aint it a joke! Savage was quite satisfied, and said he wanted me to go back to my ordinary life in everything and to go out and see people, and work, and to forget my illness. (*Letters* 1: 175)

Indeed, Victorian physicians generally discounted the content of female complaints and judged them by the patriarchal mythology of the nature of femininity:

> Expressions of unhappiness, low self-esteem, helplessness, anxiety, and fear were not connected to the realities of women's lives, while expressions of sexual desire, anger, and aggression were taken as morbid deviations from the normal female personality. The female life cycle, linked to reproduction, was seen as fraught with biological crises during which these morbid emotions were more likely to appear.

. . . The menstrual discharge in itself predisposed women to insanity, since it was widely believed that madness was a disease of the blood.[35]

Thus, the theory of female insanity reduced the value of women to their usefulness to society, not as persons seeking self-discovery, but as submissive wives and selfless mothers. An independent will in a woman "could be regarded as a form of female deviance that was dangerously close to mental illness," a rebellion which invited censure and control by the physician:

> The traditional beliefs that women were more emotionally volatile, more nervous, and more ruled by their reproductive and sexual economy than men inspired Victorian psychiatric theories of femininity as a kind of mental illness in itself. As the neurologist S. Weir Mitchell remarked, "The man who does not know sick women does not know women."[36]

Ridiculous as these opinions appear today, at the time the threat was quite real. As the nineteenth century progressed, more and more women were institutionalized: by 1875 females made up a majority of asylum inmates, and some physicians put the blame on the growing feminist movement, which advocated intellectual achievement for young women.[37] Although in private Woolf ridiculed Savage as "tyrannical" and "short-sighted" and rightly questioned his chauvinistic definition of "coherence" (*Letters* 1: 147, 159), she submitted to rest cures when ordered.

Later the Woolfs encountered psychoanalytic theory. Leonard read the first English translation of *The Interpretation of Dreams* in 1913, and the Woolfs' Hogarth Press published Freud's "Mourning and Melancholia" in the *Collected Papers* in 1925. These studies helped him to recognize the significance of the bipolarity of Virginia's symptoms and to diagnose her disorder correctly as manic-depressive illness:

> When I cross-examined Virginia's doctors, they said that she was suffering from neurasthenia, not from manic-depressive insanity, which was entirely different. But as far as symptoms were concerned, Virginia *was* suffering from manic-depressive insanity. In the first stage of the illness from 1914 practically every symptom was the exact opposite of those in the second stage in 1915. In the first stage she was in the depths of depression, would hardly eat or talk, was suicidal. In the second she was in a state of violent excitement and wild euphoria, talking incessantly for long periods of time. In the first stage she was violently opposed to the nurses and they had the greatest difficulty in getting her to do anything; she wanted me to be with her continually and for a week or two I was the only person able to get her to eat anything. In the

second stage of violent excitement, she was violently hostile to me, would not talk to me or allow me to come into her room. She was occasionally violent with the nurses, but she tolerated them in a way which was the opposite of her behavior to them in the first stage. (*Beginning Again* 161)

Leonard must also have learned a good deal of symptomatology from Karl Abraham, who published essays on manic-depressive illness in 1912, 1916, and 1924, incorporating all three in a 1927 edition of his papers put out by the Hogarth Press. And there were other sources: between 1919 and 1925 the British press published 400 articles, editorials, news items, and reviews on Freud and his followers. Psychoanalysis had become a fad, a subject for dinner conversation: "every moderately well-informed person," one reviewer in 1920 claimed, "now knows something about Jung and Freud,"[38] and Leonard himself said that Virginia made one of that number (L. Woolf, *Letters* 522).

With all this discussion of mental illness, then, why did Woolf not seek psychotherapy? Was it a kind of neurotic cowardice, as at least five Freudian critics have already suggested?[39] Was she afraid of discovering the truth about her illness because that truth was connected to deeply repressed conflicts? Did she prefer to be ill because it brought her attention and love? Does the fact that she avoided psychoanalysis prove that she was hiding something neurotic or forbidden? Or was her rejection of Freud merely childish, vindictive, and small-minded, resulting from her childhood hostility to her brother Adrian, who grew up to become a practicing psychoanalyst?[40]

I do not believe Woolf could have held much hope of finding a cure in Freud. Like Savage, he saw abnormality in social nonconformity. And, as feminist psychoanalytic critics have cogently argued, Freud's own case history of Dora, which was published by the Hogarth Press, displays his rigid, patriarchal attitude toward the organization of a patient's symptoms, at least when that patient happened to be a woman. He completely failed to understand why the adolescent Dora had not been sexually excited by the clumsy attentions of an older married man (whose wife was having an adulterous affair with Dora's father) when he had grabbed her suddenly and kissed her, pressing his body to hers. Freud reasoned that she must have felt K.'s erection through their clothing, and that she was denying she had responded in kind. This conclusion Dora flatly rejected; she found Herr K.'s actions repulsive. Freud was unaware of his own unconscious identification with K., or that he felt Dora's rejection of K. was linked to a repudiation of himself. He defensively concluded that her feelings of repulsion were evidence of neurosis. How could a normal girl resist an older man? And beneath that lay another question: how could Dora resist Freud's masterful diagnosis? The answer was, she couldn't; therefore, she must be sick. He refused to accept at face value her version of what had happened and how she had felt, turned her reproach against her father's duplicity into self-reproach, and acted as if Dora's mother were of no consequence (indeed, Freud generally minimized the role of women, particularly in his equation for the Oedipus complex).[41] In the 1920s Karen Horney clearly discerned Freud's "phallo-centric" view of women and objected to his having relegated them to a passive-masochistic sexual role.[42] Even in Woolf's lifetime it was becoming evident to feminists that Freud imposed his own unexamined views upon women, invalidating the coherence he thought he had discovered as underlying the seeming incoherence of women's symptoms.

Moreover, we cannot regard Savage's rest cure as so completely ineffective that only a neurotic would continue treatment. Recent studies at the National Institute of Mental Health (NIMH) showed that restructuring a manic-depressive's sleep cycle can effect at least a temporary remission of symptoms: in 60 percent of patients, sleep deprivation causes switches from depression to normal or manic states,[43] and recovery sleep after sleep deprivation can trigger switches out of mania. The success achieved with both "phase-advance" sleep (going to bed four to six hours earlier and rising earlier) and sleep deprivation has led NIMH researchers to speculate that manipulating the twenty-four-hour sleep-wake cycle may, in some patients, either replace or enhance drug therapy.[44] Such a hypothesis implies that a genetic defect in the brain's internal circadian (twenty-four-hour) clock is involved in the etiology of manic-depressive illness. Studies show that nights of total insomnia often precede mania, acting either to trigger an episode or to exacerbate one already begun.[45] Consequently, clinicians warn that patients need to be alert to environmental changes leading to insomnia (e.g., anxiety, excitement, grief, travel, hormonal changes). Even a single night's sleeplessness "should be taken as an early warning of possible impending mania." Patients should be counseled to avoid stressful or stimulating situations "likely to disrupt sleep" routines, and physicians should consider prescribing sedatives (such as clonazepam) to prevent significant sleep loss.[46] Overall, "the regularization of circadian rhythms through the regularization of meals, exercise, and other activities should also be stressed to patients."[47] Leonard acknowledges his belief in this premise in his autobiography, and he offers details in a 1929 letter to Vita Sackville-West:

> It was a perpetual struggle to find the precarious balance of health for her among the strains and stresses of writing and society. The routine of everyday life had to be regular and rather rigid. Everything had to be rationed, from work and walking to people and parties. (*Downhill All the Way* 49)

> Virginia has been a good deal better the last two days though she is still not right & is more or less in bed. The slightest thing is apt to bring symptoms back. But this has always been the case when she has been so near breaking point, & I think, if she keeps quite quiet, for another week, it will pass away. She has not really had such a severe attack as this for the last 3 or 4 years. It was not, of course, due to anything like influenza or sea-sickness cures, but simply to her overdoing it & particularly not going to bed at 11 for all those nights running. It has been proved over & over again in the last 10 years that even 2 late nights running are definitely dangerous for her & this time it was 7 or 8. (L. Woolf, *Letters* 236)

Since Victorian medicine believed that stress triggered "neurasthenic" episodes, Savage ordered Leonard to keep visitors, activities, and household stress at a minimum when Virginia was ill and to make sure she ate well and rested regularly. From 1913 (the beginning of a two-year period of affective episodes) to the end of 1919, Leonard kept an almost daily journal of Virginia's moods (time of onset, duration, and intensity), her sleeping and eating patterns, temperature, weight, dose of drug taken, and date of onset of menstruation. Correlations between bodily rhythms and mental states helped him anticipate what level of care she would need. In later years, whenever Virginia felt ill, Leonard returned to his monitoring, using his measurements as a predictor of impending breakdown. When she suffered from intractable insomnia, he gave cautious doses of hypnotic sedatives (listed as "chloral [hydrate]," "veronal," "medinal," "potassium bromide," and "sodium bromide" in his personal diary in his Monks House Papers, now housed at the University of Sussex). Chloral hydrate was widely prescribed for inducing sleep and calming the insane, especially manics, whose metabolism could be so hyperenergized that neither sleep nor self-control was possible.

For any sedative, it is important to recognize just how much is too much, as both Leonard and Dr. Savage understood. In 1879 Savage wrote a paper entitled "Uses and Abuses of Chloral Hydrate," in which he warned that the drug should not be applied chronically and that the advantages of sedation must be weighed against the disadvantages in each case.[48] Leonard's record of Virginia's drug schedule shows reasonable restraint. Virginia took sleeping draughts when insomnia persisted but stopped when full sleep returned. Often Leonard noted that Virginia needed only half a dose, regarded this as a positive sign, and began tapering off. Thus, in 1914, after a year of recurrent affective episodes, Leonard recorded in his diary that Virginia took sedatives eight times,[49] ceasing in July, when manic symptoms remitted. Early 1915 marked the return of mood swings, and dose frequency rose accordingly, with seventeen draughts in the month between February 18 and March 19.[50] On March 25 Virginia became so ill that Leonard decided to move her into a nursing home. Since symptoms preceded medication, they could not have been induced by the drugs themselves, as DeSalvo speculates.[51] Sedatives may indeed exacerbate a depressed mood already present, as Woolf herself noticed on one occasion in 1938: "I knew the break [a short vacation at Rodmell] would be a jangle; but not that I should feel the mixture of humiliation & dissolution wh. I feel today, after a sleeping draught" (*Diary* 5: 181). But for manic episodes in prelithium days, hypnotic sedatives were often helpful and sometimes life-saving. Such use of drugs was very different from that of some manic-depressives today, who indiscriminately abuse drugs, both legal and illegal, to intensify the pleasant "highs" of hypomania or as a form of self-medication.[52] Using "uppers" (e.g., cocaine, amphetamines, or alcohol) to combat depressive lows and "downers" (e.g., barbiturates, tranquilizers, or alcohol) to dampen manic flights is no substitute for lithium therapy, because these drugs are short-acting and cannot be correlated accurately to unpredictable mood swings. This was, perhaps, why Leonard so carefully charted the timing and intensity of Virginia's mood swings.

Whatever we may think of Leonard as a person (and opinion varies widely among critics, some of whom see him as a loving saint and some as a petty tyrant), we must remember that it is not easy to live with a manic-depressive, who may, without self-awareness, in one mood judge a situation, desire, or destiny in ways that diverge considerably from a judgment made in some other mood. Love of life, of spouse, and of self may change swiftly and without warning to suicidal despair, paranoid hostility, or grandiose self-indulgence. Subtler shifts can be even more alarming and destructive of trust in personal relationships. The domestic and personal tribulation wreaked by bipolar disorder, one researcher reports, "inevitably

has powerful and often painful effects on relationships," particularly marriages, and yet these patients desperately need a stable relationship. Those
who lead chaotic lives or have poor or unpredictable social-support systems
usually fare badly. Manic-depressives find they must rely on their families
during difficult times, but the benefits go both ways: "The involvement
of family members and friends can lessen the need for hospitalization and
increase the family's and patient's sense of control over a potentially
catastrophic situation." Control may be exerted only over seemingly minor
events, but those events often presage major episodes.[53] A memory from
Angelica Garnett, Virginia's niece, testifies to this effect:

> Leonard and Virginia's relationship was above all comradely: deeply affec-
> tionate and indivisibly united, they depended on each other. They knew
> each other's minds and therefore took each other for granted—they
> accepted each other's peculiarities and shortcomings and pretended no
> more than they could help. . . . Leonard never failed in vigilance and
> never fussed; neither did he hide his brief anxiety that Virginia might drink
> a glass too much wine or commit some other mild excess; he would say
> quite simply, "Virginia, that's enough," and that was the end of it.
> Or, when he noticed by the hands of his enormous watch that it was
> 11.00 in the evening, no matter how much she was enjoying herself,
> he would say, "Virginia, we must go home," and after a few extra
> minutes stolen from beneath his nose, she would rise and, as though
> leaving a part of herself behind, follow him and Pinka to the door.[54]

And Louie Mayer, who cooked for the Woolfs at Rodmell from 1934
until long after Virginia's death, remembers:

> Sometimes Mrs Woolf was quite ill while working on a book and had
> acute headaches. Mr Woolf then had to ration the number of friends
> who came to the house. Or, to those who did come, he had to say
> that she would only be able to talk to them for a short time. He did
> not like doing this but he knew that if she did not have enough rest
> she would become very ill.[55]

To some readers, Leonard's behavior looks petty and tyrannical. As
we have seen, however, alcohol, fatigue, and changes in sleep patterns do
affect a manic-depressive's vulnerability to breakdowns, and Virginia's
doctors presented Leonard with a similar cause-effect relationship in their
theory that mood swings resulted from weakened nerves. Both husband
and wife seem to have been behaving responsibly; but whether Leonard

was acting out of love for his wife or for domestic peace, I cannot divine. It is unfortunate that here it is the woman depending on the man, who acts as the restraining authority, for the arrangement inflames readers who are justifiably moved by Virginia's eloquent appeals for women's liberation. They mistakenly assume that such a serious psychiatric disorder as manic-depressive illness adds nothing to the dynamics of a relationship. It is, after all, common to find bipolar husbands relying on their wives for the same sense of order, continuity, and judgment. Woolf knew that "as for reason, when the mood's on, as soon might one persuade a runaway horse" (*Diary* 2: 53). She was not happy about periodically requiring supervision, but she had learned that she needed it at times, to shorten episodes and to avoid state-enforced institutionalization. To their credit, neither Leonard nor Virginia let supervision distort aspects of their lives that had nothing to do with mood swings. They respected each other's autonomy, desires, and ideas—a difficult goal, since manic-depressive illness temporarily destroys the individual's control over just these aspects of self. Manic-depressives and their spouses would all do well to learn so to discriminate between a marital power play and a practical solution to periodic affective episodes.

Ironically, then, Savage's rest-cure regime may well have given Woolf some relief, as Barbara Bagenal remembers:

> I saw her only once near to a mental breakdown. We were laughing and joking at lunch one day when suddenly she began to flip the meat from her plate on to the table-cloth, obviously not knowing what she was doing. Leonard at once asked me not to comment on her action and to stop talking to her. Then he took her upstairs to rest and stayed with her until she fell asleep and the danger was passed. At tea-time she was quite happy and composed and did not remember the incident.[56]

Woolf herself seems to have appreciated the rests:

> What a gap! . . . 60 days; & those days spent in wearisome headache, jumping pulse, aching back, frets, fidgets, lying awake, sleeping draughts, sedatives, digitalis, going for a little walk, & plunging back into bed again—all the horrors of the dark cupboard of illness once more displayed for my diversion. Let me make a vow that this shall never, never, happen again; & *then* confess that there are some compensations. To be tired & authorised to lie in bed is pleasant. . . . I feel that I can take stock of things in a leisurely way. (*Diary* 2: 125)

> I am taking, this is the last day—my weeks holiday, with very good
> results. My brain is soft & warm & fertile again, I feel fresh & free
> with energy for talk. Yes, I can even envisage "seeing" people without
> a clutch & a shudder. Odd how I drink up rest—how I become dry &
> parched like a withered grass—how then I become green & succulent.
> (*Diary* 4: 42)

> Unless I weigh 9 1/2 stones I hear voices and see visions and can
> neither write nor sleep.[57]

Woolf's association of weight with hallucinations is not unreasonable. Body
weight can drop rapidly during manic episodes, out of proportion to the
reduced intake of calories. The rest cure, with its emphasis on overfeeding,
did sometimes restore her, and even today an increase in the patient's
weight is often regarded by physicians as a herald of recovery.[58] We can
certainly criticize Savage's knowledge as a psychologist, but his medical
concerns about Virginia's weight and response to stress did benefit her.

Besides the efficacy, however limited, of Savage's rest cures, Woolf
may have dismissed psychoanalysis because both Freud and Abraham saw
manic-depressive disorder as regressive behavior, as an inability to cope
with traumatic losses in childhood. Regression has been defined generally as a retreat of the libido to an earlier period in the individual's life
because he is unable to function at a higher level, but some analysts
in the past have phrased it more indelicately: "Regression means failure." Manic speech—energized, extravagant, loosely associated, sometimes
even rhyming—was seen as "a childish babyish vocabulary," and the
exuberant physical behavior of manics—the frenetic or outlandish movements, gestures, and spontaneous dances—was compared to "the behavior of primitive man."[59] Metaphorical similarity implies identity, but
also operating here is psychoanalysis's preoccupation with the pathological, as Woolf noted in 1918 in her diary after a discussion of Freud
with Lytton Strachey: "It's unfortunate that civilisation always lights
up the dwarfs, cripples, & sexless people first" (*Diary* 1: 110). Early
Freudian theory would only have ratified Woolf's fear that her breakdowns
revealed a self-indulgent defect of character, a narcissistic weakness exacerbated by the loss of her mother, the sexual abuse inflicted by her half-
brothers, and so on. By this time she was already exploring her illness
through her fiction, seeing provocative connections between madness and
modernism. She would not have been likely to seek out rehashed Victorian
reproofs of her inadequacies.

Unfortunately, not all biographers and critics have likewise advanced beyond Freud's orientation. Quentin Bell downplays Woolf's liberal politics and feminism, as well as her apparently passionate love affair with Vita Sackville-West. He prefers to portray his aunt as childlike, ethereal, terrified, frozen in defensive panic by sex. The result is a Woolf who is not a "heroine" but, as one of Bell's reviewers put it, a "stubborn and sometimes querulous self-starving madwoman."[60] This bias has seriously affected the literary criticism of Woolf's novels. When DeSalvo and Elizabeth Heine, for instance, trace the manifold revisions of Woolf's first novel, *The Voyage Out,* they see not *evolution* of method but *dilution* of a deeply fantasized self-annihilation that kept seeping into her writing: they regard the novel's puzzling equivocations and subterfuges as an elaborate masquerade to disguise forbidden desires.[61]

Sometimes critics must directly contradict Woolf in order to fit her life and her fiction into their psychodynamic theories. When Mark Spilka puzzles over Rachel Vinrace's "odd," "mysterious," and "senseless" death, he looks to Woolf's own suicide (which occurred twenty-six years after the publication of *The Voyage Out*) for an answer, concluding that both author and character must die because they could not face "painfully blocked emotions"; he argues that Woolf's intense, sexual, and apparently unblocked feelings for Violet Dickinson and Ethel Smyth should be devalued as "neurotic attachments to older women," poor substitutes for her dead mother.[62] Behind this reasoning lie unexamined and unenlightened attitudes about women, older women, gay women, and sexual love that seem strikingly opposed to Woolf's professed beliefs.[63] But neurotics are not expected to be consistent, and so her passion for women is renamed frigidity. As the archetypal neurotic female, Woolf has become in literary journals what Jane Marcus rightly calls "a case study of female failure," a bogeywoman used to frighten little girls who flirt with the idea of becoming artists. How can we celebrate the life of a woman whose vision is disparaged as "deadly" and "disembodied" because she decided when to die, whose passion is neuroticized because it is given to women, and whose veracity is continually questioned because it is assumed that such a defective person could not, or would not, discover the truth about herself?[64] Once again we have Dr. George Savage's view of the patient as a kind of moral lesson on how not to behave.

Not only does neurosis, more than manic-depressive illness, provide a suitable explanation for a woman's art and behavior, but formidable difficulties stand in the way of a diagnosis of manic-depressive illness. Woolf's various doctors failed because, until 1904, no one had even been able to catalog the often bewildering array of symptoms which, in many ways, seem to mimic those of neurosis. Although some of the symptoms of mood disorders have been observed and discussed ever since Hippocrates first coined the term *melancholia* in the fourth century B.C., by the end of the nineteenth century psychiatric workers "were floundering helplessly around in a morass of symptoms for which they were unable to find any common denominators."[65]

The great German psychiatrist Emil Kraepelin (1856–1926), head of the department of psychiatry at the University of Munich, studied 459 manic-depressive patients and was the first to recognize a pattern in the manic-depressive illness that distinguished it from schizophrenia and melancholia, but as a clinical tool his diagnosis was slow to spread; it was not until 1921 that an English translation of his book, *Manic-Depressive Insanity and Paranoia*, was available. Kraepelin's model encountered stiff opposition from the Freudians because it described manic-depressive illness not as an unconscious conflict but as a familial disorder resistant to psychoanalysis. Kraepelin, a meticulous and objective observer of behavior, limited himself to phenomenological descriptions of clinical data and questioned the validity of intuitive hunches about mental events. Although he did not exclude psychological or social stresses as triggers of mood swings, and although his diagnostic system eventually prevailed (and is still used today largely intact), his "disease model" of manic-depressive illness struck Freudians as too conservative because he took symptoms at face value, categorizing them according to observable data. He did not discuss them as encoded emblems of pathological "meaning," nor did he consider "the talking cure" an effective treatment for a disorder that clearly could run through family lines.[66]

The early twentieth century thrilled instead at Freud's provocative "psychological" model, which promised to explain behavior in terms of a patient's unconscious thoughts, feelings, and reactions to life events. According to Freudian theory, a neurotic tries to forget the past by repressing it, but then is condemned to repeat these old patterns of behavior (the "repetition compulsion") in the form of symptoms that reassert the traumatic scene in a cleverly disguised form—so clever, in fact, that the patient is blind to the meaning of the symptoms. Freud felt that an illness that seemed meaningless could nevertheless be read for its unconscious message, and that once the patient realized what it meant to the sufferer personally, he or she would be cured. Reading an illness involved deciphering the symptom's symbolic component. Everyone thus became a text awaiting an authoritative reading—a welcome respite from the age of the machine, which darkly hinted that people were also mere biological mechanisms. Freud's cure brought art back into life and reassured people that "mind" held creative primacy over body. Often Freud's therapy worked: one of his patients, for instance, suffered from facial neuralgia and felt what seemed to be true organic pain, but Freud could find no organic basis for it. During analysis, while exploring a remembered argument with her husband, the patient suddenly realized that something he had said had bitterly insulted her, had felt "like a slap in the face," whereupon she put her hand to her cheek and made the psychic connection: her facial pain was a metaphor for her psychological pain. The insult had become "inscribed" in facial neuralgia, displacing affect from psyche to soma.[67]

The "talking cure" offered what initially seemed to be the primary key to understanding and curing all abnormal behavior. The promise, however, led to misapplication. Freud himself could not resist seeing a "psychological" meaning in symptoms that we know today are purely or largely neurologically based. And his followers continued that tradition. Earlier in this century, illnesses such as schizophrenia, autism, Gilles de la Tourette syndrome, rheumatoid arthritis, tuberculosis, tertiary syphilis, parkinsonism, neurodermatitis, ulcerative colitis, essential hypertension, temporal lobe and petit mal epilepsy, and premenstrual syndrome were thought by some to be psychological in origin and therefore suitable subjects for psychoanalysis.[68] Psychoanalysis contains no mechanism for correcting this kind of "overreading," the almost literary activity of viewing physical symptoms as metaphors for mental states—a kind of pathological transcendentalism. Freud hoped that eventually neurology and psychology would converge, but biotechnology was so primitive then that he had little data on which to propose a model that might incorporate the two. Metapsychology, however, did not need to wait.

Perhaps the best example of Freud's overreading is his 1928 speculation that Dostoevsky's epilepsy was neurotic, an hysterical expression of a wish too terrible to be brought to consciousness. Because Freud saw symbolic meaning in the violent convulsions and muscular rigidity of an epileptic seizure, he concluded that the writer's physical symptoms served as a metaphorical self-punishment for having wished his father were dead; falling helplessly ill, therefore, was a symbolic form of self-castration, which in turn suggested sexual ambivalence and a desire for a homosexual union with the father.[69] In this sense Dostoevsky, and indeed every patient, desired to be ill. Freud arrived at this conclusion by tying symptoms together, for he assumed that the same desire inspired all of them. Symptoms that seemed meaningless individually could be deciphered if they could be related to other symptoms or aspects of the patient's life. Building a case history, then, is essentially an exercise in fiction: fitting disparate phenomena into some organized and comprehensible whole with a beginning, middle, and ending (and a satisfying ending at that) requires the analyst to call upon narrative abilities as well as scientific knowledge. Since the patient's verbal report is assumed to be itself symptomatic of his illness, and therefore insufficient due to distortion or amnesia, it is up to the analyst to find the buried or missing threads to the story and weave them into a "compelling" explanation.[70]

Freud's handling of Dostoevsky's life followed this method exactly. He tied together epileptic symptoms with what he knew about Dostoevsky's relations with his cruel father and his subsequent hostility toward father-figures (including the tsar), which vanished mysteriously after he was imprisoned. Unconscious conflict does seem to explain his unexpected submission to authority as symbolic of his having accepted guilt for his parricidal wishes, and so psychobiographers since Freud have generally depicted Dostoevsky as a man with strongly repressed, violent drives which erupted spasmodically and elicited various self-destructive reactions, including his nearly fatal seizures. Now, I do not argue against the psychoanalytic view that Dostoevsky was parricidal or that his gambling implies self-hatred: the biographical evidence seems to support these interpretations. But Freud confused this "psychological" explanation with Dostoevsky's neurological symptoms. Seizures are not symbolic: they involve a paroxysm of uncontrolled electrical discharges in brain cells that typically produces the symptoms Freud observed but misinterpreted. Today we no longer consider the epileptic patient to be guilty of having wished his disorder into existence; rather, we regard him as a victim of a neurological disease that can produce psychological disturbances as well—disturbances we have learned to separate from the physical.[71] This new knowledge has led psychobiographers to reevaluate Dostoevsky's illness in terms of how medical history and literary history have intertwined.[72]

The Freudian interpretation of manic-depressive illness mirrored its evaluation of epilepsy. While Kraepelin patiently studied family histories, the Freudians embarked on the more colorful hunt for the elusive latent meanings or unconscious conflicts which presumably "caused" mania and depression, conflicts the disorder's abundant and varied symptoms seemed to suggest. Freud argued that depression resulted from a self-destructive impulse of the ego, which hurt itself with despair in order to punish the lost love object (usually a parent) with whom it unconsciously identified. Abraham focused on a blocked libido in infancy, expressed in the depressive's excessive dependence on others for affection and consolation. Other analysts blamed unrestrained narcissism, disappointment with and/or idealization of one's parents in infancy, a sadistic fixation of the ego to the state of infantile helplessness, guilt over unpardonable sexual sins in childhood, inappropriate infantile adaptive patterns extending into adult life, and anxiety and aggression.[73]

These theories are all valid descriptive categories, vivid metaphors for very real behaviors. When, for instance, a depressed patient appeared to regress to the point of allowing himself to be destroyed by his own passivity, preoccupied with his endless pain, it seemed logical to analysts that a masochistic wish tied to neurotic guilt had caused the depression and its physical symptom of a general psychomotor slowdown.[74] Could not physical symptoms be viewed as a kind of metabolic suicide? Since the patient acted like a dependent infant starved for love and reassurance, it seemed reasonable to suppose an infantile origin for his behavior; it is, after all, in infancy that self-esteem begins. And when a depressed patient suddenly switched into a highly energized, euphoric, manic mood that appeared to free him from despair and dissolve his guilty thoughts, psychoanalysts theorized the obvious: that the patient consciously or unconsciously *wished* mania into existence in order to escape or deny the painful depression. Clinicians read *intent* into manic-depressive symptoms, assuming that symptoms were tied to unconscious wishes or conflicts by more or less direct, logical lines of cause and effect. It made dramatic sense that a person who unconsciously felt inadequate, evil, or unworthy would act out this self-hatred in the form of a self-destructive depression. It seemed far less likely that a depressed person would experience his mood as negative perceptions and feelings and would consequently see himself as inadequate, evil, and unworthy—because then a nonpsychological origin for the illness would have to be found, and that would not only postpone closure but would also devalue the psychoanalyst's therapy. For much of this century, analysts followed Freud's formula, probing the minds of manic-depressives for thoughts that could cause mood shifts. A critic could argue with confidence that Virginia Woolf's suicidal depressions were caused by a self-destructive *desire* for punishment, aroused by "self-dissatisfaction, self-reproach, and guilt."[75] As in the case of Dostoevsky, psychological origins were presumed to produce physiological disturbances. After all, that is how metaphors usually work in literary texts—turbulent skies express turbulent emotions in overwrought protagonists.

In the real world of the clinic, however, cure rates were disappointing. Some manic-depressive patients never improved; others would seem to recover and then relapse periodically after repeated and seemingly authentic theory-compatible insights had been gained through months or years of psychoanalysis. The rise of biological psychiatry changed all that with an unexpected therapeutic discovery. In 1949, an unknown Australian psychiatrist named John F. Cade, working alone in a small hospital, made a startling discovery: administration by mouth of lithium carbonate, not a drug but a common mineral salt, produced a significant remission of symptoms in his manic patients. One of these patients, a fifty-one-year-old man who had been hospitalized for five years for chronic mania and who was regarded by the staff as "the most troublesome patient in the ward," got well so fast he was discharged in three months and returned to his family and his job.[76] American clinicians, at that time largely Freudian, at first dismissed this development, but Mogens Schou was intrigued and began tests in Denmark in 1954, and by 1958 trials had begun in the United States. Word of success with lithium began to spread. As one psychiatrist recalls,

> an uncontrollably manic Texas professor, simultaneously writing ten books and forty research papers, was sent to New York for lithium treatment. He responded astonishingly well. . . . He was sent back to Texas "cured" on lithium, much to the amazement of the Texas psychiatrists who had been unable to subdue his frenetic, psychotic high for the better part of a year. They were so amazed at his rapid recovery that experiments in Galveston were then begun. . . . Few experiences in psychiatry are so dramatic as watching lithium carbonate in one to two weeks utterly transform a manic-depressive personality.[77]

In the 1960s, psychologists, pharmacologists, and psychiatrists joined forces in the expanding field of psychopharmacology, and by 1969 enough genetic and pharmacological evidence had accumulated to persuade the American Psychiatric Association to recommend lithium to the Food and Drug Administration for treatment of manic-depressive illness.[78] Today over 700,000 manic-depressive Americans take lithium. Further evidence of a biological basis for manic-depressive illness came in 1987, when the first gene implicated in the transmission of the illness was identified, a discovery predicted by biochemical theory.[79]

Although its specific actions on brain chemistry are not yet fully under-stood, clinical evidence shows that lithium dampens severe mood swings, shortening attacks, lengthening remissions, and reducing the number of relapses, thus maintaining a relatively stable position between the "highs" of mania and the "lows" of depression in roughly 70 percent of patients. One study showed that patients who had relapsed once every eight months fell ill only once every sixty months when taking lithium, and the average "psychotic time" fell from thirteen weeks per year to one and a half weeks. If a patient taking lithium develops depressions (for some people, lithium is less effective against depression than it is against mania), antidepressants (such as monoamine oxydase inhibitors or tricyclics) can be added to achieve a balance acceptable to the patient. Conversely, for individuals with more severe mania (gross hyperactivity and psychotic features), neuroleptics (such as chlorpromazine or haloperidol) may be added to lithium to bolster its moderating effects. For those whose bodies cannot tolerate lithium, carbamazepine also shows promise as an anti-manic agent, as do valproic acid and clonazepam.[80]

PSYCHOTHERAPY OR DRUGS?

Since there are different types of depressions with different etiologies, no one type of therapy is applicable for all patients. For cases that do not involve genetically imposed, biochemically produced depressions, psycho-therapy is appropriate and usually helpful, whether it be psychoanalysis, cognitive psychology, behavioral therapy, interpersonal, group, or any of a number of the 250 psychotherapies existing today.[81] But clinicians must be careful; a renowned psychiatrist in this field estimates that only 10 per-cent of his depressed patients could accurately be called neurotic,[82] so the question of which type of therapy to use is important. Furthermore, many supposedly nonendogenous depressions respond to drug therapy. In one study of one hundred outpatients with mild depressive states labeled neurotic, reactive, or situational, forty developed a major affective disorder within four years, nearly half of them bipolar.[83]

Psychotherapy, and particularly psychoanalysis, is especially inadequate if applied as the sole therapy for manic-depressive illness. For the most part, manic-depressives do not exhibit secondary illnesses once their mood disorder has been managed by lithium. Conversely, in-depth psychoanalysis is not effective in the treatment of manic-depressives; the misinterpreta-tions and subtle fluctuations of mood states usually bewilder the analyst attempting to establish a stable relationship for analyzing transferences.

If, after having been stabilized by lithium, a bipolar patient has lingering problems, psychoanalysis can be tried, but manic-depressives run no more risk of being neurotic than do non-manic-depressives.[84] At most we may say that most patients need short-term psychotherapy to help them examine how the disease has affected their judgments, emotions, and memories and to encourage them to rebuild a coherent self-structure if it has been destroyed by the disease. Both mind and body must be treated to achieve a meaningful cure, but bodily intervention must come first, and mind intervention need not involve the Freudian exhumation of unconscious conflicts. Good prophylactic (preventive) management (whether it employs cognitive, interpersonal, or behavioral therapies) helps patients recognize mood swings and their effect on self-esteem, cognition, interpretation, and interpersonal relations.[85] As one patient put it:

> At this point in my life, I cannot imagine leading a normal life without both taking lithium and being in psychotherapy. Lithium prevents my seductive but disastrous highs, diminishes my depressions, clears out the wool and webbing from my disordered thinking, slows me down, gentles me out, keeps me from ruining my career and relationships, keeps me out of a hospital, alive, and makes psychotherapy possible. But, ineffably, psychotherapy *heals*. It makes some sense of the confusion, reins in the terrifying thoughts and feelings, returns some control and hope and possibility of learning from it all.[86]

It is usually not enough merely to prescribe lithium or antidepressants for mood disorders; an entrenched pattern of mood-induced misinterpretations will not be dissolved by drugs alone. Patients must explore those cognitive patterns and correct memories of previous experiences before they can reformulate other, more beneficial object-relations.[87] But, once on lithium, most manic-depressives are no longer "sick."

2 "Never was anyone so tossed up & down by the body as I am"

The Symptoms of Manic-Depressive Illness

Afflicting approximately 1 percent of the general population, manic-depressive illness is a mood disorder that can profoundly modify cognition, personality, judgment, sleep patterns, and metabolism (the chemical changes supplying energy to all body cells). Even during relatively euthymic (not ill) states, some patients experience mild variations in the intensity of their perceptions and feelings.[1] All these changes can significantly, though temporarily, affect behavior—particularly since sufferers often remain unaware of any shift in mood. Changes in affect (overall emotional state) are difficult to detect because mild mood swings are normal (the Monday morning "blues," the Friday evening "highs"); unless it presents distinguishable psychotic features, a psychiatric disorder of mood differs only in degree from those normal ups and downs. An affective psychosis is therefore defined as "a severe mood disturbance in which prolonged periods of inappropriate depression alternate either with periods of normal mood or with periods of excessive, inappropriate euphoria and mania."[2] Such terms as *excessive* and *inappropriate* should not imply that the diagnosis of an affective disorder depends on a purely subjective reaction to a patient's behavior. One of Ronald Fieve's patients has described just how fundamental—and yet how subtle—the changes can be as she slips first into hypomania (a mild euphoria), then into frank mania, and, finally, into depression:

> When I start going into a high, I no longer feel like an ordinary housewife. Instead I feel organized and accomplished and I begin to feel I am my most creative self. I can write poetry easily. . . . My mind feels facile and absorbs everything. I have countless ideas. . . .
>   . . . However, when I go beyond this stage, I become manic, and the creativeness becomes so magnified I begin to see things in my mind that aren't real. . . . I saw [them] as clearly as if watching them in real life. . . .
>   My first depression came out of the blue. . . . I seemed to get no pleasure out of living. I had no feeling toward the babies or my other two children. I tried to do extra things for the children because I felt

extremely guilty about my lack of feeling. . . . My mind seemed to be obsessed with black thoughts.[3]

Leonard saw the same phenomenon in Virginia, a discernible shift in mood from her usual perceptivity to impaired reality testing:

> I am sure that, when she had a breakdown, there was a moment when she passed from what can be rightly called sanity to insanity. On one side of this line was a kind of mental balance, a psychological coherence between intellect and emotion, an awareness and acceptance of the outside world and a rational reaction to it; on the other side were violent emotional instability and oscillation, a sudden change in a large number of intellectual assumptions upon which, often unconsciously, the mental outlook and actions of everyone are based, a refusal to admit or accept facts in the outside world.
>
> . . . suddenly the headache, the sleeplessness, the racing thoughts would become intense and it might be several weeks before she could begin again to live a normal life. But four times in her life the symptoms would not go and she passed across the border which divides what we call insanity from sanity. She had a minor breakdown in her childhood; she had a major breakdown after her mother's death in 1895, another in 1914, and a fourth in 1940. In all these cases of breakdown there were two distinct stages which are technically called manic-depressive. In the manic stage she was extremely excited; the mind raced; she talked volubly and, at the height of the attack, incoherently; she had delusions and heard voices, for instance she told me that in her second attack she heard the birds in the garden outside her window talking Greek; she was violent with the nurses. In her third attack, which began in 1914, this stage lasted for several months and ended by her falling into a coma for two days. During the depressive stage all her thoughts and emotions were the exact opposite of what they had been in the manic stage. She was in the depths of melancholia and despair; she scarcely spoke; refused to eat; refused to believe that she was ill and insisted that her condition was due to her own guilt; at the height of this stage she tried to commit suicide, in the 1895 attack by jumping out of a window, in 1915 by taking an overdose of veronal; in 1941 she drowned herself in the river Ouse. (*Beginning Again* 76–79)

Leonard's observations fit quite closely the typical profile of manic-depressive mood swings. He follows the Kraepelinean model: without attempting to ascribe meaning to her delusions, her violent outbursts, or her refusal to eat, he focuses on her symptoms themselves.

When manic-depressives fall ill, they may exhibit a multiplicity and variety of symptoms that can mystify and frustrate not only their families but their doctors as well. The variations in individual manifestations of this illness Kraepelin himself described as "absolutely inexhaustible."[4] Unipolar patients show signs only of depression; bipolar, or "circular," individuals alternate either between manic episodes and "well" periods or between mania and depression with intermittent well periods. One useful descriptive system for expressing the variable intensity of both poles employs four categories: MD (for bipolars who suffer both mania and depression at moderate or severe levels or with psychotic features), Md (for frank manias but mild depressions), mD (for mild manias but pronounced depressions), and md (for cyclothymia).[5] (MD and Md are also known as Bipolar I and mD as Bipolar II.) During her serious breakdowns Virginia experienced MD levels, but often she had milder bipolar episodes, as she noted in her diary and letters:

> I must note the symptoms of the disease, so as to know it next time. The first day one's miserable: the second happy. (*Diary* 2: 108)

> Also my own psychology interests me. I intend to keep full notes of my ups & downs, for my private information. And thus objectified, the pain & shame become at once much less. (*Diary* 5: 64)

> . . . I've been rather bad again—the result I suppose of those 4 days in London. Sleep this time—seems to have gone: and as you know this leaves me very melancholy and restless by day. . . . The Dr. said I must expect ups and downs for at least 2 months more. This is a down; but an up will come. Forgive me for being so egotistic. (*Letters* 6: 43)

Although most bipolars experience both mania and depression (frequently in cycles), the speed, duration, and intensity of the mood swings may vary greatly from individual to individual and from episode to episode in a given individual. On the average, manic episodes begin more abruptly (over a few days or hours) than depressive ones (which can take weeks to develop fully).[6] Some individuals suffer episodes of mania or depression that last for months, even years. Others make a complete bipolar circuit in a matter of minutes ("micropsychosis").[7] Still others suffer from "mixed mania," in which mania and depression are experienced concurrently; these patients report feeling both euphoric and despairing, lethargic and energized,[8] which suggests that mania and depression are not merely chemical alterations in one system of neurons but involve at least two systems that can malfunction simultaneously and produce opposite effects. As Quentin Bell notes of an interval in 1910 between rest cures:

> [Virginia] seemed very self-confident, she was elated and excited about the future, looked forward to fame and marriage; at the same time she was irritated by trifles, exaggerated their importance and was unable to shake off her excessive concern with them.[9]

Leonard noted that Virginia experienced various durations and intensities of mood shifts, although, for the most part, she was euthymic (see also Appendix, below):

> "normally" my wife was no more depressed or elated than the normal, sane person. That is to say that for 24 hours of, say, 350 days in the year she was not more depressed or elated than I was or the "ordinary person." Normally therefore she seemed to be happy, equable, and often gay. But (1) when she was what I called well, she was extremely sensitive to certain things, e.g. noise of various kinds, and would be much more upset by them than the ordinary person. These upsets and depressions were temporary and lasted only at the most a few hours. (2) Whenever she became overtired and the symptoms of headache, sleeplessness, and racing thoughts began, the symptoms of depression and elation began. (3) In (1) and (2) I do not think that anyone would have thought the nature or depth of the depression or elation was irrational or insane, but in the two cases in which, in my experience, the symptoms of headache, sleeplessness, and racing thoughts persisted and ended in what to me seemed insanity, the depression and elation, in nature, content, depth, seemed to become irrational and insane.
> (L. Woolf, *Letters* 548–49)

Mood swings can begin in adolescence—some even in childhood, though in muted form.[10] Diagnosis before adulthood is difficult. Early manifestations of bipolar disorder can be masked by the ups and downs of adolescence; mild mania can easily be misdiagnosed as hyperactivity, and mixtures of mania and depressions may look like conduct disorder or schizophrenia.[11] Full-blown manic psychosis does not appear before puberty. One hypothesis, that an immature nervous system is incapable of expressing frank mania, seems to be supported by the fact that prepubertal children do not exhibit a marked euphoric response to amphetamines, whereas adults do.[12]

Manic-depressive illness is a recurrent illness.[13] From 85 to 95 percent of patients who have an initial manic episode suffer recurrences of either depression or mania; 50 percent to 85 percent of patients who experience one major depression will undergo subsequent depressions.[14] These later episodes need not occur frequently. Clifford W. Beers, a famous American manic-depressive who wrote a book in 1907 about his experiences, was institutionalized only twice in his lifetime: once in his twenties and again in his sixties. In the forty-year interval, he lived a happy and productive life.[15] Some bipolars, however, especially women, fall ill more often as they grow older, and those who, like Virginia, are classed as "mixed" or "cycling" run a risk for chronic illness four times that of the other groups.[16]

Rarely does a breakdown result in an important personality defect or psychological deficit, though the experience itself can be quite upsetting. The "madness" is temporary and seems not to be related in any meaningful way to the individual's normal personality.[17] Leonard's observations of Virginia bear out this assertion:

> When Virginia was quite well, she would discuss her illness; she would recognize that she had been mad, that she had had delusions, heard voices which did not exist, lived for weeks or months in a nightmare world of frenzy, despair, violence. When she was like that, she was obviously well and sane. (*Beginning Again* 79)

Virginia recognized that she experienced drastic alterations in perspective, judgment, and self-esteem as she dropped from a mild mania into a mild depression:

> one night we had a long long argument. Vita started it, by coming over with [George] Plank, & L. (I say) spoilt the visit by glooming because I said he had been angry. He shut up, & was caustic. He denied this, but admitted that my habits of describing him, & others, had this effect often. I saw myself, my brilliancy, genius, charm, beauty (&c. &c.—the attendants who float me through so many years) diminish & disappear. One is in truth rather an elderly dowdy fussy ugly incompetent woman vain, chattering & futile. I saw this vividly, impressively. (*Diary* 3: 111)

For Woolf, this problem of relatedness—the connection between the "sane" Virginia and the "insane" Virginia, the brilliant one and the incompetent one—was crucial. She was quite aware of her instability: "You know how cameleon I am in my changes—leopard one day, all violet spots; mouse today" (*Letters* 5: 209). And, like other manic-depressives, she needed to know that somewhere beneath the bewildering panoply of symptoms (the "Jekyll and Hyde syndrome," as one patient put it)[18] lay a real Virginia, that central, wedge-shaped core Lily Briscoe feels intuitively is the hidden essence of Mrs. Ramsay, that subterranean self Mrs. Dalloway sinks into when personality has become mere chatter, vanity, and invention. Woolf sought the pure being that she hoped lay below her ever-changing (and, as she called it, "egotistical") consciousness. This issue of how identity is tied to mood and perception was especially crucial for a woman who struggled to throw off Victorian dogma that limited who and what a woman could be. It was a challenging task. In a diary entry in 1923, Woolf discusses the problems of such a search for pure being. She meditates on a sudden depression that had sprung up after a short holiday. Such depressions

> make my life seem a little bare sometimes; & then my inveterate romanticism suggests an image of forging ahead, alone, through the night: of suffering inwardly, stoically; of blazing my way through to the end—& so forth. The truth is that the sails flap about me for a day or two on coming back; & not being at full stretch I ponder & loiter. And it is all temporary: yet. . . . One must throw that aside; & venture on to the things that exist independently of oneself. Now this is very hard for young women to do. Yet I got satisfaction from it. . . .
>
> I will leave it here, unfinished, a note of interrogation—signifying some mood that recurs, but is not often expressed. One's life is made up, superficially, of such moods; but they cross a solid substance, which too I am not going to hack my way into now. (*Diary* 2: 221–22)

Fifteen years later she again faced the same abyss of depression (this time worrying about critical attacks upon *Three Guineas*), and she used the same reasoning to overcome her fear that she was merely a walking shadow, not a whole human being:

> Now the thing to remember is that I'm an independent & perfectly established human being: no one can bully me: & at the same time nothing shall make me shrivel into a martyr or a bitter persecution maniac. . . . I mean to stand on my own feet. (*Diary* 5: 163)

Are these the words of a repressed neurotic afraid to face ugly truths about herself? I argue that Woolf had nowhere to go for help but back into her own mind, calling upon her own reserves to assay the meaning of a perplexing disorder, to establish a sense of self that resembled neither Savage's submissive drudge nor Freud's emasculated male. To establish an identifiable sense of self is especially difficult for manic-depressives, for changes in mood and perception can be drastic or mild, brief or drawn-out, with various symptoms, each posing a problem in perception and interpretation.

MANIA

The manic phase is characterized by an elevated and expansive mood (patients describe it as "going high"), but, because various biologic components (endocrine glands, electrolyte metabolism, peptidergic hormones to "fine-tune" brain activities, and electrical and chemical systems in brain cells, among others) are involved, mania can be mild, moderate, or severe, with or without psychotic features (hallucinations and delusions, marked formal thought disorder, or grossly disorganized behavior).[19] Moreover, psychosis is not necessarily related to the depth of the mood. The manic mood may range from dreamy or infectious cheerfulness to ecstasy and exaltation. Or joy and love of mankind may change without warning to vitriolic hatred marked by verbal abuse.

Manics often evidence low tolerance for frustration coupled with explosive anger, "affective storms" that resemble temper tantrums or extreme touchiness, what Quentin Bell has called Virginia Woolf's ability to turn "purple with rage" and create "an atmosphere of thunderous and oppressive gloom."[20] As bipolars fall in and out of moods, their tempers fluctuate. Duncan Grant remembered that, although Virginia was sometimes "very shy" and quiet in company, there was also "the danger of sudden outbursts of scathing criticism," and Elizabeth Bowen described Woolf's flashes of temper as "fleetingly malicious, rather than outright cruel" or prolonged.[21]

The manic's irritability lies at the center of a critical debate in Woolf studies. Freudians typically read intent in Woolf's manic rage, as if it revealed the real feelings of the real Woolf, not the ill one. Susan M. Kenney, for instance, argues that "surely her violent aversion to Leonard Woolf during other attacks was a reaction against the silent reproach she felt in his actions," that is to say, his supposed moral disapproval of her having fallen ill.[22] But Leonard himself said he believed that there was "nothing moral" about her breakdowns (*Letters* 191) and that manic-depressive illness "really is a disease" that was "not really under [Virginia's] control."[23] Furthermore, modern medicine warns us that, since we cannot know whether statements made by a manic in the throes of an affective episode represent attitudes held by the individual when normal, we should amend Kenney's "surely" to read "perhaps" and look for more convincing corroborating evidence than Leonard's silence. Manic rage is usually unrelated to the patient's long-term feelings; it seems to be a component of the manic's potential for paranoia. In an apologetic letter to Ethel Smyth, Woolf specifically connects an outburst of temper to madness:

This no doubt seems to you wantonly exaggerated to excuse a fit of temper. But it is not. I see of course that it is morbid, that it is through this even to me inexplicable susceptibility to some impressions suddenly that I approach madness and that end of a drainpipe with a gibbering old man. (*Letters* 4: 298)

Not all manic outbursts end so peacefully. In rare cases, patients feel so fearful and persecuted that they attempt suicide to escape, thinking that their loved ones intend to murder them.[24] Both manic delusions—either that the world is full of magical people and things, or that it is full of demons and tyrants—result from the distortion produced when elevated mood and dysregulated brain chemistry mediate perceptions in uncharacteristic ways over which the individual has no control. When reality testing fails completely, in severe mania, hallucinations result.

Mild mania (hypomania), however, can be fairly pleasant, especially in social situations. Manics are "people seekers": they love attention. In return, they can be sociable, witty, and inventive, the life of the party, the "bubbly, and elastic individual who bounds into a room vigorously inquiring about everybody and everything," producing a torrent of ideas and words connected by complex webs of associations, rhymes, puns, and amusing irrelevancies.[25]

The manic's entertaining social behavior can escalate into the startling or absurd. Manic speech may become theatrical, elaborated by dramatic mannerisms and even singing.[26] Uninhibited impulsivity can lead to accidents. Her mishaps earned Virginia the family nickname of "The Goat," and Barbara Bagenal remembers that Virginia "had a strange, rather clumsy way of moving," but friends who saw her in other moods commented on her grace, elegance, and fluidity of movement.[27] Manics may also embarrass their companions by ignoring social protocol, behaving rashly, or dressing in colorful or strange clothes. Lyndall Gordon opines that Woolf acted "the cracked Englishwoman" by dressing in extremes: either in drab, dowdy outfits or in outrageous creations of her own, one of which made her look "like a young elephant," and Madge Garland remembers that "there was a presence about [Virginia] that made her instantly noticeable. But what also attracted my attention was that she appeared to be wearing an upturned wastepaper basket on her head," a basket that turned out to be a hat.[28] Even without egocentric clothing, Woolf attracted attention when she drifted through the streets "staring, entranced." Bystanders reacted predictably to her "unaffected strangeness": they "tended to laugh" at her or feel "uneasy."[29]

Many manic-depressives, Woolf included, feel humiliated by their involuntary effect on other people. Manics frequently become public spectacles because they are energized, unabashedly self-confident and exuberant, exhibiting a noisy hilarity and spouting high-flown ideas. Though mania seduces them into mistaking the ridiculous for the sublime, later, when they have shifted out of mania, they may remember their eccentric behavior with shame at its undiluted vanity. Over time, they come to fear the smile that mocks, the gaze that condemns, the friend who forgives with lingering suspicion, and they may decide to avoid intimacy, public display, even photographers, to spare themselves further embarrassment. But such resolutions usually last only until the next manic episode.

Ninety-nine percent feel the "pressure of speech." With or without an audience, they talk rapidly, tying together myriad ideas and leaping from topic to topic (known as a "loosening of associations").[30] Manic thought disorder strings ideas together, "extravagantly combined and elaborated," with many irrelevant intrusions that appear either inappropriately flippant or desperate.[31] As one patient remembered:

> My thoughts were so fast that I couldn't remember the beginning of a sentence halfway through. Fragments of ideas, images, sentences raced around and around in my mind like the tigers in Little Black Sambo. Finally, like those tigers, they became meaningless melted pools. Nothing once familiar to me was familiar. I wanted desperately to slow down but could not. Nothing helped—not running around a parking lot for hours on end or swimming for miles.[32]

Manics generally feel unable to control their racing thoughts, as if they have been inspired by a divine Muse. Some do become highly productive, but others find that the combination of overstimulation and insomnia merely spins their wheels. In a letter to Ethel Smyth, Woolf explains that, though her brain is "teeming with books I want to write," none of these visions translates into action. Rather, she feels frightened:

> Never trust a letter of mine not to exaggerate thats written after a night lying awake looking at a bottle of chloral [a common prescription for mania and insomnia at that time] and saying no, no, no, you shall not take it. Its odd why sleeplessness, even of a modified kind[,] has this power to frighten me. Its connected I think with those awful other times when I couldn't control myself. (*Letters* 6: 44)

In mania the imagination seems to go into overdrive, finding great significance in ordinary events. The individual experiences seemingly profound but inexpressible insights (e.g., the meaning of life), delusions, or vivid hallucinations. Hyperalert, patients may misinterpret actions by doctors and nurses as evidence of a sinister plot against them. When family or experience contradicts these misreadings, manics may withdraw into their own world or engage in even more desperate attempts to "read" their environment, to discover the elusive "truth" that will explain all, imposing meaning and a sometimes highly idiosyncratic order upon a world spinning out of their control:

> Our patients were labile and frequently angry. Their "world" was not
> stable and rosy but changing without reason and frustrating. . . . [The
> typical patient] frequently had insight into the fact that he was ill, often
> at the same time he was expressing delusional or grandiose ideas. . . .
> For the most part, the patients remembered being wound up and
> unable to stop, not feeling tired but aware that something was wrong,
> upsetting their families, and not being able to stop.[33]

Manics often experience extremely vivid hallucinations, and even when they are not hallucinatory, their accelerated psychomotor activity and intensified sensory perceptions make their perceptions or visions seem profoundly meaningful: objects *look* significant.[34] John Custance, a British manic-depressive who, like Clifford Beers, achieved notoriety by writing a book about his illness, when manic had "a rather curious feeling behind the eyeballs, rather as though a vast electric motor were pulsing away there," with the result that electric lights looked "deeper, more intense" and were surrounded by a "bright starlike" effect which reminded him of the Aurora Borealis. The faces of hospital staff seemed "to glow with a sort of inner light." His senses of touch, smell, and taste heightened: "even common grass tastes excellent, while real delicacies like strawberries or raspberries give ecstatic sensations appropriate to a veritable food of the gods." Heightened perceptions inspired "animistic conceptions," in which objects literally became such entities as time, love, God, peace: "I cannot avoid seeing spirits in everything."[35] Colors were so intense that they seemed to signify real threats or blessings, messages from the devil or Christ, hints which Custance felt obliged to decipher as if he were explicating a literary text:

> There was a time when I was terrified of green, because it was the
> signal to go, and the only place I thought I could be going to was
> Hell. However I eventually got out of Hell [when he recovered from

his depression] and at present green has no terrors for me . . . . [I]t stands for grass and growth.

. . . Red is the Devil's colour, and perhaps I am not quite safe from him yet. Red also means stop, and I don't in the least want to stop here for ever. However, with a certain amount of effort, concentration and prayer, I conquered the red with the help of the green and felt safe.

The next day the colours had suffered a kaleidoscopic change. Gone were the reds and the greens; there was nothing but blues, blacks and greys, with an occasional purple. The sky, which had been bright and clear, was overcast; it was raining. This new combination of colours constituted a new threat, with which I had to deal.[36]

Delusional beliefs occur in a wide range of clinical conditions (seventy-five, by one count). They are frequently seen in schizophrenia, affective disorders, substance abuse disorders, and organic psychoses, in all of which sensory experiences can be so puzzling that even impossible delusions serve an explanatory function. In a sense, delusions are necessarily unusual ways of coping with unusual circumstances.[37] Because perception is so greatly altered by mania, the patient's beliefs about his situation may become quite bizarre. When his often inappropriate or impossible, though to him reasonable, requests are not carried out, he may feel frustrated and angry, and withdraw even further into himself. As the mania becomes more severe, the world outside matters less and less, whereas attempts to explain it become increasingly important in themselves. The manic self feels dominant, creative, full of incipient meaning that is imposed willy-nilly upon perceptions of the world.[38] He may feel mystically "at one" with the universe, but in fact self has divorced the world.

Manics rarely speak of mood spontaneously or examine it critically—rather, they live out their moods.[39] Filled with great plans and designs, manics may appear supercilious and haughty, claiming to have profound visions of life's meaning which they plan to codify in some future work. One patient, a successful artist, was extremely productive during mild manias, but when his moods soared higher his work suffered from impaired reality testing:

He would think he had done something original only to discover later that his "inspiration" was ridiculous. His political and religious theories suffered from the same lack of critical perspective during his psychotic highs. He would conceive them in a flash of enthusiasm only to discover later that they were absurd.[40]

Heightened mood and a stimulated imagination give rise to delusional belief in the self's power and importance. Woolf herself noted that mania intensifies both confidence and creativity:

> Curious how all ones fibres seem to expand & fill with air when anxiety is taken off; curious also to me the intensity of my own feelings: I think imagination, the picture making power, decks up feelings with all kinds of scenes; so that one goes on thinking, instead of localising the event. All very mysterious. (*Diary* 4: 176)

But she was wary of unrestrained elations and their doubtful products, as, in a dreamy, hypomanic mood, she considered how to write *To the Lighthouse:*

> The thing is I vacillate between a single & intense character of father; & a far wider slower book—Bob T[revelyan]. telling me that my speed is terrific, & destructive. My summer's wanderings with the pen have I think shown me one or two new dodges for catching my flies. I have sat here, like an improviser with his hands rambling over the piano. The result is perfectly inconclusive, & almost illiterate. I want to learn greater quiet, & force. But if I set myself that task, don't I run the risk of falling into the flatness of N[ight]. & D[ay].? (*Diary* 3: 37)

Understandably, manics can become intrusive, irritating, or violent if balked in their pursuit of the marvelous. Euphoria can quickly change to irritability and even anger, especially if the mania is mixed or alternates with microdepressions. Beneath the surface elation may lie deep pools of black despair:

> If one allows a manic patient to talk, one will note that he shows fleeting episodes of depression embedded within the mania ("micro-depressions"). He may be talking in a grandiose and extravagant fashion and then suddenly for thirty seconds breaks down to give an account of something he feels guilty about. For instance, he may be talking vigorously and in the midst of his loquacity he may suddenly talk about the death of his father for which he has felt guilty for some time. His eyes will fill with tears but in 15 to 30 seconds he will be back talking in his expansive fashion.[41]

In one study, half of the manic patients displayed pervasive depression.[42] Such manics can be, as Woolf herself was, "very vulnerable and childishly sensitive to criticism," for the base of their inflated confidence is hollow.[43] Criticism strikes deep because the manic-depressive's worst fear is that at any moment he may permanently and unknowingly lose his judgment, his sanity.

Because manic delusions and hallucinations create and/or accompany ideas of sometimes cosmic proportions, they are frequently interpreted as religious experiences, especially by those who have been raised in a religion. The patient may believe that she has been chosen by God—why else would she suddenly feel so captivated? When euthymic (not ill), John Custance recognized that his religious delusions and visions were similar to the pseudo-revelations induced by nitrous oxide and other drugs, but when manic, he fervently believed that "depth beyond depth of truth" had been revealed to him, that the mystery of the universe had been "unveiled" and become "certain beyond the possibility of a doubt."[44] Such mystical experiences of universal communion can also be induced by mescaline, LSD, and other hallucinogenic substances that alter the biochemistry of the brain.[45]

Perhaps because abnormal brain chemistry is inherently unstable, religious delusions tend to be short-lived and variable. They seem to be used by patients as explanations for the way they feel: a mystical theory explains the elevated mood, and as moods change, explanations must change too. William Cowper (a favorite of Virginia Woolf's) explained his shifts between mania and depression in terms of Calvinist theology. When manic, he attributed his euphoria to God's saving grace; when depressed, he reasoned that he must have unknowingly rejected God and committed the sin of apostasy.[46] The manic typically engages in immoderate projection, reading as real emotions and ideas that exist only in his mind. Strong emotion skews perception, creating an obscure symbolism, solipsistic and misleading, that convinces because it is congruent with the experienced emotion. Thus, a sudden vision of life's true meaning or God's intentions or the hearing of voices seems to explain what the manic is feeling at that moment. These explanations are both true, because they bring coherence to experience, and false, because they are merely mental constructs. They are pieces of fiction that, like all fiction, are meaningful only if we understand their objective and subjective components; they are neither empirically real nor irrelevant and false, but products of the self that incorporate and reveal an inner truth. But in manic-depressive illness this inner truth is not under the individual's integrative control. When we read or write fiction, we try to balance what we know is objectively true (that we are not the book's hero or heroine, that this rendition is not a history) and what we feel is subjectively true (we identify with the protagonist and are moved emotionally by the adventures as if they were real). But manics live in a room of mirrors and do not see the inconvenient discrepancies between what they project and what they perceive. They re-create the world. To outsiders they appear self-indulgent, vain, egotistical, but it is an ego that no longer owns its identity, because it is incapable of insightful introspection and the self-control that insight brings.[47]

Woolf's manic episodes ran the gamut from lively sociableness to wild and incoherent gibberish, from pure ecstasy to mixed mania. When merely hypomanic, Woolf felt energized and creative, and fiction came easily to her—"my body was flooded with rapture and my brain with ideas. I wrote rapidly until 12" (*Letters* 3: 428); "& these curious intervals in life—I've had many—are the most fruitful artistically—one becomes fertilised—think of my madness at Hogarth—& all the little illnesses" (*Diary* 3: 254). She seems to have detected the connection between the hallucinations, the heightened perceptions, and the ecstasy of more severe manic moods:

> I've had some very curious visions in this room too, lying in bed, mad, & seeing the sunlight quivering like gold water, on the wall. I've heard the voices of the dead here. And felt, through it all, exquisitely happy. (*Diary* 2: 283)

When severely manic, she was unable to distinguish between fact and fiction, as Leonard remembers:

> But one morning she was having breakfast in bed and I was talking to her when without warning she became violently excited and distressed. She thought her mother was in the room and began to talk to her.
> . . . she talked almost without stopping for two or three days, paying no attention to anyone in the room or anything said to her. For about a day what she said was coherent; the sentences meant something, though it was nearly all wildly insane. Then gradually it became completely incoherent, a mere jumble of dissociated words. After another day the stream of words diminished and finally she fell into a coma. (*Beginning Again* 172–73)

Custance, too, connected mild mania with pleasant hallucinations of the dead, a "sense of communion [that] extends to all mankind, dead, living and to be born. That is perhaps why mania always brings me an inner certainty that the dead are really alive and that I can commune with them at will."[48] But in severe mania, the same sense of consuming communion between self and object frightened him. He saw

> demons and werewolves, strange faces of forgotten gods, and devils, while my mind played unceasingly on everything it remembered of myths and magic. Folds of the bedclothes suddenly became the carven

image of Baal; a crumpled pillow appeared as the horrible visage of Hecate. I was transported into an atmosphere of miracle and witch-craft, of all-pervading occult forces, although I had taken no interest whatever in these subjects prior to my illness.[49]

Woolf, too, as her mania intensified lost the beneficial, nurturing images and entered a paranoid world in which Leonard and her nurses had formed a conspiracy against her.[50] Her racing mind imposed the illusion of coherence on bird songs (they seemed to sing in Greek) and on noises from the garden (they sounded like King Edward VII uttering muffled profanities), and it vividly projected memories of her dead mother (con-versing with one's past is a way of thinking about it, but it is a diminished kind of thinking that cannot result in a conclusion that benefits the patient). Paranoia explained why sickroom attendants whispered to each other and why she was being restrained. Although her interpretations were uncorrected by reality testing (so that neither a royal visit nor birds that spoke seemed unlikely), they followed a logical process shared by us all. But what of the interpretations themselves? Can we decode them? Do they evidence an unspoken hostility toward men? Frigidity? An unhealthy obses-sion with sex, or with her mother, or both? When psychoanalyst Shirley Panken tries to make sense of Woolf's hallucinations (in order to "demystify" them), she reads them for symbolic significance. Her premises include: King Edward, who is a father-figure, stands for Leslie's "incest-uous" invasiveness; birds have hard beaks, so they might refer to the phallus; the Greek songs (by a tangled web of literary allusions to a Greek myth about two sisters who are turned into birds) symbolize Woolf's dead mother; bird imagery appears in *Mrs. Dalloway;* Septimus Warren Smith commits suicide in that novel. Panken reaches a conclusion by simple arithmetic: bird=phallus=death. A number of explanatory interpretations now present themselves: "Does the [bird] myth evoke Woolf's guilt regard-ing her mother's death? Woolf's silence regarding her half-brothers' lovemaking? Her frustrated longing to find a voice to express her repressed rage?" The list goes on: birds are resilient and passionate, Panken decides, whereas Woolf feels fragile and frigid; birds are small and victims of hunters, and so Virginia may be identifying with them; in a letter, Vanessa once compared Virginia to a bird, and, as children, the Stephens had bird nicknames, often ascribed by Leslie. Panken brings us back to the father because repetition implies repression: Leslie must be the organizing center of the hallucination. Theory demands it.[51]

But in whom does the repetition compulsion lie, Woolf or Panken? Since her patient is dead and cannot acknowledge, deny, or correct these symbolic connections supplied by the analyst, Panken speculates without hindrance or adequate information, using Woolf's conscious associations (bird imagery used deliberately in her novels and essays) as if they were identical to unconscious connections. But it is Panken's associations, not Woolf's, that dominate here. In a sense, the psychoanalyst is behaving like the manic-depressive, the ill Custance who does not have privileged access to why he is hallucinating and therefore must free-associate with bits and pieces of remembered lore, hoping that he will hit upon the meaningful connection. The trouble is that too many seemingly meaningful connections can be found too easily. Doubtless, both Custance and Panken construct ingenious explanations, but ingenuity is no proof of insight. To apply such ingenuity to hallucinations seems misguided, since neurotics, who might be supposed to make such associations, rarely hallucinate, and manics, who often do, are driven by biochemistry, not by mental trauma.

Complete hallucinatory and delusional manic breakdowns were, fortunately, relatively rare for Virginia Woolf. For the most part, she experienced hypomania, best exemplified by what Quentin Bell labels her "conversational extravagances":

> This was one of the difficulties of living with Virginia; her imagination was furnished with an accelerator and no brakes; it flew rapidly ahead, parting company with reality, and, when reality happened to be a human being, the result could be appalling for the person who found himself expected to live up to the character that Virginia had invented.
> . . . she must have reduced many poor shop assistants to the verge of blasphemy or of tears, and not only they but her companions suffered intensely when she found herself brought to a standstill by the difference between that which she had imagined and that which in fact was offered for sale.[52]

Bell's illustration is negatively charged; hypomanics can also be great fun. Virginia would use "a prosaic incident or statement to create a baroque mountain of fantasy," a childlike "freedom from banality" which her friends loved.[53] In a letter to Leonard, Barbara Rothschild asked him to "tell Virginia that we long to see her too and to be led again into the tortuous and torturing mazes of indiscretions into which she lures the carrot followers."[54] Lyndall Gordon describes Virginia's "mercurial public manner" at Bloomsbury parties:

With a little encouragement she threw off words like a musician impro-
vising. Her voice seemed to preen itself with self-confidence in its verbal facility as she leant sideways, a little stiffly in her chair, to address
her visitor in a bantering manner. She confounded strangers with wildly
fictitious accounts of their lives or shot malicious darts at friends, who,
the night before, she might have flattered outrageously.[55]

Most of Virginia's friends considered her fantastic stories "a splendid
game," "dazzling performances," "burlesque, a love of exaggeration for
its own sake." They saw that she indulged in "wild generalizations based
on the flimsiest premises and embroidered with elaborate fantasy . . . sent
up like rockets."[56] Nigel Nicolson valued them for precisely that reason:

> Virginia had this way of magnifying one's simple words and experiences.
> One would hand her a bit of information as dull as a lump of lead. She
> would hand it back glittering like diamonds. I always felt on leaving
> her that I had drunk two glasses of an excellent champagne. She was a
> life-enhancer. That was one of her own favorite phrases.[57]

Christopher Isherwood, noting the Tennysonian impression of unhappy
fragility in Virginia's physical appearance, contrasts her "fairy-story princess
under a spell" look with her liveliness:

> We are at the tea table. Virginia is sparkling with gaiety, delicate malice
> and gossip—the gossip which is the style of her books and which made
> her the best hostess in London; listening to her, we missed appoint-
> ments, forgot love-affairs, stayed on and on into the small hours, when
> we had to be hinted, gently, but firmly, out of the house.[58]

David Garnett reported that Virginia "had the gift for sudden intimacy"
(also a common manic trait), which both "flattered and disturbed" people,
for her interest in details—central or irrelevant—was intense. However much
her gaiety charmed and entertained, it also suggested depths. Madge
Garland noted that "Virginia could be a very enchanting person," but
"there were times when I felt . . . that she was more nearly *enchanted*.
This was when she seemed removed from the people she was talking to—
almost dreamlike." Another friend (and a psychoanalyst), Alix Strachey,
observed that Woolf's need to know every detail of other people's lives
was connected to her experience of estrangement, of being "different":
"it seemed to me that her wish to know all about them sprang ultimately
from a feeling of alienation from reality—an alienation which she was trying to overcome."[59]

Mania has trade-offs; one ascends to visionary heights by distancing ordinary things. Still, we must not underestimate the assets of hypomania. Like most bipolar patients, Woolf enjoyed her flights, and her pleasure is by no means sure evidence of a neurotic attachment to being ill. "Who would not want an illness," K. R. Jamison asks rhetorically, "that numbers among its symptoms elevated and expansive mood, inflated self-esteem, more energy than usual . . . 'sharpened and unusually creative thinking,' and 'increased productivity?'"[60] Woolf saw quite clearly the creative advantages of her mood swings, even though she also knew (as is suggested by Garland and Strachey's observations) that their usefulness would be undercut by lopsided object-relations until her euthymic periods, when she could reconnect mind and world, balanced the unrestrained imagination with an external coherence. The result then was a "moment of being":

> The way to rock oneself back into writing is this. . . . [O]ne must become externalised; very, very concentrated, all at one point, not having to draw upon the scattered parts of one's character, living in the brain. Sydney comes & I'm Virginia; when I write I'm merely a sensibility. Sometimes I like being Virginia, but only when I'm scattered & various & gregarious. (*Diary* 2: 193)

Woolf recognized that the manic state stimulated her already rich imagination to create and project fictions that had little basis in reality but that explained (or at least embodied, if obscurely) her experienced moods. In mania, she mistook her subjective world for the objective, imposed what was inside her mind upon what was outside, and learned later through disappointment that perception was neither reliable nor simple, as she shows in two penitent letters to Leonard after one of her abusive scenes:

> Dearest, I have been disgraceful—to you, I mean. . . .
> You've been absolutely perfect to me. Its all my fault. . . . I do want you and I believe in spite of my vile imaginations the other day that I love you and that you love me. (*Letters* 2: 34)

John Custance felt much the same way about his religious vision:

> Only now and then, when I am in an excited state bordering on acute mania, will it emerge from its elusive retirement and allow me to get it down. Unfortunately, when I come to read what I have written in cold blood, after the manic excitement has passed, I can barely make head or tail of it and very often its appalling egocentricity nearly makes me sick.[61]

Shame and self-doubt frequently visit the morning after a night of magical vision, boundless joy (or paranoia), and absolute certainty that one has seen the "truth," if not about the universe, then at least about oneself. Imprudent marriages, rash purchases or career changes, and adulterous flings may seem romantic and "fated" in mania, only to become tawdry and empty and undesired after mania has passed.

What could Woolf have learned from episodes that seem extravagant and meaningless? The reconnection between mind and world threatened her with a sudden, dispiriting deflation of self. The shock of falling out of solipsistic mania taught Woolf the integrity of objects, their intractable solidity, their "otherness," independent of the illusions her "unreal" self could foster about them. When well, she could invite the external, objective world into her internal, subjective world, while still maintaining the power to create fiction; it was then that she felt she could find an all-embracing coherence that was neither self-destructive nor solipsistic. She recognized that she could not control a "moment of being"; such a moment could be frightening, but it offered a "representative" and "arranged" lesson about the nature of object-relations: "we are sealed vessels afloat upon what it is convenient to call reality; at some moments, without a reason, without an effort, the sealing matter cracks; in floods reality" (*Moments of Being* 142). The image here of incipient drowning is frightening because how she responded to this flood of reality was crucial: she had to be careful neither to disregard it, as she did in mania, nor to be overwhelmed and destroyed by it, as she was in depression. And yet both mania and depression, as I will argue in Chapter 6, taught her valuable lessons about what this moment of being was. Often characters in her fiction experience similar disillusionment and deflation of wishful thinking while still remembering the value, the truth, of illusion. James Ramsay, for instance, who finally sees the lighthouse building as it really is, white and stark on the black rock, blends this fact with his idealization of his childhood and his self-serving hatred of his father until all views become facets of truth: "So that was the Lighthouse, was it? No, the other was also the Lighthouse. For nothing was simply one thing. The other Lighthouse was true too" (*To the Lighthouse* 277). Inevitably, such insights into how meaning is made and unmade, never finished, yet satisfying, are life-affirming.

DEPRESSION

The manic projections of bipolar patients, however enlightening, are eventually undermined by mood swings in the other direction. Depressive symptoms range from sadness to despair, from an uncontrollable tearfulness to a despondency beyond tears. The word *depression* cannot convey the nightmarish pain involved. It is, as William Styron has recently put it, "a true wimp of a word for such a major illness," with its "bland tonality." Styron prefers *brainstorm* to denote the "veritable howling tempest in the brain" impossible for those who have not experienced depression to imagine.[62]

In contrast to manics' exuberance and inflated self-esteem, depressives can feel hopeless, lethargic, or suicidal. Self-deprecatory comments reflect the low self-esteem that accompanies the general loss of energy, and no outside stimuli are capable of ameliorating the helpless sadness: neither the family nor the patient has any control over the depression, and this lowers spirits further on both sides. The depressed patient feels chronically miserable, worried, discouraged, irritable, and fearful.[63] Many experience great fatigue, insomnia, or repeated early morning waking (described by Woolf as "starts of terrified about nothing waking" [*Letters* 6: 376]), slowness in thinking or in motor skills,[64] loss of interest or pleasure in usual activities, and, in three-quarters of these patients, decreased sex drive— symptoms which usually strike the patient as evidence not of depression but of something else. One patient, a prominent lawyer, shared Woolf's private conviction of damnation. He

> denied being depressed. Rather, he complained of having "no feelings of any sort. . . . I have no soul, I am dead inside." When pressed, he confided that he believed he suffered from a case of "moral decay of the soul—sin sickness," as he termed it during a flash of his old court-room eloquence. "The sentence should be electrocution rather than shock treatments." However, after receiving the latter, he no longer believed he deserved to be electrocuted; indeed, in six weeks, he was able to return to the practice of law.[65]

Just as the elated manic may be either sociable or assaultive, so too the depressive may be either passive or aggressive, sad or angry. Some lie in bed, immobile, despondent, completely helpless in the face of despair and guilt. Others become extremely agitated by their black thoughts, fidgeting restlessly, wringing their hands, feeling shaky inside, experiencing heart palpitations but denying despair. These contradictory syndromes led clinicians to define two autonomous states of depression, a retarded anhedonic type (with a pathologically decreased capacity to anticipate and enjoy experience, especially on a sensory level) and an agitated delusional type (with increased anxiety and hostility).[66] The two states can both be seen in the same patient.[67] K. R. Jamison notes that the cyclothymia suffered by Hector Berlioz combined agitated and retarded depressions: "an active, painful, tumultuous, and cauldronous one (almost certainly a mixed state), and another type, characterized by ennui, isolation, lethargy, and a dearth of feeling."[68] The agitated depressive is so upset that he looks as if he is fighting back against total despair, and he may resemble irritable manics in nervous energy and paranoia. Quentin Bell records that Woolf suffered one such episode of agitated delusional depression in an 1896 breakdown:

> [Virginia] became painfully excitable and nervous and then intolerably depressed. . . . She went through a period of morbid self-criticism, blamed herself for being vain and egotistical, compared herself unfavourably to Vanessa and was at the same time intensely irritable.[69]

Anhedonia, by contrast, overwhelms patients with what appears to be "pure" depression, a debilitating sorrow which includes "vegetative" symptoms characterized by a general psychomotor retardation: they have little to say, interact poorly with others, and tire easily, complaining of exhaustion, "tight" headaches, or muscle aches. Constipation is very common and sometimes severe; even nail growth may stop.[70] William Styron remembers that his voice seemed to "disappear" as his depression deepened: "It underwent a strange transformation, becoming at times quite faint, wheezy, and spasmodic—a friend observed later that it was the voice of a ninety-year-old."[71] Sleep is disturbed. Most depressives experience insomnia and early morning waking, but some become hypersomnolent, sleeping longer at night, sleeping during the day, or taking excessive naps.[72] Loss of appetite is typical of a general slowdown in bodily processes. Some patients complain of a bad taste, a dryness of the mouth, heart palpitations, or "the feeling of a [tight] band round the forehead,"[73] as did Woolf:

> I was walking down the path with Lydia. If this dont stop, I said, referring to the bitter taste in my mouth & the pressure like a wire cage of sound over my head, then I am ill: yes, very likely I am destroyed, diseased, dead. Damn it! Here I fell down. (*Diary* 3: 315)

> The galloping horses got wild in my head last Thursday night. . . . Then my heart leapt; & stopped; & leapt again; & I tasted that queer bitterness at the back of my throat; & the pulse leapt into my head & beat & beat, more savagely, more quickly. (*Diary* 4: 121)

Sensory perceptions also change. Where mania exaggerates, depression dulls, leaving physical and mental worlds monochromatic.[74] As John

Custance noted, any object—food, clothes, one's own body—inspired "repulsion," "intense disgust," and "unpleasure" in depression, whereas in mania these same objects elicited "intense joy," "attraction," and "pleasure."[75] Because metabolic changes in manic-depression can be so profound, physiological symptoms often coincide with psychological ones, and so many patients' reports will associate the two, using one to bring significance to the other. In other words, patients usually seek to explain their loss of desire by associating it with some other depressive symptom, such as lowered self-esteem—reasoning, to cite only one example, that they no longer want to eat because they are unworthy of taking food from others. Self and world both appear manifestly degraded, evil, repulsive, and to perpetuate such a dismal situation by incorporating even more of the world into oneself would be unendurable.[76] As a psychological theory, the depressive's explanation fulfills the Freudian paradigm: it produces meaning by filling the gap that occurs between two symptoms ("I have no appetite" and "I feel so bad"), and it assumes that the physical symptom expresses a psychological state, which is its cause.

To us, anorectic conscience appears delusional, or at best a rationalization, and we may dismiss it as absurd—but delusions, like scientific theories, have an explanatory power that seems as compelling to the psychotic as objective physical evidence does to the individual whose pain results from visibly lacerated skin or a broken bone. We all need to provide a continuous narrative for our experiences; this is the basis of consciousness, and anomalous or bizarre experiences call for unusual explanations to connect the dots, to account for fragmented or incomplete events.

The symptomatic form manic-depressive illness takes, however, usually reflects the individual's experience.[77] Here biology and psychology combine. In depression there is often some reference to the patient's life (for example, a normally confident pharmacist may worry obsessively about accidentally poisoning her customers), but in severe mania the individual may lose all contact with his euthymic state (a loving husband may be unfaithful to his wife and unconcerned about his children). Like anyone else, the individual tries to formulate an explanation for his experiences; the more anomalous the experiences, the more bizarre may be the explanation, especially since a mood disorder fulfills its own prophecies by affecting what evidence the subject attends to and how he interprets it. Environmental and social factors often combine with biochemically induced delusional beliefs when the patient attempts to account for himself:

For example, suppose you are having mood swings that seem unconnected with events in your life. If you have read something suggesting
that hormones (or blood sugar, or magnesium) affect mood, and you
have social support for this idea, you may be less likely to conclude
that some abstract force is controlling you. Similarly, if you are skeptical of miracles (or magic) to begin with, you should be less likely to
conclude that a visual experience is the blood of Christ, and more
inclined to look for other possibilities. Delusions should be affected by
patients' cultural and social experience, particularly when the delusions
are not sufficiently driven by perceptual experience to determine their
character and are not constrained by alternative possibilities that are
salient because of prior experience. Especially important may be the
availability of alternative explanations for people's own *feelings*.[78]

In worldwide surveys of delusional themes, researchers have found that
Kuwaiti patients have significantly more delusions centered around supernatural phenomena such as sorcery or the devil; lower-class Egyptians are
more apt to have religious delusions such as a conviction of being
Mohammed or a great prophet; upper-class Egyptians display more
secularized delusions such as being affected by computers, X-rays, elec-
tricity, or government spies; and Irish-Americans develop sex, sin, and
guilt preoccupations.[79]

Delusional patients not only produce odd accounts for themselves; they
also try to read them to discover what they might mean. Clifford Beers,
for instance, combined paranoid and anorectic ideas in his refusal to eat.
He theorized that the mental hospital in which he had been placed had
been secretly infiltrated by ingenious, Kafkaesque police detectives who
were seeking a confession from him for an unspecified crime (though he
remained ignorant of the accusation, Beers nevertheless felt it was deserved):

> They now intended by each article of food to suggest a certain idea,
> and I was expected to recognize the idea thus suggested. Conviction or
> acquittal depended upon my correct interpretation of their symbols,
> and my interpretation was to be signified by my eating, or not eating,
> the several kinds of food placed before me. To have eaten a burnt crust
> of bread would have been a confession of arson. Why? Simply because
> the charred crust suggested fire; and, as bread is the staff of life, would
> it not be an inevitable deduction that life had been destroyed—destroyed
> by fire—and that I was the destroyer?[80]

Such deductive ingenuity would be worthy of a Freudian, but for all
this theorizing, Beers could not discover why he felt so despondent and

guilty in the first place. Nothing he had done had caused him to be manic-depressive. For all its plausibility, food proved to be neither the answer nor the significant, therapeutic symbol. Virginia Woolf also had problems with the association of food and guilt, as Quentin Bell notes:

> she thought people were laughing at her; she was the cause of everyone's troubles; she felt overwhelmed with a sense of guilt for which she should be punished. She became convinced that her body was in some way monstrous, the sordid mouth and sordid belly demanding food—repulsive matter which must then be excreted in a disgusting fashion; the only course was to refuse to eat. Material things assumed sinister and unpredictable aspects, beastly and terrifying or—sometimes—of fearful beauty.[81]

Virginia makes the same connection when describing a passing depression but notes that it does not hold up once she is euthymic:

> I think the blood has really been getting into my brain at last. It is the oddest feeling, as though a dead part of me were coming to life. I cant tell you how delightful it is—and I dont mind how much I eat to keep it going. All the voices I used to hear telling me to do all kinds of wild things have gone—and Nessa says they were always only my imagination. They used to drive me nearly mad at Welwyn, and I thought they came from overeating—but they cant, as I still stuff and they are gone. (*Letters* 1: 142)

Attitude toward eating clearly differentiates Freudian and psycho-biological approaches to manic-depressive illness. Critic Louise DeSalvo takes the purely psychological view when she decodes Woolf's loss of appetite:

> As [psychotherapist] Alice Miller has learned, symptoms are a form of communication. To starve yourself means that someone has starved you. Virginia's feelings were also frozen—she knew that if she showed rage, anger, nervousness, she would be medicated into submission. Moreover, cutting off feeling is one way of handling sexual abuse; the results, however, are deadening.[82]

Ironically, DeSalvo engages in the same kind of speculation that expresses Beers's paranoia, for she assumes that meaning underlies symptoms in a more or less direct line of logic. Because she assumes that Woolf's depression is a coping mechanism chosen, consciously or unconsciously, by a victim of incest, DeSalvo feels she has arrived at the symptom's origin and meaning simultaneously, by merely reversing the definition of who is starving whom. Such a scenario might be true of a non–manic-depressive: childhood deprivation and sexual abuse may be the "message" of purely psychological symptoms created by an ego unable to cope with hurtful feelings in any other way. But how, then, do we distinguish this form of communication from a symptom the ego has not invented, the deadening of appetite and feelings and love of life produced by abnormal brain chemistry? The "message" of anorectic conscience in this case would not be "I was sexually abused" but "I feel as bad as if I had been sexually abused," or, in Woolf's case (as I will argue in Chapter 6), "I feel bad when depressed, just as I did when I was sexually abused: depression is like that, a victimization, an inescapable emptiness and hunger where even food is tasteless, repulsive, poison." Psychoanalytic critics need to familiarize themselves with modern neuropsychiatry in order to be aware that our subjective lives are complicated mixtures of mind and brain, the freely chosen and the brutally imposed, the meaningful and the unintelligible.

Hypochondriacal preoccupation with bodily functions and the belief in some physical cause for their psychological pain occur in a third of depressed patients—not surprisingly, since mood disorders are so closely linked to metabolism. Styron sensed a direct connection between brain and mind: "What I had begun to discover is that, mysteriously and in ways that are totally remote from normal experience, the gray drizzle of horror induced by depression takes on the quality of physical pain."[83] Many patients particularize vague depressive fears by worrying about disease, commonly focusing on heart disease, cancer, and, most recently, AIDS, because in Western culture these most forcefully symbolize a personal doom. The general loss of physical energy can also affect their judgment: they consider their work and activities as trivial and their past life as a failure. Any evidence to the contrary is dismissed or misinterpreted to fit their despondent mood. Since depression interferes with memory and the brain's ability to concentrate and evaluate (Clifford Beers remembers being unable to read a newspaper, for it "appeared an unintelligible jumble of type"), the patient's work usually does suffer, adding to his conviction of inadequacy.[84] Studies show that when depressives are exposed to new material, they are less likely than controls to link novel information to preexisting knowledge, a result that indicates some hindrance to the fundamental human capacity for recognizing significance consistently over time.[85] Depressives' memory of events becomes jumbled, and unintegrative habit begins to dominate thought. They fall back on uncreative and inflexible routines, which feeds their developing nihilism and pessimism; life indeed becomes empty and fragmented.[86] While hypomanic, an employee may outperform every competitor, creatively solving problems by discovering hidden connections or correlations and by energetically exploiting opportunities. But the same individual will lose all that talent and stamina when depressed, as both John Custance and Virginia Woolf noted:

> Instead of the light of ineffable revelation I seem to be in perpetual fog and darkness. I cannot get my mind to work; instead of associations "clicking into place" everything is an inextricable jumble; instead of seeming to grasp a whole, it seems to remain tied to the actual consciousness of the moment. The whole world of my thought is hopelessly divided into incomprehensible watertight compartments. I could not feel more ignorant, undecided, or inefficient. It is appallingly difficult to concentrate, and writing is pain and grief to me.[87]

> This is the worst time of all. It makes me suicidal. Nothing seems left to do. All seems insipid & worthless. (*Diary* 3: 186)

Depressives habitually look on the gloomy side of any question. They come to believe that their very existence bodes ill for themselves and their families. The future is perceived as grim, empty, hellish, and death seems the only escape. Deeply depressed patients are unable to feel emotions at all; the brain is unable to process even pain. Often, as if to explain to themselves why they feel so low, they accuse themselves of terrible sins, or of being responsible for family tragedies. Sometimes they hear voices which make these accusations for them, and experiencing these hallucinations further convinces them that they are deservedly losing their minds.[88] The messages of these voices are usually related to the content of their particular delusion concerning (or explanation of) their experiences. If a patient explains his depressive fears as feelings of persecution ("I feel so scared, someone must want to kill me"), the voices are usually berating or derogatory. If he finds thematic unity in a general nihilism ("Life is terrible, worthless; total nuclear annihilation is unavoidable"), the voices may threaten doom and destruction.

Because any theory used to explain our personal experience affects how we make decisions, the decision to die is thus a frequent feature of the depressive state. At least 15 percent of manic-depressives, if left untreated, commit suicide; this is thirty times the rate found in the general population and is higher than for any other psychiatric or medical risk group.[89] But Winokur found that an overwhelming 82 percent of his depressed bipolar patients had suicidal ruminations.[90] Thus, it is difficult to tell who will attempt suicide and who will not: even seemingly strong people with a wide range of personal assets may, when depressed, reinterpret those assets as liabilities (e.g., ambition is no longer seen as a positive sign of success but as an empty gesture or rude pushiness or an unforgivable crime at the expense of others). Suicide itself is not a reliable indicator of strength of character or neuroticism, or the quality of the suicide's previous life, or the amount of support and love given by family and friends.[91] For some patients, it is the memory of happiness once known, or even the potential for future happiness that now seems beyond reach, that makes their despair seem unendurable.[92] Pointing out a depressive's available resources or opportunities for satisfaction (the love of his family, his potential for success, etc.) may only exacerbate his sense of the internal abyss that separates him from what he feels he needs most. Some suicidal patients are very adept at disguising their hopelessness, especially if a resolution to end their misery offers them their only hope, in which case they can appear calm and in better spirits shortly before they kill themselves.[93] Moreover, suicidal tendencies are often masked; they can occur in the absence of delusions, hallucinations, or psychomotor retardation, and the patient may not voice self-destructive wishes.[94] Clinicians and family members must look for other, subtler symptoms: alcoholism, insomnia, loss of weight and appetite, irregular heart rhythm, recklessness, social withdrawal.

Why did Woolf kill herself? Psychoanalyst Alma Bond devotes an entire book to the question of *Who Killed Virginia Woolf?* and finds, predictably enough, too many readily available answers: the threat of a German invasion, Virginia's fear of becoming an inescapable burden to her Jewish husband, her belief that her sister, Vanessa, was withholding her love, her knowledge that her lesbian lover was unfaithful, her anger that Leonard was domineering, her despair at the thought that she might lose the power to write. With so many reasons for suicide, wouldn't an emotionally weak woman be overwhelmed and offer us a compelling, dramatic climax to a life of neurotic conflict? Bond's speculation begins well enough: she wonders why Woolf killed herself when so many other people at the time endured similar trials. Because she is a Freudian, Bond explains Woolf's vulnerabilities by privileging (first hypothesizing the existence of) unconscious conflicts. Invasion, infidelity, loss, self-devaluation—all become more than Virginia can bear, not because they are in themselves unbearable but because they replicated her untimely weaning as a six-week-old baby, her mother's emotional distance, the infant Virginia's masochistic wish to surrender to a defensively idealized mother, the daughter Virginia's envy of her father's penis, and the sister Virginia's sexual abuse at the hands of her half-brothers. As usual in a Freudian landscape, family life is hell; why else would anyone fall ill? Bond still relies on Freud's sixty-five-year-old description of psychosis as an unreconciled conflict between the ego and an intolerable reality and on Jacobson's thirty-three-year-old idea that manic-depressives experience pronounced shifts in mood and self-esteem because an immature superego has failed to modulate psychic energy (primarily anger toward parents, in mania, and anger toward self, in depression).[95] Asserting, with confidence, that "*all delusions reflect the central conflict* of a tormented psyche," Bond works backward to reconcile what would appear to her (indeed, to anybody who enjoys a reasonable sense of reality granted by sanity and stable brain chemistry) to be the only "meaningful" conflict.[96]

"Nobody has explained to my satisfaction what brought on that last attack" of 1941, Bond states. If personal satisfaction is the prime requisite, the closure of death requires an artful, even melodramatic explanation:

> Virginia Woolf was not an integrated individual. She labored all her life to consolidate her personality, with only temporary success. . . .
>
> In my opinion, there was one means left to Virginia to unite her discordant selves: In her death she discovered the way to integrate the "orts, scraps, and fragments" (Woolf, 1941, p. 215) of her splintered soul. Then at last the important strains of her life—including the untimely disruption of the symbiosis with her mother and her early loss again through death, the highly ambivalent relationship with her father, the sadomasochistic interaction with her sister Vanessa, the loss of Vita as her lover, Virginia's disillusionment with Leonard and the "puncturing" of the family myth, the frightful experience of the war in the light of her inability to deal with aggression, and the death of Thoby and many of her friends, which reenacted the early traumatic deaths of her adolescence—all intermingled to culminate in her final act at the river Ouse.[97]

Like the conclusion of a melodramatic Victorian novel, Bond's version of Woolf's death threads disparate strands together in an aesthetically satisfying ending. Do manic-depressives think about suicide in such pathetic terms? Sometimes, but only when depressed. Elaborated reasons for a tragically appropriate end fill in the blank nothingness of depression, expressing its corrosive power of shaping perception and cognition so that past events seem ominously prophetic. When the patient is euthymic or manic, these same memories take on entirely different connotations: "My

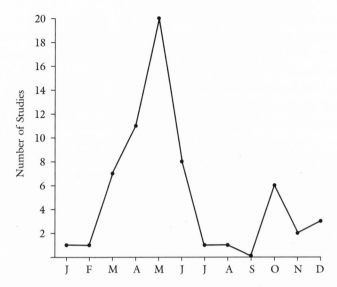

Figure 1. Peak Occurrence of Suicide by Month
(Based on review of 61 studies. Jamison [*MDI* 243])

mother's death blighted my life forever" then becomes "My mother's death hurt, but it taught me to appreciate life more." Unfortunately, psychoanalysts are compelled by Freudian theory to view a patient's euthymic disavowal of unhappiness or despondency as a manic defense, or at least a neurotic repression. This theoretical position assumes, arbitrarily and destructively (for the patient), that the *depressed* view is the "*true*" expression of the patient's deepest, most authentic feelings. By focusing on depression, Freudians reduce the three states of bipolar disorder (manic, euthymic, depressive) to one state and inadvertently encourage the patient to think of his depressed self and its sad history/fiction of fated disappointments as most central to his identity. This clinical exaggeration of the significance of the patient's ill thoughts over his well thoughts can lead, tragically, to even more suicides.

Why did Woolf die? We must relinquish the demand for an answer that satisfies *our* need for narrative unity. Studies suggest that the frequency of manic-depressive relapses increases with age,[98] so perhaps Woolf died for nothing more meaningful than the fact that the biochemistry of aging bodies changes and intensifies depression. Or perhaps it was the season. There is a striking peak incidence of suicide in May, a rise that begins in March (see Figure 1), as do the rates of hospital admissions for depression;

affective disorders are intimately connected to the body's circadian and seasonal rhythms. So perhaps Woolf died because age and winter combined to exacerbate depression. A third possibility exists: Woolf's last physician, Octavia Wilberforce, suspected in 1940 that her patient might be an alcoholic. If Woolf, like 35 percent of other manic-depressives, medicated herself with alcohol in the last year of her life, the resulting neurochemical changes could have contributed to the severity of her last depression and increased the risk of suicide.[99]

In the end, we cannot hope fully to explain Woolf's suicide by means of traumatic events in her life. Depression alters the patient's perception of the story line of those events, and it would be a matter of blind luck (or an expression of mood disorder in ourselves) if we could empathize so completely as to see her death with her eyes. It is tempting to approach psychotic thinking as if it were just a matter of conflicted thinking resolvable by therapeutic insight, to assume that delusions reliably provide the curative clue. But such a perspective obliterates the troubling *différance* of insanity (the depressive lives in the same world of blue skies, comfortable houses, clean parks, bountiful malls, and loving families that you and I do but, perversely, feels tortured and damned by it all). Our superior attitude toward people who resort to suicide tells more of our needs and wishes than of those of the deceased. Ironically, although suicide can seem the most personal of all our life decisions, it can also be the most impersonal, for the biology of our brains operates in ways that may seem most inhuman. To explain why Woolf died we must explain why anyone dies—of disease, of injury, of birth defects. . . . Our free will is only one element in a complex configuration of forces interacting in ways that are often beyond our understanding. To dramatize this violation of ego's need for continuity in psychobiography, my discussion of Woolf's death appears here, rather than in the last chapter of this book. It ends without conclusion, as so much in life does.

Biology has profound personal consequences that invade the most private realms of our souls, our character, our self-insight. Perhaps this is nowhere more floridly depicted than in depression's power to induce a false sense of guilt. Ruminations on guilt are seen in one-third of depressed patients.[100] First, they feel ashamed of losing control, of behaving bizarrely, of indulging in violent outbursts against those they love the most. If they do permanently alienate their loved ones, desertion and chronic loneliness may be taken as proving depression's insidious whisper that they are unlovable and unforgivable. If the loved one does not understand the impersonal origins of these eruptions of rage or distortions of personality and desire, he or she may, implicitly or explicitly, reinforce the depressive's nearly unbearable self-condemnation. We read of the suicides of estranged spouses and rejected lovers in the newspapers every day, but we usually do not think beyond a tepid condemnation of their weakness of character or lack of foresight. We forget Satan's admonition in *Paradise Lost* that "the mind is its own place, and in itself, / Can make a heav'n of hell, a hell of heav'n."[101]

Second, depressives feel guilt for which they cannot find a valid cause. They tend to think back over the years and center obsessively on some past event—an unpardonable sin (to explain their hopelessness and guilt), or a traumatic experience (to explain their helplessness and life's emptiness), or the loss of a significant person (to explain their extraordinary sense of abandonment and loneliness). Here emotion often serves as an informational cue: bipolars tend to remember positive experiences when in a positive mood, negative experiences in negative moods.[102] An emotional state may influence memory storage and access.[103] Studies have found that depressed patients are better able to recall words with negative content or negative experiences than positive words or experiences.[104] The tragedy that seemed to Woolf to explain her emptiness, despair, and lack of a stable self-structure was the loss of her mother in 1895. Julia's sudden death apparently triggered Virginia's first manic-depressive breakdown, but, more important—for Woolf and for us—it became Woolf's metaphor for the birth of a bipolar identity, the stream in which she pictured herself as a fish, fixed, "held in place" by "invisible presences" (*Moments of Being* 80). It offered a coherent story line for experiences that would otherwise seem senseless and impersonal.

If personal history provides no such emblematic event, some depressives will castigate themselves for sins that are entirely imaginary or that they themselves cannot remember. After an unsuccessful attempt at suicide (like Woolf, he jumped out of a window), Clifford Beers interpreted everything that happened to him in terms of his despondency and guilt. When doctors applied hot poultices to his broken feet, his "very active association of mad ideas convinced me that I was being 'sweated'"—given the "third degree" by police intent upon gaining a confession from him for an unknown crime; "with an insane ingenuity I managed to connect myself with almost every crime of importance of which I had ever read."[105] It is not the sin itself that is important, not even as a hypothetical, unconscious wish. The patient seizes upon sin as the only cause to be found for an indefinable despair. One patient admitted to having committed the unforgivable sin but when [the psychiatrist], very interestedly, tried to find out the awful details, he replied "That's just it, I don't know what it is". The content of these ideas and delusions is consonant with the patients' personalities and activities. Thus a television newscaster felt that he was involved in a recent murder that had evoked much publicity. A conscientious doctor was convinced that he had poisoned a patient (actually alive and well) with an overdose of a drug in his prescription.[106]

Leonard had suspicions that Virginia's depressed guilt had no simple origin:

> Pervading her insanity generally there was always a sense of some guilt, the origin and exact nature of which I could never discover. . . . In the early acute, suicidal stage of the depression, she would sit for hours overwhelmed with hopeless melancholia, silent, making no response to anything said to her. (*Beginning Again* 163)

Other depressives fill the void by developing fixed false beliefs that symbolize their present mental states: they are guilty of having wished their parents dead, God has refused to forgive them for alienating the affections of a past lover, they are being spied on and persecuted, they have no intestines, their brains are rotting, the furniture in a room has been altered simply to irritate them, they have become the focus of universal abhorrence, or the world itself is disintegrating or plunging toward Armageddon because of their personal inadequacies and failures.[107] In such a moral nightmare, suicide would seem a welcome release or at least an appropriate conclusion to a narrative of utter hopelessness. No wonder, then, that Freudians described such negativity as a self-induced attack on the ego. Since, as they saw it, all matters of punitive conscience arose from the superego, depression served to convince them that the superego could be vicious, even homicidal. But since neuroscience shows us that a depressive symptom can be elicited by the administration of certain drugs, by illness, or by brain injury, we must wonder if the attack is always "motivated": can the superego be turned on and off by physical changes? A specific depressive symptom may be the result of an unconscious conflict and be a good candidate for psychoanalysis, but global despair more likely has its source in a neuronal system that mediates all perceptions, feelings, and beliefs.

Because depressives are convinced they have been singled out for their personal shortcomings, they feel doomed, disconnected from the world, yet vulnerable to attack.[108] Depressives' striking passivity led Willard Gaylin to describe the symptoms of depression as "non-symptoms." Normally, in neurosis, symptoms are attempts to compromise one's way out of a conflict situation; they are reparative maneuvers executed by the threatened ego. But in endogenous depression, Gaylin observed, reparative mechanisms are at a minimum. Depressives are not victims of illusions: they have no illusions—and no protection against a dark world that is empty of meaning because the self has no power to create a satisfactory meaning.[109] This produces a problem for the analyst, who must rely in part on the patient for his diagnosis. Depressed patients cannot always give true accounts of themselves, for mood is difficult to gauge; it undermines the brain's capacity to achieve self-insight, interpret experience, and make judgments about whether a present mental state conflicts with past states.[110]

In the manic state the omnipotent subjective world dominates the objective, but the depressive state reverses these positions, rendering self powerless, hopeless, worthless, and uncreative, without even the desire to defend itself against its own perceptions. When biochemistry falters, the brain's ability to distinguish incoming from self-generated stimuli is undercut; interpretations become either predominantly positive or predominantly negative, depending on mood. If they are negative, the self feels impotent and the world seems hideously empty and malevolent. Although the patient may seem the picture of uncontrollable tearfulness and bitter sorrow, to him his emotions may seem "blocked" or "frozen," and so he may experience his self as unreal or as an open wound that will never heal.[111] He feels truly depersonalized, self-less. Suicide looks attractive because the mind is already experiencing a death of the soul.

Woolf's depressions exhibited most of these symptoms, and she distinctly perceived their physical dimension:

> I know the feeling now, when I can't spin a sentence, & sit mumbling & turning; & nothing flits by my brain which is as a blank window. So I shut my studio door, & go to bed, stuffing my ears with rubber; & there I lie a day or two. And what leagues I travel in the time! Such "sensations" spread over my spine & head directly I give them the chance; such an exaggerated tiredness; such anguishes & despairs; & heavenly relief & rest; & then misery again. Never was anyone so tossed up & down by the body as I am, I think. (*Diary* 3: 174)

In fact, many of her descriptions of symptoms that precede breakdowns emphasized physical changes: headaches or numbness in the head, insomnia, nervous irritation, a strong impulse to reject food.[112] More important, she recognized that such physical changes had psychological consequences:

> This is the worst time of all. It makes me suicidal. Nothing seems left to do. All seems insipid & worthless. . . . Mercifully, Nessa is back. My earth is watered again. I go back to words of one syllable: feel come over me the feathery change: rather true that: as if my physical body put on some soft comfortable, skin. (*Diary* 3: 186)

The physicality of manic-depressive illness can help us differentiate it diagnostically, in four ways, from the Freudian notion of neurotic depression. First, Woolf usually connected her depressions to physical changes or ailments that accompanied or preceded mood swings, an association research has shown does exist in mood disorders with strong biochemical components, though seldom in psychological mood disorders. Second, she was often able to state the time of onset of illness: whereas neurotic-reactives find it difficult to determine when they shift moods, manic-depressives can sometimes date onset to within the hour:

> I woke to a sense of failure & hard treatment. This persisted, one wave breaking after another, all day long. We walked on the river bank in a cold wind, under a grey sky. Both agreed that life seen without illusion is a ghastly affair. Illusions wouldn't come back. However they returned about 8.30, in front of the fire, & were going merrily till bedtime, when some antics ended the day. (*Diary* 1: 73)

Third, neurosis rarely interferes with reality testing (that is, it is not accompanied by visual hallucinations), and it is often seen by the patient himself to occur as a response to a traumatic life event. Manic-depressive illness, in contrast, often inhibits reality testing and frequently occurs without any discernible exterior "psychological" cause unless physical stress accompanies it. And, fourth, in endogenous mood swings, symptoms tend to be more severe and more frequent than in neurosis. The patient perceives his illness more clearly as a distinct change from his usual self and complains more often of a loss of pleasure in activity and a loss of reactivity to usually pleasurable stimuli,[113] as in these descriptions by Woolf of two depressions and their effect on her sense of self:

> Here is a whole nervous breakdown in miniature. We came on Tuesday. Sank into a chair, could scarcely rise; everything insipid; tasteless, colourless. Enormous desire for rest. . . . [A]voided speech; could not read. Thought of my own power of writing with veneration, as of something incredible, belonging to someone else; never again to be enjoyed by me. Mind a blank. Slept in my chair. Thursday. No pleasure in life whatsoever. . . . Character & idiosyncrasy as Virginia

Woolf completely sunk out. Humble & modest. Difficulty in thinking what to say. (*Diary* 3: 103)

[It's] a physical feeling as if I were drumming slightly in the veins: very cold: impotent: & terrified. As if I were exposed on a high ledge in full light. Very lonely. L[eonard]. out to lunch. Nessa has Quentin & don't want me. Very useless. No atmosphere around me. No words. Very apprehensive. As if something cold & horrible—a roar of laughter at my expense were about to happen. And I am powerless to ward it off: I have no protection. And this anxiety & nothingness surround me with a vacuum. (*Diary* 5: 63)

Like Rhoda in *The Waves*, the depressed Woolf feels naked and vulnerable, stripped of all illusions, as empty on the inside as the world seems to be on the outside. It has long been noted that depressed patients often identify the self with the external world,[114] and this confusion between inner and outer destroys the perceiver's sense of an autonomous identity. All of Woolf's worst fears seem validated by what she perceives. In both of the episodes quoted above, self is blank, with no capacity to generate meaning or fiction, which would at least provide evidence that self existed. The situation is doubly difficult for a female depressive, since society tends to deny value and power to women's selves. Fiction, however, could, like a mother, like the mother Virginia had lost, validate and nurture. Thus Julia became a crucial emblematic part of Woolf's fictional world, which she consciously and repeatedly used to explore both her illness and her wellness.

Woolf needed to rework her experiences in fiction because in depression perceptions defy synthesis: the brain is incapable of integrating the full spectrum of the individual's feelings and desires, past or present. A wall of overly negative perceptions is raised that frustrates attempts by the therapist to cheer the patient. Helpless and overwhelmed by despair, Woolf felt as if the "veils of illusion" had been drawn, leaving her "to face a world from which all heart, charity, kindness and worth had vanished" (*Letters* 3: 50), feeling a "horror—physically like a painful wave swelling about the heart—tossing me up . . . spreading out over me. . . . One goes down into the well & nothing protects one from the assault of truth" (*Diary* 3: 110–12). Yet, even in the depths of despair Woolf found something of value to work with in her novels, a "truth" not glamorized or distorted by human illusions and human vanity. This truth was thus potentially inhuman, perhaps even inexpressible but certainly felt, and it contained the essence of reality that the "egotistical" manic Woolf overlooked. Just as the manic's "truth" reveals rampant subjectivity, with wishes and illusory theories leveling out ambiguities and distinctions, the depressive's vision seems to him to unveil a severely objective truth, the world of stark objects unmolested by wishful thinking or vanity, as Woolf reports:

> The depression however now takes the wholesome form of feeling perfectly certain that nothing I can do matters, so that one is both content & irresponsible—I'm not sure that this isn't a happier state than the exalted state of the newly praised. At least one has nothing to fear. (*Diary* 1: 214)

IDENTITY AND BIPOLARITY

If our sense of self is expressed in our words and actions, then Woolf's problem as a writer was to find a self underlying her disparate experiences, what she called "a core" in this 1921 letter to Sydney Waterlow:

> You say people drop you, and don't want to see you. I don't agree. Of course I understand that when one feels, as you feel, without a core—it used to be a very familiar feeling to me—then all one's external relations become febrile and unreal. Only they aren't to other people. I mean, your existence is to us, for example, a real and very important fact. (*Letters* 2: 455)

Woolf understood Waterlow's situation because mood disorders have a powerful effect on a patient's sense of self, as one psychiatrist has observed:

> I contend that because of the nature of this illness affective patients emerge with particular problems in organizing a sense of self that are specific to this illness. . . .
>
> When a patient has a major affective episode, his or her normal self disappears. The patient becomes someone foreign, another self. By definition, this self has a different affective organization from the normal self. There are different thoughts, behaviors, and personality traits. Physiological rhythms and drives are dramatically altered. . . .
>
> Unipolar patients have two personae: depressed and euthymic, "psychobiologese" for out-of-episode. Bipolars have three: depressed, manic or hypomanic, and euthymic. . . . The spectre of a recurrence can become a vivid phantom self, something or someone who might again take them over. Who, then, is the real self for someone who has been up and down and in between? Is the real self who one is when one is euthymic? Is it possible or even necessary to construct a whole self out of an amalgam of the "self-in-episode" and "self-out-of-episode"? Can this integration ever achieve the same coherence of self-structure that the patient previously took for granted?

. . . To switch unpredictably into highs and lows that are not in your control, when you have no clear sense of stable, differentiated identity to start with, leaves you without a critical anchor in a very treacherous storm.[115]

To the manic-depressive, experience is polarized, the oppositions undercutting (deconstructing, as it were) each other. Because mood swings interfere with both cognition and memory, patients are left with little consistent evidence out of which to integrate disparate experiences of self. The euthymic self seems transparent compared to the vivid manic ups and depressive downs.[116]

Manic-depression showed Woolf how subject and object interact to make meaning; it did so by periodically revoking meaning, by polarizing subject-object relations. Although euthymic manic-depressives can look back over a mood-disordered episode and see how wrong they were to make deeply gloomy or grandiose assessments of the value of life, patients who are in the midst of an episode find it difficult, if not impossible, to gain self-insight, since they typically over-identify with the world they see. A magically expanded world of miraculous meaning is allied with an exalted experience of the manic self perceiving that world, while a degraded, empty self either sees the world as being as barren as itself or, if objects are idealized, a world too good for the likes of the depressive. Fiction allowed Woolf to examine the pieces separately before she put them back together in a pattern of her own choosing.

But what pattern was right? As they move repeatedly from ill to well, manic-depressives tend to "seal over" memories of episodes of acute illness;[117] undesirable or even "alien" experiences or behaviors are easily denied or fitted forcibly into an explanatory model that filters out the radical divergences of self and world that once were so compelling. The patient's attempts to protect a vulnerable self-identity may result in an intolerance for ambiguity or novelty[118]—a temptation Woolf herself seems to have resisted successfully by acknowledging the value of the divergence itself:

But it is always a question whether I wish to avoid these glooms. In part they are the result of getting away by oneself, & have a psychological interest which the usual state of working & enjoying lacks. These 9 weeks give one a plunge into deep waters; which is a little alarming, but full of interest. All the rest of the year one's (I daresay rightly) curbing & controlling this odd immeasurable soul. When it expands, though one is frightened & bored & gloomy, it is as I say to myself, awfully queer. There is an edge to it which I feel [is] of great importance, once in a way. One goes down into the well & nothing protects one from the assault of truth. . . .

I wished to add some remarks to this, on the mystical side of this solitude; how it is not oneself but something in the universe that one's left with. It is this that is frightening & exciting in the midst of my profound gloom, depression, boredom, whatever it is. . . . Life is, soberly & accurately, the oddest affair; has in it the essence of reality. I used to feel this as a child—couldn't step across a puddle once I remember, for thinking, how strange—what am I? (*Diary* 3: 112-13)

Woolf gained her perspective on depression by contrasting it to her manic episodes and by comparing both to the process of creative writing, which involves a similar alternation of creative construction with critical revision:

I tried to analyse my depression: how my brain is jaded with the conflict within of two types of thought, the critical, the creative; how I am harassed by the strife & jar & uncertainty without. This morning the inside of my head feels cool & smooth instead of strained & turbulent. (*Diary* 4: 103)

She found it very difficult to write fiction (as opposed to critical reviews) when she was depressed:

Its odd how being ill even like this splits one up into several different people. Here's my brain now quite bright, but purely critical. It can read; it can understand; but if I ask it to write a book it merely gasps. How does one write a book? I cant conceive. It's infinitely modest therefore,—my brain at this moment. (*Letters* 3: 388)

But she also realized that hypomania's energized and inventive fluency was not enough to produce lasting fiction. And so she noted, preparing to return to her writing after three weeks of headache and depression:

now I must press together; get into the mood & start again. I want to raise up the magic world all round me, & live strongly & quietly there for 6 weeks. The difficulty is the usual one—how to adjust the two worlds. It is no good getting violently excited: one must combine. (*Diary* 4: 202)

Depression, the critical, counterbalanced hypomania, the creative. Depression concentrated and contracted the gregarious Woolf who had felt scattered, buoyant, unheedful of anything outside of her own subjective world. What Woolf needed, therefore, was a subjective-objective view that integrated the critical and the creative. She knew that only a flexible self—neither a depressive, rigid one nor a manic, scattered one—was capable of artistic fusion. Elucidating this view became a central concern in her novels.

None of Woolf's doctors could satisfactorily explain how the sane and the insane Virginias were related, because they did not even recognize clearly the symptomatic changes: in their eyes, her illness merely produced an incoherence or self-indulgence that was best left unexamined. Indeed, one of Savage's colleagues, Thomas Clifford Allbutt, recommended against much analysis or discussion of mental illness with clients: "we must beware of putting notions into the patient's head; . . . we must avoid giving the child, or the childish adult, the 'formula for his defects,' lest he act up to the character."[119] When Dr. Sainsbury prescribed "Equanimity—practise equanimity Mrs Woolf" (*Diary* 2: 189), Virginia considered the advice superfluous. In her diary, she continued to probe madness: "what use is there in denying a depression which is irrational?" (*Diary* 2: 232). That is a good question, but her doctors were not prepared to ask it. Leonard was curious, but until Virginia was past thirty years old he was unable to see a pattern in her symptoms. By then she had begun exploring symptoms in her fictional characters.

Woolf's knowledge of her illness was nonmedical, the result of an acute sensitivity to what she felt, not of scientific analysis. She particularized the problem of her illness in terms of discovering or creating a sense of self in spite of, but also recognizing the validity of, the multiplicity of her experiences. In her diaries and letters she evidenced her awareness that mood shifts caused her to act against her normal desires and perceptions. To Dora Sanger she apologized for previous hostility:

> Your letter to Leonard makes me very angry with myself. How can I have been such a fool as to spoil those days with "merciless chaff"? It must have been some idiotic mood—probably nervousness—on my part. I do hope you will forgive me and believe in the sincerity of my affection. (*Letters* 4: 135)

It was with this subjective experience of the multiplicity of manic-depressive illness that she worked. "After being ill and suffering every form and variety of nightmare and extravagant intensity of perception" (*Letters* 4: 231), Woolf questioned her "terrible irregularities," her "spasms of one emotion after another" (*Letters* 5: 29). But instead of discounting the "mad" feelings as incoherent and irrelevant (as Savage had done), or imposing a phallocentric Freudian explanation, she turned the issue around and questioned all mental states—normal or abnormal, in herself and in others—and the unexamined assumptions about their integrity:

> and then there's the whole question, which interested me, again too much for the books [*Night and Day*] sake, I daresay, of the things one doesn't say; what effect does that have? and how far do our feelings take their colour from the dive underground? I mean, what is the reality of any feeling?—and all this is further complicated by the form, which must sit tight, and perhaps in Night and Day, sits too tight; as it was too loose in The Voyage Out. (*Letters* 2: 400)[120]

The experience of mood swings challenges our fundamental belief in the authenticity of identity and the reality of emotion, for the dividing line between well and ill feelings is surprisingly tenuous. Many manic-depressives know by experience that a seemingly normal depressive reaction (to bad news, the loss of a loved one, a marital squabble) can sometimes deepen into a major episode of psychotic proportions, or that a feeling of well-being, or happiness and creativity, can sometimes escalate into hypomania or mania:

> Many common emotions range across several mood states, spanning euthymia, depression, and hypomania. For example, irritability and anger can be a part of normal human existence or alternately can be symptoms of both depression and hypomania. Tiredness, sadness, and lethargy can be due to normal circumstances, medical causes, or clinical depression. Feeling good, being productive and enthusiastic, and working hard can be either normal or pathognomonic of hypomania. These overlapping emotions can be confusing and arouse anxiety in many patients, who may then question their own judgment.[121]

The relationship between ill and well emotion was made further significant for Woolf because her father, Leslie, treated his own mood swings as if they were legitimate responses to real conditions. He demanded from his family consistent support and care when anxieties struck him, for he did not question the reality of those "bad thoughts," or any of his feelings, though he knew they were at variance with his convictions at other times. Carried away by the conviction of a mood, he angered and alienated loved ones, which only exacerbated his already shaky self-esteem when depressed. When well, he did not look beyond his expanded self-confidence to examine critically what he had previously felt: he left his exhausted family and vigorously climbed alpine mountains. Woolf admitted her divided feelings by noting that "all interesting people are egoists, perhaps; but it is not in itself desirable" (*Diary* 1: 152) to impose one's subjective world on others. She admired her father's mind even as she hated his seemingly infantile dependency. Clearly, she chose a different path from his: to think about her mental states, to scale inner mountains rather than outer. Even as early as January of 1915, after two years of recurrent and severe bipolar episodes, Woolf realized that there was a qualitative difference between "sane" feelings and "insane" ones: "I thought how happy I was, without any of the excitements which, once, seemed to me to constitute happiness" (*Diary* 1: 20). An essential element of "natural happiness," as opposed to "intense happiness," she noted in 1925, was that she felt "stabilised once more about the spinal cord" (*Diary* 3: 73, 43). Such discriminations helped her realize that if feelings can be fictional, then self is not a given (not given by birth, or by mother, or guaranteed by exaggerated support from a coerced family) but a creation—and, at that, not the old ego-centered self of traditional novelists. A "modern" self, especially the self of a feminist and a manic-depressive, must be continually created and re-created and reevaluated. The power to give birth to herself lay solely in her own hands.

In order to "authorize" herself, Woolf continually probed this connection between normal and abnormal mentality, letting each one inform the other, questioning not only emotion but the self—sane or insane, what was it? Rocked back and forth between subjective omnipotence and depersonalized impotence, she wondered whether self was merely an illusion, a phantom shadow shaped like a human being:

> How much I dictate to other people! How often too I'm silent, judging it useless to speak. I said [to Katherine Mansfield] how my own character seemed to cut out a shape like a shadow in front of me. (*Diary* 2: 61)

What she sought in her fiction, therefore, was a marriage of these two modes of perception, manic and depressive, the ability to imagine wedded to a lucid recognition of reality, an epiphanic moment when her inner being and the outer world cooperated with each other, each ratifying the existence and the worth of the other, so that self became more than a walking shadow or an inflated ego; it became both real *and* invented, like a work of art: "I thought, driving through Richmond last night, something very profound about the synthesis of my being: how only writing composes it: how nothing makes a whole unless I am writing" (*Diary* 4: 161); "[I] write rather to stabilise myself" (*Diary* 3: 287). Perhaps she was thinking here of Katherine Mansfield: " 'Nothing of any worth can come of a disunited being', [Mansfield] wrote. One must have health in one's self" (*Granite and Rainbow* 75). Woolf too saw the connection between art and mentality, but, as I will argue in the next chapter, she questioned the value of achieving closure and certitude in either.

3 "But what is the meaning of 'explained' it?"

Countertransference and Modernism

As an experience, madness is terrific I can assure you, and not to be sniffed at; and in its lava I still find most of the things I write about. It shoots out of one everything shaped, final, not in mere driblets, as sanity does. And the six months—not three—that I lay in bed taught me a good deal about what is called oneself.

(*Letters* 4: 180)

Writing fiction was good therapy for Woolf because, like bipolar integration, fiction deals with subject-object transactions that make a whole, a meaning that ratifies the integrity of both self and text. It involves authors and readers alike in the difficult task of *creating and yet discovering* a meaningful reading, of reconciling our experience of the text with the objective text. As we read we must avoid the twin errors of "depressive" underreading (passively receiving information without projecting into it a beneficial meaning) and "manic" overreading (taking our interpretive projections to be in fact the text). Virginia was well aware of the bipolar structure of misreading (*Diary* 1: 184), as was her Aunt Anny (the novelist Anne Thackeray Ritchie), who in 1874 warned readers that studying human character, whether in real life or in fiction, required a paradoxical combination of impartiality and empathy:

> It is difficult, for instance, for a too impulsive student not to attribute something of his own moods to his specimens instead of dispassionately contemplating them from a critical distance, or for a cold-hearted observer to throw himself sufficiently into the spirit of those whose actions he would like to interpret. (*Toilers* 38)

I believe that Woolf's experience of mood shifts between these two positions helped her to see that through an integrative alternation between reception and projection, a creative but not deluded reading might be achieved. Fiction is intrinsically good ground for exploring manic-depressive illness; in both, making interpretations is the crux of the problem.

Interpretation is a function of identity, as Norman N. Holland has argued, since each reader brings to the experience of a text a habitual style of coping with the world. What we see is related to who we are; our reading tends to replicate ourselves. Holland theorizes that all readers adapt perceptions defensively in the service of infantile, distorted, and conflicted adaptive strategies in order to protect their "identity theme" from incongruent experience.[1] I agree that many readers do misread, but not all, and not all the time; neither self nor text is static in everyone. Marshall W. Alcorn, Jr., and Mark Bracher argue that literature induces some readers to confront ideas and feelings that are alien to their habitual ways of seeing the world. Alcorn and Bracher base their argument on Georges Poulet's idea that "when one reads any text, one's own identity is set aside and the text constitutes a new subjectivity within oneself" that initially is disturbing. Since "reading introduces alien thoughts into consciousness" and since " 'every thought must have a subject to think it, this *thought* which is alien to me and yet in me, must also have in me a *subject* which is alien to me.' "[2] Thus, literature helps us to experience previously undiscovered parts of ourselves, parts which *can* feel and empathize and understand alien experiences; if we tolerate the insecurity and chaos attending incongruence and if we resist defensive strategies, then we may re-form the self by consciously integrating what had been unrecognized. Once we are "occupied" by the thoughts of the author, we draw new subject-object boundaries, discovering or re-forming our habitual self by taking in what had been the "not-self."[3]

Like the manic-depressive who seeks the inclusive self by repeatedly confronting the misinterpretations of the ill selves, readers need to deal with the inevitable, irreducible, and inexhaustible discrepancies between the text's objective features and the self's subjective response to that text before they can begin to understand the text and themselves in new ways. Literature is, then, more than a mirror passively reflecting our image: it is like D. W. Winnicott's notion of a "good enough" mother (and the "good enough" psychotherapist) who offers her child the opportunity to interact with her, misread her, correct misreadings by confronting her objective reality and recognizing the child's own part in projecting self-deceptive meaning onto her, and thus come to discover and define itself through its object-relations with her.[4] What is essential, in understanding both literature and manic-depressive illness, is the ability to open oneself up to experiences, reactions, emotions, and ideas that do not slavishly reinforce our defensive, narrow, entrenched strategies for coping with self-world transactions.

Perhaps this affinity between art and mood shifts explains why so many artists suffered from affective disorders. Donizetti, Beethoven, Mahler,

Rachmaninoff, Dickens, Ruskin, Hopkins, Dante Gabriel Rossetti, Van Gogh, Pollack, Poe, Emerson, Hemingway, Sexton, Roethke, Robert Lowell, Jean-Jacques Rousseau, Johnson, Byron, Shelley, Goethe, Chopin, Chekov, Schumann, and Cowper are but a few who experienced pronounced variations in mood that seemed to contribute to their creativity.[5] Although unipolar depressions occur in only 5 percent of the general population, and bipolar in a mere 1 percent, a recent study of forty-seven accomplished British writers and artists found that 38 percent had been treated for an affective illness; three-fourths of those treated had been given antidepressants or lithium or had been hospitalized. The great majority of the subjects (89 percent) reported hypomanic states during intense, creative moments, and a third experienced severe mood swings.[6] A similar survey of writers at the University of Iowa Writers' Workshop, the oldest and most widely recognized creative writing program in the United States, found a strong association between creativity and mood disorders: 80 percent of the writers had had a mood disorder at some time in their lives, compared with 30 percent of the control subjects. Moreover, a surprisingly high percentage (43 percent) of these illnesses was bipolar, in comparison with 10 percent of the controls (schizophrenia had no association with creativity). The study concluded that mood disorder may be "both a 'hereditary taint' and a hereditary gift."[7] Fully 90 percent of the hypomanic writers and artists in the British study themselves stated that such moods were either integral and necessary (60 percent) or very important (30 percent) to their work.[8]

Other studies have shown that creative persons experience a heightening of senses typical of hypomanic states and have an enhanced capacity for feeling and a keener awareness of mood swings (both of which provide fresh material for their creative work). Mood swings, whether mild or severe, intensify and vary the individual's expectations, beliefs, and insights into human nature, life, and God. As one patient put it:

> So why would I want anything to do with this illness? Because I honestly believe that as a result of it I have felt more things, more deeply; had more experiences, more intensely; loved more, and been more loved; laughed more often for having cried more often; appreciated more the springs, for all the winters; worn death "as close as dungarees," appreciated it—and life—more; seen the finest and the most terrible in people, and slowly learned the values of caring, loyalty, and seeing things through. I think I have seen the breadth and depth and width of my mind and heart, and seen how frail they both are, and how

ultimately unknowable they both are. . . . And I think much of this is related to my illness—the intensity it gives to things and the perspective it forces on me. I think it has made me test the limits of my mind.[9]

A mood disorder brings depth to an artist's work and sense of reality, focusing attention critically in the lows, expanding his or her scope in the highs, integrating Alcorn and Bracher's "alien subject" into his or her habitual, euthymic identity.[10]

In terms of cognitive style, creative persons share a number of characteristics with hypomanic patients: expansiveness of thought, grandiosity of mood, and unusual fluency of words and ideas.[11] Creative thinking, like mild mania, demonstrates word fluency, associational fluency (production of synonyms), expressional fluency (rapid juxtaposition of phrases), ideational fluency, spontaneous flexibility (ability to produce a great variety of ideas across various categories), and adaptive flexibility (creating unusual solutions to problems).[12] Finally, creative individuals engage in far more divergent than convergent thinking. In convergent thinking there is almost always one conclusion that is regarded as uniquely right; efforts are channeled in the direction of that answer. In divergent thinking there is much searching about or going off in various directions; no unique conclusion is expected or sought. This kind of "free writing" is exemplified in a playful, aimless and hypomanic entry to Woolf's diary in 1925:

> A disgraceful fact—I am writing this at 10 in the morning in bed in the little room looking into the garden, the sun beaming steady, the vine leaves transparent green, & the leaves of the apple tree so brilliant that, as I had my breakfast, I invented a little story about a man who wrote a poem, I think, comparing them with diamonds, & the spiders webs (which glance & disappear astonishingly) with something or other else: which led me to think of Marvell on a country life, so to Herrick, & the reflection that much of it was dependent upon the town & gaiety— a reaction. However, I have forgotten the facts. I am writing this partly to test my poor bunch of nerves at the back of my neck—will they hold or give again, as they have done so often?—for I'm amphibious still, in bed & out of it; partly to glut my itch ("glut" and "itch"!) for writing. (*Diary* 3: 40)

Intensified sensory perceptions and a love of the sound of language combine with associational play to defy (or at least postpone) closure in an uncontrolled narrative. Pointless but pleasurable, hypomanic thoughts continually enrich and delight.

These two cognitive styles, convergent and divergent, are divided according to mood in creative work. In one study, nineteen spontaneous drawings were obtained from a rapid-cycling (every twenty-four hours) manic-depressive patient. The drawings showed that different colors, linear styles, configurations, organization, and affect were associated with mania and with depression. The drawings produced during depressive days centered on prisons, cages, tombs, and coffins, whereas manic days resulted in images of bursting out. Depressive symbols tended to be concentrically and tightly organized, forms within forms, while manic symbols often were energetic spirals with much motion:

> manic drawings were more likely to be vivid, full of motion and bold lines, busy, confused, and characterized by anger, sensuousness, wildness, and ebullience. Depressed drawings were pale, tentative, static, tight, and characterized by listlessness, hopelessness, emptiness, less affect, and a sense of being trapped or enclosed.[13]

Such shifts in style and structure help artists achieve fluency with their material, "pushing back the envelope" before worrying about content. Mood disorder itself, of course, cannot produce art; the artist must have talent and must be able to integrate the "wild" with the "enclosed."[14] But depression is a definite asset if it teaches timely restraint and object-relational humility, whereas hypomania provides increased energy, enhanced performance and perception, freer thought processes, and, perhaps most crucially, the exuberant self-confidence to risk one's most private vision and skill in a public medium. Even the vision itself threatens the sense of security:

> From virtually all perspectives—early Greek philosopher to 20th century specialist—there is agreement that artistic creativity and inspiration involve, indeed require, a dipping into untapped irrational sources while maintaining ongoing contact with realities of "life at the surface." The degree to which individuals can, or desire to, "summon up the depths" is one of the more fascinating of individual differences. . . . Individuals also vary enormously in their capacity to tolerate extremes of emotions and to live on close terms with darker forces.[15]

Woolf described the creative process as a summoning up from the depths, from what she called her "dark underworld," which "has its fascinations as well as its terrors" (*Diary* 2: 126), and she experienced her mild manias as creative and enjoyable, as being "once more washed by the flood, warm, embracing, fertilising" (*Diary* 2: 192). In writing novels, she did not simply transcribe her delusions or hallucinations—madness itself is not creative, and she disapproved of overtly confessional fiction for herself (*Letters* 6: 404)—but she did learn from her anomalous experiences how thought and feeling could themselves be fictions shaped by mood and that literary fiction had to incorporate both convergent and divergent thinking, coherence and incoherence, the wild and the enclosed, in order to be truly alive: "Suppose one can keep the quality of a sketch in a finished & composed work? That is my endeavour" (*Diary* 2: 312).

Somehow art must embody in an organized form that which is manically and magically unorganized, undifferentiated, and endlessly suggestive. But it can do this only when it is not restricted (in writing, "the only thing that matters is a thing that you cant control" [*Letters* 1: 361]). For Woolf, manic-depressive illness periodically destroyed control ("I dont think you can get your words to come till youre almost unconscious; and unconsciousness only comes when youve been beaten and broken and gone through every sort of grinding mill" [*Letters* 5: 408]) and so permitted her to return to the creative process unencumbered by the illusion that meaning lay in order alone. Perhaps this is another reason why she objected to psychoanalysis: she may have feared it might systematize the vital disorder of mentality and mood. The secondary benefits of such upheavals often keep manic-depressives from seeking help, for they are unable or unwilling to conceptualize their mood swings as a psychiatric illness requiring a cure. Rather,

> some view their serious mood problems as part of the human condition, the price one pays for being "too sensitive," for having an artistic temperament, or leading an artistic lifestyle. Indeed, in many such individuals, emotional turmoil is seen as essential to their identity as performing or creative artists. Additionally, many writers and leaders are concerned that psychiatric treatment will erode or compromise their ability to create or lead.[16]

Kay Redfield Jamison argues that elated or euphoric states are "highly potent reinforcers," that many patients on lithium therapy miss the productive highs, and that clinicians should not automatically condemn these patients as shortsighted, regressive, or escapist, since hypomania does bring very real benefits. As one clinician enthusiastically put it:

> If we could extinguish the sufferers from manic-depressive psychosis from the world, we would at the same time deprive ourselves of an immeasurable amount of the accomplished and good, of color and warmth, of spirit and freshness. Finally only dried up bureaucrats and schizophrenics would be left.[17]

Contrary to popular assumption, creative patients generally function much better on lithium if their mania produces disordered work or if mood swings destroy their personal lives and with it the desire or opportunity to write. Robert Lowell's literary output increased with lithium therapy. Lowell had suffered from severe bipolar disorder, and his repeated hospitalizations resulted in lost productivity as well as personal anguish ("frightful humiliation and waste," Lowell wrote). After eighteen years of annual episodes of insanity, he began lithium treatment in the spring of 1967 and noticed a remarkable change: his breakdowns stopped, his personal life improved, he felt happier, and between June and December of that year he wrote seventy-four sonnetlike fourteen-line poems.[18]

Neuroscience combined with Woolf's metacritical explorations of the problems of interpretation challenges our traditional approaches to her life and work. In general, we do not question the reality of any feeling unless we already have some "more" real meaning to fill the void. This, as Marshall Edelson has recently argued, is essentially the Freudian perspective: "The mental phenomenon that does not make sense is both caused by, and is the realization of, a set of relations among hypothetical (i.e. unconscious) psychological entities or intentional states, which do make sense."[19] Under such a premise it is unthinkable that powerful emotions, delusions, or statements of explosive hostility have no reality outside a mood-disordered episode. We may doubt Woolf's ability to know her true feelings, but a Freudian takes it for granted that true feelings exist, submerged and veiled in enigma though they may be, and he tries to infer them from suspicious behavior, unguarded words, or seemingly autobiographical novels. We tend to assume that emotion is grounded in identity and cannot be faked or accidental: it always reveals, one way or another, the authentic self.

Manic-depression upsets this reliable connection, and it brings into sharp relief a problem inherent in all biography: the imposition of meaning. As biographers, we hope to detect a pattern in the evidence of our subject's life, but what pattern we recognize depends in part on our preconceptions of what an artist is, what mentality is, and what an individual's mentality is. True objectivity is impossible, because the story of our subject's life is partly the result of our having imposed a convergent order on the evidence as we gather it, an order that we can fail to remember is fictitious. When Freudians give priority to Woolf's suicide or her sexual traumas or her mother's death, when they think the meaning of her life is encoded symbolically in these events, then they have substituted a theory

for evidence, a theory claiming that all feelings are authentic and quanti-
fiable; it is a theory biased to read a madwoman's life as contained, one-
dimensional, a dead end. This is not good psychoanalysis, which has the
potential for a far greater scope, as Shoshana Felman argues:

> Does psychoanalysis, then, aspire to meaning—or to truth? . . . This
> question . . . this now unavoidable question of *the meaning of psychoanalysis*,
> is in fact a contradiction in terms, since "meaning" is forever but a
> fiction and since it is psychoanalysis itself which has taught us that. But
> contradiction, as we know, is the mode of functioning par excellence of
> the unconscious, and consequently, also of the logic of psychoanalysis.
> To reckon with psychoanalysis is to reckon with contradiction, including
> its disequilibrium, without reducing it to the specular illusion of
> symmetry or of a dialectical synthesis.[20]

François Roustang aptly states the problem when he asks a startlingly
simple question: How do you make a paranoic laugh at himself? The
answer is, you can't. Paranoia cannot admit such a discontinuity; any
attempt would be interpreted by the patient as persecution. Roustang
suspects that psychoanalysis cannot laugh at itself either, because "it claims
to have the last word in every discussion, the decisive explanation in every
interpretation." Such a "successful paranoia," like any good theory, resists
rupture and cure; it cannot bear being the enemy of its own thought,
though it should: "The psychoanalyst's sole task is to put all possible
theories in doubt. Indeed, a psychoanalyst who adheres to anything
resembling an intellectual construction can only reinforce the symptomatology of the paranoiac."[21] This situation is ironic because, early in his
career, before he became entangled in theory, Freud himself argued that
both patient and doctor must achieve a "negative capability," a suspension
of assumptions and prejudices that censor disturbingly chaotic or seemingly
irrelevant thoughts. Relaxing the grasp of convergent, secondary-process
thought allows the analyst to respond to primary-process thinking[22]—or
any untoward, uncatalogable thinking—a very difficult thing to do since
sometimes that response takes the shape of fear, anger, denial, hopelessness,
or guilt. Explaining a patient's depression by accusing him of playing for
pity, for instance, when in reality the therapist is unwilling to endure the
unpleasant sense of feeling manipulated, burdened by yet another hopeless
patient, is doing no good for the analysis. We may grow intolerant, even
angry, at the sight of the homeless on our city streets, but to react with
a snap psychoanalytic formulation (e.g., "at some level they must want

to be poor") brings no insight. It is only a defense of our identity theme inscribed in a monolithic reading of their despair.

How do we know when we are reading a text or a life history in all its disruptive multiplicity, and when we are only imposing a coherent and habitual theme acceptable to our own supposedly stable identities? Our version of the meaning of an artist's life may indeed reveal a biographical truth, but it may instead be a kind of countertransference, an unconscious response that, if left unacknowledged and unanalyzed, will create a defensive misunderstanding, an analytical fiction that protects us against meaning and interferes with our ability to read more fully. In psychoanalysis, countertransference can be useful, for the therapist's responses may illuminate the hidden nature of a patient's behavior—but only if the analyst becomes aware of this spontaneous and largely unconscious interpretation occurring simultaneously with his theory-driven, consciously mediated interpretations. The most common countertransference state is one that the psychoanalyst Christopher Bollas calls the "not-knowing-yet-experiencing one."[23] When nameless feelings and unidentifiable ideas create psychic pain, it is hard to fend off the need for the security and closure that psychoanalytical formulas provide. But it can be done, and it needs to be done if we are to become aware of material that does not neatly fill theoretical slots, if we are to go beyond official decoding like that of the bird=phallus=death formula discussed in Chapter 2. Bollas describes this sensitizing process as tolerating a "generative split in [the] analytic ego" that remains open to the threat of incoherence by delaying the security of analysis:[24]

> I am receptive to varying degrees of "madness" in myself occasioned by life in the patient's environment. In another area of myself, however, I am constantly there as an analyst, observing, assessing, and holding that part of me that is necessarily ill.[25]

He is "ill" because indeterminacy robs him of his habitual and personal sense of identity. But by living out this form of "self-relating" in the presence of a patient, by, paradoxically, tolerating disorder while detecting patterns, new material for analysis can be found in the therapist's own divided subjectivity. Interpretations, in other words, are "meant to be played with—kicked around, mulled over, torn to pieces" by both patient and analyst.[26]

Such transactions occur in reading as well. Like the patient who "uses the analyst as an object in the transference in order to put the analyst into the patient's mind,"[27] the reader uses the author (via the text) to bring a combined mental world into being. Readers live out a form of self-relating in the presence of a text, with one part of them functioning as a source of "alien," inchoate, "manic" material (like the patient in analysis), and another, more "depressive" part functioning as critic (like the analyst). When self-relating fails, however, the analyst/reader reverts to making "official psychoanalytic decodings" that reductively impose coherence upon the patient/author/text. A literary interpreter can thus easily develop a " 'pseudo-methodology' since his rational strategies will then be as much an unconscious defense against inner disruption as a cognitively suitable reaction to the external world."[28] Reasoning along these same lines, Steven Marcus concludes that Freud's analysis of Dora failed because Freud remained unaware of a countertransference—his identification with Herr K. Freud could not accept Dora's rejection of K.'s advances and defended himself by accusing her of resisting psychoanalysis. The order he imposed on the fragments of her life story was more appropriate to his own life story. But instead of accepting the problematical character of his reading of her narrative, he resorted to revising for the sake of coherence. Her narrative was superseded by his.

The same problem arises in psychobiographical literary analysis. Both Leon Edel and Noel Chabani Manganyi have recently warned us that any life history must be considered only a provisional attempt at truth, since the biographer is easily swept up into an intricate and intimate relationship with the subject: "a biographer in seeking the truth of his subject must seek his own truth simultaneously."[29] Although Manganyi and Edel consider heroization the most likely culturally activated transference between biographer and subject, I contend that psychobiographers run an equal risk of the opposite distortion, that of reducing the subject to a mass of neurotic failings by discounting contradictory, inconclusive, or unintelligible evidence as evasions and disguises. This pattern seems most common when the subject is a woman. Manganyi advises us to give our subjects precedence as authoritative witnesses to their lives; I further recommend that applying a neurotic theory of behavior inevitably undercuts the integrity of those self-reports.

Woolf apparently understood countertransference, at least in terms of a collusion between personal style and unrecognized needs. In her diary she describes Ethel Smyth's defensive reaction to Woolf's manic-depressive illness, zeroing in not only on Smyth's need to reduce disorder with a theory but on the relationship between theory and identity:

Ethel again—All my ills, such as they are, spring from liver: I am a very
strong woman, who needs calomel. After swallowing this terrific insult
to the celebrated sensibility of my nervous system, I try to find out
what motive lies behind Ethel & her calomel. I think; (but then I am
not a psychologist) that she wants me to be everlasting: that she wants
me to be unhurt by any amount of talk about the Prison [Smyth's
musical composition]: that she wants to have things—to her own will:
that she dislikes other peoples illnesses which interfere with her vitality;
that she likes to rationalise everything: that she suspects, on principle,
all shrinking, subtlety & sensibility. Also she is remorseful for having
sent me the picture of a sick monkey, but feels that if she can prove
that the monkey was not sick but shamming, she is absolved. I dont
know. It is very characteristic, & akin to the methods she pursues
about her music. There too, to explain her lack of success, she
fabricates a theory. (*Diary* 4: 29)

Smyth's personality expresses itself in the way she filters out certain perceptions and imposes theories upon others. She fails in interpretation because
a threatened self dominates the world instead of reading it.

As for literary analysis, Woolf reasons, anticipating Norman Holland,
that it can also become a defensive misunderstanding in the service of the
critic's personal needs:

To the psychologists a writer is an oyster; feed him on gritty facts, irritate
him with ugliness, and by way of compensation, as they call it, he will
produce a pearl. The genealogists say that certain stocks, certain families,
breed writers as fig trees breed figs—Dryden, Swift, and Pope they tell
us were all cousins. This proves that we are in the dark about writers;
anybody can make a theory; the germ of a theory is almost always the
wish to prove what the theorist wishes to believe. (*"The Moment"* 129)

Can we blithely dissect the writings of this mind, so aware of our need
to protect ourselves, by imposing theories she was perfectly capable of
anticipating? If what Woolf writes threatens our habitual and comfortable
ways of dealing with texts or with the woman who writes the texts, what
better defense than to approach the work already thinking of her as an
hysterical neurotic who did not always know the unconscious subtext of
what she was saying? Is it any wonder that Quentin Bell could amass two
volumes of biographical data on his own aunt, a woman who was active
in women's education, the feminist movement, and the group of conscientious objectors to the First World War, and still insist that Woolf was not
political? It is a fundamental irony, but one which Woolf herself thought

was almost irresistible, that the more we need to hear a writer's revolutionary message—and the more subversive that message is—the deafer we become. Cultures survive intact because individuals habitually filter out whatever would truly upset the status quo. Can we, then, possibly read what the writer writes? Woolf thought we could if, paradoxically, we tolerated disorder while detecting patterns; by combining disorder and pattern, convergent and divergent thinking, we might see something new. What, exactly, would that new thing be? It doesn't matter, just as long as we start seeing what previously could not be seen, the *différance* of the text, the voice of the Other, which urges us to question every assumption we hold sacred, especially those we do not know we hold.

The case of Virginia Woolf provides a good illustration of what can go wrong with psychobiography. Too much has been read into Woolf by analysts unconsciously wishing to find the coherence of neurosis in genius and to establish Woolf's complicity in her own madness. Her breakdowns are notable for their almost bewildering array of symptoms, seemingly a fertile field for interpretation but for that very reason a dangerous one, since manic-depressive symptoms do not reliably reveal any deep-seated conflict. The biographical relevance of this illness is limited. This point is particularly crucial in the analysis of Woolf's guilt feelings and self-recriminations, which usually centered on her parents; when depressed, she believed she had killed them simply by wishing them dead. Mark Spilka offers two likely interpretations:

> Did she want her mother to die, as some Freudians might conjecture, and was she therefore secretly pleased (and later overcome by guilt) when life granted her wish? Or was she angry with her mother for dying, for depriving her of life, and . . . was she then unable to grieve (and later overcome by guilt), as still other Freudians . . . might argue?[30]

Spilka candidly admits to having held both views, theorizing that Woolf wrote novels about her mother as obsessive restitutions for the unconscious crime of repressing her grief.

Susan Kenney and Edwin Kenney reason along similar lines when they claim that Woolf periodically went mad as "an escape or temporary respite" from her intense guilt at not having felt enough grief.[31] The Kenneys see Woolf as a fearful child who

> did not want to move forward out of childhood, away from being taken care of. . . . [S]he felt herself being pulled forward out of that comfortable cocoon she had never quite managed to kick loose. It is

necessary to view [her breakdowns] as a desperate response to a desperate fear, that she would have to grow up when she didn't want to and felt she couldn't.[32]

Louise DeSalvo and Shirley Panken take this theory a step further: according to them, when fiction failed to resolve Woolf's conflicted feelings and she realized the illusion of restitution for matricide through imagination, she attempted suicide—the ultimate act of avoidance.[33] But is it? All these biographers assume that guilt causes mental disorder. Thus, for them, meaning and order are restored once it is made clear that Woolf brought on her own tragedy. The uneasy fear that madness can strike anyone, randomly, unjustly, has been explained away. Like Milton's God, psychoanalytic critics pronounce that Woolf had been given all she needed to live correctly, but she perversely chose not to do so—not to grieve, not to resolve her conflicting emotions, not to seek therapy before the composed face of the psychoanalytic truthgiver. To Edward Albee's question, "Who's afraid of Virginia Woolf?" we may answer, "Any sane person, but there are various ways to handle our fear. We need not blame Woolf for making us afraid."

Perhaps the problem of countertransference lies not so much with the critics as with mood disorders themselves, which seem to bring out the worst in people, and particularly in the psychoanalyst attempting to make sense out of a subtle yet pervasive dysfunction that defies depth psychoanalysis.[34] According to Jamison, "the potential for power struggles with bipolar patients is virtually limitless" in the analytic setting, because therapists face such a difficult task: they must objectively assess the patient's limited control over his own illness, remain sensitive to his pain, his complaints, and his appeals for help, while simultaneously resisting being manipulated.[35] On the one hand, extroverted manics do not feel in the least ill and do not take kindly to being treated or questioned; the analyst, who by either profession or temperament is likely to be a more sensitive, introspective person, may feel outflanked and outperformed by someone so colorful, energized, and confident. On the other hand, an introverted, depressive patient will seem to resist therapeutic efforts, be slow to respond, and feel unable to fill in the gaps of a memory ravaged by the disorder. Rapid-cycling patients frustrate efforts at forming a stable transference relationship: "the patient who appears at a session angry and irritable might produce a reaction in the therapist, whose feelings may then persist longer than the patient's fleeting mood."[36] Being pulled about by patients who are chronically ill but constantly shifting, who moan shamelessly about their pain or boast of their superiority, therapists may respond with overt or covert hostility, by demonstrating their impatience or by eliminating bipolars from their private practice altogether.[37] Psychotherapists can just as easily overidentify with patients, particularly the successful manics, who may provoke denial or overprotectiveness.

Jamison lists five major problematic issues in countertransference with manic-depressive patients, which I will explain parenthetically. First, moods can be contagious (therapists must not allow themselves to identify with the patient's depression and yet must not lose patience with someone who is continually hurting; similarly, they should not mistake the good feelings of hypomania for therapeutic progress, as the patient usually will). Second, it can be difficult to distinguish subtle fluctuations in mood states from characterological problems (the therapist must determine whether a statement, feeling, or idea is a permanent feature of the person being treated, or a state-dependent symptom that will disappear when the current mood ends). Third, depressions should not be misinterpreted as resistance (nothing so inspires therapists' anger or unwarranted analysis as the suspicion that patients are not responding as they should because they are hiding something unconsciously, and analysts can easily be tempted into supplying the hidden secret themselves: are these patients blocking feelings we suspect they have, or do they really not feel them? It is too easy to assume that anyone who suffers so much pain must be deeply flawed). Fourth, hypomania can induce special sensitivity to vulnerabilities in the therapist (mild manics are so sensitive to stimuli that they can quickly zero in on the therapist's own flaws and foibles, an invasion the doctor may react to with fear, hostility, or the blind imposition of superior authority and rigid doctrine). And, fifth, the hypomanic state can make certain illegitimate emotional appeals to the therapist—for example, it can evoke envy, projective identification, collusion with lithium noncompliance, or guilt or concern over depriving patients of a "special state" (trying to cure someone of mania, sometimes the most pleasant, stimulating, and productive mental state one sees in a medical career, can seem cruel, especially when the patient clings to such "highs" after suffering the agonies of deep "lows").[38] I would add to Jamison's list a sixth issue relevant to Woolf studies: the literary critic, disturbed by his subject's inconsistent behavior, odd perspectives, and creative superiority, and by the uncertainties of analyzing across gulfs of time and space, may find it easier to impose a theory than to remain sensitive to the text.

Most important, clinicians trained in psychoanalysis must not overestimate the patient's control over his feelings and ideas. In this sense, manic-depressive illness usurps the psychoanalyst's authority as the "subject presumed to know" how patients make themselves sick. Once it has been ascertained that a chemical dysfunction is the cause of a particular patient's mental illness, therapists must be cautious not to assign guilt for behaviors the patient cannot master:

> Most analytic treatment carries with it a strong implication that it is a major analytic task of the patient to accept responsibility for his actions. In the psychoanalytic view, this responsibility is nearly total. We are even responsible for incorrectly or exaggeratedly holding ourselves responsible. It is our job to change our harsh superegos, and it is our job to do battle with unacceptable impulses. However, it now seems likely that there are patients with depressive, anxious, and dysphoric states for whom the usual psychodynamic view of responsibility seems inappropriate and who should not be held accountable. . . . It may be that we have been coconspirators with these patients in their need to construct a rational-seeming world in which they hold themselves unconsciously responsible for events. Narcissistic needs may lead these patients to claim control over uncontrollable behaviors rather than to admit to the utter helplessness of being at the mercy of moods that sweep over them without apparent rhyme or reason. An attempt at dynamic understanding in these situations may not only not be genuinely explanatory, it may be a cruel misunderstanding of the patient's effort to rationalize his life experience and may result in strengthening masochistic defenses.[39]

Distinctions must be made between psychological conflicts and those disturbances arising out of a strong biochemical predisposition.

For manic-depressive illness, this whole issue of the relationship between therapist and patient, and between critic and subject, becomes crucial. The easy assumption of a psychodynamic cause-and-effect relationship (event leading to illness, repression leading to symptom) is not valid. Indeed, it has been reversed. Guilt cannot cause manic-depressive illness; it is the other way around. Depression is a vicious cycle because it can fabricate evidence justifying itself. Such evidence is not a reliable indication of a repressed suicidal wish, and guilt may be only the result of a temporary neurohormonal disturbance, not the cause of it. Thus, both Simon O. Lesser and Shirley Panken err when they conclude that Virginia's "lack of inner assurance . . . was undoubtedly one of the causes of [her] depressions."[40] It is much more likely that her lowered self-esteem was caused by a depression. When not depressed, Woolf was "by nature" confident, creative, and life-affirming, as evidenced by the testimony of her husband and friends.

What evidence, then, can the biographer use? What a manic-depressive thinks about or experiences during a breakdown may reveal inner conflicts—or it may not. Did Woolf perceive her body as repulsive, the "sordid mouth and sordid belly demanding food," and refuse to eat because of a lifelong frigidity and self-hatred created by sexual trauma or the loss of her mother? Or does this perception of the body effectively express the uncontrollable and inexplicable feelings of emptiness and degradation that manic-depressives have when their biochemistry falters?[41] Is it "highly likely," as Panken asserts, that Virginia's 1913 depressive breakdown "was precipitated by her sense of personal inadequacy and inability to cope,"[42] when both symptoms are *consequent* to a metabolic slowdown? If biographical and autobiographical writing explains as it chronicles, we must be very careful not to confuse cause and effect, or else the deep-seated conflict we are looking for may be ours instead of hers.

If we *liberate* ourselves to read as Woolf writes, and if we *confine* ourselves to what is known about manic-depressive illness, fiction no longer appears to be a neurotic attempt to restore lost parents or deny repressed guilt. It is not a symptom or a disguise but a transformation. Since none of Woolf's doctors could explain how her manic and depressive personalities were related to each other or to the sane Virginia, I argue that she wrote novels in order to explore her own symptoms in the characters she created; that, like Emil Kraepelin, she found it helpful to examine without reduction what appeared to be hopelessly disorganized:

> Its odd what extreme depression a little influenza & a cold in head
> produces. Happily, I'm interested in depression; & make myself play a
> game of assembling the fractured pieces—I mean I light a fire, &
> somehow dandle myself over it. (*Diary* 5: 215)

In this, she duplicated both the scientist's and the biographer's work of marshaling evidence, but with one advantage: by not specifying how she assembled the pieces (it is done "somehow," and it is not even done seriously but is only a "game"), she situated herself in two opposed states—sickness and health—simultaneously. Choosing as her organizational form fiction, which is both serious and playful, fully assembled but not according to a specific formula, enabled her to avoid reducing the complexity of life experiences in the service of a psychological model.

Woolf had a healthily skeptical attitude toward any theory that restricted creativity: "I am much of Hardys opinion that a novel is an impression not an argument. The book is written without a theory; later, a theory may be made, but I doubt if it has much bearing on the work" (*Letters* 5: 91). And she admired Byron's *Don Juan* because of "the springy random haphazard galloping nature of its method . . . a[n] elastic shape which will hold whatever you choose to put into it" (*Diary* 1: 181). From Woolf's perspective, theories are merely defenses to deny the chaos of real life. Even autobiographies can be theoretical, in that they contain and secure order within a human life. In her diary she criticizes Herbert Read's autobiography as unreal because it is "weathertight, & gives shelter to the occupant," but

> his self that built the castle is to me destructive of its architecture. A mean, spiteful Read dwells outside. What is the value of a philosophy which has no power over life? I have the double vision. I mean, as I am not engrossed in the labour of making this intricate word structure I also see the man who makes it. I should say it is only word proof not weather proof. We have to discover the natural law & live by it. We are anarchists. We take the leap (glory that is) from what we know to the instinctive. (*Diary* 5: 340)

As a literary anarchist, Woolf smashes comfortable, word-proof cocoons to see what odd, unexpected, even alien truths come out in the way the pieces fall. For this reason her work is often puzzling and difficult; it is meant to mystify because it is designed to represent a perplexing disorder in perception and mood. A conventional narrative would not suffice because, as Evelyne Keitel agrees, no intersubjective knowledge of psychoses is available for traditional forms to impart to the reader:

> there is no established formula for processing psychotic experience in literary discourse . . . the author of a pathographical text is forced to make innovations of literary form. He can do so, however, only to a limited degree for, as information theory tells us, it is scarcely possible to communicate a new subject area (in this case a psychosis) by means of absolutely unfamiliar, unprecedented formal innovations.[43]

Keitel reasons that since it is impossible to communicate in language experiences beyond the margins of discourse, writers must translate the complexity of psychosis into "a schema of textual strategies."[44] Tension created by unconventional form, randomness, even meaninglessness (all opposed to the fundamental goal of reading, which is that of communication) frustrates the reader's need for consistency, his desire to make a comprehensive whole out of the disparate fragments, and so effectively reduces the reader's identity as "not at all ill." The reader, too,

> participates in the protagonist's attempt to create identity out of contradictory incidents and experiences. His reading aims—as all reading does—at building consistency, and in order to build consistency he himself must provide the missing links between the separate but interacting textual perspectives.[45]

If this proves difficult or impossible, the reader shares an aesthetic version of a psychotic episode with the author—not madness itself but a representation that can still be quite disturbing.

"Form in fiction," Woolf wrote to Roger Fry, "is emotion put into the right relations" (*Letters* 3: 133). If this is so, then disturbances in emotion require of fiction an asymmetrical form; its incoherence is not a neurotic evasion, not a loss of control, but a translation, an expressive discourse similar to the visual disjunctions of the surrealists.[46] Reading such a work is a test of our ability to read the unreadable without reducing or systematizing or translating it into coherent, nonmad discourse:

> How can we read the unreadable? . . . This question . . . subverts its own terms: to actually *read* the unreadable, to impose a *meaning* on it, is precisely *not* to read the unreadable *as unreadable*, but to *reduce* it to the readable, to interpret it as if it were of the same order as the readable. . . . [H]ow does the unreadable mean?[47]

> In seeking to "explain" and *master* literature, in refusing, that is, to become a *dupe* of literature, in killing within literature that which makes it literature . . . the psychoanalytic reading, ironically enough, turns out to be a reading that *represses the unconscious*, that represses, paradoxically, the unconscious it purports to be "explaining."[48]

For Woolf, both art and madness embody what cannot survive dissection, what exists in a state of incoherence, unread and unrecognized by the habitual ego, but with a power to help readers explore within themselves Alcorn and Bracher's elusive, embryonic "alien subject" and so, perhaps, to revise self-structure,

> to live and live till we have lived out those embryo lives which attend about us in early youth until "I" suppressed them. . . . Incomprehensibility

has an enormous power over us in illness, more legitimately perhaps than the upright will allow. In health meaning has encroached upon sound. Our intelligence domineers over our senses. But in illness, with the police off duty . . . if at last we grasp the meaning, it is all the richer for having come to us sensually first, by way of the palate and the nostrils, like some queer odour. Foreigners, to whom the tongue is strange, have us at a disadvantage. The Chinese must know the sound of *Antony and Cleopatra* better than we do. (*"The Moment"* 18–19)

Our reading, then, becomes *our* illness, but only if it is "an intoxicating reading," if we are "drawn into the dizzying whirl of [our] own reading," where deciphering the text involves deciphering our dreams of the text (even if they are only the sounds of a language we cannot understand) and recognizing that incoherence speaks as loudly of ourselves and the author as does the ordered, the symmetrical, and the intelligible.[49] Psychoanalytic critics like Panken who desire "to demystify the aura surrounding [Woolf's] emotional oscillations" must learn to tolerate and even value disorder if they are to understand the manic-depressive's world.[50]

To describe the multiplicity of the subject and the elusive contact between self and world, Woolf deliberately knotted and twisted her own narrative style "in conformity with the coils in my own brain" (*Letters* 1: 300). The pattern of the "coils," though unknown, could still be expressed, but not in traditional narrative order. And so her depiction of character consisted "not of a single integrated ego but rather of separate states of awareness," a discontinuity which implies that human "identity change[s] with each new set of perceptions."[51] Woolf attempted to make literature radial rather than lineal, to describe the waves which were the motion of mood, the turbulence of self, the uncertainty of perception:

I attain a different kind of beauty, achieve a symmetry by means of infinite discords, showing all the traces of the minds passage through the world; & achieve in the end, some kind of whole made of shivering fragments; to me this seems the natural process; the flight of the mind. (*Passionate Apprentice* 393)

In a letter to a friend she praised the poetry of Gerard Manley Hopkins for its similar respect for discord and "nonsense":

Have you read the poems of a man, who is dead, called Gerard Hopkins? I liked them better than any poetry for ever so long; partly because they're so difficult, but also because instead of writing mere rhythms and sense as most poets do, he makes a very strange jumble;

so that what is apparently pure nonsense is at the same time very beautiful, and not nonsense at all. Now this carries out a theory of mine; but the poor man became a Jesuit, and they discouraged him, and he became melancholy and died. I couldn't explain this without quoting however, and now I must go and wash. (*Letters* 2: 379)

Typically, Woolf's "explanation" trails off, for her theory resists stasis and statement; it is defined by its own indefinable and perpetual undercutting of any single perspective.

In her critical essay "Modern Fiction" she advises other writers likewise to tolerate ambiguity, lack of structure, bewildering confusion if need be, in the hope that some truth lies beneath the multiplicitous appearances:

The mind receives a myriad impressions—trivial, fantastic, evanescent, or engraved with the sharpness of steel. From all sides they come, an incessant shower of innumerable atoms; and as they fall, as they shape themselves into the life of Monday or Tuesday, the accent falls differently from of old. . . . Life is not a series of gig lamps symmetrically arranged; but a luminous halo, a semi-transparent envelope surrounding us from the beginning of consciousness to the end. Is it not the task of the novelist to convey this varying, this unknown and uncircumscribed spirit, whatever aberration or complexity it may display, with as little mixture of the alien and external as possible? (*Common Reader* 154)

The semi-transparent envelope is not merely an aesthetic metaphor: it is the perceptual envelope that constantly surrounds us, the fluid plane of demarcation between what is outside us and what is inside, between object and the brain's sensation/interpretation of that object. The shape of the envelope constantly alters, so that from one moment to the next we do not know how far we extend into the external world, how close we have come to touching or understanding an object, or how plastic and insubstantial our subjective world may be. It is an osmotic envelope of sensitive uncertainty, casting only the vaguest of shadows where our self is presumed to be. Thus, Woolf's fiction tends to use symbols and images (which, in a neurotic writer, might serve as interpretable symptoms of his or her psychology) to create more ambiguity and incoherence than they can resolve: "I am sure that this is the right way of using them—not in set pieces, as I had tried at first, coherently, but simply as images; never making them work out; only suggest" (*Diary* 4: 10–11).

The danger with such an approach, of course, is that it can degenerate into shapelessness, a harlequinade of patches alternating between meaning and meaninglessness. This was a problem Woolf felt had dogged her first novel, *The Voyage Out* (*Diary* 2: 17):

> What I wanted to do was to give the feeling of a vast tumult of life, as various and disorderly as possible, which should be cut short for a moment by the death, and go on again—and the whole was to have a sort of pattern, and be somehow controlled. The difficulty was to keep any sort of coherence. (*Letters* 2: 82)

But indeterminacy is worth the risk, because it avoids the imposition of a coherence that obscures—"Directly you specify hair, age, &c something frivolous, or irrelevant, gets into the book" (*Diary* 2: 265)—a method which deliberately frustrates those analytical readers who expect to stick "little horns manfully into facts . . . the steely intellectuals who treat literature as though it were an ingenious picture puzzle, to be fitted accurately together" (*Diary* 2: 214). The subjective life of a manic-depressive is divergent, and so should be the experience of readers who can open themselves up to the pluralistic experience of literature. Woolf's modernistic method is a necessary counterbalance to the dry suffocation of convergent thinking: "Prosaic judgement, whether by a psychiatrist or a narrator, is an attempt to freeze, to immobilize," an imposition incompatible with real life; "[f]iction must deal in ambiguity, the impossibility of judgement; it must avoid the formulaic definition of character."[52] Conventional form falsifies through a linearity and closure imposed by the authoritative, unified, omniscient narrator. It is a configuration of Freud's death instinct—the desire for an absolute reduction of tension[53]—and is antithetical to modernism's heterogeneity.

To shape her fiction to express what her manic-depressive experience taught her about subject-object transactions, Woolf invited our countertransferences. Only by struggling with the problem of interpretation will readers experience the asymmetrical complexity of life as Woolf knew it. When Woolf "explains" the significance of Lily Briscoe's painting in *To the Lighthouse,* she aims not to confine but to enlarge beyond rationality's capacity to establish an intelligible order:

> I meant *nothing* by The Lighthouse. One has to have a central line down the middle of the book to hold the design together. I saw that all sorts of feelings would accrue to this, but I refused to think them out, and trusted that people would make it the deposit for their own emotions—which they have done, one thinking it means one thing another another. I can't manage Symbolism except in this vague,

generalised way. Whether its right or wrong I don't know; but directly
I'm told what a thing means, it becomes hateful to me. (*Letters* 3: 385)

Even in her autobiography she wisely avoids analysis, as when she comments on the therapeutic action of writing *To the Lighthouse*:

> I suppose that I did for myself what psycho-analysts do for their
> patients. I expressed some very long felt and deeply felt emotion. And
> in expressing it I explained it and then laid it to rest. But what is the
> meaning of "explained" it? (*Moments of Being* 81)

Freud might have viewed the coy question as evidence of Woolf's failure
to see the unconscious subtext beneath the surface of this text—yet another
example of neurotic denial, not a real laying to rest. Indeed, why does
she refuse to explain her emotion to us? Syntactically Woolf equates
"explained" with "expressed." Critics may ignore surface structures
embodying multiplicitous experience, but Woolf finds value in embracing them wholly, without searching for an organized rationalization in
line with the ego's penchant for hegemonic fictions. Heterogeneity,
indeterminacy, endless suggestiveness and openness: these qualities nurtured the living truth about Woolf's psyche and provoke us, first to
respond and then to question our response. By self-relating we may
experience another subject within us and so share with her a richer world.

Woolf's fiction continually draws attention to our attempts to clarify
and systematize ambiguous texts. By applying the same principle to her
self, embracing the "shivering fragments" that her doctors ignored or the
Freudians reduced and arranged, in order to "make a whole," she found
that the power to authorize self was no longer limited to her mother's
body or a long-lost, unredeemable past:

> I will go on adventuring, changing, opening my mind & my eyes,
> refusing to be stamped & stereotyped. The thing is to free ones self; to
> let it find its dimensions, not be impeded. (*Diary* 4: 187)

To dramatize symptoms was not regressive but adaptive; it gave Woolf
the opportunity to explain her illness, to represent it, without simplifica-
tion. This helped her to accept not only her illness but her wellness too:
the sane and the insane, differentiated yet one, the one Virginia Woolf.
Critics must likewise learn to be suspicious of psychological preconceptions that reduce complexity to simplicity by eliminating the meaning of
complexity. When a psychological profile makes too much sense,
something has been ignored.

4 "In casting accounts, never forget to begin with the state of the body"

Genetics and the Stephen Family Line

Now if there's any truth in Darwin,
And we from what was, all we are win,
I simply wish the child to be
A sample of Heredity
      (James Russell Lowell to his
  goddaughter, Virginia Stephen, 1882)

The evidence for genetic transmission of manic-depressive illness is quite strong. If one identical twin has manic-depressive illness, the other runs a 67 percent chance of having it too, whereas a fraternal twin has only a 20 percent chance—roughly the same ratio as for many other inherited diseases. Of children with one bipolar or unipolar parent, 27 percent will be bipolar or unipolar themselves. When both parents have an affective disorder, and one of them is bipolar, 74 percent of offspring will suffer a major affective disorder.[1] Studies of manic-depressive offspring who had been adopted and separated from their parents show that more than 30 percent of the absent, biological parents displayed clear signs of the disorder, but only 2 percent of the adoptive parents did.[2] There is no relation between bipolar rates and rural-urban status, marital status, religion, or race.[3] Thus, the disorder is not primarily an environmentally induced or learned pattern of behavior.

Manic-depressive illness does not afflict every family member. Although some genes can cause disease almost 100 percent of the time, most require a specific bodily environment for expression, factors often created by other genes.[4] But it is important to remember that, whether or not some or all of these genes are ever expressed in behavior, they can be passed on to future generations, even by seemingly normal individuals. Recent studies have identified a gene implicated in the etiology of manic-depressive illness in some groups of individuals, and more are expected to be found in these and in other groups.[5] It is likely that several genes are involved (since several mechanisms and neurochemicals influence brain states) and that manic-depressive illness, like diabetes, results from a number of different genetic combinations interacting with a number of bodily factors. Such genetic heterogeneity may also account for manic-depression's several phenotypes, various levels of severity, and myriad symptoms, as well as for its association with other disorders (alcoholism, generalized anxiety, cyclothymia, and schizo-affective disorder) with which it may share certain, but not all, genes.[6]

Who will inherit the disease and when the patient's normal mood will change are not yet predictable. Sometimes a breakdown is triggered by a stressful event, but many shifts of mood or even complete breakdowns cannot be traced, either by analyst or by patient, to an exterior or psychological cause. An event can activate a genetically determined, preexisting affective vulnerability, usually in the first few episodes, but once the disorder has been established, life events usually play little or no role in new breakdowns.[7] This may explain why manic-depressive illness can resemble a neurosis (initial appearance of illness following trauma), but in fact the central ingredient of neurosis—repression leading to symptom substitution—is missing. Biology, not psychodynamics, is the primary mechanism of predisposition; life events can trigger but not cause madness, and many breakdowns are initiated by purely biological changes. It is also possible that traumatic life events only appear to precede affective episodes, that breakdowns begin biochemically and subtly, skewing the patient's perception of and reaction to a subsequent event, causing him or her to misinterpret and magnify its causative power.[8]

It is commonly assumed that Woolf's breakdowns were always tied to specific events: the death of a loved one, the publication of a novel, or the anticipation of unfavorable reviews. It is true that when vulnerable to depression, she did react sensitively to criticism (just as Leslie did when he was depressed), but when the reviews of *Jacob's Room* appeared, she noted how little impact it had on her: "The reviews have said more against me than for me—on the whole. Its so odd how little I mind—& odd how little I care much that Clive thinks it a masterpiece" (*Diary* 2: 210). Quentin Bell reports that some traumas, such as Thoby's death, produced no illness (1: 61, 111). And Woolf herself records a series of depressions unrelated to any stressful event:

> The interesting thing is that one does, normally, keep up a kind of
> vibration, for no reason whatever. Equally for no reason whatever, the
> vibration stops. Then one inquires why one ever had it, & there seems
> no reason why one should ever have it again. Things seem clear, sane,
> comprehensible, & under no obligation, being of that nature, to make

one vibrate at all. Indeed, its largely the clearness of sight which comes at such seasons that leads to depression. But when one can analyse it, one is half way back again. I feel unreason slowly tingling in my veins. (*Diary* 1: 298)

We have been to Rodmell, & as usual I come home depressed—for no reason. Merely moods. (*Diary* 2: 119)

   Intense depression . . . which does not come from something definite, but from nothing. (*Diary* 3: 111)

I cant tell you how down in the mud and the brambles I've been— nearer one of those climaxes of despair that I used to have than any time these 6 years—Lord knows why. Oh how I suffer! and whats worse, for nothing, no reason thats respectable. (*Letters* 5: 67)

Unless we discount her veracity or the accuracy of her euthymic self-observation, we must conclude that Woolf was justified in not seeking a purely psychological cure.

Consequently, there need be no "reason," conscious or unconscious, why Virginia suffered a breakdown soon after her marriage to Leonard. Psychoanalyst Alma Bond, in typical Freudian fashion, ties these two events together thematically:

If one were to read only Virginia's diaries and the words of her family (i.e., Bell, that marrying Leonard was the wisest decision she was to make in her lifetime), one might be inclined to wonder why, during the honeymoon of this "happiest of marriages," the bride would suffer the most severe breakdown of her life.[9]

Virginia's diaries contain numerous references attesting to her content-ment with and respect for Leonard. Since a bipolar episode can occur either randomly or in reaction to stress and does not reliably symbolize censored messages from below, it seems doubly reckless to discount Virginia's (and her family's and friends') own words. But, because Bond operates accord-ing to the Freudian theory that manic-depressives would not be sick if they were not already unconsciously lying to themselves, it is easy for her to dismiss any contrary evidence. In a like manner, Panken admits that "Woolf never acknowledged the possibility that her neurasthenia masked emotional disturbances" and then proceeds to ignore the possible truth of Woolf's position by presenting theory-driven conflicts as an explana-tion of why she fell ill.[10]

Genetically, Virginia Woolf's family history (see Figure 2) tallies with studies showing that relatives of manic-depressives are more likely than

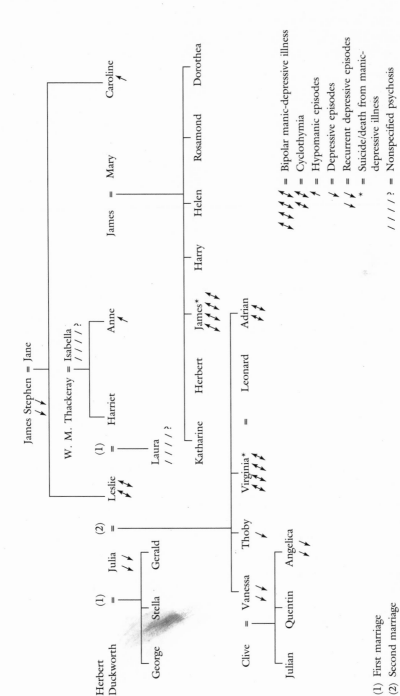

Figure 2. A Partial History of Stephen Family Affective Disorders.

the general population to exhibit affective illnesses (mania, depression, cyclothymia, schizo-affective disorders).[11] Leslie's nephew, Virginia's cousin James Kenneth Stephen, developed bipolar symptoms in his late twenties, four years after a head injury. Switching between "violent states of excitement & states of utter apathy," each lasting some months, indulging in "childish and absurd pranks" that terrorized his friends, James gradually became so "wildly extravagant" in his behavior that he was unable, despite a brilliant career at Cambridge and prestigious family connections with the legal profession, to secure employment in government.[12] Virginia remembered her cousin's manic behavior:

> That great figure with the deep voice and the wild eyes would come to the house looking for [Stella], with his madness on him; and would burst into the nursery and spear the bread on his swordstick and at one time we were told to go out by the back door and if we met Jim we were to say that Stella was away.
> . . . He was mad then. He was in the exalted state of his madness. He would dash up in a hansom; leave my father to pay for it. The hansom had been driving him about London all day. . . . I suppose madness made him believe he was all powerful. Once he came in at breakfast, "Savage has just told me I'm in danger of dying or going mad," he laughed. And soon he ran naked through Cambridge; was taken to an asylum; and died. (*Moments of Being* 98–99)

In November of 1890 Dr. Savage warned James by letter that as his disease progressed he would spend and borrow money rashly, "buying useless things," "dress in unconventional ways," and consider having to repay his debts as "a grievance"—typical manic characteristics.[13] On November 21, 1891, James was institutionalized under emergency order at St. Andrew's Hospital in Northampton. He had been referred by his family doctor, Lawrence Humphrey, and was put under the care of the then medical superintendent, Dr. J. Bayley. James's brother, Herbert, told the admitting doctor that James had for three years "been subject to attacks of loss of self-control followed by fits of depression and inaction."[14] The attending physician diagnosed "extreme depression—almost mute," with previous episodes of depression "lasting some months followed by periods of unusual excitability. This morning [prior to his admittance to the hospital] (at home) threw a looking glass into the street and stood naked in the window. Believed there was a warrant out for his detention" for unspecified crimes. Nudity or sexual exposure occurs in 28 percent of manic patients,[15] and Victorian doctors, ever vigilant against sexual perversity, took the symptom seriously. At admission James was described as "tall well built & muscular in good condition (inclined to be stout)." An eye exam revealed normal reaction to light, but his pulse was 104 and his complexion sallow. James stated that there was nothing the matter with him except that he suffered from constipation (a common depressive symptom),[16] for which he had taken opium but with no effect. Despite other medications and repeated enemas, James remained constipated for a week. He had the delusion that there was a plot against him. He struck out at an attendant and then fell into a "violent state of excitement & destroyed his furniture & clothes," after which he became unconscious. Thereafter James was depressed and quiet again, socially isolated, and neither medicines nor enemas could move his bowels satisfactorily for the next two months.

By January 1st James had improved, was almost cheerful, played billiards, and took regular exercise, but he relapsed on the 15th, becoming reserved and irritable, pacing about his room and refusing all food until he had to be fed by tube. He became incontinent, urinating in bed and in chairs, and gradually weakened from lack of nourishment, mumbling "It's too late." His pulse rose to 123, though his temperature remained at 98. Finally, he died on February 3, 1892. Dr. Bayley listed the cause of death as "mania, refusal of food, and exhaustion." In prelithium days, in-hospital deaths of manics were not uncommon. In one 1933 study, 40 percent of the deaths of hospitalized manic patients were attributed to "manic exhaustion," many of these compounded by refusal of food.[17] Summing up the case in a recent review of James's medical records, Dr. K. L. K. Trick, the current deputy medical director of St. Andrew's, concludes: "In modern terms it would seem that he suffered from Manic Depressive illness and this final episode was one of agitated depression with delusional ideas which gradually turned into a retarded depression with mutism and refusal of food."

James suffered from manic-depressive mood swings, but was their origin genetic, or were they a result of the head injury four years earlier? It is not certain how severe the physical trauma was. He was struck by a windmill sail that turned a pump, but he did not lose consciousness; he received a bad cut, which healed, but there were no reports of paralysis, amnesia, or aphasia from the five doctors (one of whom was the renowned neurologist Hughlings Jackson, and another Hack Tuke, the president of the Neurological Society) who examined him in 1890 and found him to be in good physical health with no discernible brain disease or damage to his nervous system.[18] If the injury had been severe, unipolar mania could have resulted from an intracranial cerebral lesion, but James definitely shifted between mania and depression. In the absence of any neurological symptoms, it is more likely that the trauma only activated a genetic vulnerability for mood disorder that James had inherited from the Stephen family line.[19]

Leslie's unpredictable mood swings, although infamous among family members, were never severe enough to incapacitate him and were therefore most likely cyclothymic. Although milder than manic-depressive illness and sometimes called a "subsyndromal" mood-swing disorder, cyclothymia's chronically fluctuating moods (in short cycles, usually lasting no more than days) resemble manic-depressive mood swings but without frank psychotic episodes. Cyclothymic mood shifts range between irritable depression and high excitement, arrogant overconfidence and shaky self-esteem, creative spurts of energy and industry alternating with hypersomnolence and intellectual aridity. Family members often describe patients as "high-strung," "explosive," "moody," "sensitive," or "irritable." Cyclothymia is thought to involve predisposing genetic and biochemical components in common with manic-depressive illness: manic-depressives tend to have more cyclothymic relatives than the general population, and if one identical twin is manic-depressive, the other, if not manic-depressive too, is very frequently cyclothymic. Often cyclothymia appears as a "premorbid" precursor to full-blown breakdowns in manic-depressives, and lithium is beneficial to some 60 percent of cyclothymic patients.[20]

Leslie's symptoms were typical of the nonpsychotic mood swings of cyclothymia. According to his mother's diary, he was extremely volatile in childhood, "violent in temper" and erratic in health. He would burst into tears if reproached ("A word or even a look of blame puts him into an agony of distress") and hide in shame.[21] Even in his forties, he was hypersensitive to reproach, becoming depressed when his housekeeper "looked and spoke unpleasantly" to him.[22] Leslie's mother, Jane, found that her son was so sensitive that he refused to listen to "stories with unhappy endings."[23] Although he was at times "impetuous" and "turbulent," his mother noted, he could also become "abashed at a look and seems to have scarcely courage to ask for what he wants." Though "self-willed" and passionate, he could not "endure to hear of the boys being naughty or even the animals in a make-believe story."[24] He grew pale and distressed when he heard "of any suffering or sorrow." Jane concluded that he was "the most sensitive child I ever saw" and that being reassured of her love gave him "peculiar pleasure," as did order:

> "Leslie was rather amused with the stories at first, but when I had finished it, he told me he wished I would not read that kind of book that went *wiggling* from one subject to another; he liked a book that was more steady and settled, like that long thing (the 'Library of Entertaining Knowledge'); he liked to have a great deal on one subject and in regular order." Subsequent experience did not make him fonder of books that "wiggle."[25]

Throughout his life, the security of order and love reassured Leslie whenever he was depressed; he felt that his very existence depended on carefully insulating himself from the hostile, dangerous world (both inner and outer) created by his unpredictable black moods. When newly married to his first wife, Harriet ("Minny") Thackeray, he described himself in pathetic terms: "I feel like a frozen animal that has been taken in and thawed by benevolent people."[26] He responded to disorder—even seemingly trivial irritations, such as noisy children—as if it were an attack upon himself: "He was always overly sensitive about noise and disorder, feeling that they were somehow designed to make him personally uncomfortable."[27] Not surprisingly, Leslie coped with emotional disorder by combining these saving graces of love and order in family life:

> Love for Stephen was a simple emotion. Passion, obsession, delusion could never steal upon him unseen, breed about his heart and possess him. The fascinating and alluring, and those attractions which are mysteriously generated by the temperament and physique, were alien to his nature and repelled him. Love meant devotion: to adore and to be adored.[28]

Leslie's depressions frightened him by distorting his judgment about the status of all he relied upon for security. He worried excessively about his health, the value of his work, and the family budget, though all were sound. When accounts were presented to him, he would "roar" and "beat his breast" and claim he was "dying." He suffered from extreme melancholy, guilt feelings, insomnia, hypochondria, and alternating constipation and diarrhea. When acutely depressed, he was haunted by "hideous morbid fancies" he knew to be "utterly baseless";[29] he believed that life was "ghostly, meaningless, and unreal," "a confused and purposeless mess of odds and ends," and that he was a "mere formless ghost." News of crop failures abroad sent him into "overwhelming worry," yet food would appear to him as "a dingy, idiotic whity brown, with no vivid colour in it."[30] Describing himself as a "harmless misanthrope," he overworked himself to avoid boredom and loneliness, or he sulked in isolation in a "comatose" state, or he flew into violent rages, which he called his "Berserker Fits."[31]

But, typically, cyclothymics can shift quickly out of their bad moods and become happy and productive. When not depressed, Leslie worked and wrote well, felt healthy and climbed mountains, played with his children and loved life. Between 1865 and 1871 he had well periods in which he could write three or four articles a week, complete a six-thousand-word essay at a sitting, and boast: "It is one of my weaknesses that I cannot work slowly; I must, if I work at all, work at high pressure."[32] Leslie could be "enchanting" when in the right mood. He delighted his children with animal stories and drawings, recited poems, and discussed literature with them. He saw them as beautiful and intelligent,[33] and he taught them that life could be exciting, as Virginia remembers:

> On a walk perhaps he would suddenly brush aside all our curiously conventional relationships, and show us for a minute an inspiriting vision of free life, bathed in an impersonal light. There were numbers of things to be learnt, books to be read, and success and happiness were to be attained there. (*Moments of Being* 45–46)

When depressed, Leslie condemned himself as a pathetic failure, even though he was obviously an accomplished man. He had established a reputation as "a critic of literature and religion; a philosopher and historian of British thought; a biographer; a Cambridge tutor and Anglican clergyman; an alpinist and mountaineer; and an editor and author" who was knighted in 1902.[34] He had the courage to act on his convictions and resigned his church office, proudly wearing the label of agnostic in an age of fervent belief and conformity.

Thus Leslie came to be regarded by his family as two men: one was tough-minded, rational, persevering, and independent; the other was childishly insecure, irrational, excessively sensitive, and self-pitying. Virginia was well aware of her father's two personae: the public Leslie was strong, sensible, sympathetic, and resourceful, but the private paterfamilias grumbled, whined, worried, and howled. He was ashamed of his weaknesses. His insecurities, his needs, and his distemper he displayed only to his family, which, as a Victorian husband and father, he felt it was his right to do. But it earned him his family's rage as well as their pity.

Leslie was aware of his moodiness and tried to reassure Julia, in an 1887 letter, that his fits of ill temper and misery had nothing to do with her or with their marriage:

> you know, I hope, that though you cannot give me a fresh set of nerves, all my tantarums [*sic*] and irritabilities, & oaths & lamentations are (comparative) trifles; & that I have always a huge sense of satisfaction underneath.[35]

Although, like most depressives, he blamed himself for his weaknesses, he also likened himself to his own father, from whom he felt he had inherited components of his character:

> I would sometimes awake in a fit of "the horrors"—in a state, that is to say, of nervous excitement and misery—with the erroneous impression that I had been awake for hours and a conviction that I should not get to sleep again.
> . . . I am, like my father, "skinless": over-sensitive and nervously irritable. . . . I have so often forgotten things that have been told me, when I was more or less in this state, and declared by way of excuse that I had never been told, that it became a standing joke against me. I am inclined too to be often silent. . . . At the time of my nervous depression in particular I became fidgety and troublesome in a social point of view.
> . . . My humours and vagaries were part of my character and, though many men are far better than I, I could not become another man. This at least I can say. My irritability implied nothing worse. I have been led to speak this way only because in my morbid state, when my own shortcomings have risen up before me, I have tried to disperse them by recalling the reality.[36]

Indeed, in prelithium times he could not become another man or change his "nerves," but at the same time Leslie's response to his disorder was not in his family's best interests. It sensitized Virginia to the whole issue of just what rights and duties family members had to each other, sick or well.

Leslie was right to compare himself to his father, the gloomy, self-mortifying, "intensely pessimistic," workaholic Sir James (1789–1859), who suffered from recurrent but unipolar depression.[37] Sir James had at least three major nervous breakdowns, in 1824, 1832, and 1847, the last of which was so severe that his doctors and close friends advised him to retire early from his post as under-secretary of state at the Colonial Office.[38] In a March 3, 1841, letter to his wife, the normally stoic Stephen, who was so convinced of his ugliness that he could not bear to look into mirrors, described the "bad thoughts" that threatened him with dissolution:

> Living alone I am sometimes oppressed by myself. I seem to come too closely into contact with myself. It is like the presence of some unwelcome, familiar, and yet unknown visitor. This is a feeling for which I have no description in words. Yet I suppose everyone has now and then felt as if he were two persons in one, and were compelled to hold a discourse in which soliloquy and colloquy mingle oddly and awfully.[39]

In another letter, written in February, 1853, he again failed to find adequate words to express his sense of blank depression, though he did tie it to a loss of self-esteem:

> What a strange thing it is that the blank of downright helpless inaction should be so very dismal a blank! Why can't one go quietly and contentedly through a fit of nothingness? Because it is not mere nothingness, but a wretched revelation to oneself what a bankrupt one is the moment one cannot draw any longer on things without.[40]

Like Leslie, Sir James had a "naturally ascetic turn of mind" and an obsession for ordering inner chaos with "systematic and clearly articulate . . . thought," insisting upon "the utmost precision of language." Both father and son were haunted by the fear of penury, and both wrote self-consciously about their nervous condition: "My mind," Sir James noted in a March, 1847, letter, "is as sensitive as my eyes, and as soon pained, irritated, and darkened by any kind of glare." Like many agitated depressives, he was especially vulnerable to criticism, to being proved wrong, under which he "suffered so much" that his friends quietly avoided questioning his judgment; he, in turn, "dreaded" the thought that his very presence "cast a gloom over others."[41] Although he was nicknamed King Stephen by his colleagues, and, with Sir Henry Taylor, "virtually ruled the colonial empire" during some momentous years in British history,[42] he was so shy that he developed "a nervous tick" in his eyes, which deceived one stranger into thinking Stephen was blind. Sometimes he stared at the ceiling, "with a dreamy, far-away look," while talking to others. He was "scrupulously neat in dress, and even fanatical in the matter of cleanliness," but he moved awkwardly and was manually incompetent, cutting himself repeatedly with a razor and struggling even to tie his shoes.[43] Depression sapped him of both finesse and self-esteem.

We also know that Leslie Stephen's first daughter, Laura (Virginia's half-sister), was born prematurely on December 7, 1870, and was institutionalized from the early 1890s until she died of intestinal cancer on

February 9, 1945, at The Priory Hospital, Southgate. Hospital regulations on patient privacy prevent The Priory from releasing any details from Laura's medical records. All information on her comes, therefore, from family members, who viewed her condition as either psychosis or mental retardation. The variance of these reports may have been due to differing opinions given by different doctors. Nineteenth-century physicians often misdiagnosed affective disorders, schizophrenia, and infantile autism as retardation because mood, metabolic, and thought disorders interfere with attention, cognitive performance, and memory; indeed, Victorian psychologists considered retardation "a fundamental characteristic of depressive mood."[44] Furthermore, the sentimental Victorians preferred to think of abnormal children as retarded rather than insane, as babyish rather than psychotic, and Leslie apparently shared this popular belief. His description of Laura confuses mental deficiency and insanity: he refers to her as "obviously a backward child" and "mentally deficient," but he also notes her "strange waywardness and inarticulate ways of thinking and speaking," regressive behavior his biographer Noel Annan specifies as "baby-ways and apathy."[45] Laura could do "disconcerting things—calmly throw a pair of scissors into the fire,"[46] sing nonchalantly when Leslie tried to get her attention, stare "vacant-eyed" (*Moments of Being* 182), complain of choking throughout her meals, or spit the meat out of her mouth.

Laura developed no overt problems in the first five years of her life, although Leslie had noticed some subtle (but unspecified) indications that his daughter was developing too slowly. She was sent to kindergarten, but the school's mistress told Leslie that Laura "would never learn to read." He tried to teach her himself, but she succeeded in reading only "after a fashion";[47] in 1921 Virginia said that Laura "could hardly read" (*Moments of Being* 182). When she was a teenager, Laura suffered from nervous tics and speech impediments. Her learning difficulties, her "strange mannerisms" of straining and boggling over words in a "lockjaw way of talking," her "spasmodic" utterances and "queer squeaking" caused the short-tempered Leslie to complain about her "sluggishness" and call her an "idiot" (as did Virginia Woolf [*Moments of Being* 182]), but he also reported that at times she could be an exceptionally verbal child, talking quickly ("as fast as a pack of hounds"), noisily, and persistently. Sometimes she made irrelevant remarks with "the most provoking good temper," but she could fall unexpectedly into tantrums of wild howling. Her father was particularly alarmed by her "grotesque waywardness," "perversity," and lack of "moral sense"[48]—although, ever the Victorian gentleman, he did not illustrate such observations with specific examples. This is unfortunate, since even today affective disorder in adolescents is frequently mistaken for conduct disorder if symptoms are not adequately specified.[49]

But what kind of mental illness was this? In his family memoir, *Sir Leslie Stephen's Mausoleum Book,* Leslie wrote of his suspicion that Laura had inherited her maternal grandmother's insanity: in 1840 Isabella, William Makepeace Thackeray's wife and mother of Leslie's first wife, Harriet, fell into a postpartum psychosis from which she never recovered. Although she had always been "eccentric" and notoriously absent-minded, it was only after Harriet's birth that Isabella began to suffer from "an extraordinary state of languor and depression" and constipation.[50] Then she began to alternate: on some days she seemed better, on others much worse. Periods of normalcy were recurrently succeeded by "the usual reversal"—weeks when she seemed nearly recovered followed by episodes of excessive violence.[51] William noted immediately that her mental state was unstable: "at first she was in a fever & violent; then she was indifferent, now she is melancholy & silent." Soon she switched between sluggishness, agitation, and moments of happiness, but was "especially" and "curiously" low in the mornings—a common feature in biochemical depression. She experienced difficulties with concentration, complaining in a letter that she lost her train of thought ("I feel myself excited[,] my strenght [*sic*] is not great and my head flies away with me as if it were a balloon"—a confusion William also noted: "she has been clouded & rambling again"; "she knows everybody and recollects things but in a stunned confused sort of way." She apologized for her dark thoughts but at the same time asserted their truth: "I try to think my fears imaginary and exaggerated and that I am a coward by nature, but when people do not raise their expectations to too high a pitch they cannot be disappointed." Then she attempted suicide by throwing herself overboard from a ship.

She subsequently lost interest in her new baby and in the rest of the family. William noted that at times she was "devoured by gloom" and wept over faults and past mistakes.[52] She thought herself "a perfect demon of wickedness—God abandoned," in a period of acute despair that progressed from "apathy to fits of rambling gloom, wallowing in a '*moral melancholy*', deploring her own unworthiness, thinking she had entailed all manner of misery on her husband, that she never had been fit to be a wife."[53] William concluded that Isabella's melancholy had "augmented to absolute insanity," leaving her "quite demented."[54]

After much care and many treatments, Isabella's episodes became less severe, as William writes:

There is nothing the matter with her except perfect indifference, silence and sluggishness. She cares for nothing, except for me a little, her general health has greatly improved: her ideas are quite distinct when she chooses to wake from her lethargy. She is not unhappy and looks fresh, smiling and about sixteen years old. To-day is her little baby's birthday. She kissed the child when I told her of the circumstance, but does not care for it.[55]

Eventually, Isabella settled into "gentle, childish ramblings" and a daily routine of simple domesticity, socially withdrawn and unconcerned with thoughts of her family. She lived for thirty years after William's death in 1863, maintaining "the same placid, retired life," unable to recognize her grandchildren as her own.[56]

If Isabella did suffer, as seems likely, from a psychotic depression triggered by the major changes in hormonal levels brought about by childbirth,[57] then both sides of Laura's family had a history of affective illness, which dramatically increases the odds for the daughter of such a union to suffer from some form of it as well. Leslie noted that by the time she was in her early twenties Laura, like Isabella, was unable to recognize her family clearly.[58] In 1921 Virginia wrote to Vanessa that Laura's guardian, Katharine Stephen, had visited the fifty-two-year-old patient in the asylum and reported that she "is the same as ever, and never stops talking, and occasionally says, 'I told him to go away' or 'Put it down, then', quite sensibly; but the rest is unintelligible" (*Letters* 2: 492). This is not the typical family profile of mental retardation, which would not, at any rate, oscillate so markedly in severity. Nor does it support DeSalvo's alternate view that Laura was actually sane, her learning disabilities and strange behavior merely a "refusal to use her mental abilities" at the behest of an abusive father who wanted to control her, and that she was imprisoned in a mental asylum for over fifty years because Leslie wanted to punish her for misbehaving.[59] DeSalvo reads Leslie's confused rendering of Laura's problems as a deliberate obfuscation of the facts. But we must remember that even Victorian specialists frequently conflated the symptoms of what we now know to be different disorders, and Leslie's own doctor, George Savage, publicly espoused the belief that "an insane parent may have an insane, idiotic, wicked, epileptic, or somnambulistic child," as if all those traits were genetically connected.[60] Given Savage's views, even Minny's death by "convulsions" (probably eclampsia caused by complications during pregnancy, rather than epilepsy) would have suggested to both men that an inherited link existed between Isabella's disorder and Laura's.

Leslie's conclusion was theory-coherent for the times. His lapses prevent us, however, from establishing a firm diagnosis—Laura's symptoms occur with several brain disorders, including the childhood psychoses and autism—but we can at least avoid the temptation of dismissing Leslie's or Julia's testimony altogether for the sake of a conspiracy theory that spans over fifty years of medical supervision and the deaths of both parents and the admitting doctor. Diagnosis aside, Leslie's observations were probably accurate; at least one study shows that parents of psychotic and autistic children do usually succeed at estimating in general, nonpsychiatric terms the abilities and disabilities of their offspring.[61] And recent history provides abundant evidence that parents of children with psychotic, autistic, or developmental disorders have been unjustly and cruelly victimized by those who seek simplistic answers—indeed, the simplest answer of all, that *someone* must be blamed for abnormality in children. Unless biological mechanisms can beyond a reasonable doubt be eliminated as the cause of a child's mental problems—especially when those symptoms appear in disorders known to be biologically based and unconnected to childrearing practices—blaming the parent is merely a witchhunt masquerading as science.

Leslie's second wife, Julia, herself exhibited chronic depressive symptoms (as I will explore in more detail in Chapter Five), and their children were also afflicted with varying levels of affective disorder. Both Virginia's brothers, Adrian and Thoby, had episodes of depression, as did her only full sister, Vanessa. In 1894 Thoby reportedly attempted suicide during delirium induced by influenza; he died of typhoid in 1906.[62] Adrian's much longer life gives us a more complete picture of chronic, nonpsychotic depression. Leonard and Virginia described him as being "extremely lethargic and critical," "passive, inert, depressed and aloof" (L. Woolf, *Letters* 531), always looking on the dark side (V. Woolf, *Passionate Apprentice* 192), needing "constant reassurance," lacking in vitality, subject to "tantrums," having had his life "crushed" out of him before he was born, "moping & glooming" and dwelling too much on the past (V. Woolf, *Diary* 1: 187; 2: 186; 2: 277; 3: 227; 4: 103). Vanessa was intermittently crippled by severe depressions, "different in effect but not perhaps unrelated to Virginia's instability," and her only daughter, Angelica, was hospitalized for severe depression.[63] Across three generations, then, we find five depressives, two nonspecific psychotics, two manic-depressives, and one cyclothymic: an impressive display of familial pattern.

Why should there be such diversity? Affective disorders are not genetically identical, just as they are not biochemically identical, but they do tend to appear in the same families, and so they must have some genetic components in common that combine in various ways in different individuals. With the exception of identical twins, each individual receives from the parents a different combination of mood-disorder genes. Some combinations produce the various forms of manic-depressive illness, and others produce related mood disorders: pure mania, pure depression, cyclothymia, and schizo-affective illness, all of which can vary markedly in severity. None of Julia's three children (two sons, Gerald and George, and a daughter, Stella) by her first husband, Herbert Duckworth, showed any signs of affective illness, but since Julia herself suffered from chronic depression, we can assume that her own mood-disorder genes contributed to or abetted Leslie's in their children, all of whom displayed depressive symptoms.

An individual's genetic make-up is a complicated business, for it combines selected genes from each parent, neither of whom may display the full range or strength of the characteristics they pass on to their children. A gene coded for mood disorder may be either abetted or inhibited by the addition of other genes in the formation of each new human being. Genes are switches and may be turned either on or off, permanently or temporarily, by the presence of other genes or by even smaller nucleotide switches within the gene's DNA.[64] It is therefore possible that what Jane (who was not ill) bequeathed to her son Leslie was an inhibiting gene that prevented full-blown manic-depressive illness in him, a gene which may either not have been passed on to Virginia or have been switched off in her by a gene contributed by Virginia's mother, the depressive Julia. Julia's predisposition to depression may in turn have been switched off in her first three children by Herbert's genes.

Because manic-depressive illness is more readily passed from father to daughter or from mother to son and daughter than it is from father to son, it has been hypothesized that in some families one of possibly several primary genes responsible for predisposing individuals to full-blown bipolar illness is transmitted via the female sex chromosome.[65] If this sex-linked gene was involved in Virginia Woolf's illness, then the likelihood would be that Leslie had inherited only non-sex-linked mood-disorder genes from Sir James (enough to contribute to his cyclothymia, his father's depressions, and Laura's mental difficulties, but not enough to produce frank manic-depressive illness in any of the three).[66] According to this model of inheritance, the missing sex-linked gene, by itself insufficient to produce illness, might have come from his mother, Jane, to augment the Stephen family genetic code loaded for mood disorders.

Thus, two routes for Virginia's inheritance are possible: Leslie's and Julia's genes may have combined to cause frank bipolar disorder in Virginia, or Leslie could alone have transmitted a full complement of genes to Virginia even though he himself suffered only the milder but related cyclothymic mood swings. Again, it is important to remember that, like most genes, mood-disorder genes do not have complete penetrance (the percentage of cases that carry the gene who do in fact show its effect in any degree); that is to say, only a minority of those who inherit these genes ever exhibit full-blown manic-depressive illness. Pure mania, pure depression, cyclothymia, and schizo-affective illness can occur in separate individuals in a family that later produces a manic-depressive. Thus, whereas 66 percent of bipolar patients have a family history of mood disorder, only 15 percent of them have a bipolar parent. Thorough family studies are needed to determine the distribution and degree of risk of inherited mood disorder.[67] Anyone worried about the chance of inheriting an affective disorder should seek genetic counseling. Genetic mechanisms produce the great variability that is essential for evolutionary adaptation and survival, but they complicate questions of inheritance.

5 "How completely he satisfied her is proved by the collapse"

Emblematic Events in Family History

If Virginia Woolf suffered from a manic-depressive illness with such important genetic and biochemical components, is nothing left for the psychobiographer? Are we now, because we cannot question genes, to be denied speculation about the psychological significance of her life and work? The diagnosis of manic-depressive illness may explain her breakdowns and the form of her symptoms, but it does not mean Woolf was unaffected by life events or did not incorporate their significance into her work. Nor is it a guarantee of immunity from psychological conflict. A mood disorder is an emotionally wrenching experience, and some sufferers may develop phobias, obsessions, or neurotic strategies to cope with these disturbances; at the very least, they develop a preoccupation with psychological concerns that can be illuminating. We can still talk about Woolf's psychodynamics so long as we are careful to distinguish between psychodynamic conflicts and the manic-depressive syndrome. Psychiatrists approach this problem by looking for adaptive or constructive, as opposed to regressive or evasive, behavior in the euthymic personality (between episodes). Teaching the patient how to recognize and cope with endogenous illness minimizes the psychological damage and allows the analyst to address any neurotic conflicts that may be present—although we must remember that manic-depressives are no more liable to be neurotic than the general population is.[1]

Within the psychiatric rubric, Woolf may be classified as adaptive: rather than allowing herself to be overwhelmed by an incurable illness, she explored it with great sensitivity, courage, and intelligence. How she did understand it is a legitimate object of study for the psychobiographer, because her explanation in part resulted from her own experiences, in part from seeing similarities between herself and other family members. Personal history can be used as a context in which to consider Woolf's ideas about her disorder, for her art was not an evasive or conflict-ridden mediation of unconscious drives: she deliberately shaped her novels to explore her anomalous experiences and to express her insights about them.

114

• • • • •

Most manic-depressive episodes occur spontaneously, but, since brain activity is so closely tied to bodily processes, breakdowns are sometimes associated with traumatic events that produce great stress.[2] Although the symptoms are not symbols of an unconscious conflict presumed to have generated the breakdown, a link exists in the minds of patients who, like Freud, try to understand their despair in terms of an emblematic biographical event. Normal individuals react to the death of a parent, for instance, with sadness, mourning, and loneliness, but for the biochemically depressed this event takes on a huge biographical significance. Suffering an intense sense of abandonment and certain doom, convinced that they alone are inadequate and impotent, and feeling as helpless and as vulnerable as infants, these patients often look back nostalgically to what now seems to them an idyllic childhood union with an idealized parent, as they bemoan their loss or blame themselves for this fateful turn of events. It was this constant appeal for reassurance and nurturing from others, particularly from therapists, that led the early Freudians to label the depressive as narcissistic and to focus on oral symptoms, for they assumed that traumatic loss during the oral stage of infancy had originally caused the neurosis.[3]

We must not underestimate the psychological effect of loss on the Stephens, however. They endured a succession of deaths, illnesses, and disappointments that would have tested the mettle of any family. Loss created a psychological pattern Woolf felt she had, to some degree, inherited, a pattern of alternating highs and lows, idealization and disillusionment, that colored her view of what her manic-depressive symptoms meant, of who she was and who she wanted to be.

Both Leslie Stephen and Julia Jackson brought to their marriage firmly established traditions of depressive response to loss. Julia's first husband, the attractive and romantic Herbert Duckworth, died suddenly of a burst brain abscess when she was pregnant with their third child, Gerald, in the fourth year of their marriage. The Duckworth marriage had been a passionate one, which even the skeptic Leslie declared had given Julia happiness that was "unqualified" and "perfect." Herbert was remembered not only for his "sweetness of temper" but also for Julia's "complete surrender of herself in the fullest sense" to a union so idyllic that "there was to be no shadow of difference or discord."[4] The guilt and grief Julia felt at Herbert's death were severe and forever imprinted on the family consciousness the Herbert myth with its moral that perfect happiness lay always out of reach. As Woolf herself argued in 1940,

> how completely [Herbert] satisfied [Julia] is proved by the collapse, the
> complete collapse into which she fell when he died. All her gaiety, all
> her sociability left her. She was as unhappy as it is possible for anyone
> to be. (*Moments of Being* 90)

Julia responded to her loss with a stoic but mechanical devotion to her
family. She lost her religious faith and defended her agnosticism in print
by claiming it was earthly life, not the hereafter, that contained the real hell:

> Judgement comes to us while we live. The distant flames of Hell can
> surely not cause the agony which remorse brings on us. The sorrow we
> have caused those who love us best, the misused opportunities of our
> lives, the wasted energies line up against us and torture us more than
> the words of the preacher.[5]

Julia was haunted by persistent melancholic and even suicidal thoughts
that turned her into a "chronic mourner" and an indefatigable nurse.[6]
She never forgot her idealized past, and neither did the Stephen family:
it became the central image of a pervasive belief that a perfect union is
always followed by devastating loss, a sequence that both Stephen family
history and Virginia's own bipolar breakdowns repeatedly revived.

Julia's extended mourning went hand in hand with her nursing: the
sick and dying served for her as Herbert-substitutes. She felt a "morbid
guilt" for having survived Herbert and confessed to Leslie her fear that
she could only "wound but not heal" others who risked loving her.[7]
For some time she refused Leslie's proposal of marriage on the grounds
that his love for her would eventually do him harm.[8] Only the seriously
ill ran no risk from her attentions, and for the rest of her life, therefore,
she was tireless in her visiting of sickrooms. Quentin Bell blamed her
early death on her nursing.[9] She died in 1895, at the age of forty-nine,
technically of rheumatic fever but essentially of exhaustion.[10] Leslie
certainly knew that her need to serve others was closely connected to
widowhood and grief:

> As it seems to me, she had learnt so thoroughly in her dark days of
> widowhood to consider herself as set apart to relieve pain and sorrow
> that, when no special object offered itself for her sympathy, when there
> was no patient to be nursed or bereaved friend to cheer, she had a
> stream of overflowing goodwill which forced her to look out for some
> channel of discharge. A child's birthday or any little occasion or present
> presented itself to her as a chance of adding something to the right side
> of the balance in the long and too often mournful account of pain and
> happiness.[11]

As Leslie suspected, it was not for their sakes alone that Julia was motivated to nurse others. In her book on nursing techniques, *Notes from Sick Rooms*, Julia herself admonishes nurses to love nursing but not the patient: "It ought to be quite immaterial to a nurse whom she is nursing. . . . The genuine love of her 'case' and not of the individual patient seems to me the sign of the true nursing instinct." Since devotion should be impersonal, a nurse should be able to affect cheerfulness and become adept at wearing a "face." "Cheerfulness," Julia declares, "is a habit"; if a patient asks questions that may result in unhappiness, a nurse should "lie freely."[12] For Julia, nursing became a hiding place as well as an expiation.

Herbert's death had destroyed Julia's illusion of life's unalloyed goodness. Woolf describes her mother as having been

> happy as few people are happy, for she had passed like a princess in a pageant from her supremely beautiful youth to marriage and motherhood, without awakenment. . . . [S]he had lived with a man, stainless of his kind, exalted in a world of pure love and beauty. The effect of his death then was doubly tremendous, because it was a disillusionment as well as a tragic human loss. (*Moments of Being* 32)

The loss numbed Julia, left her empty of feeling and depressed. In a letter to Leslie she explained:

> And so I got deadened. I had all along felt that if it had been possible for me to be myself, it would have been better for me individually; and that I could have got more real life out of the wreck if I had broken down more. But there was Baby to be thought of and everyone around me urging me to keep up, and I could never be alone which sometimes was such torture.[13]

Prevented from experiencing her grief in its full intensity, from sinking down into herself to feel *real* emotions, perhaps even "alien" emotions unbecoming a Victorian widow and mother, Julia had to assume a dissembling "face" for the sake of others to whom she would lie freely— about her cheerfulness, the value of life, and self-worth:

> I was only 24 when it all seemed a shipwreck, and I knew that I had to live on and on, and the only thing to be done was to be as cheerful as I could and do as much as I could and think as little.[14]

Julia sacrificed her time and her emotions for others but did not really give herself to them, not because she was ungenerous but because she felt as if there were nothing left inside her to give, as if her innermost self had died with Herbert. She wrote quite candidly to Leslie that she felt "callous" and "horribly unsentimental" about their engagement to be married.[15] Perhaps this was why she felt such an affinity for the sickroom. As Leslie writes:

> She argues with sweet sophistry that I am more "tender" than she, because I can try to sympathize with the happy [healthy] whereas she puts them "on a sort of mental shelf when they are bright again." When she had saved a life from the deep waters, that is, she sought at once for another person to rescue, whereas I went off to take a glass with the escaped. . . . It seemed to me at the time that she had accepted sorrow as her life-long partner.[16]

Julia's melancholic view of life, her "restrained" manner, and her reticence about telling her husband that she loved him, convinced Leslie that she had been "numbed and petrified by her grief," but her emotional paralysis was not unacceptable to his Victorian notion of the nature of femininity: "woman-like she had accepted sorrow, a life of sorrow, or let me say a life clouded by sorrow, as her permanent portion."[17] Depression is easier than mania for spouses to endure. The energized misbehaviors of mania are experienced as "exceedingly disruptive to the overall family system," whereas depressive withdrawal causes "relatively little marital disruption."[18] Subdued by her depression, selfless and dutiful, Julia was—as she appears in images that recur in Virginia's novels—"like a person reviving from drowning . . . [who] sometimes feels . . . that she must let herself sink."[19] In her letters to Leslie during their courtship, she talked of entering a convent (though she was by then an agnostic) because such a life meant the "spirit of submission" to superiors who would relieve her of the necessity of thinking about her life.[20] Julia sank into self-sacrifice, into the Victorian role of "angel in the house" which Virginia would grow up to fear and hate.

Julia had emptied herself, or had been emptied, of a positive identity that her daughter could have emulated. Her depression, however, was something they could share. Virginia remembered her mother as someone who could be talked to: "I think her service, when it was not purely practical, lay in simply helping people by the light of her judgement and experience, to see what they really meant or felt" (*Moments of Being* 35). Their relationship had not been intimate, but Woolf did not posit her mother's potential for service on intimacy or demonstrable love: the emphasis is on "judgement" (for Virginia too saw life as brutal) and on "experience," the experience only another depressive could understand.

Sir Leslie Stephen, by Beresford, 1902. By permission of the National Portrait Gallery.

Harriet ("Minnie") Thackeray, by Julia Margaret Cameron, 1862. By permission of the Tate Gallery Archive.

Julia Duckworth, by Julia Margaret Cameron, 1867. By permission of the Gersheim Collection, Harry Ransom Humanities Center, University of Texas at Austin.

Anne Thackeray Ritchie, by Julia Margaret Cameron, 1867. By permission of
the National Portrait Gallery.

Virginia Stephen, 1903. By permission of the Tate Gallery Archive.

Virginia Woolf, n.d. By permission of the Harvard Theatre Collection.

Ironically, Julia's composure in the face of suffering fulfilled Leslie's public (but not private) ideals. In an 1876 letter to Charles Eliot Norton, Leslie admitted his failure to accept with dignity Minny's death:

> The worst of it is that, as you so truly say, the hideous mass of commonplace life thrusts itself in between me and my old happiness, and further—what is an unfortunate tendency of mine—that unhappiness tries my temper. I am more fretful and irritable by disposition than you perhaps know, and sometimes I bully my best friends shamefully. The problem of making sorrow ennobling instead of deteriorating is a terribly hard one.[21]

Both father and daughter disliked self-indulgent displays of emotion or morbid sensitivity; both felt degraded by their "weakness" of character when in the throes of despair; both admired Julia's stoical decorum. Virginia praised her mother's "inimitable bravery" because it involved facing

> a deep sense of the futility of all effort, the mystery of life. You may see the two things in her face. "Let us make the most of what we have, since we know nothing of the future" was the motive that urged her to toil so incessantly on behalf of happiness, right doing, love; and the melancholy echoes answered "What does it matter? Perhaps there is no future." Encompassed as she was by this solemn doubt her most trivial activities had something of grandeur about them; and her presence was large and austere, bringing with it not only joy and life, exquisite fleeting femininities, but the majesty of a nobly composed human being. (*Moments of Being* 36)

In the final pages of his 1896 book, *Social Rights and Duties,* Leslie seems to speak of Julia's life, echoing Virginia's admiration in his account of how grief can be turned to good account:

> Suppose, now, that one so endowed is struck by one of those terrible blows which shiver the very foundations of life; which make the outside world a mere discordant nightmare, and seem to leave for the only reality a perpetual and gnawing pain, which lulls for an instant only to be revived by every contact with facts. Sorrow becomes the element in which one lives and moves. . . . Yet the greatest test of true nobility of character is its power of turning even the bitterest grief to account . . . . It knows instinctively that grief, terrible as it is, is yet, in another sense, an invaluable possession. The sufferer . . . acquires a deeper and keener sympathy with all who are desolate and afflicted; and the natural affections become blended, if with a certain melancholy, yet with that quick and delicate perception of the suffering of

others which gives the only consolation worthy of the name—the sense of something soothing and softening and inspiring in the midst of the bitterest agony. . . .

A lofty nature which has profited by passing through the furnace acquires claims not only upon our love but upon reverence.[22]

Both Leslie and Virginia felt that Julia's nature was loftier than their own, but whereas Leslie succumbed to his grief, Virginia examined her despair by creating fictional versions of her mother that focused on two seemingly contradictory characteristics of her mother's depressions. They were dangerous, because despair is self-negating (her mother lived, Woolf wrote, "as though she heard perpetually the ticking of a vast clock and could never forget that some day it would cease for all of us" [*Moments of Being* 35]), and yet they were protective, for they prevented further disillusionment. The realization that, because she felt dead already, she had nothing to fear from others' dissolution, gave Julia the strength to carry other people's burdens, other people's pain, accepting "that sorrow is our lot, and at best we can but face it bravely" (*Moments of Being* 32).

Julia's sense of partial immunity has been shared by other depressives. In some patients the self-devaluation typical of anhedonic depression seems to have a passive-defensive function as well as a self-destructive one: it tempers the perfectionist tendency to form high expectations or even manic illusions that run the risk of further deflation. For example, one young pregnant woman who had created the exalted fantasy of "a perfect, idyllic union between mother and child" had that fantasy "traumatically shattered" by the realities of birth, child rearing, and parental responsibilities. Her initial exaggerated enthusiasm gave way to a despair that insured against future disillusionment.[23]

In her novels Woolf explores the relationship between idealization and disillusionment, especially the advantages and disadvantages each offers. Julia can appear in any character who sinks in order to survive depression with dignity. Her last words to Virginia ("Hold yourself straight, my little Goat" [*Moments of Being* 84]) were, not a rebuke nor a dismissal, but the kind of advice Virginia needed from a fellow sufferer of depression. They suggest, too, why Virginia came to depend so much on Vanessa, who was, as her daughter Angelica remembers, "self-reliant almost to a fault, producing an effect of rocklike stability that was not as secure as it seemed."[24] Julia's influence seems neatly illustrated by another memory provided by Angelica, who, in the absence of Leonard, helped her aunt Virginia to bed one evening at the onset of a headache:

It was the only time I ever saw her near a breakdown. I had been shielded from knowledge of these. . . . Seeing her suddenly threatened left me with the impression of a stoic vanquished only for the moment, as brief a moment as she could make it. In spite of her fragility Virginia had enormous resilience.[25]

Leslie had less. He responded to the sudden death of his first wife, Harriet ("Minny") Thackeray, with a remarkable indulgence in grief, becoming "wrapt in gloom, companionless, and silent," exhibiting a perpetually "mournful manner." But rather than feeling guilty for having survived his mate, as Julia had done, Leslie pitied himself and intensified his search for a protective, maternal figure to assuage a dependency that had been cultivated in him by his mother years earlier, when he was a weak and sickly boy. Jane had encouraged his cyclothymic tendency "to worry excessively about signs of ill health, and to feel that he was a creature greatly deserving pity."[26] Unlike the anhedonic Julia, Leslie feared dissolution:

Julia had been numbed and petrified by her grief. . . . I[,] though plunged into deep melancholy[,] always resented or resisted the thought of a complete abandonment of the hope, at least, of happiness. I still somewhere, deep down in my nature, was able to carry on a struggle against the dominion of grief.[27]

His cyclothymia manifested itself in an assortment of physical as well as psychological complaints typical of agitated depression, such as waking up in the middle of the night with "fits of nervous depression," an insomnia which required narcotics. But, beyond these symptoms imposed by nature, Leslie quickly realized that his most effective maneuver to persuade self-styled nurse Julia to marry him was to act helpless or sick whenever he lacked her constant attention.[28] It was a dependency he enjoyed: "To be nursed by her, I know it alas!, was a luxury even in the midst of suffering."[29]

Evidently Julia found the relationship congenial: Leslie was a willing patient, she was a willing nurse, and both were depressed. In a March 4, 1870, letter to Charles Eliot Norton, Leslie described this interest he shared with his new bride:

We want rest, protection from the outside world—a quiet domestic life with the least possible proportion of anything bordering upon gaiety. This sympathy between us grew up in a common sense of suffering.[30]

Such a combination is by no means uncommon. A tendency for assortative mating (people with similar disorders marrying each other) has been "reported repeatedly" in research on affective disorders.[31] They seek each other out, perhaps because "normal" mates find it difficult to understand the depressive's world. Julia and Leslie found in each other a mutual history of disappointment, a patient sympathy, a consoling tolerance for unhealed wounds, a shared belief (connected to their declared agnosticism) that life had no guarantees, that no benevolent providential design could explain away the senseless pain of Herbert's and Minny's deaths. More important, each granted the other the right to be depressed without censure and the right to require care (to soothe Leslie's nerves) or distance (to let Julia forget herself by nursing others). Before the availability of antidepressants, such a mutual policy at least allowed depressives some integrity for their feelings—an attitude far different from that embodied by the tyrant of proportion and conversion, Dr. Bradshaw in *Mrs. Dalloway*. So, after much evasion, Julia finally agreed to marry Leslie—and exactly for the reason he propagandized, not love necessarily, but to provide for him the mothering he craved and to give herself another chance to keep a husband alive.[32]

The Stephen marriage, then, was a compact between two people who, overwhelmed by depression's debilitating pain, substituted need for romantic love. However much we may sympathize with their very real suffering, we must examine critically (as their daughter Virginia did) the destructive aspects of their strategy, for each coped with loss and sorrow not by exploring their inner resources but by filling up the emptiness inside with relationships outside, by nestling into domestic bonds. Ironically, in an age that extolled self-help and rugged individualism as public values, the structure of the private Victorian family offered security by making self-reliance, even self-actualization, unnecessary. Clung to as a refuge from a competitive society, family life was idealized beyond its real value, particularly by Leslie, who sanctified Julia's role as mother:

> He worshipped Julia [and] desired to transform her into an apotheosis of motherhood, but treated her in the home as someone who should be at his beck and call, support him in every emotional crisis, order the minutiae of his life and then submit to his criticism in those household matters of which she was mistress.[33]

There was a curious balance in this relationship between dominance and submission. Leslie both worshipped Julia and controlled her, principally through her role as a mother, which allowed him to idealize her and yet use her, as if he valued his vision of womanhood over Julia herself. Leslie felt obliged to "extract" nurture from Julia through various ploys: feigning dependence, placing her on the defensive through accusations, or implying that she was stingy with her affections, that she made him coax or trick her into loving him. Like an infant, he knew nothing but his need. He felt that his gestures of self-pity "were valid indications of love, for they showed how profoundly he needed her," and he did not mind dominating her when pity was not forthcoming.[34] Julia, in turn, submitted to her husband's demands, but she took complete control in the sickroom.[35] As he grew more demanding, she withheld herself, becoming rigid, numb, and more internalized. Leslie periodically lost control when he felt defenseless; if despair threatened him, he either tried to fight back or whined, asserting himself through domination or manipulation. Julia then contracted her spirit and bore the pain stoically.

It is important to make the distinction here between mood and desire: the depressive mood, imposed by brain chemistry, was not under Leslie's control, either consciously or unconsciously, but how he responded to that despair when euthymic was shaped by mind, by Leslie the person who experienced himself as threatened and could decide how best to handle his fear and his pain. Certainly, Leslie's mother had encouraged the display of such needs, but his cyclothymic depressive moods increased their severity. Psychoanalyst Sandor Rado, who observed the same behavior in his depressed patients, theorized that they become inordinately reliant on others for narcissistic gratification and for maintaining the self-esteem that depression destroys. Ultimately, Rado reasoned, the depressive's desire to be passive can be satisfied only by an all-giving "other" whom he can control and tyrannize. That desire to be passive is thus a composite of what the depressed Leslie could not choose and what he did choose. His strategy for coping with mood swings failed (especially in Virginia's eyes) because he laid upon his family so much of the burden to make sense and order in his life. He expected Julia to restore his sense of security and self-esteem when depression made him feel unloved and inadequate. After her death, he turned to his children to act as buffers between himself and the cruel world. Paraphrasing one of his unpublished letters, Jean Love reports that Leslie "said that as long as he could surround himself with the children, like an 'animal in a burrow,' nothing could hurt him—an inverted and frightening concept of fatherhood."[36] Instead of distancing himself from his moods to observe them critically (as Virginia was later to do with her own mood swings), Leslie allowed himself to be swallowed up by them, to believe that every momentary feeling, whether it was fear that he would sink without Julia's constant care or fear that he was a miserable failure and did not deserve Julia's care, represented objective truth. Attending wholly to himself, he became self-centered, egotistical, and more miserable.

Contraction and control, surrender and domination, in reaction to the threatened losses of despair and selflessness, would later become major motifs in their daughter's novels. But Virginia tried to evolve a different strategy for herself, that of exploring her own resources and resisting dependence on her mother. Mother and father stand for more than real or fantasized parents or even the whole of childhood: each figure embodies distinct object-relational characteristics. Although she sought short-term nurture and support from other women to allay acute depressive insecurities, and although she relied on Leonard to manage practical affairs in the sickroom, Virginia did not pretend that mother and father, affection and order, solved the very personal and existential problem posed by manic-depressive illness. Virginia made no one but herself responsible for establishing her sense of identity. Through writing she filled up the emptiness inside without entrapping others in a self-deceptive game; by facing despair alone, she felt she could disarm it, at least in part. Fiction facilitated autonomy because it helped her to both mother and father herself.[37]

Leslie's domination was in fact a reaction research suggests is fairly common in depressed patients. Although he sometimes responded to loss and deprivation with fear and trembling, giving up his self-integrity as depression washed away subject-object boundaries, he often exploited the more potent alternative of dominating chaos through obsessive intellection. Depression may mask itself in behaviors not overtly gloomy: instead of a discernible black mood, the patient may exhibit a need to dominate interpersonal relationships. He or she may manifest meticulous work habits, rigidity of view (making black-and-white distinctions, with little tolerance for ambiguity), nervousness, anxiety, irritability, fear of financial impoverishment, hypochondria, and digestive disorders such as alternation between diarrhea and constipation, a chronic symptom of Leslie's.[38] John Custance noticed that in mania he cheerfully embraced paradoxes and out of fragments synthesized cosmic visions of wholes; in his depression, by contrast, his tendency was to "divide and differentiate, analysis as opposed to synthesis." Custance theorized that his mania operated on what he called the Dionysian principle, which he defined as a "frenzy" of divergent thinking that "dissolves the ego and unites man with his brother-man as well as Nature"; depression, the Apollonian principle, involved Logos, thinking by "measure, number, limitation and order, the separation of the individual from the mass by a process of individuation, the separating out of the elements of experience by orderly analysis."[39] Although Custance here oversimplifies (agitated manics, for instance, may not feel united with humanity but may just as easily experience alienation and intense paranoid hostility, while anhedonic depressives may lose mental concentration and complain that they are "dissolving"), mood shifts do affect cognition, and Custance's formula describes many bipolar experiences. In general, the agitated depressive can react to despair by demanding control, order, and vindictive analysis, whereas the manic may display a hapless belief in magic and disorder and an inflated view of the self's powers of intuition.

Like the depressed Custance, Leslie tried to live his life rationally, keeping chaos at bay by imposing his own "infallible" sense of order at the expense of others. Reason and realism became the sole arbiters of what was true or tolerable in life; whatever was imaginative, chaotic, or emotional was illusory, untrustworthy, or undignified.[40] Leslie's arguments with Anne Thackeray Ritchie, Minny's sister and a successful novelist, were notoriously combative. Although he admired Anne for inheriting William Thackeray's "genius" and thought her "quick sympathies and her bright perceptions made her one of the most delightful persons in all social intercourse," he heatedly condemned her "unmethodical" mind, her disrespect for "facts and figures," the lack of "proportion and neatness" in her novels, her tolerance for a "chaotic jumble" of notes while writing novels, her habit of "jumping from one topic to another" in conversation, and the "intricate and apparently absurd processes" by which she solved problems.[41]

Anne defended her mercurial temperament and her expansive thoughts by attributing them to extreme sensitivity:

> I care for too many things ever to do one perfectly. At one moment I'm mad to be an artist, the next I languish for an author's fame, the third, I would be mistress of German, and the fourth practise five hours a day at the pianoforte. . . . [T]hings seem to pierce through and through my brain somehow, to get inside my head and remain there jangling.[42]

She was exquisitely responsive to life's little joys, as she shows in this 1891 letter to her husband, written while traveling:

> O what kind ladies!
> O what a delicious dinner!
> O what a nice room!
> O how extraordinarily rejuvenated and cheered I feel!
> . . . The best of everything is not too good for one. The sun is
> shining, the air is delicious! I like the climate of Manchester!!![43]

Leslie was hypersensitive too, but for him, being "thinned-skinned" opened the floodgates to anxiety and chaos; he could never tolerate the cacophony Anne loved. Whereas Leslie was haunted by depressive worries of penury and reproved any unnecessary expenditures, Anne spent money rashly, forgot to pay her bills, and roared with laughter at his objections.

Anne's reported behavior—her vivacious outbursts of good humor, her "extraordinary capacity" for cheerfulness, the many plans for "a clutch of novels," the "floods" of words in conversations, her "resilient optimism," "ebullience," and "recklessly extravagant" spending sprees— suggest hypomania, especially considering that both her mother and her niece were institutionalized.[44] We must take this conclusion with caution, however: manics do repeatedly and floridly talk around the point, as Anne did, digressing rather than logically developing an argument, and spending money recklessly is another, and rather notorious, symptom of mania, but two symptoms are slim evidence for a firm diagnosis. Anne did experience "immense bursts of energy, followed by nervous exhaustion," but she never became psychotic or dysfunctional.[45] This is a borderline case. She may simply have had "an uncommonly buoyant, optimistic temperament" that stood out in stark contrast to the brooding Stephen family, or she may indeed have inherited from Isabella a predisposition for mild mania exacerbated by her "thyroid trouble," for which she underwent an operation in 1898.[46] Disorders in thyroid function are frequently accompanied by changes in mood, especially in genetically vulnerable patients, including those who would never have developed a mood disorder had they not experienced some extraordinary biochemical stress.[47] But unless more corroborating evidence is uncovered, Anne can be labeled only as "possibly" manic.

No matter what the cause, Anne's exuberance left a permanent and positive impression upon people, as Virginia boasted:

> The most ingrained Philistine could not remain bored, though bewildered she might be, by Miss Thackeray's charm. For it was a charm extremely difficult to analyse. She said things that no human being could possibly mean; yet she meant them. She lost trains, mixed names, confused

numbers, driving up to Town, for example, precisely a week before she was expected, and making Charles Darwin laugh—"I can't for the life of me help laughing," he apologised. (*"The Moment"* 195)

Woolf's account of her aunt's vivacity and creativity focuses on mild mania's characteristic features of energy and playful synthesis:

> [Anne's] most typical, and, indeed, inimitable sentences rope together a handful of swiftly gathered opposites. To embrace oddities and pro-duce a charming, laughing harmony from incongruities was her genius in life and letters. (*"The Moment"* 195)

Like the hypomanic Woolf, Ritchie evolved an approach to writing that grew "through the intensity of her absorption in particular moments and scenes which set her memory alight and her imagination afire."[48]

It was precisely this expansiveness, which Woolf celebrated in her portrait of Mrs. Hilbery in *Night and Day*, that irritated Leslie, for he could not tolerate divergent thinking. He readily admitted his intellectual despotism:

> I had a perhaps rather pedantic mania for correcting her flights of imagination and checking her exuberant impulses. A. and M. used to call me the cold bath from my habit of drenching Anny's little schemes and fancies with chilling criticism. . . .
>
> (I observe parenthetically that Mrs. Jackson [Julia's mother] said afterwards that my behavior to Anny always puzzled people: but that after living in the house with us, she sympathized with me, for Anny was always the aggressor and could not keep silence. Upon Julia reporting this, I confess that Anny's aggressions were not very irritating, and that she was like a person forced to live in a den with a fretful beast and persisting in stroking it the wrong way.)[49]

Disregarding Leslie's imploded sense of reality, Anne replaced reality with the constructions of her expansive imagination. The imposition additionally infuriated Leslie, because he wanted women to be maternal figures who represented solidity and security and embraced life as it was, empirically and unquestioningly. Anne, in contrast, was a competitor who refused to submit to his interpretations of what constituted "meaning." Her "exuberant" and "flighty" imagination could disdain his cold rationalism because both imagination and rationalism are, in fact, mere mental constructs—not the truth about life but only artificial orders designed to impose sense upon life according to mood.

Woolf also felt this conceptual competition with her father keenly:

> Father's birthday. He would have been 1928
> $$\underline{1832}$$
> $$96$$
> 96, yes, today; & could have been 96, like other people one has
> known; but mercifully was not. His life would have entirely ended
> mine. What would have happened? No writing, no books;—
> inconceivable. (*Diary* 3: 208)

Indeed, she could not have competed with Leslie, for his fictions could tolerate no one else's, and least of all a woman's. It was "inconceivable" because conceptions were solely his province, and they could be nonthreatening only if they were fixed, rational, and convergent—everything a manic finds impossible to maintain. Quentin Bell sees a similar trend throughout the Stephen family line:

> They were all writers. . . . But they wrote like men who are used to
> presenting an argument, who want to make that argument plain but
> forcible; seeing in literature a means rather than an end.
> Their minds are formed to receive facts and when once they have a
> fact so clearly stated that they can take it in their hands, turn it this
> way and that, and scrutinize it, they are content; with facts, facts of
> this kind, they can make useful constructions, political, judicial or
> theological. But for intuitions, for the melody of a song, the mood of
> a picture, they have little use.[50]

Woolf's explorations of divergent cognitive styles that defy formulation and habitual belief would also have been greeted with Leslie's chilling baths of logic. Anne laughed them off, but Virginia was bipolar; her father's criticism would have found a potent ally in her periodic depressions, as Woolf's own description of a garden party in 1899, "a terrible oppressive gathering of Stephens," suggests:

> The others are all Stephens. . . . They all bring with them the atmos-
> phere of the lecture room; they are severe, caustic & absolutely
> independent and immoveable [*sic*]. An ordinary character would be
> ground to a pulp after a weeks intercourse with them. . . . They
> acknowledge that it is drizzling & grey, that their guests are depressed
> & think the whole party a bore; they can bear the knowledge of these
> facts & support the discovery without turning a hair. (*Passionate
> Apprentice* 146, 149)

In contrast, Julia's family line, the Pattles, "had no aptitude for words" and were chiefly remembered for their personalities and beautiful features, which Julia had passed on to Virginia. Bell writes that Woolf was quite conscious of having inherited two opposed traditions, one dominant, rational, and critical, the other recessive, intuitive, and beautiful. As the product of two such family traditions, and as a manic-depressive, she found it helpful to integrate the subject-object patterns passed on to her: Anne's creative, "absurd processes," Leslie's "proportion and neatness," Julia's obscure depths.

Thus, Virginia was born into a morass of despair and dependency, idealized unions and disillusioning separations, control and contraction, dominance and surrender, divergent and convergent thinking—all of which had direct consequences for her life and her writing. Leslie's needs and Herbert's memory demanded too much attention from Julia for her to be able to attend to her children. Ironically, in a family devoted to the illusion of perfect mothering, Virginia was weaned after only ten weeks,[51] and her memories of Julia show little intimacy:

> What a jumble of things I can remember, if I let my mind run, about my mother; but they are all of her in company; of her surrounded; of her generalised; dispersed, omnipresent, of her as the creator of that crowded merry world which spun so gaily in the centre of my child-hood. . . . Can I remember ever being alone with her for more than a few minutes? (*Moments of Being* 84, 83)

This figure of the mother, elusive, magical, central, yet one whose truest happiness belongs to a long-dead husband, positions Virginia herself as an outsider, in orbit around Julia but never touching, never realizing the promise of good mothering.

For any infant, parental care is extremely important. As Nancy Chodorow has argued, the mother first serves as an "external ego," mediating the infant's total environment until the child can develop an effective and identifiable ego of its own. But the effect of mothering continues long after weaning:

> The quality of care also conditions the growth of the self and the infant's basic emotional self-image (sense of goodness or badness, allrightness or wrongness). The absence of overwhelming anxiety and the presence of continuity—of holding, feeding, and a relatively consistent pattern of inter-action—enable the infant to develop what Benedek calls "confidence"

and Erik Erikson "basic trust," constituting, reflexively, a core beginning of self or identity.[52]

Fred Pine adds that developing an identity also has a cognitive component.
At first the infant is nonself-conscious; it does not experience itself in the act
of perception. Early events occur "long before the sense of ownership can
be identified as such by the infant. These experiences are passive in the sense
that they are not something that the infant *shapes,* but rather something
that *happens* (or not) to the infant." Even feelings may appear to come
from outside the self. Self-consciousness crystallizes when the child develops
the capacity to "own" experiences, to feel the self as the experiencing and
integrating center of his or her world, when the infant is no longer a
"passive container" of sensations and emotions. By locating experience
phenomenologically in the self, the child learns to master events, principally through mirroring (e.g., setting up a circular reaction with the
mother in which the infant actively produces repeated behavior the mother
rewards) and playful rehearsals or repetitions (in play the self initiates all
the action, including that action supposedly initiated by external objects).
In this way, the child discovers continuity and familiarity in experiences
of both external and internal events; identity is then felt to be "owned,
self-directed, and self-consistent." Self-consistency can develop inappropriately. Such faulty development displays itself as overinclusiveness of self-
experience, a manic omnipotence and grandiosity with irrational feelings
of power, responsibility, or guilt about events beyond the domain of the
actual self-as-actor—the same symptoms found in adult manic-depressive
illness. In this sense, the adult disorder, even though it is a different disorder
with a different etiology, recapitulates early issues of identity and perception everyone faces.[53]

We cannot guess how much anxiety the infant Virginia experienced
during her early weaning. Unlike Betty Kushen, I am unwilling to speculate
until we have corroborating evidence that "without consciously intending it, Julia or her nurse successor, probably held the infant Virginia at
a distance or handled her roughly."[54] Basing her assertion on the fact that
during her breakdowns the adult Woolf refused to eat, Kushen argues for
a neurotic cause-and-effect relationship: that the infant's oral fixation can
cause madness later on. Since she has no firm evidence about Woolf's
weaning, Kushen works backward by using adult psychosis as proof that
something bad must have happened years before. This is tantamount
to using Freudian theory itself as proof, turning it into a self-fulfilling

prophecy. Moreover, mood disorders can cause anorexia whatever the patient's nursing history, and oral symbolism in manic-depressive symptoms does not reliably or literally refer to early feeding patterns, but, more likely, to the emptiness, emotional hunger, and sense of abandonment a depressed mood produces.

It would be more useful to see how the crucial issue of self-image, originating in the mother-child relationship, can help us, as it helped Woolf, to understand the wild fluctuations of mood in manic-depressive illness that, in effect, recapitulate the initial, universal loss of security and goodness during weaning (whether good or bad, in Woolf's childhood or anybody else's). To Woolf, this "first severance," the loss of the sustained sense of continuity that the nursing Julia brought to the infant Virginia's self, seemed to recur whenever mania gave way to depression; it was a disconnection that Julia's death and Virginia's madness made a lifelong curse. Had she lived longer, could Julia have counseled her daughter in the finer points of depression and despair and made less horrifying Virginia's own periodic contraction of spirit? Did Woolf see her mother as a kindred spirit who could have empathized with her daughter's need to feel "real emotions" that others, including her doctors, dismissed as perverse or irrelevant? I think the answer is yes. A consideration of Woolf's novels (in Chapters 7 through 11, below) will show us how mother and daughter did connect in fiction, what this meant to Woolf, and how she created for herself the confidence with which to build an identifiable core of self.

Quentin Bell remembers Woolf said of her mother, "Her death was the greatest disaster that could happen" (*Moments of Being* 40). What did Julia's death "mean" to Virginia? To begin with, she was not allowed to mourn her mother; only Leslie could indulge in grief openly. Virginia followed her mother's tradition of feeling guilty about grief, with the rationale that to mourn was "vain, selfish, and egotistical," because it focused attention on her feelings rather than the feelings of others, whom a dutiful daughter should want to console.[55] Owning feelings openly was a double-edged sword: Victorian propriety demanded demonstrations of false concern, and manic-depressive mood swings demonstrably undercut authentic emotions. Moreover, while Virginia felt compelled to control herself (and was deeply ashamed of losing control in mania or depression), Leslie indulged in an extravagant mourning, melodramatically exclaiming to his family at the breakfast table that he wished he were dead, and receiving in his study the visitations of countless friends for communal weeping (*Moments of Being* 40–41). From his daughters he demanded the sympathy he had wrung out of their mother, behaving as if female selves were inexhaustible stores of supportive and positive feelings, a supposition the depressive Virginia knew from painful experience was false.[56] After Leslie's death, Virginia worried that she had not given her father the comfort he needed, though she knew his appetite for it was unquenchable (*Letters* 1: 130). Julia's death and Leslie's dependence drove home Virginia's fear that she did not possess all the emotional reserves she would need to be the good daughter, the good wife, the "good enough" mother. Julia could no longer stand as proof that a woman's self was always strong enough to survive.

Leslie's grief was not limited to real life but entered the sphere of fiction as well. His memoir, *Sir Leslie Stephen's Mausoleum Book,* begun two weeks after Julia's death, distorted the past with his sentimentalism. Virginia soon felt unable to remember her mother accurately; her father now exerted ultimate control over Julia's self by replacing it with the "unlovable phantom" of an idealized mother. The revision has been interpreted as an "elaborate defensiveness" to disprove the unspoken accusation that he had worn Julia to death,[57] but it was also an act of the imagination asserting itself against a keenly felt despair, generating illusion to fill the emptiness of depression. Virginia, finding no comfort in Leslie's depiction of Julia as an angel of the house, summoned up her own image of her mother. Both father and daughter took comfort in fiction, as if their creations could mother them, could mirror back a supportive, nurturing image, not of Julia, but of themselves. A revised past conferred not only a sense of ownership over Julia but a renewed sense of the owner, the "I" who remembers and recasts. Memory, as a self-created, inner experience, helped to correlate identity with experience. Leslie apparently never questioned the authenticity of his narcissistic portrait; he was content with his illusions, having subordinated memory to desire. But Woolf, as we shall see in later chapters, continually reexamined the maternal characters in her novels, the portrait changing as Woolf's self-confidence and self-knowledge grew, until at last, in *The Waves,* she was able to represent her inner world in all its multiplicity without summoning up her mother's image at all. Identity must rely not only on corroborating memories but on the ability to wean the self from an excessive reliance on others to mediate experience or make interpretations for us—in short, to give us ourselves.

For the young Virginia, convinced of her inadequacy by her first breakdown and, through Leslie's operatic monopoly on grief, cheated of legitimately expressing her feelings, Julia's death occasioned another threat.

When Leslie capitulated to helplessness, Virginia discovered her own real vulnerability as a female. Once dead, her mother could not act as a restraining influence on George and Gerald Duckworth, whose sexual advances and authoritarianism filled Virginia with anger and disgust. She had no defense against them. Family members and friends considered them to be model brothers, taking over Leslie's authority after the father retired from family life to his upstairs study to become a full-time mourner. Not even Dr. Savage objected strenuously when told of Woolf's victimization.[58]

This early tendency to adopt a silent, passive position (modeled by her mother, enforced by her half-brothers) and to think of herself as having inherited her father's neurasthenia was further reinforced by her rest cures. The Weir Mitchell treatment of intensive mothering (extended bed rest in a darkened room and a diet of milk, cream, and eggs) undermined her independence and induced a very real sense of helplessness in exchange for a quicker remission of symptoms. Shortening illness would have been enough reason for her to endure it, but there were cognitive rewards as well. Re-creating the mothering she had lost and acting out Leslie's role of a helpless infant may have seemed a satisfying therapy if only for its symbolic value, for it tied a seemingly incoherent illness to familiar (and familial) sources, especially to Julia's nursing and her wish to sink completely instead of remaining afloat, rigid, defensive, numb. Weighed against the terrors of bad thoughts and hellish visions, the rest-cure connection—to parents, to family history, to old, established, psychological patterns—may have been reassuring, even if somewhat demoralizing. When "mad" and out of control, Woolf could not create comforting fictions, but she at least had the assurance that one had been prepared for her. As Jane Marcus has aptly remarked: "For Virginia Woolf the art of being ill was essentially the art of letting go."[59] It was an art her mother had wished she had.

In the following chapters I argue that Woolf's own explanations of her manic-depressive symptoms incorporated and symbolized the patterns of unsatisfactory intellective control, self-reproach, manic projections, and dependency rife in her family. Her early, abrupt weaning and the lack of intimacy with her mother, as well as her frightening violations by George and Gerald, brought home to her her crucial need to develop an independent, confident, adaptive self that could tolerate life's disappointments and the body's mood shifts without resorting either to Leslie's defensive control, to Julia's selfless surrender, or to Anny's flights. Fiction became a source of nurture because it could mirror back to her a creative self that was not contracted, numb, infantile, or self-deluding.

6 "How immense must be the force of life"
The Art of Autobiography and Woolf's Bipolar Theory of Being

Although it might seem unlikely that fiction devoted to expressing the experience of a specific illness in terms of a particular family's psychology could appeal to many diverse readers, in fact Woolf's mood swings and her interpretive struggles, while extreme, are shared by all of us to some degree. For any infant, development of an identifiable self hinges on learning to discriminate between subjectivity and objectivity. The first lesson comes when the child loses the initial, blissfully "manic" fusion with its mother and establishes transactions with her as a separate object.

Melanie Klein first presented her pioneering research in childhood object-relations in England, in a lecture in July, 1925, at the home of Woolf's brother and sister-in-law, Adrian and Karin Stephen.[1] That work provides us with two useful constructs for understanding the early relationship between self and object during perception. Essentially, Klein argues that *all* children go through a transitory manic-depressive state, which she considers a defense, through the use of manic omnipotence and control over others, against early infantile loss. Normal children work through this "natural affective overreaction" by completing the separation-individuation process; pre-manic-depressive children, in contrast, continue to experience alternating moods, and even major disruptive storms, that will later develop into full-blown psychotic shifts.[2] Thus, the experiential difference between manic-depressive and normal development in childhood is largely a matter of degree, not kind.

Klein focused her research on how the first two years of an infant's life create a pattern of object-relations that extends into adulthood. Initially, the baby is cognitively narcissistic: experience of self is the same as experience of everything else in the world. When an infant comes to recognize the mother as a separate, independent, yet absolutely necessary object, he also discovers his utter dependence on her and his own helplessness. As an isolated entity, the child is doomed to emptiness unless filled by someone else. Successful weaning gives the baby confidence to believe that separateness need not be traumatic while allowing him to realize that, since subject and object are intrinsically distinct, his inevitably ambivalent feelings about his mother had no hand in creating the separation and did not destroy his source of perfect nurture.[3] In other words, it was not some "original sin" that banished the infant from bliss. The lesson to be learned here by the child is that feelings, wishes, and fantasies are contained *within* the infant and that they can sometimes be quite unrelated to external circumstances. The subjective self can now be seen as one world, while objective reality is another world, seemingly unrelated and sometimes hostile, although transactions between the two can occasionally bring about a satisfactory sense of unity. This reassuring understanding averts the intense separation anxiety that can cause infants to form unconscious fantasies that they have virtually devoured their mother and will be endlessly hungry, empty, and depressed from now on.

Significantly, psychoanalyst Otto Fenichel has observed that the unconscious—and conscious—ideas of depressed patients are "filled with fantasies of persons or parts of persons they may have eaten." Early psychoanalysts mistakenly theorized upon such evidence that manic-depressive illness was caused by narcissistic trauma during the oral stage of infancy.[4] But Klein believes that we all form such fantasies when, as infants, we struggle with the problems of dependence and nurturing, the "manic" desire for perfect satisfaction, the "depressive" fear of endless hunger, the primacy of subjectivity, and the insignificance of the subject. Perhaps, then, endogenously depressed patients, feeling empty and doomed, symbolize their inner state by recapitulating this early, similar experience we all share. Oral images may be spontaneous metaphors by which certain elements of a manic-depressive's experience may be expressed. The manic who declares himself to be God because he feels godlike is not necessarily and neurotically regressing back to the infantile stage of omnipotent bliss. Rather, the similarities between the two mood states are exploited by a brain whose disturbed perceptual apparatus reads external and internal stimuli, past and present events, reality and belief as one and the same. Neurologically, making connections is a fundamental way of knowing.

If weaning is not successful, Klein argues, the infant may fear he has damaged the mother on whom he is totally dependent, especially if, disappointed and fatigued, she withdraws her attentions and imposes separation awkwardly or ruthlessly. The baby's internal world fragments as well, destroyed by his ambivalent feelings about her and about himself. When that ambivalence is not recognized as an inner state but is perceived as an outer fact, subject-object distinctions become confused, leading to self-destructive and self-deceptive misinterpretations. Feelings of helplessness and anger are transmuted into a sense of an empty and hostile universe, and the depressed infant mourns the loss not only of his former happiness but of his self.[5] Outer lack equals inner. This can have long-term repercussions:

> The infant comes to define itself as a person through its relationship to [mother], by internalizing the most important aspects of their relationship. Its stance toward itself and the world—its emotions, its quality of self-love (narcissism), or self-hate (depression)—all derive in the first instance from this earliest relationship.[6]

Any symbolic attempt, in art or in play, to restore the lost object increases trust in self-love and self-confidence; the self becomes good again because it demonstrates its power to create a valued object. But reparation, Klein warns, is a slow process, and the infant knows only its urgent need. Manic defenses (which should not be confused with mania) are faster and, by denying dependency and helplessness, can protect the ego from despair. "Manic control," the infant's omnipotent wishes, orders the world and makes it dependable. The child determines to extort care from the mother through manipulative behavior. Self dominates object, transforming it according to self's wish and need. However, if any satisfaction is gained, it is illusory, as insubstantial as Mr. Ramsay's alphabetical conquest of facts in *To the Lighthouse,* as harmful as Leslie's cold baths of logic splashed on Anny's exuberant imagination.[7] The mother who must be coerced by threat of tantrum or tears is a mirror of the truly worthless self. As long as Leslie had to coax affection from Julia (or impose order upon chaotic experience), he could not increase his self-esteem.

Klein's model of infant development illuminates a critical personal and aesthetic issue for Woolf that lies at the heart of a series of central memories in her autobiographical work "A Sketch of the Past." Klein, like her mentor Freud, tends to view the creative act as an illusion, a substitute gratification rather than a way of knowing the world and establishing a nurturing transaction with it. But her formulation of the manic and depressive modes as reactive and originating in infancy does articulate what Woolf learned from the subjective experience of her manic-depressive breakdowns, which were endogenous and limited to adulthood. It also explains why sometimes in Woolf's fiction a moment of creative perception results in conflict rather than resolution. Two incompatible entities, self and object, and the mechanisms accompanying transactions between the two interpretative postures of manic projection and depressive objectification must be integrated, or insight will fail. Creativity challenges the self to risk its autonomy in the hope of strengthening itself by binding its inner world of meaning to the outer world of objects. Art allowed Woolf to explore her illness by returning her to those initial crossroads where she was obliged to handle reality both as a thing in itself and as an artifact of imagination—a skill her illness periodically revoked but her writing and our reading reinstate. Although reading her novels cannot induce the illness in us, it can recapitulate that early and formative event we share with Woolf if we allow ourselves to experience a problematic reading, achieving a fluid balance between perceiving the literal meaning of words and fabricating a subjective meaning unique to ourselves but not foreign to the text. Fiction is as much a test of our powers as of the author's, and in her most difficult novels Woolf deliberately taxes our interpretive skills to help us become more conscious of how we read.

· · · · ·

"A Sketch of the Past" is an obscure, digressive, and fragmentary autobiography written to provide relief from the author's "drudgery of making a coherent life" of Roger Fry's biography (*Moments of Being* 85). Stressing its casual nature, Woolf introduces her sketch with a curious apology:

> There are several difficulties. In the first place, the enormous number
> of things I can remember; in the second, the number of different ways
> in which memoirs can be written. As a great memoir reader, I know
> many different ways. But if I begin to go through them and to analyse
> them and their merits and faults, the mornings—I cannot take more
> than two or three at most—will be gone. So without stopping to
> choose my way, in the sure and certain knowledge that it will find
> itself—or if not it will not matter—I begin: the first memory. (64)

This passage is odd because, while Woolf claims not to shape a pattern for her narrative, she assures us that a pattern will emerge—"or if not it will not matter"—thus implying that what she wants to communicate cannot wholly reside in the text itself. Our apprehension of a structure that connects a seemingly disjointed sequence of events depends on our ability to supply meaning, or on the text's ability to invite it, or on Woolf's desire not to destroy it by imposing her own analysis—or on all three. We are never sure what to think about our role in reading this text. We have not been invited to apply convergent thinking on objective, biographical facts, but to read scenes that arrange themselves and so become "representative, enduring," emblematic of something other than an historical fact. Such "informality" has been shown to be the product of careful art, not inattention; by foregrounding the technique of working through the past by scene-making, *Woolf focuses upon herself as the one who experiences,* which is what identity formation is all about.[8] I shall now extend that insight by showing how the experiences themselves are emblematic of bipolar mood components.

In the first ten pages of her sketch, Woolf gives us seven childhood memories to illustrate her discovery of "being": a momentary, profoundly truthful interpretation of a perception that validates the unity of the perceiver without explicitly tying any of the memories together, resisting the pamphleteering Stephen family tradition of marshaling evidence to argue a point. Instead, she asks her readers to experience her memories as unordered, incoherent, suggestive but not definitive, while we remain aware that we are simultaneously engaged in the problematical activity of reading, in which meaning is traditionally equated with order. Both the content and the form of Woolf's autobiography focus our attention on the difficulties of interpretation, as if the real source of biographical knowledge about Woolf lay as much in how we handle meaninglessness as in what we do with meaning. Her deliberate reticence and the text's ambiguity test our tolerance for a "failed" reading. If we are to know *her* and not just the facts about her, the rainbow as well as the granite, we must be careful neither to impose order arbitrarily on what we read nor to sink into an unshaped collection of data. We must let the memoir "find itself"—but that too involves our unspecified help.

Obviously, such a method defies conventional Freudian strategies for reading autobiography. Previous authors of psychoanalytic studies of "A Sketch of the Past" have seen only evasion or disguise in the text's ambiguities and lapses in continuity, and a brief consideration of how they arrived at their readings will illuminate the bipolar structure of Woolf's memoir. Virginia Hyman, for instance, sees the difficulty of interpreting "the vast quantity of disparate and sometimes contradictory information," warning readers that any memory may be reworked and that the narrative may have more validity than the experience it is supposed to render:

> If any recollection is in itself a distortion, and if a recollection of a recollection is further removed from the original experience, how can we arrive at the truth about the original experience? The obvious answer is that we cannot.[9]

Good so far, but will Hyman relinquish her need for a convergent truth? She continues:

The best we can do is to construct what Roy Schafer (1980) calls a "second reality" which is more coherent and inclusive than the narrative itself. . . . To construct this second reality, we must juxtapose what we know of the writer's present circumstances against the story that he is telling us.[10]

The word *against* implies that we must discount Woolf's text as untrustworthy and prevaricating whenever it and Freudian theory conflict. Since there are many points of conflict, Hyman finds Woolf to be a frightened woman whose adult world is collapsing and who flees to the past to escape her present difficulties. This regression is presumed to be neurotic and distortive, and so Hyman reasons:

If we accept the fact that the scenes Woolf describes are defenses against the experiences, and at least as much created as perceived, we must alter our interpretation of them as direct and valid recollections of the original events. . . . [W]e can construct a second reality that is more coherent and inclusive than the first.[11]

Again, the word *against* characterizes Hyman's attitude toward autobiography: not only should we array our knowledge against Woolf's, but Woolf herself is depicted as opposing her own past in order to create comforting illusions about what really happened. Freudian theory, like the infant's manic control, reorders evidence to avoid cognitive dissonance.

Hyman's original insight is good; as an autobiography, "A Sketch of the Past" is fragmented, ambiguous, a recollection of recollections, and it may therefore not be valid as objective history. But her need for a more coherent and inclusive reality than Woolf is willing to give us leads her to replace Woolf's story with, in effect, an "unlovable phantom," just as Leslie replaced Julia in his memoir with a wife more suitable to his personal needs and his culture's values. Leslie certainly seemed defensive in his revisions, and in his version of his life history he carefully covered over gaps and contradictions.[12] Woolf, in contrast, *foregrounds* the fragmentedness of her recollections, as if to draw our attention to what cannot be told systematically. But Hyman cannot accept lapses in narrative as anything but defensive omissions; like the badly weaned infant, she denies the experience of lack by forcibly manipulating the text and extorting a more comforting order than the one Woolf thinks best expresses her multiplicitous life. That order comes in the form of a theory: because Woolf "treats herself as a perceiver acted upon by external forces" instead of imitating autobiographers who record triumphs, Hyman concludes that Woolf is so pathologically passive she cannot face her feelings honestly.[13] The "external forces" become mere neurotic projections of repressed emotion.

My interpretation will offer no narrowly convergent "truth" of Woolf's early life that she could not have known. Like the nursing mother weaning her dependent infant, Woolf withholds ready satisfaction for our own good—and for hers. We must learn to accept her as she is, and accept the fact that her memories may have been reworked because memory is not reliably objective in anyone. The brain refines and abstracts all it perceives; no memory is epistemologically privileged. Moreover, Woolf's is an autobiography that explicitly introduces itself as a problematic history: in the first paragraph Woolf refuses to analyze content (which memories she will select) or form (why her memoir is written just this way). Seemingly haphazard, this sketch can have only one purpose: to express Woolf's own sense of her identity, that which somehow orders the material. Thus the fragments tell a more profound truth than either unadorned fact could express or defensive ego could impose. To see this subjective-objective view, this emblematic history of being, we must let her instruct us.

Beginning with her earliest memory, a purely visual impression of her mother's dress—red and purple flowers on a black background—as seen from her mother's lap, Woolf digresses into another memory of lying in a nursery at St. Ives, hearing the rhythm of the ocean waves, and feeling "it is almost impossible that I should be here . . . feeling the purest ecstasy I can conceive . . . of lying in a grape and seeing through a film of semi-transparent yellow" (65). The womblike security of these images of fruitfulness (the flowers on Julia's breasts, the grape, the ever-present, comforting, rocking rhythm of the waves) is belied by the ominous statement that Virginia finds it hard to believe she is really there. The ecstasy is real, but she herself is not: "I am hardly aware of myself, but only of the sensation. I am only the container of the feeling of ecstasy, of the feeling of rapture" (67). The experience is so pleasant, she confesses, that she sometimes wishes she could return to the pure ecstasy she associates with infancy, without shame or repercussions. She is careful here to tell us, though, by a series of qualifiers, that she knows such recapitulation can never be real:

> At times I can go back to St Ives more completely than I can this morning. I can reach a state where I *seem* to be watching things happen *as if* I were there. That is, I suppose, that my memory supplies what I had forgotten, so that it *seems as if* it were happening independently, though I am really making it happen. (67; my italics)

The adult Woolf knows that self is more real than mood. But in the grip of mania (or in the state of infancy), ecstasy seems to have an existence independent of her willingness to conjure up images. Mania denies her ownership of her own experiences, but the sensation is so rewarding that she hopes science will someday invent a machine to trace such states and present them as pure experience, without the egotistical misbehaviors she knows accompany adult episodes:

> I shall fit a plug into the wall; and listen in to the past. I shall turn up August 1890. I feel that strong emotion must leave its trace; and it is only a question of discovering how we can get ourselves again attached to [the past], so that we shall be able to live our lives through from the start. (*Moments of Being* 67)

Clearly, the past is seductive for Woolf, a blessed time before the onset of an illness that proved the problematic and disturbing nature of the self, but it is also emblematic of the myth of pure happiness, of an idealized construction equal to Leslie's remembrances of Julia and to Julia's memory of Herbert. Woolf speculates that if she could only learn how to "fit a plug," and, conversely, to "pull the plug" (when mania gets out of control and becomes self-destructive), she might enjoy the assets of mania without becoming ill. Like an infant before weaning, the manic Woolf feels as if she has entirely subsumed nurturing goodness into herself and yet is still engulfed by it, buoyed and bathed as by a friendly wave. Nurture, in mania, is inexhaustible, and so omnipotence is a given. The yellow meat of the grape softens perception, privileges impression over fact, smudges subject-object boundaries, and erases separateness.

How should we view this idealized portrait? Freudians react with a peculiar mixture of scientific detachment and moral disapproval. Alma Bond concludes that mania is merely a defense mechanism:

> In order to escape unspeakable pain and grief at terrible crises of her life, Virginia Woolf experienced a tremendous pull back to her early paradise. She faced a double jeopardy: Regression meant loss of self, while growing up meant loss and despair. To avoid these twin disasters, Virginia "chose" the middle path of mania. . . . In my opinion, Virginia Woolf, as all manics, distorted one of nature's most beautiful and creative growth periods, that of the "love affair with the world," into a hideous travesty.[14]

Leaving aside Bond's hostile countertransference that manics choose to lose touch with reality, or that shifting into mania is a perverse and unnatural act, should we regard Virginia Woolf's memory as a defensive blind spot? Is it here because she habitually severs the connection between self and its emotions? The answer, Woolf tells us enigmatically, may lie in a second memory: at six or seven years old, she got into the habit of looking at her face in a hall mirror, a self-indulgence of which she felt deeply ashamed. Attributing her sense of shame not to any personal conflict but to an "instinct" inherited from the Stephen family line, she refers to a story about her self-denying, depressive grandfather, "Sir James, who once smoked a cigar, liked it, and so threw away his cigar and never smoked another" (*Moments of Being* 68). He, apparently, did not indulge himself, despising egotism, nor did he long for self-induced bliss; his control was absolute and rigid, exaggerating the separation between a unmergeable self and the object it controlled. A digression now follows, which includes a discussion of Woolf having inherited "puritanical" prohibitions (she too feels compelled to control herself and refrain from the egotism of self-indulgence), her admission of intense shame about femininity and dress (for most of her life, she, like Sir James, found it difficult to look at her image in a mirror), and then a confession that she could feel "ecstasies and raptures spontaneously and intensely and without any shame or the least sense of guilt, so long as they were disconnected with [her] own body" (68). Mania is enjoyable and guilt-free as long as it is not acted out as vanity, as long as it is childlike and given to her by someone or something else.

Focusing on the mirroring of her body serves as a personal metaphor for a self-indulgent mania, the punishment for which is depression. As we saw in chapter 2, John Custance noted that depression made him feel guilty about having enjoyed his egotistical manic states; he too felt "repulsion" for himself:

> [Depression] invades the personality in the form of intense disgust for oneself, horror of one's body, of seeing one's reflection in a mirror and so on. Clothes and personal property associated with oneself become objects of repulsion, whereas in the manic phase clothes and other property take on an extraordinarily attractive aspect; I have often felt them imbued with magical powers, filled with "mana" as it were. At the same time one takes a narcissistic delight in one's own body.[15]

Most manic-depressives experience acute shame and humiliation, particularly over self-indulgent actions performed during mania: monopolizing conversations, ignoring the feelings of others, or indulging in spending sprees, sexual transgressions, or violence. Mood swings are often viewed by patients as lows that naturally and inevitably counterbalance unreasonable highs.

For Woolf, depression came as a period of penance for "great egoism and absorption and vanity" (*Letters* 1: 470), typically as a morning headache and melancholy after too much socializing the night before:

> Variable as a barometer to phychical [*sic*] changes, my wits flutter & frizzle & I can get no work out of them. . . . I've been gadding . . . gadding too much for the health of my five wits. They soon jangle. (*Diary* 2: 258)

When her life revolved too intensely around her own personality—too much clever talk, too many parties, too much admiration—depression taught her to question the arrogance of personality:

> [W]hy is not human intercourse more definite, tangible. . . . Something illusory then enters into all that part of life. I am so important to myself: yet of no importance to other people: like the shadow passing over the downs. I deceive myself into thinking that I am important to other people: that makes part of my extreme vividness to myself: as a matter of fact, I dont matter; & so part of my vividness is unreal; gives me a sense of illusion. (*Diary* 3: 188)

Loving the euphoria but condemning the egotistical expansion of mania, the depressed Woolf tried to see herself in minimalist terms, not as an everlasting thing or a beautiful face in the mirror, but as a container waiting to be filled with something that really was valuable, real, and life-giving. For the evangelical Sir James, that source of blameless bounty was his God, whose blessing was a joy about which he did not need to feel ashamed. Woolf expected no such divine intervention. What, then, would fill up the inner emptiness left by her passing moods? "A Sketch of the Past" will tell us—but not just yet.

Two more memories—also unexplained and tied up with self, shame, and mirrors—follow in quick succession. In the first, about the time that Virginia began to admire herself in the hallway mirror, near that hallway eighteen-year-old Gerald Duckworth explored her private parts: "I remember resenting, disliking it—what is the word for so dumb and *mixed* a feeling?" (*Moments of Being* 69, my italics). In a letter on the same memory, she describes her feelings after this violation as "shame" (*Letters* 6: 460) and attributes her discomfort to "all sorts of subterranean instincts," stressing her allegiance to the ancestral moral code, inherited by all Stephens, that condemns egotistical self-indulgence—which, unfortunately, was another Stephen inheritance. Caught between inheritances, between manic indulgence and depressive control, she moves on to the second memory and relates a childhood dream, vaguely explaining its relevance ("for it may refer to the incident of the looking-glass") in which, while staring at herself in the hallway mirror, "a horrible face—the face of an animal—suddenly showed over [her] shoulder" and frightened her (69).

The dream seems rather straightforward, too easy in fact, and Woolf leaves unsaid the connection the reader is tempted to make: that the dream illustrates Woolf's sexual response to Gerald's abuse, that she was ashamed of the sexual feelings he supposedly stirred up in her, that the previous mirror encounter was therefore autoerotic. Thus, the animalistic face belongs to Gerald (who is acting "beastly") or perhaps even to Virginia (who desires his beastliness but, neurotically, cannot admit the fact). Jean Love argues successively for both views, concluding that Woolf's shame stems from having demeaned herself by enjoying the caresses of someone who repulsed her.[16]

Out of shame, of course, come frigidity and madness, and so the neurotic basis for manic-depressive illness seems to have an autobiographical corroboration. But biological research shows that frigidity does not cause manic-depressive illness; it is often a result of the disorder. And we must ask ourselves whether, like Freud who insisted that Dora must have been sexually attracted to Herr K. because she had felt his erection, we too are supplying feelings the subject does not have. Freud did not doubt the power of the phallus to inspire desire in a woman, and so he regarded Dora's denial of desire as resistance and her subsequent dreams as deceitful representations. If we treat the absences or gaps in Woolf's text as resistance, are we too not assuming that sex can drive a young woman insane? Woolf does connect Gerald and beast, but the Freudian reading leaves much unexplained, and especially the issues of mothering, mirroring, and mania which permeate this whole section. Moreover, the portrait of Woolf's "devastating frigidity" has been ably challenged by Blanche Wiesen Cook, who has analyzed Woolf's euthymic letters to Violet Dickinson and finds expressed there not a coldly dispassionate love but a warm, convivial lust. We should follow Vita Sackville-West's suggestion that what Woolf disliked about men was not their desire for sex but their "possessiveness and love of domination,"[17] and we should remember Woolf's critical evaluation of Ralph Partridge:

> Ralph comes twice a week or so, an indomitable, perhaps rather
> domineering, young man; loves dancing; in the pink of health; a healthy
> brain. He described a brothel the other night—how, after the event, he
> & the girl sat over the fire, discussing the coal strike. Girls paraded
> before him—that was what pleased him—the sense of power. (*Diary* 2: 75)

Gerald may have turned Woolf against the alliance of power and sex in men, but not against passion. Eros takes many forms, and a woman's desire for another woman is not, in itself, evidence of neurosis, let alone of frigidity. If Woolf had not been manic-depressive, her sexual preference would not be viewed as a convenient symptom of stunted development.

How, then, should we view this memory of a dream? Significant memories or dreams in our lives, the ones we remember as emblematic, need not be—indeed, usually are not—sexual in nature. As one critic reminds us: "If Freud teaches us anything, it is not that 'desire is primarily sex,' but that we never know what desire is, or what sex is."[18] The dream research of the past two decades suggests that the word *transformation* would better carry Freud's formulation of how dreamwork functions than would *distortion* or *censorship* of forbidden unconscious wishes. These "transformations may subsequently be understood by the waking psyche in ways that make them classifiable as disguises," but "they may also be understood by the waking psyche in ways that make them classifiable as revelations or expressions or inspirations or compensations or creative insights or what have you."[19] Dreams, fantasies, and even hallucinations are ways of thinking about ideas, the world, ourselves, but there is no reliable formula for deciding how the connections are being made.

Ironically, it is precisely with this problem of dream analysis that psychoanalytic thought has been most creative in recent years. Freud had devalued the manifest content of the dream:

> it is bound to be a matter of indifference to us whether it is well put together, or is broken up into a series of disconnected separate pictures. Even if it has an apparently sensible exterior, we know that this has only come about through dream-distortion and can have as little organic relation to the internal content of the dream as the façade of an Italian church has to its structure and plan.[20]

For Freud, the literary function of a dream's manifest narrative was tantamount to secondary revision: it was simply a deceptive cover for the true meaning. But Phillip McCaffrey asserts that the dream is structured in so many ways like art that if its full meaning is to be grasped it must be judged by aesthetic criteria as well as psychoanalytic ones. McCaffrey doubts the accuracy of Freud's version of Dora's dream. Freud attributed meaningful order exclusively to latent content, dismissing Dora's manifest dream as mere "jumbles of likely clues, disorganized assortments of pregnant hints" that were unimportant in themselves. But since the missing message of the dream is ultimately supplied by the therapist, who replaces gaps with theoretically congruent substance, the risk of minimizing or even distorting what the patient has made of the dream message, the artfully crafted dream itself, is high. For McCaffrey, the dream is not a screen designed to disguise but a stage on which to represent what the patient wants to say on both conscious and unconscious levels. He cites Freud's analysis of Dora's dream as paradigmatic: Freud concluded that Dora dreamt her father was dead because she wanted to exact revenge upon him for enjoying the pleasures from Frau K. that Dora unconsciously wanted from Herr K. Moreover, Freud decided that Dora terminated her analysis to gain revenge against him, for she desired him as well. But McCaffrey notes that both Dora's manifest dreams and her actions clearly represent another, not unconscious, motive. She left father and Freud behind because both had betrayed her by refusing to believe her version of what had happened with Herr K. The crucial issue for Dora was not sex but respect.[21]

In order not to betray Virginia Woolf ourselves, we must follow her lead through her associations and transferences, remembering that these appear in an aesthetic context with an informative legitimacy of its own. Her assertion that she was ashamed of the sexual aspect of Gerald's violation is only one element interwoven with other memories in a text that is self-conscious about the aesthetic and psychological issues of biography. Thus, this event has important object-relational meanings as well. Viewed as a transformation rather than a disguised evasion, Virginia's dream of the mirror scene can be seen aptly to dramatize the sensations of a mood shift into depression—an inexplicable transition very like a narrative gap. A magical, maternal world has filled the child in the grape with an unself-conscious bliss, but the child at the mirror wants to fill herself *by* herself and *with* herself, going against the dictates of inherited Stephen morality (exaggerated by depression's "puritanical" self-abnegation as embodied in Sir James). In her dream, therefore, she finds only horror, a reflection of an animal, a body without a self, a body that devours selves. Woolf's conclusions: some manias are bad because they are self-indulgent and solipsistic; what appears to be magically profound is, in reality, only self-delusion, an inflated image of the self; the beast is emblematic of the emptiness of depression lurking behind the illusion of fullness that mania (symbolized by cosmic mothering) miscreates out of nothing. Woolf is frightened when her deepest depressive fear—that she does not actually exist behind the face in the mirror—is made real by mood shifts, even pleasant ones.

Here mirroring seems more important than desire—not only Virginia's desire, but Gerald's too. In both scenes Virginia is being looked at. And just as she is ashamed to see the Virginia in the mirror gazing back at her, responding to her beauty with damning "pride and pleasure," so too Gerald is an equivocal mirror that responds, evaluating her as a desirable object. Behind this surface appreciation lurks a terrible emptiness: he treats her as an object, beauty without substance, a body without a self, and reinforces her worst fear (as a victimized woman and as a manic-depressive): that she is not really there. Like a mirror, he reflects nothing of her inner self, which seems to melt away into "dumbness"; numbed by emptiness, she cannot even summon up the words to name her emotions. She loses ownership of her emotions as she loses her identity; the silence that lures Freudians into filling up gaps also dramatizes eloquently her inner state of nonbeing. Depression destroys her sense of self and self-worth just as the animal head threatens to devour her. The scene is not primarily sexual (and modern attitudes toward incest and rape now more accurately reflect their nonsexual, violent character) but perceptual and deadly. For the rest of her life, the depressive Woolf, like the depressive Sir James, suffered unbearable anxiety when she saw someone looking at her, evaluating her, as if a look had the power to invalidate self because others could see her as she was, or, rather, as she was *not* ("Sketch" 68).

Mirroring is ambiguous because it is bipolar: it can create either fullness and ratification of being or emptiness and invalidation, the death of the soul. Woolf uses this metaphor to dramatize the manic-depressive's search for a therapeutic mirroring "Other" to correct interpretations and to establish identity. Real mirrors are inadequate, because they cannot establish a bipersonal field on which to illuminate the reciprocal nature of mood and projection. Their failure is evidenced in a memory:

> There was the moment of the puddle in the path; when for no reason I could discover, everything suddenly became unreal; I was suspended; I could not step across the puddle; I tried to touch something . . . the whole world became unreal. (78)

Compare the depth of Woolf's existential perception with Louise DeSalvo's simplistic Freudian interpretation:

> She cannot explain why she couldn't step across the puddle, but the act of opening her legs wide enough to stretch across a puddle of water was horrifying to her possibly because she would be able to see in the puddle a reflection of her legs, open wide, which she might have associated with her abuse.[22]

DeSalvo puts to poor use such a rich metaphor. Self and the universe it lives in are mirror images. Without a core, Woolf cannot find meaning in the outside world; reciprocally, a meaningless world proves there is no core in Virginia to make meaning. Body alone cannot ratify spirit, and when that body is female in a patriarchal culture that discounts a woman's value, physical mirroring of woman-as-body symbolizes a great loss. What could Woolf have seen in the mirror, in Gerald's eyes, in the depths of her depressions, but an object to be possessed and devoured, an image of nonbeing and worthlessness, a madwoman? Where could she find a reciprocal mirror that dependably ratified self, opened it up safely to insight, when manic-depressive mood shifts made and unmade perception and belief with dizzying unpredictability? She would find it in fiction, in the doubled bipolar field established by writer/text and reader/text, and, significantly, she would fulfill Christopher Bollas's criteria for good psychoanalysis:

> The psychoanalytic process is a unique therapeutic procedure because it enables the person to represent the transference to the self as object and to crystallize those features of being and relating which are counter-transferential expressions. . . . Frequently [the patient's] reproaches or enthusiasms will be followed by another response which is a reaction to his own narration—a reaction, that is, to the transference aspects of the relation to the self as object, and his responses will be in the nature of a countertransference.
>
> . . . When the patient lives through the discourse of the transference experience within the analytical setting, a discourse where the trans-ference addresses of the patient's object world and defensive makeup both impl[y] an other and evoke aspects of the self and other within the analyst's countertransference, the person gradually discovers the private language of the self. . . . [T]he patient gradually hears news of himself through the experience of the other.[23]

Woolf "heard the news" of Gerald's experience of her as "Other," as nothing but a glassy hole in the world into which she might at any moment fall.

But "A Sketch of the Past" is not merely a cautionary tale, and manic-depressive illness is not just a disability. It is also a gift. It can occasion "fun." The three memories that follow the first mirror scene are all used by Woolf to illustrate a "moment of being," the centerpiece of her ideas about fiction, her version of the circuit of transference between subject and object, which she feels will also "explain" her psychology and the previous memories. But clearly her idea of what an explanation should do is unconventional; she merely groups three memories together in an ambiguous way. In the first she and her brother, Thoby, are on the lawn, pummeling each other:

> Just as I raised my fist to hit him, I felt: why hurt another person? I dropped my hand instantly, and stood there, and let him beat me. I remember the feeling. It was a feeling of hopeless sadness. It was as if I became aware of something terrible; and of my own powerlessness. I slunk off alone, feeling horribly depressed. (*Moments of Being* 71)

In the third memory, having heard of a family friend's suicide, Woolf walks out to the garden by the apple tree and is paralyzed with terror:

> It seemed to me that the apple tree was connected with the horror of Mr. Valpy's suicide. I could not pass it. . . . I seemed to be dragged down, hopelessly, into some pit of absolute despair from which I could not escape. (71)

Years later, after Stella's death, when Stella's fiancé Jack Hills visited the grieving family, Virginia thought again of the tree as standing for her depression: "And the tree outside in the August summer half light was giving me, as he groaned, a symbol of his agony; of our sterile agony; was summing it all up" (*Moments of Being* 141). Like Woolf's symbol of the lighthouse, the apple tree "sums up," standing for all sorts of meanings. No metaphorical similarity is required, and so no Freudian analysis of the tree's phallic shape will help us understand Woolf's feelings.

What Woolf gives us is a bipolar sequence. The second memory, sandwiched between these depressive episodes, ends happily. Looking at a flower bed, she says out loud to herself, "That is the whole," and feels quite satisfied:

> [I]t seemed suddenly plain that the flower itself was a part of the earth; that a ring enclosed what was the flower; and that was the real flower; part earth; part flower. (71)

Such an aesthetic solution to grave psychological problems may at first strike us as a sidestep, an evasion or denial. But in terms of object-relations—which are, as we have seen, central to the manic-depressive's dilemma—it makes good sense. Working from the theories of Melanie Klein and D. W. Winnicott, Christopher Bollas argues that to assume that the world is there to be experienced and understood, that a meaning awaits us there, is the basis of sanity. Woolf's "moment of being" is equivalent to Bollas's "aesthetic moment," when "the subject feels held in symmetry and solitude by the spirit of the object," a wordless occasion, "notable for the density of the subject's feeling and the fundamentally non-representational knowledge of being embraced by the aesthetic object. . . . [S]elf and object feel reciprocally enhancing and mutually informative." To the perceiver, "uncanny moments" seem to be "partially sponsored by the object" itself, as if it were "the hand of fate" leading us to some unspecified involvement.[24] Woolf calls this uncanny sponsorship "a third voice":

> The lemon-coloured leaves on the elm tree; the apples in the orchard; the murmur and rustle of the leaves makes me pause here, and think how many other than human forces are always at work on us. While I write this the light glows; an apple becomes a vivid green; I respond all through me; but how? Then a little owl [chatters] under my window. Again, I respond. Figuratively I could snapshot what I mean by some image; I am a porous vessel afloat on sensation; a sensitive plate exposed to invisible rays. . . . I fumble with some vague idea about a third voice; I speak to Leonard; Leonard speaks to me; we both hear a third voice. Instead of labouring all the morning to analyse what I mean, to discover whether I mean anything real, whether I make up or tell the truth when I see myself taking the breath of these voices in my sails and tacking this way and that through daily life as I yield to them, I note only the existence of this influence; suspect it to be of great importance. (*Moments of Being* 133)

The resulting sense of transcendental fusion cannot be dissected or analyzed: it "is an experience of being rather than mind, rooted in the total involvement of the self rather than objectified via representational or abstract thought," the sort of thought typical of strictly ego-dominated actions. Such perceptions are aesthetically structured, like McCaffrey's model of the manifest dream, and tell their story in ways that are beyond the grasp of the analytical conscious mind. They are "outside cognitive coherence."[25] And, as Clarissa Dalloway will note after hearing of Septimus's death, such moments are "fun" (284).

Bollas explains the "uncanniness" of such moments of being as "a form of *déjà vu*," an experience of unthought but known familiarity, the feeling of having a deep and even sacred "rapport" between subject and object harkening back to the first time we wrestled with the problem of perceiving anything. That time was overseen by our mothers, who filled us when we were empty, touched us when we were lonely, and showed us that rapport was possible. Bollas considers all aesthetic experiences as transformational because, like the image of the mother for the infant who believes in her magic, "the transformational object seems to promise the beseeching subject an experience where self fragmentations will be integrated through a processing form." Because the mother is the teacher of the ecstasy of special moments, she seems sacred, formative, ideal—regardless of what cold hard facts we know about her objectively. Woolf's "obsession" with her mother (her repeated use of the mother figure in fictions dealing with just these issues of perception) is not in itself evidence of pathology. Nor is the "illusion" (such a pejorative word for such a reverential experience) of the sacred and magic moment/mother a defensive projection or evasion of ugly truths: it expresses, in the only terms possible or aesthetically satisfying, a preverbal, prerepresentational perception. Since we experience mother before we can "know" her (as a person, a being like ourselves, or a member of a category), she is called up as an emblem of experiences that also resist analysis, particularly linguistic analysis.[26] Is it any wonder that a manic-depressive, whose disorder can arbitrarily induce or destroy that sense of uncanny rapport in seemingly authentic perception, would explore her own multiple sense of being in repeated re-creations of mothering and mirroring?

"A Sketch of the Past" is, then, a metafiction, so self-reflexive that it lays before us all its parts in a heap. If it is forcibly organized, it yields up only paltry ideas about repressed guilt and thwarted desire that tell us nothing of why Woolf's work is so splendid, so compelling, and so much fun. This text is not a formulized schematic; it awaits a magical moment, a creative reading that is also *déjà vu*—unbidden, uncanny, yet deeply personal to each reader, regardless of what happened to him or her in childhood. Only when we can encompass the diversity of bipolar memories, moments of ecstasy and unity, moments of despair and fragmentation, without resorting to neat and tidy analysis, can we experience the autobiography of a manic-depressive.

Woolf does not analyze her aesthetic resolution of object-relations. She says only that the flower is more than a mere flower; it is an indefinable reconciliation of formerly fragmented parts, the world's objective flower and the imagination's subjective flower. Aesthetic wholeness mirrors back an image of the one who sees as ordered and coherent and thus increases the seer's self-confidence: "I was not powerless. I was conscious—if only at a distance—that I should in time explain it" (*Moments of Being* 72). By making the experience "whole" Woolf can feel whole herself, for it is partly by *her* power that the moment of understanding and the feeling of oneness with the world come about. Because she and the uncanny object jointly create the moment of authentic perception, experience "has lost its power to hurt [her]," to destroy her sense of self—as Gerald did—by treating her merely as an object, by mirroring back only fragments. This transaction produces a new sense of self-continuity and self-importance that is different from the illusion of manic egotism, for it is object-related, reality-related:

> So I came to think of life as something of extreme reality. And this of course increased my sense of my own importance. Not in relation to human beings: in relation to the force which had respected me sufficiently to make me feel [what was real]. (137)

In a "moment of being," life and Virginia Woolf co-create a space in which self and world can exist (71–72). They are mutually enhanced, made whole and good by what D. W. Winnicott calls "play," what Erik Erikson calls "interplay": a transaction that shapes identity and establishes modes of relationship with the environment by involving, paradoxically, the features of a mutual fusion and a gain in distinctiveness. Between purely subjective "primary creativity" and "objective perception based on reality testing," a transitional space is created where the self experiences "fusion with that which is beyond the self in order to achieve higher and higher degrees of self-definition."[27] Boundaries between self and object are both blurred and re-formed. In a like manner, manic and depressive modes of perception are reconciled when subject and object connect but are not completely subsumed in each other. It is only then, and not by looking directly into the mirror (which aggrandizes egotism or destroys ego, depending on mood), that the truth is captured. For Woolf, focusing on the object mirrors the subject because

> one can't write directly about the soul. Looked at, it vanishes: but look at the ceiling, at Grizzle, at the cheaper beasts in the Zoo which are exposed to walkers in Regents Park, & the soul slips in. (*Diary* 3: 62)

World and self must meet.

Significantly, what Woolf did in writing duplicated what psychoanalysts attempted, before lithium therapy, to do in their treatment of manic-depressives. Both Otto Fenichel and Edith Jacobson, for instance, reported that helping their patients establish good object-relations (by understanding the transferences that occur between patients and therapists which affect patients' ability to make interpretations) was crucial in order to begin analysis. Jacobson felt that the biggest hurdle lay in overcoming the "highly illusory, magic quality of [the manic-depressive's] transference feelings [and] his exaggerated idealization and obstinate denial of possible or visible shortcomings of the analyst."[28] When the patient's mood determined how the progress of analysis was perceived, he could not see that he was (or was not) improving, and the analyst felt helpless. Reconnecting the patient to the world by breaking through a misleading transference allowed true insight to begin, even if it could not prevent further mood swings.

Woolf valued the same breakthrough. It is true that the perfect, unwilled, automatic bliss of grapelike infancy is gone (the plug has been pulled permanently), but separateness can be overcome by an imaginative-perceptual reach which has the advantage of not reducing one to infantile dependence. There is a positive alternative to having one's mother back. Woolf seems to connect all these elements by concluding her childhood explorations of perception with her mother's death and the onset of her first breakdown:

> How immense must be the force of life which turns a baby, who can just distinguish a great blot of blue and purple on a black background, into the child who thirteen years later can feel all that I felt on May 5th 1895—now almost exactly to a day, forty-four years ago—when my mother died. (79)

The loss was severe and keenly felt, but her mother's death came at a time when Virginia more distinctly realized that what one could know about the world depended a great deal on how one felt about it and about oneself. Self-knowledge was strength:

> The tragedy of her death was not that it made one, now and then and very intensely, unhappy. It was that it made her unreal; and us solemn, and self-conscious. We were made to act parts that we did not feel; to fumble for words that we did not know. It obscured, it dulled. It made one hypocritical and immeshed in the conventions of sorrow. Many foolish and sentimental ideas came into being. Yet there was a struggle, for soon we revived, and there was a conflict between what we ought to be and what we were. (95)

Julia's death intensified Woolf's struggle to establish her own identity, a struggle complicated by mood swings, misinterpretations, and erratic behavior and thoughts. Woolf's preoccupation with her mother thus stood for more than a neurotic longing to escape into the past. Julia became an emblem for Woolf's search for self. Psychotherapy can likewise help patients rebuild a cohesive, reality-related, object-related self if the therapist can create a "maternal matrix" to mediate between self and world. Psychoanalysis is, after all, a highly interpersonal affair, and it is in this bipersonal field that a "mothering" analyst and the patient can recapitulate the separation-individuation process, repair faulty schemata by which perceptions have been organized and interpreted, and establish mutually satisfying interpersonal relations, all of which facilitates a renewed sense of core identity. In order to accomplish so much, the analyst must, like a good mother, help the patient explore interpretations without intruding on the patient's autonomy (by providing or imposing interpretations) or allowing herself to be intruded upon (allowing unchecked transferences to distort the patient's view of the therapist). Mutual autonomy allows the patient room to define his or her own identity and determine self-world boundaries.[29] Similarly, art allowed Woolf to replace her mother's mirroring with her own, to explore moods and make interpretations. The power to nurture was no longer limited to the mother's body. Through a "second severance" (*The Waves* 125), art weaned Woolf from dependence on an unobtainable source of life; it recapitulated the balance between individuation and fusion that the first weaning accomplished years before. By thinking in terms of mothering, mirroring, and weaning, Woolf could cope with a bipolar disorder that otherwise baffled even the specialists of her time.

This emphasis on the mutual autonomy of subject and object strikes some readers as too inactive. Indeed, "A Sketch of the Past" embodies the principle of autonomy as a whole in its refusal to specify anything essential about Woolf as subject. Like Virginia Hyman, Daniel Albright complains that Woolf's autobiographical impulse differs significantly from that of other confessional writers, such as D. H. Lawrence or James Joyce: whereas the male writers describe "a vigorous ego [that] fights to realize its proper self," Virginia Woolf "does not struggle toward selfhood; instead, a self is thrust upon her." Because Woolf seems to emphasize passivity throughout the text, Albright concludes that much of the formation of her personality began when she was sexually abused by her half-brothers, and subsequent catastrophes reinforced a lifelong pattern of victimization that culminated in her theory of the true artist's anonymous self: "[A]ccording to Virginia Woolf's doctrine the artist is most in touch with art when attenuated, abnegated, a colorless vehicle of revelation. Properly the artist should have no self, be nobody, for there is no expresser, only an expression."

For Albright, such impersonality does not guarantee good art: "[T]he whole edifice of fiction is threatened by collapse if its architecture has no one's personal guarantee behind it."[30] But a manic-depressive finds the need for a guarantee highly suspect, for the aggressive ego can aggrandize its power by imposing its constructs on art. Mania destroys the object, which becomes merely a locus for imposing projections of inner desires. In contrast, the vulnerable, depressed self is incapable of producing art because it feels depersonalized by a universe devoid of meaning. Only when the moment is right can creativity put together the pieces, ordering what is outside by simultaneously ordering what is inside (though the order itself remains unspecified), ratifying both self and object and the uncanny sense of belonging between the two. Woolf can do this only at the invitation of the moment—she cannot create wholeness on her own; to try would result only in a kind of manic-defense. Thus, Woolf leaves her aesthetic model deliberately vague, even paradoxical, because to tidy it up would be to violate its own prescription. There can be no formula for discovering identity or meaning either in autobiographies or in novels. Woolf employed the same method in writing her diary, as she notes in this 1919 entry:

> What sort of diary should I like mine to be? Something loose knit, & yet not slovenly, so elastic that it will embrace any thing, solemn, slight or beautiful that comes into my mind. I should like it to resemble some deep old desk, or capacious hold-all, in which one flings a mass of odds & ends without looking them through. I should like to come back, after a year or two, & find that the collection had sorted itself & refined itself & coalesced, as such deposits so mysteriously do, into a mould, transparent enough to reflect the light of our life, & yet steady, tranquil, composed with the aloofness of a work of art. The main requisite, I think on re-reading my old volumes, is not to play the part of censor, but to write as the mood comes or of anything whatever; since I was curious to find how I went for things put in haphazard, & found the significance to lie where I never saw it at the time. (*Diary* 1: 266)

This is not Albright's passive victim. Like a swimmer riding the rhythm of a wave, the creative Woolf feels both subordinate to and dominant over experience. By fostering the uncanny sense of sponsorship between self and text, Woolf allows us room to experience life's most important characteristic—its endless suggestiveness—in a moment of vision, understanding, and peace.

7 "A novel devoted to influenza"

Reading without Resolution in The Voyage Out

> Considering how common illness is, how tremendous the
> spiritual change that it brings, how astonishing . . . how we
> go down into the pit of death and feel the waters of annihi-
> lation close above our heads . . . it becomes strange indeed
> that illness has not taken its place with love and battle and
> jealousy among the prime themes of literature.
>   . . . Those great wars which the body wages with the
> mind a slave to it, in the solitude of the bedroom against
> the assault of fever or the oncome of melancholia, are
> neglected. . . . [T]he body, this miracle, its pain, will soon
> make us taper into mysticism, or rise, with rapid beats of
> the wings, into the raptures of transcendentalism. *The public*
> *would say that a novel devoted to influenza lacked plot;* they
> would complain that there was no love in it—wrongly how-
> ever, for illness often takes on the disguise of love, and plays
> the same odd tricks. It invests certain faces with divinity.
>   . . . [L]ove must be deposed in favor of a temperature of 104.
>
>   (*"The Moment"* 9–11; my italics)

In her first novel, *The Voyage Out*, written between 1904 and 1913, Woolf
explored the themes that pervade all her books: mothering, madness, and
the universal human need for a meaningful therapeutic mirroring of self-
continuity in a world that can, at any moment and for no reason, inflict
pain, loss, and powerlessness. Although Lytton Strachey was right in calling it a "very, very unvictorian" book, it was not yet modernist.[1] Woolf
had been hoping to "re-form the novel and capture multitudes of things
at present fugitive, enclose the whole, and shape infinite strange shapes"
(*Letters* 1: 356), but she had yet to experiment with narration, point of
view, and interior monologue as ways to dramatize her sense of the
multiplicity of self and life. Instead, she used a rather traditional narrator
to tell a story that seems conventionally biographical—the growth and
education of a young woman—and her attention to detail, continuity of
action, and dialogue were a far cry from her series of highly experimental
and abstract books that began with *Jacob's Room* in 1921.

The Voyage Out is an uneasy mixture of the new and the old: "[W]e get a story with action and plot in the conventional sense, a story which by its *form* depends for its meaning on the sequence of events, whose real meaning nevertheless depends on the author's throwing, by a variety of devices, all sorts of contradictory meanings into the *content*."[2] The novel's aesthetic tension has been attributed to its irritating tendency to frustrate conventional expectations, illustrated best by the "apparently pointless sacrifice of Rachel."[3] In general, critics tend to view its shapelessness and lapses as evidence either of Woolf's neuroses creeping into the text or her inexperience with plotting.[4] But I will argue that the novel's inconsistencies are part of a deliberate strategy to invite the reader to experience a *failed* reading and to deal with the frustration of pointlessness when critical acumen meets an intractable text—the first step toward understanding the manic-depressive's world.

Although few critics agree on the meaning of *The Voyage Out,* its plot is fairly straightforward. Twenty-three-year-old Rachel Vinrace, naive, motherless, raised by a patriarchal father and thoroughly conventional Victorian aunts, embarks on a voyage of self-discovery to the little South American resort of Santa Marina. A small company of shipboard travelers influence her development: Richard Dalloway, former member of Parliament, masculine, domineering, suave, a grasper of objective fact and convergent thinking, furtively gives Rachel a kiss, her first lesson in a male's sexual desire and in depression; Clarissa Dalloway, Richard's idealized wife, adoring, feminine, maternal, seems to understand intuitively Rachel's inexpressible yearnings and fosters in the young girl an exalted faith in the goodness and bounty of life; Helen Ambrose, Rachel's depressive aunt, educates her niece in the deceitfulness of life and the brutality of emotion; Ridley Ambrose, Helen's husband, the remote scholar, hoarding, hypochondriacal, defensive, offers no nurturing to Rachel, for he is as needful as she is.

Throughout the voyage, Rachel's companions are unable to provide her with the answers she seeks—perhaps because she never seems able to form a coherent set of questions about the meaning of her life. The Dalloways have disembarked in Portugal before Rachel can resolve the ambivalent feelings of excitement and despair that Richard has aroused in her. Helen teaches Rachel through cool, ironic, detached observation, producing a sharper, more critical intellect and a more independent self, but one that feels isolated from others and disillusioned with the world. In Santa Marina, Rachel confronts the same dichotomy in feeling, first by befriending St. John Hirst (who is so isolated and critical himself that he has become miserable and misogynist) and then by falling in love with Terence Hewet, would-be modernist, dreamer, and moody lover who yearns for a profound, benevolent fusion with the world and with a woman. In an Edenic tropical forest, where natural affections flourish and life seems most promising, she and Terence become engaged and try to work through the maze of feelings separating them. Rachel suddenly develops a high fever, suffers profound perceptual disturbances for ten days, and dies. The last two chapters of the novel focus exclusively on how the English colony there first mourns her death and the cruel termination of the lovers' plans and then settles back into mundane concerns.

Even in this short summary we can see several elements from Woolf's life exploited in fiction. Like Virginia, Rachel lost her mother before she could develop an adult's independence; now she seeks nurturing fusions with Clarissa, Helen, and Terence just as Virginia did with Stella, Vanessa, and Leonard. Richard Dalloway, like Gerald Duckworth, teaches the young woman a somber lesson about powerlessness and vulnerability as the male prerogative to make fumbling advances fills the object of his desire with anger and fear. The happy Clarissa, like the young Julia in love with the "stainless" and romantic Herbert Duckworth, does not remain long enough to counsel Rachel or to give her a lasting model of joyous selfhood to imitate, but instead leaves her in the care of the depressed mother-figure, Helen, an older Julia. St. John Hirst, Ridley Ambrose, and Willoughby Vinrace, sharing a number of Leslie Stephen's characteristics, are isolated, patriarchal male figures who, because they do not question their assumptions about what and who women are, fail to understand and nurture females; the inner lives of women remain as much a mystery to them as does the dense jungle. And, like "A Sketch of the Past," *The Voyage Out* presents moments of being, when self and world seem to fuse and enhance one another, as well as moments of failure, when self and world cannot join, when identity fragments, manic illusions spring up, or depression sweeps over the self like a suffocating wave.

At the heart of *The Voyage Out* is Stella Duckworth. She had been a dutiful Victorian daughter: selflessly she tended the family and supported Leslie emotionally, and she too declined in health from exhaustion, becoming "pale as a plant that has been denied the sun . . . bowing to the inevitable yoke of her sex."[5] After Stella's death, Virginia and Leslie relied on the younger Vanessa for mothering, but Vanessa, like Helen Ambrose, was "as quick to detect insincerity of nature as fallacy of argument," and she rebelled (*Moments of Being* 54, 56). When Stella died, the last living vestige of Julia's image died with her. It was an important loss for Virginia.

Like Stella, Rachel was a tintype of her mother, a minor likeness to the idealized Victorian original. Neither Stella nor Rachel felt at all idealized herself. Naive and inexperienced, with little self-confidence, both hoped an external change (a happy marriage) would fill internal needs. When Stella became engaged to Jack Hills, Virginia rejoiced in her good fortune in terms reminiscent of Julia's idyllic life with Herbert: love seemed to be like an exalted manic dream, and, indeed, coincided with what she remembered as her first hypomanic "vision":

> And it was through that engagement that I had my first vision—so intense, so exciting, so rapturous was it that the word vision applies—my first vision then of love between man and woman. It was to me like a ruby; the love I detected that winter of their engagement, glowing, red, clear, intense. It gave me a conception of love; a standard of love; a sense that nothing in the whole world is so lyrical, so musical, as a young man and a young woman in their first love for each other. (*Moments of Being* 105)

In Jack, Stella had found "rest and support" as well as growth; she became "more positive, less passive" (*Moments of Being* 106). Stella, Virginia concluded, "had come to stand by herself, with a painful footing upon real life, and her love now had as little of dependence in it as may be . . . as though Jack had finally convinced her of her worth" (*Moments of Being* 50–52).

Stella was betrayed, however, just as life seemed most promising. Pregnant, she died of peritonitis contracted (perhaps during sexual intercourse) while abroad on her honeymoon.[6] In *The Voyage Out,* Rachel contracts a fever after she and Terence acknowledge their love for one another. Love and death, optimism and pessimism, are tied together in a disturbing, bipolar way, violating our conventional expectations of romance. In her diary, Virginia recorded feeling a terrible rage followed by inertia and depression—both reactions, she said, to the "stupid damage" Stella's death inflicted. It was, she wrote in 1940, a "shapeless catastrophe" (*Moments of Being* 55) because it seemed so meaningless in comparison with her expectations of

> Stella's happiness, and the promise it held for her and for us of escape from that gloom [after Julia's death]; when once more unbelievably—incredibly—as if one had been violently cheated of some promise; more

than that, brutally told not to be such a fool as to hope for things; I remember saying to myself after she died: "But this is impossible; things aren't, can't be, like this." (*Moments of Being* 124)

I remember saying to myself this impossible thing has happened:—as if it were . . . against the law, horrible, as a treachery, a betrayal—the fact of death. The blow, the second blow of death, struck on me tremulous, creased, sitting with my wings still stuck together, on the broken chrysalis.[7]

Stella's death was a violation of desire (for a world responsive to our inner needs, for a real landscape in which to realize our dreams) and self-confidence (would the young Virginia even be given the chance to try her own wings?). But, as such, did this shock not also hold a lesson to be learned, one especially valuable for a manic-depressive?

I would reason that if life were thus made to rear and kick, it was a thing to be ridden; nobody could say "they" had fobbed me off with a weak little feeble slip of the precious matter. So I came to think of life as something of extreme reality. (*Moments of Being* 137)

Are we deluded to expect good out of life simply because we can conceive of a benevolent pattern we think it should follow? Two more deaths in 1904, and a third in 1937 may help illustrate the meaning this unanswerable question held for Woolf. In one week, two acquaintances died. One death was an accident: Margaret Hills (significantly, Jack Hills's sister-in-law) was riding a bicycle when it slipped on a wet road. The other resulted from a chronic illness: Charles Furse succumbed to tuberculosis at the age of thirty-six. "Of the two," wrote Woolf, "Margaret's death is the sadder," because "her death seems merely aimless and cruel," whereas an identifiable and predictable disease *explained* why Furse died. His widow, Woolf reasoned, "must have known what a risk she was taking when she married him" (*Letters* 1: 150): she did not fall victim to an illusory expectation of happiness. In 1937, Vanessa's eldest son, Julian Bell, died in the Spanish Civil War. It was "as if he were jerked abruptly out of sight, without rhyme or reason: so violent & absurd that one cant fit his death into any scheme" (*Diary* 5: 122).

Woolf objected, not to the necessity of death, but to its pointlessness. We feel betrayed by accidental death because it appears so unrelated to the individual's personality or character. Apparently arbitrarily imposed, it destroys our conventional expectations about what life means, who we are, and what destiny we deserve. The life that has ended is, in a way, trivialized because chance—a slippery road, a shallow tread, a tropical germ picked up somewhere—predominates. Have we been deluded all along, like the overconfident manic, about our power over our lives, about our ownership of ourselves and our identity? And this phenomenon we call the human self, the whole fascinating and significant inner universe of consciousness which legislates what rules life should follow and what destiny character deserves, is this too proven to be ephemeral when a rise in temperature or a change in blood chemistry can distort it until self seems barely recognizable, until we are quite mad? Whenever the physical world intrudes on our existential sense of self-integrity, our identity, we lose ownership of ourselves until we can integrate the traumatic event into a rationale that implies a consistency in life's events and self's understanding of those events. We are continually engaged in the effort to see design in the real world. Religion, philosophy, art, literary theory—so much of civilization is meant to protect us from the haunting suspicion that life may have no transcendent direction that can explain why things happen as they do.

This is the real subject of *The Voyage Out*: how do we deal with a death that threatens us and with a reading that defies us? When life (or a novel) is so intractable that it defies even our wish to understand, we may feel compelled to keep our guard up always, to impose meaning where we cannot find it, to wrench the text if need be, lest we throw down the book in despair. One critic complains that the plot of *The Voyage Out* "is so slack, woven with such slender threads, that if one tries to analyse it one is caught between two dangers either to see it disintegrate, or to see it stiffen into a coarse, inflexible framework whose pattern confuses or even destroys the essential lines of the work."[8] Manic-depressives are most familiar with these two reactions, but we need not suffer a mood disorder ourselves to recognize how Woolf felt about the meaninglessness of Hills's death or her own illness. We need only read a novel that resists our habitual interpretive strategies.

The Voyage Out undermines our control by inviting us to face an intractable fact: that seeking the bliss of subject-object fusion, the ruby of love, may for no reason at all make one *pregnable,* a word that, like this novel, is disturbingly equivocal. The novel's themes are connected to Rachel's infected body. As a metaphor for the self, it signifies a frightening vulnerability:

> If Woolf thought her mother's early death was due to her womanhood
> —the many births, the energy absorbed by her large family and
> relentlessly demanding husband—, then how much more must Stella's

death have given her forebodings about sexuality, about marriage, about the ability of her body to change and her inability to control that change?[9]

Woolf's body imposed bipolar disorder and gender on her without her permission, and with these *irreducible* biological facts came arbitrary cultural determinations of what madness and femaleness meant that threatened *to reduce* and trivialize her inner life. We should not, as readers, try to explain away this threat to Woolf or to ourselves when death or madness or sexism makes no sense. When we feel helpless in the face of an intractable fact, we share Woolf's experience as a female manic-depressive victimized by what she could not change.

Is Woolf suggesting that we retreat into a pessimistic stoicism, because life is aimless and we are too vulnerable?[10] She certainly took her mother's death seriously and generalized from it, especially when she was depressed, ominous propositions about the world's treachery. Yet she also believed, especially when manic, in life's potential for happiness. When, a year before she began to write *The Voyage Out,* her closest friend and lover, Violet Dickinson, lay ill with fever for ten days (the length of Rachel's illness), Woolf described fate in depressed terms, as "a brutal sledge hammer, missing all the people she might knock on the head, and crashing into the midst of such sensitive and exquisite creatures as my Violet. I wish I could shield you with my gross corpse" (*Letters* 1: 81). Yet, other letters from this same period reveal a profound love of life, a joyful curiosity about it, a willingness to abjure shielding. In January of 1913 Vanessa praised Virginia's ability to cheer her up:

> I am sometimes overcome by the finest qualities in her. When she chooses she can give one the most extraordinary sense of bigness of point of view. I think she has in reality amazing courage & sanity about life. I have seen so little of her lately that it has struck me here.[11]

Obviously, any observer's impression of Woolf's worldview would depend on what mood she was in at the time, but Vanessa's evaluation at least demonstrates that at some points her sister was anything but pessimistic or morbid. Virginia's own letter of August, 1906, attests to the same attitude: "Really it is worth while to take a spirited view of the future. Things are bound to turn up" (*Letters* 1: 233). It was only four months later that Thoby died of typhoid fever contracted on holiday in Greece.

An irresolvable uncertainty pervades *The Voyage Out*: should we or should we not embrace life, untrustworthy as it is? It is a difficult question for a manic-depressive to answer. Woolf's youthful spirits were dashed by tragic deaths at fairly regular intervals: 1895 (Julia), 1897 (Stella), 1904 (Leslie), and 1906 (Thoby). In each case, death seems to have followed moments of great promise and evident security,[12] and the resulting uncertainties, the cyclic highs and lows, could appear in nonpsychotic forms in any personality that experienced such successive losses. The complication here is that these shifting perspectives are also specific to, and magnified by, manic-depressive illness, with or without actual losses, for mood shapes the evaluation of events. How are we to read Woolf's philosophy of life, when biography and biology blend indistinguishably into one another? How are we to view pessimistic or even suicidal statements about the meaninglessness of life when certainly the deaths she endured, the breakdowns she experienced, the sexual abuse she suffered—all senseless, incomprehensible, undeserved—might convince even a non–manic-depressive that existence was periodically a hard business? And what do we do with the other passages in her diaries and letters: the ecstasies, the triumphs, the exultant sense of life's abundance and her own creative power to surmount obstacles? Are these merely hypomanias, or are they the pleasures of a flourishing and productive creative genius enjoying life when it is good? Seeking one totalizing answer offers us too great a temptation merely to impose upon life's discord the false orders of our own unexamined, mood-mediated, need-fulfilling assumptions. Fate is difficult to read for both external and internal reasons. But it is this difficulty that makes doubly interesting a fiction written by a manic-depressive about reading fate. Woolf's novels will not present us with congruent answers to separate "real" from "unreal" events, perceptions, feelings, or ideas. They will only help us appreciate the problem of asking unbiased questions:

> I don't admit to being hopeless though—only the spectacle is a profoundly strange one; & as the current answers don't do, one has to grope for a new one; & the process of discarding the old, when one is by no means certain what to put in their place, is a sad one. (*Diary* 1: 259)

Hope is a bias, but then so is hopelessness; both induce a false sense of certainty in "reading" life. A novel that confronts the aimlessness of life and death will necessarily be a puzzling and frustrating exploration of just how difficult it is to read anything.

Because reading should be a struggle, *The Voyage Out* contains a rather large number of flat characters whose primary function is illustrate simplistic object-relations: they either surrender—becoming passive, selfless, hapless, or hopeless—or fight—becoming unmergeable hard cores that deny vulnerability and uncertainty. One who immediately succumbs without contest is the servile and featureless Susan Worthington, reputed to have "no self" (134), who becomes engaged to the equally dull Arthur Pennington. Proper, fossilized, neither wrestles with uncertainty; culture has provided them with ready answers to every problem, so that even Rachel's tragic death can be "smoothed over" with "tactful" conversation (363). By surrendering individuality immediately, Susan and Arthur become blessed nonentities wrapped in cotton wool, an institutionalized form of nonbeing. Without depth, there can be no drowning.

Rachel herself periodically succumbs to selflessness. After reading a perplexing play by Ibsen, she feels as if she has shrunk:

> "What's the truth of it all?" . . . It was all very real, very big, very impersonal, and after a moment or two she began to raise her first finger and to let it fall on the arm of her chair so as to bring back to herself some consciousness of her own existence. She was next overcome by the unspeakable queerness of the fact that she should be sitting in an arm-chair, in the morning, in the middle of the world. . . . And life, what was that? . . . Her dissolution became so complete that she could not raise her finger any more, and sat perfectly still, listening and looking always at the same spot. It became stranger and stranger. (123–25)

Rachel's dissolution reduces her to paralysis and magnifies the impersonal world; it is perceived as queer and unreal, because she cannot believe in her own subjective reality. James Naremore is correct in reading such events as frightening examples of loss of self, though he has wrongly seen them as Woolf's urging us to seek purely objective knowledge—if that were even possible.[13] The death of the soul is not Woolf's moment of being. When Rachel as subject is a mere blank, an empty container incapable of contributing meaning to her perceptions, the world is alien and unreal to her. The only advantage to anhedonic depression lies in the fact that it empties one of illusion;[14] it allows Rachel to ask the most fundamental questions of existence. Her periodic dissolutions cleanse the soul—an asset if one is adaptive enough to understand how such cleansing comments on the unexamined assumptions of sanity.

Other minor characters fight despair and vulnerability, not by dissolution and surrender, but by imposing themselves. The determined Miss Allan orders her environment, preferring the security of closed curtains to the open night sky (151) and the hoarding of a bottle of crème de menthe as a "charm against accidents" (254). Like Leslie Stephen, Miss Allan seems perfectly suited temperamentally to the large task of categorizing the lives of great writers for her *Primer,* yet at the same time she finds it difficult to express their originality, to say "something different about everybody" (316). The agitated depressive has a knack for imposing order, but at the same time tends to obliterate individuality by constraining responsiveness—an unfortunate lesson to be giving readers new to the study of great literature. Ridley Ambrose likewise stifles emotion with "the continuity of the scholar's life," closeting himself for hours like a misanthropic hoarder of self, caring deeply only about Pindar, food, and digestion (199). Mrs. Flushing, "upright and imperious" (259), assaults art (198); in her own paintings, "all perfectly untrained onslaughts of the brush upon some half-realised idea suggested by hill or tree," her highly organized and inflexible personality dominates, permitting little of the external world to show through (234).

Perhaps most revealing is the intensely defensive William Pepper, gloomy, cross, severe, who has disciplined himself until his heart has become "a piece of old shoe leather" (19) and who abjures the freedoms of life in a spacious villa for the constraints of the hotel because he fears infection from improperly cooked vegetables. Pepper may seem just a crank, a petty academic at whom Woolf can poke fun for his ludicrous egotism,[15] but he serves a very important function in the novel: he expresses before an assembled company of major characters what seems to be a convenient piece of narrative foreboding. At first, when he withdraws from his friends, Helen fears she has somehow angered him. She would have tried to change his mind

> if William had not shown himself inscrutable and chill, lifting fragments of salad on the point of his fork, with the gesture of a man pronging seaweed, detecting gravel, suspecting germs.
>   "If you all die of typhoid I won't be responsible!" he snapped.
>   "If you die of dullness, neither will I," Helen echoed in her heart. (93)

Pepper's paranoia seems justified by Rachel's subsequent death by fever, and this connection might lead some readers to conclude hastily that Pepper's survival and Rachel's death are linked to how they live their lives, for it is conventional to presume that a fictional character's fate comments on his/her wisdom or folly, sanity or morbidity. Does Pepper's caustic contraction of spirit save him? If so, then does Miss Allan's bottle of crème de menthe actually prevent accidents? Assuming that Pepper is rightly defensive, why does the novel avoid specifying the origin of Rachel's fever to substantiate his attitude? But if Rachel's death is unrelated to Pepper's defensiveness, why does Woolf have him specify typhoid fever, which Rachel's illness seems to resemble? To complicate matters even more, Helen's silent retort rings true: Pepper is dead inside. So what does this novel want to say? Is a safe life worth living? Or is a romantic adventure up tropical rivers worth dying for? Susan stands as proof that nonbeing is not always actually fatal, but she scarcely invites the reader's admiration. Throughout, Woolf remains curiously noncommittal, making suggestions that are indirectly and invariably undercut.

As readers, we find ourselves forced into a corner by Woolf's unwillingness to resolve this problem about the relative value of different states of mind. The novel shows that pernicious defensiveness and self-destructive surrender can, under certain circumstances, work equally well. Each mood, even those we may find repellent, has certain assets. (Who would be more likely to survive a first-strike nuclear attack than the paranoid depressive whom we dismissed as a kook because he moved his family to southern Oregon to live in a well-stocked bomb shelter?) What a manic-depressive feels exaggerates what we all feel—and should feel—about life's essential equivocation. "There is no irony in Nature," the elderly George Meredith wrote to the dying Leslie Stephen in 1904. "We who have loved the motion of legs and the sweep of the winds, we come to this. But for myself, I will own that it is the Natural order."[16]

The Voyage Out re-creates this most lifelike condition of contingency whenever it deals with how characters find meaning in their lives. Thus, Clarissa may extol life's abundance ("when you're my age you'll see that the world is *crammed* with delightful things" [58]) with an exuberance that infects Rachel briefly ("it seemed indeed as if life which had been unnamed before was infinitely wonderful, and too good to be true" [61]), but in fact, in this particular case, it *is* too good to be true: Rachel dies, and Clarissa's own exalted visions of a noble husband and an ennobling England are undercut by the tawdry realities of his philandering and the spiritual emptiness of his politics. Yet we cannot use these tragedies as evidence for the opposite conclusion, that life is inherently bad, for Rachel benefits as much by Clarissa's idealized image of life's goodness as she does by Richard's demonstration of its badness, and the novel does not specifically reduce the paradox. Both views, irreducibly contradictory, help Rachel realize what the world is like and what she needs from it.

It is significant, then, that Rachel's object-relational style can at times seem closely related to Pepper's; by creating an unmergeable self, she defensively rejects communion with the world. When, for example, she realizes that prostitutes are desired by men as sexual objects, and that the same instinct which exploits them is the desire Richard Dalloway felt toward her (remember Ralph Partridge's desire for power mixed up with his desire for sex), she immediately recoils. "It *is* terrifying—it *is* disgusting," she asserts with considerable hatred, and then concludes suddenly: "So that's why I can't walk alone!"

> By this new light she saw her life for the first time a creeping hedged-in thing, driven cautiously between high walls, here turned aside, there plunged in darkness, made dull and crippled for ever. (82)

This is essentially the conclusion reached in her dream, the night of Richard's kiss, of lying as still as death before the gibbering man. Freudian critics often focus on the dream as a neurotic disguise for Rachel's (and Woolf's) fear of sex: the gibbering man is identified as Gerald hiding at the end of a moist vaginal tunnel. But such an interpretation presumes that symbolism works in only one direction, from manifest image toward repressed sexual desire, supposedly where the "real" meaning lies. If, instead, we follow recent advances in sleep research suggesting that dreams are transformative and adaptive ways of thinking rather than the products of an unconscious censor,[17] we can see that this fictional dream may be using sexual imagery to represent something nonsexual: the walled-in "no exit" hell of depression with all its attendant helplessness, terror, and despair. Replicating Pepper's leathery interior, Rachel must pretend to be dead, emptied of a living self, or the dwarfish man will attack her. The fear of vulnerability to such a depressive state is an agony that ruins sleep, because selflessness *is* a nightmare. Unfortunately, Rachel's initial response to attack is to create a defensive image of the self as unassailable:

> The vision of her own personality, of herself as a real everlasting thing, different from anything else, unmergeable, like the sea or the wind, flashed into Rachel's mind, and she became profoundly excited at the thought of living.
>
> "I can be m-m-myself," she stammered, "in spite of you, in spite of the Dalloways, and Mr. Pepper, and Father, and my Aunts, in spite of these?"
>
> "In spite of every one," said Helen gravely. (84)

This idealization of individualism at first seems positive, because it emboldens Rachel, but control is a defensive denial of vulnerability, not a solution to it, and it must obstruct a beneficial and creative fusion with others.[18]

Against a backdrop of minor characters embodying elements of various fixed moods, Rachel moves, a sensitive, unformed human being, indefinitely drawn, gathering experiences. Because of her vagueness as a character, she is plastic enough to be intensely aware of subtle changes in her own moods.[19] This is her function in the novel—to be difficult to pin down, to chart the aimless waters of mood shifts, life's ambiguous nature, and self's constantly changing relationship to it, as the ship *Euphrosyne,* to which she is often compared, plies the waters to an uncertain fate: "The sea might give her death or some unexampled joy, and none would know of it. She was a bride going forth to her husband, a virgin unknown of men; in her vigour and purity she might be likened to all beautiful things, worshipped and felt as a symbol" (32). Deliberately obscure, this image of veiled purity is not simply a foreboding of Rachel's death; it also predicts the equal possibility of unexampled joy. It is the noncommittal omen of an "inscrutable destiny."[20]

Thus, *The Voyage Out* is a hodgepodge of emotions and views that do not sort themselves out into any convenient order. Rather, reading this novel invites us to see that the subjective world of perception, mood, and judgment is one of organized and organizing "meaning," whereas the objective realm of physical nature is one of "truth" we glimpse only occasionally and then find disconcertingly divergent and unresolvable. This is why the omniscient narrator philosophizes about the myriad bootless activities of landbound Britons who cut flowers, fell in love, admired the day, and "prognosticated pleasant things about the course of the world," none of which seems to carry much weight. "Some said that the sky was an emblem of the life they had had," the narrator notes without emphasis; "others that it was the promise of life to come" (31). Terence himself, desperate to deny the seriousness of Rachel's illness, also indulges in unsupported interpretations, one of which seems meant for the reader to apply to this novel: "According to him, too, there was an order, a pattern which made life reasonable . . . for sometimes it seemed possible to understand why things happened as they did" (299). There may indeed be a meaningful pattern behind the chaos of events in our lives, but our understanding of it is marred by the limitations of our psychic apparatus, by invisible moods largely outside our control, by the way we order our rooms, wash our vegetables, and digest our food. Consciousness is shaped in so many ways. How, then, can we discern the pattern that will make Rachel's destiny "reasonable"?

No one in this novel possesses an "authoritative" reading of events. At first Rachel (and the reader) looks to Helen for guidance. Mild depressives do have a special and, at times, valuable talent for debunking illusion, which the inexperienced Rachel requires, for she "would believe practically anything she was told, invent reasons for anything she said" (34). Helen's perspective on Richard Dalloway's kiss helps Rachel understand that it was both stimulating and banal, not a transcendent event but not a fatal one either. However, Rachel finds that even the formidable Helen has her limitations. Halfway through the novel, Helen falls into a deeper, more debilitating depression which seems to have no cause and against which she has no defense:

> Always calm and unemotional in her judgments, Mrs. Ambrose was now inclined to be definitely pessimistic. She was not severe upon individuals so much as incredulous of the kindness of destiny, fate, what happens in the long run, and apt to insist that this was generally adverse to people in proportion as they deserved well. Even this theory she was ready to discard in favour of one which made chaos triumphant, things happening for no reason at all, and every one groping about in illusion and ignorance. (221)
>
> Mrs. Ambrose looked and listened obediently enough, but inwardly she was a prey to an uneasy mood not readily to be ascribed to any one cause. . . . She did not like to feel herself the victim of unclassified emotions, and certainly as the launch slipped on and on, in the hot morning sun, she felt herself unreasonably moved. (277–78)

Helen's depression consists of "unclassified emotions" she cannot analyze or name, a vacuum she finds uncomfortable. Just as she had played Freud to Rachel's Dora by interpreting Rachel's depression after Dalloway's adulterous kiss as "the most natural thing in the world" (81), so now Helen explains her own depression as the result of having seen beneath appearances to a truth seldom glimpsed. But she cannot name that truth.

Although Helen's worst fears are eventually realized by Rachel's death, it would be a mistake to view them as a clumsy narrative device of foreboding,[21] or as Woolf's only philosophy of life. Helen is no "fate figure" (though depressives typically fear that they are), just as Pepper's phobia about germs is no virtue offered for our imitation (though he would argue so). Helen exhibits symptoms typical of depression, which Woolf knew by experience could occur independently of life events—even though life does occasionally prove the depressive's view to be correct. There can be no reliable litmus test for how realistic our feelings are when feeling itself distorts the results. The text tests our ability to interpret, not by giving us a heavy-handed Freudian disguise to decode, but by underscoring the fundamental dilemma of all perception: the need to avoid solipsism on the one hand and meaninglessness on the other, even though both are necessary components of reading. When Freudian critics interpret Helen's foreboding morbidity as evidence of Woolf's inability to keep her neurotic fears out of the text, they undermine not only the author's control over her story but our responsiveness to it. When we must wrest artistic control from Woolf in order to explain away the sense of uncertainty and multiplicity that she deliberately creates, then we have become defensive ourselves. We have become Pepper.

One such defensive posture is Mitchell Leaska's argument that Helen's bleak outlook is really an attempt to punish Rachel for deserting her to form a heterosexual attachment with Terence. Helen's despair is a

> desperate, unconscious effort to poison the atmosphere with irrationality and gloom and death; her inclination to feel victimized and defeated, and hopelessly to want to massacre all that is, or could be, happy and flourishing. Whatever satisfaction in life or in love Helen Ambrose may have been denied must also be denied to others, particularly to Rachel whose increasing independence deprives Helen of her most cherished substitute for real satisfaction: transitory fulfillment through others.[22]

Leaska does not feel the need to sympathize with Helen's pointless suffering or to examine the possible truth of her tragic vision; he dismisses both as evidence of veiled aggression, a sick need to control others. Psychotherapists often experience similar countertransference reactions when dealing with depressed patients, whose despair (which they often generalize into gloom-and-doom predictions for the whole world as well as for their families) can be interpreted as disguised, self-destructive rage. A physician's own anger and frustration at what he perceives to be the patient's resistance to therapy may be manifested as a defensively vindictive condemnation of the depressive's seeming collusion with his disease.[23] It is hard to sympathize with someone whose victimization seems global, unnecessary, and self-advertised. But sympathize we must if we are to see that Helen's morbidity is neither jealousy nor Woolf's supposed unconscious fears about lesbian love (is it likely that a woman who seemed so conscious of, and so satisfied with, her feelings about other women would have much to repress?). We must prepare ourselves for the possibility that the text means what it says—that consciousness is a puzzle without resolution.

Terence Hewet also seems to be constantly victimized by his unclassified emotions. Although initially enthusiastic about organizing an expedition up a mountain, he loses his desire as he walks to meet his companions:

> "But why do we do it?—is it to prevent ourselves from seeing to the
> bottom of things . . . making cities and mountains and whole
> universes out of nothing, or do we really love each other, or do we,
> on the other hand, live in a state of perpetual uncertainty, knowing
> nothing . . . ?" (127)

What is "the bottom of things" he should be seeing? Once he starts the climb he quickly forgets his depressive speculations, recovers his spirits, and gains the hilltop. But no sublime conclusion awaits him at the overview. Instead, he "became, for no reason at all, profoundly depressed" and fell to meditating once again on how insipid and cruel all his guests really were (134), though moments before he had judged them "noble" (132). He had climbed the mountain but gained no ground in the struggle to read his own feelings.

Whereas Helen's mood swings are gradual and chronic, Terence endures many brief shifts between depression and exultation that illustrate how even rapid alterations of mood escape detection when the individual assumes that his present interpretation is always the right one. Having eavesdropped on Helen and Rachel, Terence excitedly stumbles down a path, shouting happily, "Dreams and realities, dreams and realities, dreams and realities" (188), exultant that life seems to be combining the mysterious and the real in the beloved figure of Rachel. In the next paragraph, he falls into a depression, feeling "as if he were enclosed in a square box, and instantly shrivelled up" when he enters his room. Slowly he regains some equanimity, but Evelyn's flirtation leaves him again depressed, overwhelmed by "the mystery of life and the unreality even of one's own sensations" (194), though only minutes before, with boundless optimism, he had shouted his joy at just such a mixture of subjectivity and objectivity. Mood makes all the difference: to the manic, "unreal" sensations seem a miraculous synthesis of self and world promising exciting new realms of experience; to the depressive, they are frightening confusions of self and world that minimize him and imprison him in dark cells of pain and disappointment. Terence may feel quite powerful, superior to Hirst's fear of risking contact with women, but he can also perceive his desire for communion with Rachel as a fearful prospect that makes him feel helplessly miserable. His most rapid shifts occur with Rachel, when "at one moment he was clear-sighted, and, at the next, confused," and so, when he confesses his faults to her, he concludes that he is indeed "moody." "I'm overcome by a sense of futility—incompetence" (280), he tells her, though later he boasts of inflated feelings of self-esteem and power, describing himself as "immensely solid" and claiming that the "legs of my chair might be rooted in the bowels of the earth" (293).

Mood swings are volatile: Terence is most depressed by the least incident. When Rachel complains of a headache, he is overwhelmed by depression out of all proportion to the occasion: "[H]is sense of dismay and catastrophe [was] almost physically painful; all round him he seemed to hear the shiver of broken glass which, as it fell to earth, left him sitting in open air," vulnerable, exposed (327). Our hindsight of Rachel's death tempts us to regard his depression as a conventional narrative stratagem.[24] Like the Britons, we find it all too easy to read meaning even in the equivocal sky, to suppose with unexamined confidence that life would not have given sunsets such an important function as that of ending the day with extravagant beauty if it had not intended them to symbolize something more. But what is that "more"? And on whose authority do we descry its meaning? Not Terence's, certainly. Desperate to deny the seriousness of Rachel's illness (and of his own despair), he overlooks Dr. Rodriguez's incompetence and is shocked when suddenly his evaluation changes: "His confidence in the man vanished as he looked at him and saw his insignificance, his dirty appearance, his shiftiness, and his unintelligent, hairy face. It was strange that he had never seen this before" (337-38). Strange indeed, but is this a shift in perception to a more objective view, or just another misinterpretation? What has facial hair to do with medical expertise? Has a subjective impression merely coincided accidentally with Rodriguez's actual incompetence? Why is reading this novel as problematical as reading Rodriguez's face? And where is the omniscient narrator when we need her? She remains silent on the issue here, but in her memoir to her niece and nephews, Woolf recounts how friends of her family read into Stella's face her mother's visage and character:

> People who must follow obvious tokens, such as the colour of the eye,
> the shape of the nose, and love to invent a melodramatic fitness in life,
> as though it were a sensational novel, acclaimed [Stella's] now the

divinely appointed inheritor of all womanly virtues, and with a certain haziness forgot your grandmother's sharp features and Stella's vague ones, and created a model of them for Vanessa to follow, beautiful on the surface, but fatally insipid within. (*Moments of Being* 55)

With expectations of perfect happiness for her, they wished Stella well on her honeymoon. From her journey, however, she returned fatally ill; from divine guarantee came only a "shapeless catastrophe . . . death making an end of all these exquisite preparations" (*Moments of Being* 55).

Rachel's emotional vacillations enlarge her experience of life, but they also shape belief, the premises by which she evaluates these experiences. Like Helen and Terence, she is unable to compensate for the distortions, though she does note them. One day, having walked alone along a river bank, she is suddenly "filled with one of those unreasonable exultations which start generally from an unknown cause, and sweep whole countries and skies into their embrace[;] she walked without seeing" until interrupted by a solid object, the perception of which is momentarily intensified and falsified by her energized brain. "It was an ordinary tree," the narrator tells us, "but to her it appeared so strange that it might have been the only tree in the world." This illusion of miraculous singularity is temporary; the tree "once more sank into the ordinary rank of trees" as Rachel sank out of her hypomanic state (174). Sitting in the shade and reading Gibbon, Rachel again experiences an elevated mood, but this time she attempts to understand it: "Slowly her mind became less confused and sought the origins of her exaltation." With effort, she narrows down the probable cause to Terence and St. John. Yet she cannot analyze and so control their power to affect her so drastically, because for her they are still enveloped in an idealizing "haze of wonder": "From them all life seemed to radiate; the very words of books were steeped in radiance" (175).

Questioning belief in the midst of hypomania proves to be useless. Mood manipulates belief and colors facts, even individual words, to fit itself: "She could not reason about [Terence and St. John] as about people whose feelings went by the same rule as her own did, and her mind dwelt on them with a kind of physical pleasure such as is caused by the contemplation of bright things hanging in the sun." Knowing objectively that Terence and St. John do not radiate "all life" or that the words of books are not "steeped in radiance" will not lead her to insight until she identifies the source of the reflected, blinding brightness. This Rachel does not do. Like the early Freudians, she focuses on the object of her distorted perception in the hope that it has somehow caused the shift in mood, but this gets her nowhere. Soon her mood drops again, she loses the manic ability to "juggle with several ideas," and "a kind of melancholy replace[s] her excitement," destroying even the illusion of significance: "She sank down on to the earth, clasping her knees together, and looking blankly in front of her," wondering, "What is it to be in love?" (175).

What does it mean for Rachel to be in love when she cannot be sure of her beliefs or her emotions? How can this novel be judged a tragic love story or a failed bildungsroman when the most basic issues about perception and self have yet to be resolved? Rachel thinks she sees clearly that the preacher Bax's complacent listeners have confused their notions of God with their own self-images, but it is an agonizing struggle for her merely to determine what she feels about Terence and whether or not it is even love. Each time they meet, conflicting emotions assert themselves ("when they met their meeting might be one of inspiriting joy or of harassing despair" [224]). Helen's counseling only confuses the two women further when Rachel's bipolar mood swings occasionally, but only temporarily, coincide with Helen's depression:

> [Rachel's mind] was so fluctuating, and went so quickly from joy to despair, that it seemed necessary to confront it with some stable opinion which naturally became dark as well as stable. Perhaps Mrs. Ambrose had some idea that in leading the talk into these quarters she might discover what was in Rachel's mind, but it was difficult to judge, for sometimes she would agree with the gloomiest thing that was said, at other times she refused to listen, and rammed Helen's theories down her throat with laughter, chatter, ridicule of the wildest, and fierce bursts of anger even at what she called the "croaking of a raven in the mud."
> "It's hard enough without that," she asserted.
> "What's hard?" Helen demanded.
> "Life," she replied, and then they both became silent.
> Helen might draw her own conclusions as to why life was hard, as to why an hour later, perhaps, life was something so wonderful and vivid that the eyes of Rachel beholding it were positively exhilarating to a spectator. (221–22)

Helen's attempt to understand Rachel's moods is doomed because she too assumes that ideas or events are behind them, that if she could only "discover what was in Rachel's mind," she could counteract the cognitive changes.

Like many other manic-depressives before her, Rachel suffers as much from her own moodiness as from the world's inability to understand her inner world. Frustrated and tearful, her pulse "beating, struggling, fretting" against a world of degraded human beings who cannot comprehend her emotional tumult or satisfy her demands (which mania intensifies so much that her desires cannot be adequately formulated or appeased), she becomes convinced that other people are against her, imposing their "ponderous stupidity" upon her, like Leslie Stephen drenching Anny's exuberant imagination with his "cold bath" of logic:

> All day long she had been tantalized and put off. . . . For the time, her own body was the source of all the life in the world, which tried to burst forth here—there—and was repressed now by Mr. Bax, now by Evelyn, now by the imposition of ponderous stupidity—the weight of the entire world. Thus tormented, she would twist her hands together, for all things were wrong, all people stupid. Vaguely seeing that there were people down in the garden beneath she represented them as aimless masses of matter, floating hither and thither, without aim except to impede her. (258)

Driven and visionary, the manic cannot understand that indefinable requests are impossible to fulfill. Though desire is vivid and expansive, the real world and its limitations are only "vaguely" seen through the blinding light of exalted mood.[25] Manic confidence, intensified by scattered creativity and unrealistic goals, is easily diverted into egotism and hostility.

But this denial of her aimless moodiness cannot last. Rachel's paranoid rage soon settles into its opposite, a "melancholy lethargy." Her imagined vision of a persecutory world dims, and with it the illusion of unlimited energy and profound purpose. "It's a dream," she concludes, and she subsequently discovers that the rusty inkstand, the pen, the ashtray, and the old French newspaper are really only "small and worthless objects [that had] seemed to her to represent human lives" bursting with vivacity and malice. Rachel has arrived at a momentary insight into this particular instance of mania, but has she achieved a lasting understanding of all the mood swings she has experienced? This moment of micro-depression is not definitive; it merely disillusions her of one false belief by replacing it with another. Within seconds she moves on to the next shift in mood. As before, she is overwhelmed by elevated mood, energy, and perception: the landscape seems covered with "a haze of feverish red mist," and her friends have a

> startling intensity, as though the dusty surface had been peeled off everything, leaving only the reality and the instant. It had the look of

a vision printed on the dark at night. White and grey and purple
figures were scattered on the green; round wicker tables; in the middle
the flame of the tea-urn made the air waver like a faulty sheet of glass;
a massive green tree stood over them as if it were a moving force held
at rest. (258–59)

But what is this unpeeled "reality"? Vivid and yet indefinite (Evelyn and
Helen appear merely as unrecognizable "figures"), Rachel's vision lasts
only an instant and is soon forgotten. Her exultation drops away, and she
rejoins the hotel guests for a quiet tea, during which she considers and
accepts Mrs. Flushing's invitation to the ill-fated expedition up the river.

Unable to connect present moments of intense feeling with conflicting
past moments, Rachel learns nothing that can help her understand emotion. Although Clarissa confidently predicts that Rachel is "going to find
out" why people marry (60), her engagement to Terence takes place
without much enlightenment. Their love scenes seem deliberately cast as
eerie and unreal, full of ambiguous silences and flat, unremarkable
statements spoken with a dull, lifeless quality, the diminished inflection
typical of depression:[26]

> "You like being with me?" Terence asked.
> "Yes, with you," she replied.
> He was silent for a moment. Silence seemed to have fallen upon
> the world.
> "This is what I have felt ever since I knew you," he replied.
> "We are happy together." He did not seem to be speaking, or she to
> be hearing.
> "Very happy," she answered.
> They continued to walk for some time in silence. Their steps
> unconsciously quickened.
> "We love each other," Terence said.
> "We love each other," she repeated. (271)

A dreamlike unreality so overwhelms them that they question not only
why they want to marry but whether in fact Terence had even asked her
(282). Mood shapes what is recorded in memory and how it is recorded,
making events apprehended as unreal more difficult to remember. Rachel
and Terence therefore agree to review their previous conversation, to pin
down what each one felt so that "together they would interpret her feeling"
about what had happened. But their attempt at an intellectualized
reconstruction proves futile. Rachel only becomes conscious of a new and

unfamiliar feeling running through her: "This is happiness, I suppose." This is not a Freudian novel about love or sex. This is a story about whether emotion is a fiction that can be read. Rachel accepts each of her different readings of the world because each carries with it a powerful force of conviction. Unable to analyze her perceptions, "it seemed to her that her sensations had no name," and she herself becomes a mere container for those sensations (223).

By refusing to name Rachel's fatal illness but foregrounding her delirium, which is inherently inchoate, Woolf focuses our attention on the physicality of Rachel's illness, showing us that a biological disorder has perceptual and psychological consequences that resist a "personal" explanation. When Rachel's head first begins to ache, the words of Milton, recited by Terence, begin to mean "different things" from the ordinary (as we should expect by now, Woolf does not specify what the difference is), and "the garden too looked strange" (327). Interpretation and perception have become indistinguishable; objects, especially words, have become malleable, plastic, obscurely symbolic, inexplicably significant. Rachel envisions her sickroom attendants taking flight above trees and high towers. The sickroom itself persecutes her: the walls lean malevolently toward her, harsh light assaults her, and the movement of the blinds in the wind terrifies her. These perceptions are convincingly vivid, but they fail to yield to analysis:

> For six days indeed she had been oblivious of the world outside, because it needed all her attention to follow the hot, red, quick sights which passed incessantly before her eyes. She knew that it was of enormous importance that she should attend to these sights and grasp their meaning, but she was always being just too late to hear or see something which would explain it all. For this reason, the faces,— Helen's face, the nurse's, Terence's, the doctor's,—which occasionally forced themselves very close to her, were worrying because they distracted her attention and she might miss the clue. However, on the fourth afternoon she was suddenly unable to keep Helen's face distinct from the sights themselves; her lips widened as she bent down over the bed, and she began to gabble unintelligibly like the rest. The sights were all concerned in some plot, some adventure, some escape. The nature of what they were doing changed incessantly, although there was always a reason behind it, which she must endeavour to grasp. (340–41)

Confused, Rachel resorts to unlikely explanations validated only by mood, not by fact, and though her perceptions change incessantly, she cannot stop to think that the fault lies with her. Woolf's metaphor for this most essential element of manic-depressive illness is the dream state. Both familiar and strange to readers, it emphasizes the paradoxical experience of Woolf's madness: it suspends the rules of "normal" waking mental functioning and yet sharply reveals the unexamined assumptions of those rules. Rachel's fevered mental state is described as "a transparent kind of sleep," as if she is trapped in Terence's dichotomy representing moodiness, "dreams and reality"; she is neither fully asleep nor awake and is unable to tell the difference. Though her premises are distorted, however, Rachel's mind does still function in a logical way. To paraphrase Leonard's reassurances to Woolf, Rachel is "terribly sane in three-quarters of her mind" (*Beginning Again* 164). She attempts to "cross over into the ordinary world," to know when she is experiencing a dream, when a reality, but it is difficult, for the fever has "put a gulf between her world and the ordinary world which she could not bridge" (329).

Unable to wake up, Rachel is imprisoned by subjectivity: "all landmarks were obliterated"; even the sounds of people walking on the floor above seem incomprehensible and can "only be ascribed to their cause by a great effort of memory. The recollection of what she had felt, or of what she had been doing and thinking three days before, had faded entirely" (329–30).[27] The sight of Terence takes special effort "because he forced her to join mind to body in the desire to remember something" (347)— how she felt about him, with the same beliefs and conviction, an impossible task now. In this sense she is no longer Rachel, for she loses identity when she loses her past. She has "ceased to have any will of her own" and is unable to communicate with the rest of the world, for her mind has been "driven to some remote corner of her body, or escaped and gone flitting round the room" (347). Only body, the cause of the separation, can forge the link between self and world and end the nightmare. Woolf may not have understood how biology determined mood, but clearly she experienced the connection.

As the fever progresses the mood swings intensify, and Rachel begins to hallucinate vividly. Nurse McInnis now appears to be playing cards in a tunnel under a river, a vision Rachel interprets as "inexplicably sinister" (330). The next vision expands on the theme. A waking dream that repeats elements of Rachel's nightmare after Dalloway's kiss, it replays the same message that powerlessness and vulnerability are frightening:

> Rachel again shut her eyes, and found herself walking through a tunnel under the Thames, where there were little deformed women sitting in

archways playing cards, while the bricks of which the wall was made oozed with damp, which collected into drops and slid down the wall. But the little old women became Helen and Nurse McInnis after a time, standing in the window together whispering, whispering incessantly. (331)

The women are McInnis and Helen, distorted by fever, sitting in her room; the oozing walls, her own skin shedding beads of sweat. The body's boundaries have melted and are mixed up with perceptions of separate objects. Depression and sexual abuse are connected here because each reduces Rachel to a helpless, paranoid object. Recapitulating a nightmare puts into words what is nameless and so difficult to explain—how Rachel feels when depressed.

A similar scene occurs when Terence next visits. Rachel hallucinates an old woman with a knife killing chickens (as she had earlier witnessed), a decapitation scene that has inflamed some Freudians with its lurid imagery. Shirley Panken maintains that this vision of castration expresses Rachel's (and Woolf's) neurotic and repressed fear of sexual intimacy with a man and her masked oral rage (*Lust of Creation* 83–85). But if Woolf did know what she was doing here, and if it was based on her experience of manic-depressive illness, then the focus should not be on decoding latent content for some tidy and reasonable message but on the structure of Rachel's hallucination. When Terence kisses her, she sees an old woman slicing a man's head off with a knife (339), but it is Rachel who has been cut off— by her own paranoia. She feels as if her mind is "flitting round the room." An attempt to touch, to communicate, is perceived not simply wrongly but as its opposite, as a separation, an alienation. The kiss's meaning is a florid unmeaning, just as Stella's death defied hope, just as manic-depressive illness undermines desire and character and judgment. Rachel's hallucinations and the novel's equivocations alike cry out for coherence and reduction, but at what price? If we save Rachel from an incoherent madness and a meaningless death by saving ourselves from the fundamental uncertainties of reading, are we not destroying the novel?

To tempt us further, in the characters who survive Rachel we are offered bad models for making interpretations, though no one voice rises above the rest with an authoritative, or even convincing, explanation of why Rachel dies. Miss Allan overgeneralizes sorrow into depressing pessimism: she feels "as if her [own] life had been a failure, as if it had been hard and laborious to no purpose" (356). The indomitable Mrs. Thornbury over-comes her sobs ("How could one go on if there were no reason?" [357]) by fabricating an order that beautifies death: "on the whole, surely there was a balance of happiness—surely order did prevail. . . . they were saved so much; they kept so much. The dead—she called to mind those who had died early, accidentally—were beautiful" (360). Mr. Flushing is defensive too but lacks the imagination to idealize death: he fears that his wife feels "she was in some way responsible," a suspicion he argues is "unreasonable" in a series of unfinished assertions that cover all defensive bases: "We don't even know—in fact I think it most unlikely—that she caught her illness there. These diseases—Besides, she was set on going. . . . I've no doubt myself that Miss Vinrace caught the infection up at the villa itself." Mrs. Flushing counters her grief by stiffening, regarding death as a humiliating surrender:

> When she was alone by herself she clenched her fists together, and began beating the back of a chair with them. She was like a wounded animal. She hated death; she was furious, outraged, indignant with death, as if it were a living creature. She refused to relinquish her friends to death. She would not submit to dark and nothingness. (359)

William Pepper blames Rachel's death on taking unnecessary risks with unwashed vegetables. Old Mrs. Paley agrees, referring to Rachel as "young people" who "always think they know better, and then they pay the penalty" (362). The sexist Arthur Pennington assumes that Englishwomen are too weak constitutionally to survive "roughing it," even though the soft and passive Susan flourishes physically. Evelyn denies contingency altogether: if Rachel's death were not a part of a Providential plan, she worries, "it need never have happened" (357). The rest of the hotel's inmates quickly forget their grief when a storm momentarily absorbs their attention, after which they return to their needlework and chess and novels, as if nothing fundamental had disturbed them at all.

In this way *The Voyage Out* trivializes its own ending, undermining the significance of Rachel's death by presenting contradictory interpretations ready-made according to each character's own psychological needs and strategies for dealing with threatening, pointless events. And critics have generally followed the models set out for their imitation. Some, like Mrs. Thornbury, accept the "apparent" arbitrariness of Rachel's death as evidence that some orderly pattern underlies all human experience but that it transcends the capacity of individuals to understand it; only in death will be found an idealized "vision" of truth or a perfect union with Terence—though what that vision is and why it should be so valuable is certainly not demonstrated in the novel.[28] Perhaps Rachel *prefers* death because it offers the illusion of perfect fusion with Terence, but the illusion belongs to Terence alone, not to the text, and it is subsequently exploded by a "necrophilic rage" once the reality of Rachel's death sinks in.[29] Like Mr. Pepper and Mrs. Paley, some critics moralize that tragedy results when foolish risks are taken, death being the "inevitable end of romantic dreaming" that ignores the grim realities of the world.[30] Or, like Miss Allan, they take a depressive, tight-lipped line, blaming Rachel's death on the "impossible barriers between people, barriers which in the end are triumphant."[31]

Only the Freudians share Mr. Flushing's talent for rationalizations at any cost when they try to specify a latent origin for Rachel's fever: Shirley Panken argues that Rachel dies because she capitulates, in a kind of death wish, to insoluble inner conflicts; Louise DeSalvo and others contend that sexual knowledge and sexual guilt are the real causes of death; Rachel succumbs either from fear of sex or from an unresolved, latent lesbian desire for Helen.[32] (And yet Hughling Eliot contracts a similar fever and is treated by the same Dr. Rodriguez: are we to assume he suffers from impotence or lurking homosexuality? Mrs. Thornbury reports that she fell ill with typhoid for six weeks on her honeymoon in Venice; was this too a psychosomatic reaction to intimacy? And what of the famous explorer, Mackenzie, who "had died of fever some ten years" before in the jungle [277]? Bestiality? How far are we willing to go to make sexual feelings fatal?) Finally, it has been suggested that Rachel sinks into fever because she does not resist surrender to the dark inner forces and social, sexual pressures; just as Mrs. Flushing feels that she survives by sheer will power, Leaska and Apter theorize that Rachel dies "*a self-willed death*," one that is "the ultimate expression of her personality tendencies."[33]

What are we to think about Rachel's death when so many convenient critiques have been provided us by the author herself? Rachel and Terence explicitly state that a life of happiness is a reasonable request to make of fate ("It isn't as if we were expecting a great deal—only to walk about and look at things" [301]), but *it is apparently too much to ask,* not only in this novel but frequently in real life as well. How are we to evaluate a thoroughly naturalistic event in fiction? Perhaps in response to other critics' frustration, one has voiced the inevitable conclusion that Rachel's death is arbitrary and essentially unrelated to the novel's thematic structure: "It does not seem convincing to treat the illness as the *outcome* of Rachel's emotional experiences—as a flight from sex or from the unsatisfactoriness of love." That significant admission is shared by others: the novel's ending is "unmotivated," seemingly "intended to upset all expectations of 'pattern' "; it is "gratuitous," "pointless and unnecessary."[34] And so our focus should be shifted onto why readers have such a difficult time accepting it as such, why, although admitting that Rachel's death *defies* analysis, striking the reader as a "blank fact," they try to analyze it anyway, filling in the blanks as if they were not meant to be there.[35] Mitchell Leaska sees the "tragic pointlessness" of Rachel's death, accepts that it "is intentionally made ambiguous" ("the author, however, names no proliferating organism, specifies no unwashed vegetables") and yet concludes that it is "*self-willed*," even while he wonders why we "are at liberty to speculate on why we are not able 'to give a reasonable explanation' " for it. Instead of enjoying this liberty to speculate on the meaninglessness of death, Leaska presumes that, since "*everything is there not by chance, but by choice,*" this narrative gap stands for something that is missing because it is latent, forbidden, repressed; some crucial element that will give the "real" reason for the novel's central event has been left out. Claiming that we can dip into Rachel's (and Virginia's) unconscious mind, Leaska finds discarded references to sexuality, violence, and bestiality in earlier versions of the novel and reestablishes them as motives for Rachel's withdrawal into fever, delirium, and death.

But perhaps the point is that Rachel's death *is gratuitous,* and that, faced with confusion and loss, some readers will go to great lengths to establish a rationale that will explain away tragic senselessness, making unsupported interpretations along the way (for instance, that Woolf's earlier revisions and deletions of "bestial" passages give us a privileged view into her mind "at work in the *unguarded act of creation.*"[36] Leaska follows the comforting Freudian formula of psychic determinism, the theory that no psychic event occurs by chance, and so he assumes that Rachel's death must be caused by deeper conflicts that Woolf is unwilling to confess (by definition, neurotics are not willing to examine what they have repressed). He gives himself license to supply what is not in the text, to make clear what has been left deliberately unclear, to center a decentered text, and he ignores the significance of obscurity, of absence, of meaninglessness—in essence, of modernism. Ironically, it is precisely this unlimited "end-less" state that characterizes psychoanalysis at its best—when it is still exploratory and potentially capable of tolerating the untoward chaos and pain of illness. By forcing a conclusion to Rachel's life (e.g., death by frigidity), Freudian critics not only gloss over Woolf's deliberately constructed textual strategies but also embalm psychoanalysis by prematurely explaining away contingency. Freud's dictum of psychic determinism is not a license to bury under theory all uncertainties, gaps, and elisions.

It is this liberty to speculate, without hope of an objective or conclusive answer, that frustrates Leaska and us, but it cannot and should not be avoided. Such freedom to perceive pointlessness is an integral part of subject-object relations. Often, like Woolf in "A Sketch of the Past," we face only a blank wall of nonbeing, of unmeaning (why *did* Margaret Hills die on her bicycle?). And yet Woolf obviously values these experiences, as when she tries to sum up her feelings about the deaths of Julia and Stella:

> If there is any good (I doubt it) in these mutilations, it is that it sensitises [one] . . . to be aware of the insecurity of life. . . . Did those deaths give us an experience that even if it was numbing, mutilating, yet meant that the Gods (as I used to phrase it) were taking us seriously . . . ?
> I would reason that if life were thus made to rear and kick, it was a thing to be ridden; nobody could say "they" had fobbed me off with a weak little feeble slip of the precious matter. (*Moments of Being* 137)

Death mutilates feeling. This Leslie Stephen himself said in a letter to C. E. Norton apropos of Minny's death:

> Grief like yours and mine seems to me to be not like an illness from wh. one recovers but like a permanent mutilation wh. can never be cured; though one may become accustomed to the [illegible] state of existence and lower one's ambition to suit one's capabilities.[37]

Virginia acknowledged the hurt both her father and she felt at the loss of loved ones and security, yet clearly she surpasses him when she tells us that one must remain sensitive to it nevertheless; one must tolerate uncertainty, confusion, multiplicity. Knowing that even senseless experience was "the real thing" ratified her sense of self, a self brave enough to stare into the consuming fires without resorting to the comfort of illusions or a lowering of ambition. Shirley Panken dismisses *The Voyage Out* by concluding that Woolf "seems incapable because of her inexperience and warp in development of sorting out threatening emotions";[38] I argue that this novel does indeed "sort out" confabulations of inner states and outer objects—but not in an order Panken expects or recognizes.

Perhaps because Woolf is more interested in depicting the existential contingency of mood shifts, she does not attempt to deal with madness and death as anything more than a final void that swallows up selves forever. In *Jacob's Room,* she explores the emptiness left by a character's death. By 1925, in *Mrs. Dalloway,* she shows us that even loss and death can be faced with some confidence that an essential feature of the self will remain intact;

and in *To the Lighthouse,* characters overcome the helplessness death and loss produce, touching one another across gulfs of time and mortality in ways that Rachel and Terence do not manage. *The Voyage Out* is but the first step toward depicting a self strong enough to survive the loss of meaning.

8 "Does anybody know Mr. Flanders?"

Bipolar Cognition and Syncretistic Vision in Jacob's Room

Woolf conceived the form of *Jacob's Room* before the story:

> Suppose one thing should open out of another. . . . For I figure the approach will be entirely different this time: no scaffolding; scarcely a brick to be seen. . . . [T]he theme is a blank to me; but I see immense possibilities in the form I hit upon more or less by chance 2 weeks ago. I suppose the danger is the damned egotistical self; which ruins Joyce & [Dorothy] Richardson to my mind: is one pliant & rich enough to provide a wall for the book from oneself without its becoming as in Joyce & Richardson, narrowing & restricting? (*Diary* 2: 13–14)

The unusual form of this novel both attracts and repels readers. Without an omniscient narrator, cohesive plot, or detailed characterization, the novel tells a story that falls apart. We know more about Jacob's room than we do about Jacob, who remains a ghost whose touch is felt but not identifiable.

Like *The Voyage Out,* this story is simple: a young person grows up only to die pointlessly. But whereas Rachel "gallantly . . . takes her fences" (*Diary* 2: 17) against the odds, Jacob is in no way uplifted by a journey that is trivialized by his aimlessness, his wasted destiny—a superficiality emphasized by the narration's disconcertingly comic tone. That tone leads one writer to conclude that *Jacob's Room* is not a serious bildungsroman at all, but a parody of one.[1] Jacob is presented to us not for our love or pity but as a figure that escapes us whether alive or dead. The omniscient narrator of *The Voyage Out* confides to us Rachel's thoughts, but we are given little insight into Jacob's mind. He teasingly escapes even his "biographer," who self-consciously ruminates on her limited knowledge. *Jacob's Room* questions its own validity as a biography.

Woolf's quest for a fictional order without "scaffolding" was tied to her desire to avoid the "egotistical self," that surface function of an author's psyche that subdues plot and limits psychological insight to the coherent, the demonstrable, the visible—to itself, in other words, the perfectly configured mask of the omniscient author masterfully governing his created world and falsifying the reader's experience. Ego creates meaning out of its own coherent structure, and so Woolf views its literary productions as merely self-serving illusions, proving not that reality has been grasped but that it can be replaced by an intellectualization. Fiction, she realized, can suffer by attempting to be too complete, by pretending that its wholesale surrender to the ego's need for certainty and artifice has not obscured the truth. Three years before she began *Jacob's Room,* Woolf considered critically the illusion of omniscience and power that her manic expansions created:

> Ever since I was a child . . . I've had the habit of getting full of some biography, & wanting to build up my imaginary figure of the person with every scrap of news I could find about him. During the passion, the name of Cowper or Byron or whoever it might be, seemed to start up in the most unlikely pages. And then, suddenly, the figure becomes distant & merely one of the usual dead. (*Diary* 1: 180)

It was from this rhythmical movement between believing in imaginary fullness and discovering later only deflated fact that Woolf learned to both appreciate and suspect the biographer's wish to capture a life. Once the elated mood was past, Cowper and Byron receded from her because she had never really touched them.

Jacob's Room moves beyond the carefully balanced paradoxes of *The Voyage Out* to a more daring experiment in fiction: a self-conscious expression, in both content and form, of the bipolar subject-object relations of reading fiction, transactions which go awry in manic-depressive episodes. Woolf realized that representing Jacob's soul in its totality would dangerously aggrandize the narrator's authority and make the novel as self-serving as Leslie's *Mausoleum Book*; she was as concerned with protecting her narrator from egotism as she was with depicting Jacob's tragic fall into it. Jacob and his narrator are counterparts, and an analysis of his story and her method will show how Woolf proposed to construct a fictional order that does not restrict a novel's meaning or her readers' ability to create meaning for themselves.

To encourage our self-examination during the reading process, Woolf makes discontinuity more than a fact of life; it is a fact of text. "As frequent as street corners in Holborn," her narrator reminds us, "are these chasms in the continuity of our ways. Yet we keep straight on" (96). Readers typically cover over gaps in meaning with the more consistent narrative of intention. But what is Woolf's intention here? comic? tragic? critical?

elegiac? Evidence exists to support any one of these unifying themes. Critics readily acknowledge that *Jacob's Room*'s dreamlike, spasmodic incoherence—its rapid transitions, shifting perspective, and disconnectedness—evidences Woolf's modernity, but then they resort to hunting in the few specific details in Jacob's life for clues that would help to plug up the very large holes in the text with what is supposed to be Jacob's "real" story, a more coherent story. Meaning is equated with completeness, and so even a modern novel must be patched up before it can be declared finished. Perhaps by its very nature, literary criticism is conservative: it opposes both the subversive goals and methods of modernism and Woolf's own feeling that even living characters are "splinters & mosaics; not, as they used to hold, immaculate, monolithic, consistent wholes" (*Diary* 2: 314).

If we let the gaps stand, the underemphasis of plot in *Jacob's Room* shifts the burden of storytelling to the development of imagery, which readily invites readers' subjective responses; indeed, it is in our arbitrary interpretations that Woolf is primarily interested. Perhaps this is why the novel abounds with images of order and chaos, foregrounding the question of order and disorder in fiction and in critical response. Instead of reading symbols for their latent content, I will extend Virginia Blain's insight that "*Jacob's Room* relies on connecting the apparently disparate by setting up subtle trains of imagery which shift and modulate like a mirror of the narrative voice, creating a chain of perception wherein each new image reflects and contains the preceding one."[2] I will consider how these images function as representations of the novel's structure, as self-reflexive pieces of metafiction embodying components of manic-depressive object-relations.

Opposed images of order and chaos occur throughout *Jacob's Room*: uniformity/irregularity, rigidity/fluidity, mechanical lifelessness/primitive energy, destructive rationality/vital emotions, psychic fragmentation/psychic wholeness. Woolf realizes her theory of having one thing opening out to another by clustering these images of structure around characters who read their internal, psychological states in the form of external, spatial relationships—embodiments of the mood-distorted psychological patterns of Woolf's family and her illness. Some characters want to surrender, like Julia Stephen, to life's elemental disorder—a dissolution that comes as relief, a wished-for sinking into oblivion and unconsciousness. For others, following Leslie Stephen, oblivion and uncertainty elicit a defensive fear that throws up barriers between self and object, hoarding and starving the ego imprisoned in a joyless, tidy world. A third type, like Anne Thackeray Ritchie, tolerates the insecurity of chaos, ambiguity, and dissolution without sinking into isolation and nothingness, but whether a vision of life's meaning that is not merely self-serving is achieved depends on how well manic projection and depressive introjection are integrated.

The novel begins with an immediate opposition between agitated control and a healthy adventurism. Jacob's mother, Betty Flanders, after two years still unable to accept her husband's death, mourns the loss of structure in marriage, which is compared to "a fortress" while "widows stray solitary in the open fields" (8). She feels her vulnerability keenly and reacts with horror to Jacob's sheep's skull, with revulsion toward nature in general:

> The waves showed that uneasiness, like something alive. . . . Betty, pulling [her children] along, and looking with uneasy emotion at the earth displayed so luridly. . . . [T]his astonishing agitation and vitality of colour . . . stirred Betty Flanders and made her think of responsibility and danger. (11)

Betty projects her own uneasiness onto the landscape and its "lurid" display. She associates safety with order and constructs a "scaffolding" in her personal narrative,[3] embodied in a bare front room where an oil lamp sprays its harsh artificial light in straight, regular lines across the lawn. Inside she and her servant can conduct the sterilizing duties of householding: "they were conspirators plotting the eternal conspiracy of hush and clean bottles" (13). Outside a storm lashes the house with a wild, intense energy that lacks any recognizable plot or order; it is "nothing but muddle and confusion." This strict division, spatialized as inner and outer, between meaning and unmeaning, conformity and innovation, schematizes the agitated depressive's subject-object relations. Jacob's crab circling endlessly within a bucket aptly represents the boy's life under his mother's rule. He was, as Betty complained, "the only one of her sons who never obeyed her" (23), but his wild nature, at home on the moors, is bounded by rigid circumstance shaped by her.

Similar oppositions surround the Flanders family. Betty's unofficial, married suitor, Captain Barfoot, is passionless, "military" (26), "rigid" (28), and as "regular as clockwork" (15) in his weekly calls, inspiring a sense of safety ("Here is law. Here is order" [28]). He is the perfect antidote to Betty's worries about her late husband's fate: "Had he, then, been nothing? . . . At first, part of herself; now one of a company, he had merged in the grass, the sloping hillside, the thousand white stones, some slanting, others upright, the decayed wreaths" (16). Betty fears nothingness inside as well as outside; the prospect of loss haunts her like the shadows of chaos lurking behind images of order. This dichotomy is especially well portrayed by the mechanical regularity of the town of Scarborough itself: the band plays in a Moorish kiosk, a structure mathematically precise in its decorated patterns; the music is categorized by number; the dancers have no real vitality or animality in the repetitive movements of a waltz—"all wore the same blurred, drugged expression." Yet "through the chinks in the planks at their feet they could see the green summer waves, peacefully, amiably, swaying round the iron pillars of the pier" (18).

Mrs. Flanders admires civilization's order and camouflage. She likes to climb Dods Hill and watch what appears to be, in repeated images of constriction and control, a subdued landscape: trousers are aligned in rows; flower beds are neatly laid out by the Corporation; the golden sea is "hoarded" up by a black pier; men in white coats wheel "triangular hoardings" that advertise a seaman's capture of a "monster shark" (17–18). When her eldest son, John, slaps down grass and dead leaves haphazardly into her lap, Betty "arranged them methodically but absent-mindedly . . . [thinking] the church clock was ten or thirteen minutes fast" (19). The measuring of time is a depressive denial of chaos. Three pages later, Betty reminds herself that Topaz the cat will soon have to be killed because he is so old. As she does so, she also decides not to marry Mr. Floyd (who had given Topaz to Jacob), although his proposal moves her emotionally. A husband, like an unexpected death, would introduce an uncontrollable element into her life, and so Woolf combines thoughts of the red-haired Mr. Floyd and Topaz's castration and extermination in one sentence: " 'Poor old Topaz,' " said Mrs. Flanders, as he stretched himself out in the sun, and she smiled, thinking how she had had him gelded, and how she did not like red hair in men" (22–23). Mr. Floyd cannot be gelded and must be dismissed from thought.

Mrs. Jarvis, on the other hand, wants to surrender completely. She wanders out on the moors at night, desperately yearning to sink into oblivion. Though a vicar's wife, she would exchange security and salvation for unhappiness, divorce, and loneliness—if only she could be swept away by the "universal that is." But "she does not know what she wants to give, nor who could give it to her" (27). Feeling dead inside, she finds it "difficult" even "to think of herself" as existing (132), just as Julia Duckworth, wanting the one thing life could not give back to her, felt hollow and "deadened," desiring only "to think as little" of herself as possible.[4] Attributing an exaggerated value to the unobtainable universe and underrating herself, Mrs. Jarvis hopes that losing self-consciousness will dissolve her troubling doubts and fears. She finds the tombstone epitaphs reassuring, for the dead *are* one with the moor, which "seems to hoard these little treasures, like a nurse. . . . [The] skeletons are in safe keeping" (134). But this apparent peace is the nullity of despair and depression:

> "I never pity the dead. . . ."
> "They are at rest," said Mrs. Jarvis. "And we spend our days doing foolish unnecessary things without knowing why." (131)

A true moment of being is impossible for an individual who, feeling foolish and unnecessary, wants to dissolve into nothingness. Mrs. Jarvis cannot imagine what she wants to receive or what she can give because she does not have a sturdy enough sense of self to make such a fusion productive.

Mrs. Flanders and Mrs. Jarvis represent cognitive components of two different types of depression. Mrs. Jarvis, the anhedonic depressive who feels empty, isolated, and impotent, would willingly surrender to dissolution regardless of cost; Mrs. Flanders, the unmergeable, agitated depressive self, defensively protects her isolation against the void outside. Depression, it seems, *must have a void,* but its location is variable. Neither character recognizes how mood colors perception of self and object, and so they confuse the two realms of subject and object. Betty externalizes the internal, denying fear by projecting it outside onto the landscape, whereas Mrs. Jarvis internalizes the external, desiring to bring the landscape inside to fill her emptiness.

These two women sketch out the parameters of how self relates to its own perceptions of the world within which Jacob moves. When he is out on the moor, his inner and outer worlds coincide without imposition or surrender, much the way Rachel Vinrace feels one with her music. But Jacob's cognitive growth is stunted by attending Cambridge, which, like Betty's house, is represented by harshly mechanical, orderly images the narrator pits against Jacob's Byronic moors:

> Insolent he was and inexperienced, but sure enough the cities which
> the elderly of the race have built upon the skyline showed like brick suburbs,
> barracks, and places of discipline against a red and yellow flame. . . .
> . . . the world of the elderly—thrown up in such black outline
> upon what we are; upon the reality; the moors and Byron; the sea and
> the lighthouse; the sheep's jaw with the yellow teeth in it; upon the
> obstinate irrepressible conviction which makes youth so intolerably
> disagreeable—"I am what I am, and intend to be it," for which there
> will be no form in the world unless Jacob makes one for himself. (36)

Making a "form in the world" is difficult, because Cambridge will not tolerate disorder. Dogs and women are forbidden in King's College Chapel as disruptive elements, and even light itself seems laundered and pressed:

> An inclined plane of light comes accurately through each window, purple and yellow even in its most diffused dust. . . . Neither snow nor greenery, winter nor summer, has power over the old stained glass. As the sides of the lantern protect the flame so that it burns steady even in the wildest night . . . so inside the Chapel all was orderly . . . all very orderly.

In contrast to the "civilizing" of light into geometrical, spectral, and immutable patterns, the narrator pictures a lantern set in Jacob's forest:

> If you stand a lantern under a tree every insect in the forest creeps up to it—a curious assembly, since though they scramble and swing and knock their heads against the glass, they seem to have no purpose—something senseless inspires them. (32)

The lantern can be viewed in either of two ways: as an example of defensive control, or as an irrational surrender. Perspective is everything; the object remains the same. More important for Jacob, orderliness is associated with prosaic thoughts and egotism, whereas chaos is allied with senseless inspiration and animal vitality. Jacob's destiny is not Rachel's. He is not to die in the dreamy mystery of exotic fever but in a ritualized, mechanized, meaningless sacrifice fostered by his society's need for uniformity of view, which strangles originality, tolerance of ambiguity, and the radial openness of modernism.

Woolf populates Cambridge with pedantic teachers whose qualities are antithetical to Jacob's childhood subject-object fusions. Old Sopwith, methodical in habit and thought, suffering from a "strange paralysis and constriction" of human feeling, analyzes and refines all experience as if he were minting coins, bringing order and "value" to chaos:

> Sopwith went on talking. Talking, talking, talking—as if everything could be talked—the soul itself slipped through the lips in thin, silver disks. . . .
>
> . . . Sopwith went on talking, twining stiff fibres of awkward speech—things young men blurted out—plaiting them round his own smooth garland, making the bright side show. (40–41)

The "bright side" filters out whatever inchoate meaning "awkward speech" may contain. Only Sopwith's "own smooth garland" benefits. The coin of experience bears his likeness rudely stamped upon it.

Jacob is most strongly repulsed by George Plumer, whose sixpenny weeklies reflect "the weekly creak and screech of brains rinsed in cold water and wrung dry" (35). Jacob's disgust should be reassuring, but the narrator warns us that Jacob has no language of his own to replace the conventional, uniform discourse that cannot see beyond one or two views of a lantern. "What can you do with a brain so competent that nothing resists it—because after all, it attempts only solid things—histories, and triumphant little text books[?]" Woolf asked once in a letter about Oxford dons (*Letters* 1: 319–20). With only the dead language of immobilization, how can Jacob find a "form in the world" open and fluid enough to allow the creative disorder of cognitive growth? Thus, "the extent to which he was disturbed proves that he was already agog" (35–36).

As a member of the disfranchised sex, Woolf was saved from Jacob's fate by being excluded from indoctrination into the "triumphant" and "competent" tradition of the British male intellectual. Because manic-depressive illness is a radial experience, not a linear one, she was free to find her own discourse, her own form, to resist stasis . This mood disorder does not illuminate or justify a sane point of view. Rather, it periodically deconstructs the validity and self-righteousness of "normal" interpretations. Many manic-depressives *want* to be well (for the sake of their families, their jobs, peace and quiet), but they cannot deny that, when ill, they perceive in profoundly different and sometimes fascinating ways that are denied them when well. They have experiences they find difficult to express or explain directly, without turning them into refined theories, metaphors, or symptoms. The change from mad discourse to nonmad discourse is not a transformation but a replacement—and a dispiriting one. As a result, manic-depressives often feel as if they lived in a different world from non-manic-depressives. It is not surprising, then, that Woolf chose to narrate this story as an outsider looking in, attempting neither solidity nor triumph.

Surrounded by the ego-aggrandizing, self-congratulatory, patriarchal machinery of civilized behavior, Jacob's rebellions become more trivial. He loses his natural amiability, becomes "overbearing," and strikes Bonamy in an academic disagreement over abstract terms—*good, absolute, justice,* and *punishment* (102). When he accompanies the Durrants to the Opera House, he surrenders himself to a seat:

> Only to prevent us from being submerged by chaos, nature and society between them have arranged a system of classification which is simplicity itself; stalls, boxes, amphitheatre, gallery. The moulds are filled nightly. There is no need to distinguish details. But the difficulty remains—one

has to choose. . . . Never was there a harsher necessity! or one which entails greater pain, more certain disaster; for wherever I seat myself, I die in exile. (68–69)

Jacob's choice is tragic because it shows how classification and order mold us in seemingly insignificant ways, subtly seducing us to agree that disorder is impractical or undesirable. Theater seating is emblematic of analytical thinking, which structures his object-relations in other areas of his life, even that of perception itself. It is much harder to feel the romance of senseless forest insects butting their heads against a lantern when one accepts the value of protecting a steady flame from the wild night winds.

Jacob cooperates with society's penchant for order and prosaic judgment even as he ridicules it. He must therefore develop a social self that disguises and protects what he considers his essential self. But the mask is composed of the same humbug manners Woolf had diagnosed two years before, in her essay "Cleverness and Youth," as evidence of deep self-destruction: inauthentic emotion, nonbeing, and psychic death (*Contemporary Writers* 149–51). Thus, although he is not proficient in Greek, Jacob idealizes the ancients, touting the Cambridge line. He abandons a desire to write home of his initial excitement when visiting Greece by cynically rationalizing, "I daresay this sort of thing wears off" (149). He rehearses in his mind Victorian platitudes, such as "the ruins of the Coliseum suggest some fairly sublime reflections" (136), intending to impress Bonamy with his sensibility to scene. He notes his favorite lines in Donne's poems, piecing together profundities by breaking them out of context, as if one can accumulate experience like coins with a marked value: Donne's words, like Sopwith's, become experience melted down and rudely stamped with an authoritative meaning.

Jacob's constriction of the spirit is manifested by his bifurcated relationships with women. Just as his mother dissociates herself from nature, Jacob dissociates himself from deep sexual involvement with women. Of all women he is said to "honour" most deeply the incorporeal Clara Durrant, whom he prefers to think of sentimentally as a "virgin chained to a rock" (123).[5] His sexual partners are clearly associated with primitive energy, chaos, mystery, and animality—as if they were sexual moors he intended to visit only on holiday. Florinda is "wild and frail and beautiful" (78), though as "ignorant as an owl" (79); her handwriting is chaotic, as if made by "a butterfly, gnat, or other winged insect, attached to a twig which, clogged with mud . . . rolls across a page" (94). Jacob meets her on Guy

Fawkes Day, in a incoherently structured scene, a dreamscape contrasting starkly with the precise, harshly lit world of Cambridge. Eerily lit by a wood fire, Florinda floats in a "dark vacuum," as if she were a ghost. She hurls a purple globe at a young man's head, but it magically and harmlessly crushes to powder. In the hotel dining room, inanimate objects acquire the power of life: a table "ran, as if on invisible legs[,]" across the room (75). Causal connections have broken down. In Florinda's presence Jacob feels "free, venturesome, [and] high-spirited," and he marvels at her freedom from propriety: "she had called him Jacob without asking his leave" (76). She is "entirely at the beck and call of life," whereas he is preoccupied with classifying her on the grounds of her virginity (79). He has generalized the lesson of seating in the Opera House by acting the prig here; his passion, dictated by abstractions, never precedes his categorizations. Passion has seated itself and died in exile.

Consequently, Jacob's escape to Greece is no real escape. He pursues Mrs. Wentworth, who is also a sham, a caricature of himself. She is the romantic Englishwoman seeking a controlled abandon by seducing young men while maintaining order and security in her life in the form of an imperturbable husband. They put on the appearance of profound emotion while withholding their authentic selves from each other. Soon afterward, Jacob virtually disappears as a figure in the narrative; his death is reported indirectly, at a distance. Invulnerable on the moors, he dies in the First World War, a nightmare of prosaic judgment and mechanized death.

What Jacob's death may mean is connected in the last two chapters to his friend Bonamy, who undergoes a conversion. Like the young Leslie Stephen at Cambridge, Bonamy had been "all for the definite, the concrete, and the rational" (146). Jacob had hated Bonamy's methodical, constrictive turn of mind: "I like words to be hard—such were Bonamy's views, and they won him the hostility of those whose taste is all for the fresh growths of the morning" (140). But after Jacob's death, Bonamy experiences a sudden revulsion for order and reason: he "got a very queer feeling, as he walked through the park, of carriages irresistibly driven; of flower beds uncompromisingly geometrical; of force rushing round geometrical patterns in the most senseless way in the world" (152). Bonamy is thrown into chaotic emotionalism (just as Leslie abandoned his faith and took up agnosticism), an overwhelming feeling of being "tossed like a cork on the waves; of having no steady insight into character; of being unsupported by reason, and of drawing no comfort whatever from the works of the classics" (164)—strangely, just the reaction most readers feel reading this book.

Here is Woolf's repudiation of the war, framed not only as a political statement but in terms of subject-object relations. War is evil because it unleashes onto a real landscape what should be kept in check in the mind: the self-destructive tendency of Logos to dissect, regiment, and rationalize until feeling is dead, fossilized and meaningless. The falsifying fiction of a "just war" imposes the depressive's delusion that hell is inescapable, perhaps even desirable, that the cognitive rules one must live by require a hell. War is a mental object as well as a physical one, and Bonamy's former objectivism is as much a violation, an act of war, as is Jacob's death. Both young men are casualties of the lopsided object-relations that make possible civilization's blunders and mass deceptions. *Jacob's Room* is not merely Woolf's paean to her dead brother, Thoby, but to all "dead" people, the citizens of nonbeing, paralyzed by convention, hoarded egotism, and disillusionment—to the world of depressive cognition in all its many forms.

This narrative of Jacob's failed subject-object relations is paralleled by the story of his biographer's own tribulations. We read, not a "triumphant" biography of self-congratulatory "solidity" (such as Cambridge dons would write), but the subjective account of an "outsider" who confesses she is unable—and unwilling—to present life objectively. Perceptions are unreliable, she reminds us, people are mere Platonic shadows, and the real Jacob is unreachable by either writer or reader. Only our most incoherent impressions of Jacob are vivid, but their "truth" is so subjective as to be almost incommunicable:

> [L]ife is but a procession of shadows, and God knows why it is that we embrace them so eagerly, and see them depart with such anguish, being shadows. And why, if this and much more than this is true, why are we yet surprised in the window corner by a sudden vision that the young man in the chair is of all things in the world the most real, the most solid, the best known to us—why indeed? For the moment after we know nothing about him.
>
> Such is the manner of our seeing. Such the conditions of our love. (72)

We desire more than our seeing will bear. If the depressive tries in vain to tack life down, and the manic desires more than life can grant, then mood swings imply that loss teaches a valuable lesson: the "manner of our seeing" is at odds with "the conditions of our love." We cannot know Jacob (or Virginia know Thoby) so well that losing him must be a fatal loss of self. Though self habitually feels its fate is intertwined with objects, it lives in its own subjective world and need not fear dissolution if an object is suddenly torn away. Manic-depressives must repeatedly learn to resist morbid storylines if they are to survive suicidal thoughts.

Since her Platonic attitude discounts the substance of perceptual evidence, the narrator cannot take very seriously her work as a historian. Jacob is unknowable, and books written about him must be unreadable; objectivity fails, and "what remains is mostly a matter of guesswork" (73). To overcome the lack of direct evidence, the self-conscious narrator resorts to speculation and imagination, filling in the gaps, not with Jacob, but with products of her own personality which she carefully foregrounds *as hers*.[6] She accepts the dichotomy of objective and subjective knowledge as irreducible but freely mixes the two in the hope that the reader will discern some truth incorporating both—the same ambiguous prescription Woolf gives us in "A Sketch of the Past." Just as the moor encompasses all things—the shadows we call Tom Gage or Bertha Ruck, or Mrs. Flanders's cheap brooch—the narrator and the reader must embrace fact and fancy, seeing and love.

By undercutting our interpretative strategies, *Jacob's Room* invites us to struggle with provisionality: the retentive grasp on objective, orderly data (Leslie's agitated depression), the submissive surrender of reading to chaos (Julia's anhedonic depression), and the dreamy embrace of disorder by a dilated self (Anny's hypomania). Woolf's narrator encourages us to become self-conscious as we read. What are we looking for in a fictional biography? she continually asks by implication. Would we really be satisfied if she pretended to omniscience? If we doubt ourselves, the narrator reminds us that:

> Nobody sees any one as he is. . . . They see a whole—they see all sorts of things—they see themselves. . . .
> . . . One must do the best one can. . . . It is no use trying to sum people up. One must follow hints, not exactly what is said, nor yet entirely what is done. (30–31)

If what we see in others originates in us, what knowledge have we gained? Why do we accept without question the narrator's omniscient judgments of minor characters? To urge our self-examination, she stops short at the one character we want to know most; she refuses to pin down Jacob. Standing outside his Cambridge rooms, she draws attention to her position (and ours) as an outsider, as a reader who cannot quite see the text:

> The laughter died in the air. The sound of it could scarcely have reached any one standing by the Chapel, which stretched along the opposite side of the court. The laughter died out, and only gestures of arms, movements of bodies, could be seen shaping something in the room.

> Was it an argument? A bet on the boat races? Was it nothing of the sort?
> What was shaped by the arms and bodies in the twilight room? (44)

The reader who accepts omniscient confidences about minor characters is disconcerted by the narrator's doubts and winks when it comes to Jacob.

Perhaps Woolf teases us because the Edwardian reader expected to be told everything; he was confident that he *could* have complete knowledge of a character, and a narrator's voice seemed more real to him if it confidently constructed a totalizing portrait. For this reason Arnold Bennett criticized Jacob as inadequately developed. Woolf's response accepted his logic but refuted his assumptions:

> its only the old argument that character is dissipated into shreds now:
> the old post-Dostoevsky argument. I daresay its true, however, that
> I haven't that "reality" gift. I insubstantise, wilfully to some extent,
> distrusting reality—its cheapness. But to get further. Have I the power
> of conveying the true reality? Or do I write essays about myself?
> (*Diary* 2: 248)

Woolf aimed for a reading beyond the objective and demonstrable (cheap reality), aware that at the other extreme she risked the self-indulgent solipsism of egotism or mania ("essays about myself").

Like Bennett, other readers find the tactic a strain. Mitchell Leaska, for instance, is alarmed by the slipperiness of *Jacob's Room:*

> If, as some serious readers maintain, Virginia Woolf meant us to supply
> at least as much as she suggests in *Jacob's Room,* then the serious critic
> is in serious trouble. For the implication is that the text becomes a
> different novel for each reader; and that from personal reservoirs of
> memory, experience, and feeling, a reader may furnish the otherwise
> lifeless page with whatever he pleases; that the book becomes a massive
> Rorschach test, a series of stimuli with no response *controls.* If one
> reading of a book is as valid as any other reading, then all literary
> criticism is futile.

Concerned that art cannot exist unless it controls reader response, Leaska argues that reliable ("valid") cause-and-effect holds the novel together. Woolf, he reasons, has merely reversed this order, presenting the effect before giving us the cause. His conclusion, that the subtext of *Jacob's Room* chronicles the fatal progress of Jacob's repressed homosexuality, fastens on gaps or lapses in the text (how else would a neurotic lesbian express herself but in avoidances?) and overlooks much of the novel's deliberate reticence. Leaska simply cannot believe Woolf means what she says:

> For surely, Mrs. Woolf, so delicate an analyst of human relations, would
> not have written a novel of one hundred and seventy pages merely to
> prove her point that "it is no use trying to sum up people."[7]

Validity is Leaska's God (just as proportion will be Dr. Bradshaw's in *Mrs.
Dalloway*), and so for him a novel that discounts all truth must be trying
to repress an ugly truth. For Leaska, Woolf's sexual preference is that
repressed truth missing from the text, and so he "returns" it to a position
of prominence—in effect, rewriting her novel. Perhaps this is why Leaska
repeatedly refers to her as *Mrs.* Woolf throughout his book: to underscore
her marital status and imply unconscious sexual conflict.

   Non-Freudians also react badly to a novel that does not impose its own
resolution. Joan Bennett dismisses it as immature because it

> falls apart. The reader is left with the impression of a series of
> episodes. . . . But the successive moments build up no whole that
> can be *held in the mind*. . . . [The reader's] attention is dissipated and
> diffused. Too many disassociated, or only tenuously related, demands
> have been made upon it.[8]

What is at issue here is the process of reading. Bennett, like the character
Bonamy, wants to hold a unified idea of the novel in her mind. She is
not content to let her experience exist in that "semi-transparent envelope"
Woolf calls creative perception when it can convey/elicit objective and
subjective knowledge simultaneously (*Common Reader* 154), because Bennett
assumes that reading is largely a receptive activity: it moves from author,
who supplies ideas, to reader, who holds them. Like Professor Sopwith,
Bennett regards reading as an extraction of an essential ore, a purification
of complexity. Such assumptions lead another critic to conclude that a
fictional order should not be lifelike:

> In a world which does not offer any simple connections, human
> understanding can only be achieved with great diligence. Order, if it is
> to exist at all, must be man-made, and the need to create one's own
> order, which the very form of the novel makes imperative, is insisted
> upon throughout *Jacob's Room*. . . . *Jacob's Room* is filled with people
> struggling to formulate coherent perceptions to sustain them through
> the welter of impressions and experiences constantly assailing them.
> The wide variety of human testimony we have concerning Jacob's
> appearance and behavior not only suggests the difficulty of knowing
> him but also the urgency of such a task.[9]

The "urgency" of the need to "formulate coherent perceptions" lies, not in the narrative form itself, but in the reader who imitates Betty Flanders, the Cambridge professors, and young Bonamy. Even James Hafley, who momentarily considers a provocative question ("Are there not *two* interpretations of experience" in this novel?), seeks closure by concluding that *Jacob's Room* is not "a completely accomplished work of art" because its potential for meaning exists neither in Jacob nor in the narrator.[10]

If we consider *Jacob's Room* to be a complete and deliberate work, then we must ask again, are there two interpretations of experience operating here, so that even a neutral object like a lantern set in the forest supports mutually exclusive views, is both a beacon of order and a spur to incomprehensible frenzy? In her essay "Phases of Fiction," Woolf theorizes that authors in the past beheld life as one and entire, but that modern life contains such discord and incongruity that authors can now offer only a divided response (*Granite and Rainbow*). She rates Daniel Defoe the chief of "the great truth-tellers," because he "assures us that things are precisely as [he says] they are." For Defoe's reader,

> to believe seems the greatest of all pleasures. . . . [E]mphasis is laid upon the very facts that most reassure us of stability in real life, upon money, furniture, food, until we seem wedged among solid objects in a solid universe.
> . . . Defoe presided over his universe with the omnipotence of a God, so that his world is perfectly in scale. (*Granite and Rainbow* 95–96)

Woolf argues that Defoe's readers wanted, not a record of consciousness as it was—insecure, unstable, inconclusive—but an illusory fabrication of life as it should be—predictable, ordered, and profitable—according to the capitalistic cultural values of the eighteenth century. For the modern age, however, mind and reality are no longer unities:

> Feelings which used to come single and separate do so no longer. . . . Emotions which used to enter the mind whole are now broken up on the threshold. . . . In the modern mind beauty is accompanied not by its shadow but by its opposite. (*Granite and Rainbow* 16)

We cannot reduce the multiplicity of experience (which is "infinitely beautiful yet repulsive" [12]) into a single vision, because "it is as if the modern mind, wishing always to verify its emotions, had lost the power of accepting anything simply for what it is" (16–17). Omniscience is too unreal to be acceptable in a novel that seeks to record truthfully the "shower of innumerable atoms," the "myriad impressions" (*Common Reader* 154) that constitute consciousness of modern life. Since meaning itself is "provisional" and since modern novelists doubt any form of belief, they now "are forcing the form they use to contain a meaning which is strange to it" (*Granite and Rainbow* 11), a meaning so disordered that it literally cannot be stated.

Jinny Carslake is the only character in *Jacob's Room* who achieves such a "modern" perspective. She occupies a reading space that lies between Mrs. Flanders's aggressive solipsism and Mrs. Jarvis's passive receptivity, between the critics' insistence on order and the narrator's relinquishing of authority. Jinny cherishes "a little jeweller's box containing ordinary pebbles picked off the road" and arranged in an apparently meaningless pattern: "But if you look at them steadily, she says, multiplicity becomes unity, which is somehow the secret of life" (*Jacob's Room* 131). The passage is terse and ambiguous, but, whatever Jinny thinks she sees, her method is suggestive because it ties together the novel's imagery, its narrative reticence, and modes of manic-depressive perception. Viewed objectively, Jinny's stones have no order, no unity, no meaning. Viewed subjectively, the stones uncannily invite her contributions, and any meaning is possible. Indeed, meaning itself is unimportant here. Woolf focuses on the relationship between Jinny and the stones through which some kind, any kind, of meaning is gained. Readers of *Jacob's Room* face the same problem when they move from subjective approaches (intuiting the essence of Jacob from our emotional reactions to him) to objective (deducing Jacob's character from such factual evidence as his love of Donne's poems): each perspective presents its own Jacob Flanders. Jinny has gone beyond this dilemma by recognizing an order that does exist, not in the stones exclusively, nor in herself exclusively, but *between* the two. A "hidden order," it cannot be spelled out, because it has more than one origin and more than one kind of cognitive structure. It is not the enforced unity of the depressed ego's mechanical analysis, or the uninvited disorder of pure mania, or the sole property of the stones. Its integration of all three without prejudice is the secret of life for a manic-depressive.

To begin integration we must accept chaos wholly, syncretistically. It is only then that we can create/discover a satisfying order in what we have perceived. To gain this paradoxical sense of order's origin, primary- and secondary-process thinking must be coordinated, but in a way that defies classical psychoanalysis. Anton Ehrenzweig provides us with a useful construct by defining syncretistic vision as a global, unanalytical view attained through an unconscious scanning that does not differentiate detail (as the authoritative ego acting alone would). Traditional Freudian thought viewed the unconscious as lacking structure because it "does not distinguish between opposites, fails to articulate space and time as we know it, and allows all firm boundaries to melt in a free chaotic mingling of forms."[11] Since fiction is usually regarded as the embodiment of rigorous organization (since "*everything is there not by chance, but by choice,*" as Leaska says),[12] we have traditionally assumed that a novel is primarily shaped by the conscious mind extracting bits and pieces from the boiling cauldron of unconscious thoughts (even if the ego represses latent meaning). For Ehrenzweig, however, primary-process thinking only *appears* chaotic. The artist and his audience must rely on unconscious scanning to provide the "hidden order" that conscious analysis cannot:

> The chaos of the unconscious is as deceptive as the chaos of outer reality. . . . [C]reative work succeeds in coordinating the results of unconscious undifferentiation and conscious differentiation and so reveals the hidden order in the unconscious. . . . The artist, too, has to face chaos in his work before unconscious scanning brings about the integration of his work as well as of his own personality. . . . [U]nconscious scanning makes use of undifferentiated modes of vision that to normal awareness would seem chaotic.[13]

Ehrenzweig redefines the notion of repression: some images, too personal to be shared with anybody, have been withdrawn from consciousness because of the superego's censorship of "certain offensive *contents,*" but others, so impersonal they are shared by all, become inaccessible because of their "undifferentiated *structure* alone":[14]

> What appears ambiguous, multi-evocative or open-ended on a conscious level becomes a single serial structure with quite firm boundaries on an unconscious level. Because of its wider sweep low-level [syncretistic] vision can serve as the precision instrument for scanning far-flung structures offering a great number of choices. Such structures recur regularly in any creative search.[15]

The artist discovers the hidden order of a seemingly chaotic reality by associating it with unconscious, seemingly chaotic fantasy material; when the connections are made, order is perceived and meaning is gained because perception has been personalized. Self and object are now related in a deeply personal way, which, as Jinny says, "is somehow the secret of life."

The advantage of Ehrenzweig's theory lies in his redefinition of artistic unity in concord with Woolf's experience of bipolar cognitive styles. Conscious perception tries, as Leslie's agitated depressive rationalism did, to smooth over the gaps, imperfections, or incoherence of open material; the ego's need for clarity rounds off discontinuous structures by a narrow focus on a limited number of details. Syncretistic vision, like Anne's hypomania, scans without focus and allows us to grasp widely scattered deviations without premature ordering.[16] John Custance followed roughly the same procedure when he facilitated his all-inclusive manic visions through "a sort of relaxation of the focusing of my eyes" and of his analytical powers, which allowed his energized imagination to scan visual images and bring unconscious associations to the surface:

> In periods of acute mania [visions] can appear almost like a continuous cinema performance, particularly if there are any complicated and variable light-patterns with which my optical mechanism can play the necessary tricks. These visions generally appear on the walls of my room, if these are shiny enough to reflect light. They are infinitely varied, and bear a close relation to the processes of thought passing in my mind at the time. They are obvious products of the Unconscious, which in this state is of course largely in control of my mind.[17]

Neither Woolf nor Custance locates meaning either strictly or metaphorically in the specific ideas brought up from the unconscious. They are more interested in form than in latent content, in how to integrate manic dedifferentiation (that is, global, uncritical perception of divergent detail) and depressive analysis without specifying a restrictive formula.

The modernist goal of expressing this sense of multiplicity is likewise "incompatible with [the] design and order" of the novel (*Granite and Rainbow* 143). To avoid becoming merely theory-ridden or a Rorschach test gone wild, fiction must give the reader room to experience a problematical reading that is to some extent *uncorrected and uncontrolled by the author's ego*. *Jacob's Room* provides that space in which a reader can experience discontinuity, uncertainty, ambiguity, without either feeling wedged, like Defoe's audience, by objective knowledge, or lapsing into wild projection. A subjective-objective view is possible if the author refuses to verify the reader's response on a conscious level.

How the artist can tolerate order and disorder has been described by Ehrenzweig as "the three phases of creativity." He relates these phases to Melanie Klein's manic and depressive modes of early perception as the child tries to heal the fragmentation of self and world during weaning:

[T]he dual rhythm of projection and introjection can be conceived as
an alternation between the paranoid-schizoid and depressive positions
as described by Melanie Klein. . . . The creative process can thus be
divided into three stages: an initial ("schizoid") stage of projecting
fragmented parts of the self into the work; unacknowledged split-off
elements will then easily appear accidental, fragmented, unwanted and
persecutory. The second ("manic") phase initiates unconscious scanning
that integrates art's substructure. . . . Then creative dedifferentiation
tends towards a "manic" oceanic limit where all differentiation ceases.
The inside and outside world begin to merge. . . . In the third stage
of re-introjection part of the work's hidden substructure is taken back
into the artist's ego on a higher mental level. Because the undifferentiated
substructure necessarily appears chaotic to conscious analysis, the third
stage too is beset with often severe anxiety. But if all goes well, anxiety
is no longer persecutory (paranoid-schizoid) as it was in the first stage
of fragmented projection. It tends to be depressive.[18]

By itself, mood cannot integrate self and object, but it does provide the
alterations of view needed to gather the material for creative work. It is
precisely this rhythmical movement through various levels of our mental
organization, each level informed by or responding to another, that is lacking in psychotic thinking. In psychosis, undifferentiated impulses erupt
explosively from the unconscious, dismembering self-structure, or else the
conscious mind becomes so "split off" from the unconscious that the individual seems to have lost emotional and ideational depth. What psychosis
and creativity share is

a partial dissolution of the ego. The important difference between the
two phenomena, on the other hand, is the fact that creative artists are
obviously able to alternate between contrary modes of perception.
Thus, from a psychoanalytic viewpoint, their egos must be extremely
strong, and in this they differ from psychotics, the weakness of whose
egos makes it almost impossible for them to exercise voluntary control
over the alternation between opposed kinds of thinking.[19]

These two "opposed kinds of thinking" have been defined simply in
terms of Freud's introspectively based distinction between conscious and
unconscious. Research in neuroscience, however, offers us a complication
that may enrich our understanding of why art is so multi-layered and compelling: different styles of thinking may also be divided between left and
right hemispheres of the brain. In the split-brain study, surgeons cut the
two hundred million nerve fibers in the corpus callosum, the interface
between the two hemispheres. When each hemisphere is tested separately,

distinct cognitive styles become apparent. To what extent these differences are significant is still controversial, and my summary is necessarily over-simplified, but it will show how important and exciting future research may be for establishing connections between brain function and literary theory. In general, the dominant hemisphere (usually the left) has superior analytic and verbal skills because of its talent for sequential processing; the nondominant hemisphere (usually the right) is adept at processing imagery, visuospatial, musical, and holistic data and plays a major role in responding to emotional stimuli.[20] Left hemisphere skill lies in processing with a substitutive semantic code—words—whereas right hemisphere cognition is syncretistic and analogical. Right hemisphere talents are useful in detecting novel or unexpected events, identifying patterns that are illegible or obscured by random interference, and extrapolating from incomplete information[21]—very like Ehrenzweig's structural unconscious. Because of its talent for a nonlinear mode of association rather than syllogistic logic, the right hemisphere arrives at solutions to problems based on multiple converging determinants rather than on a single causal chain; it produces metaphors, puns, and "word-pictures."[22] One psychiatrist discusses this intriguing connection between hemispheric style and global-versus-analytic cognitive styles in terms reminiscent of Leslie and Anny's temperaments:

> In the obsessive-compulsive personality, whose rigid intellectualization and penchant for detail suggest a left-hemisphere cognitive style, we find a restricted affective [mood] life with something of a negative tone. Is this a characterization of an exaggerated left hemisphere in personality? In the hysteric personality, on the other hand, whose global and undifferentiated cognitive style suggests a relatively greater right-hemisphere contribution, we find affective lability, a tendency to deny problems, and Pollyannish optimism. Are these the affective characteristics that emerge when the right hemisphere makes the major contribution to personality organization?[23]

It would seem likely, then, that the alterations in cognitive style we see in manic-depressive illness involve a disintegration of left hemisphere and right hemisphere cooperation.[24] A review of neuropsychological studies of interhemispheric activity in patients with affective illness shows a "surprising degree of consistency" in reports that people with depressive and manic-depressive illness, as a group, "typically demonstrate deficits in right hemisphere or nondominant hemisphere functioning."[25] Depression seems especially to correlate with right hemisphere impairment, which is associated with an inability to integrate thoughts or relate elements in a

complex pattern. Mania, on the other hand, is associated with left hemisphere impairment more than depression is.[26] The right hemisphere sensitivity to context may be important for the experience of emotion; without
benefit of the right-hemisphere attentional powers, the left hemisphere
may produce either flights of confused fancy and loosened logic in mania
or impoverished imagination and isolated judgment in depression.

Intriguingly, some researchers have found that they can induce manic
or depressive states by injecting sodium amytal into the blood vessels
leading to the hemispheres. Anesthetizing the right hemisphere produces
euphoria, giddiness, or a manic state; anesthetizing the left hemisphere
produces depressive symptoms. Although other studies have not consistently
replicated these results, these findings have spurred experiments which
underscore the importance of interhemispheric activity in mood states:
electroconvulsive therapy more often produces depression when applied
unilaterally to the left hemisphere and euphoric responses when applied to
the right hemisphere.[27] Could the rhythmical alternation between mania
and depression be related to a switching of dominance patterns between left
hemisphere and right hemisphere? Could we eventually explain "mixed"
states, which combine features of mania and depression, as a simultaneous
dysfunction in both hemispheres? If both hemispheres participate in the
depressive syndrome, then perhaps the right hemisphere dysfunction produces the mood component, the left hemisphere dysfunction the cognitive
and anxiety components. Dividing responsibility for the production of
mood disorders between the hemispheres might explain, first, why manic-
depressives fail to introspect the cause of a mood shift (and so arrive at
specious explanations), for the word-fluent, model-building left hemisphere
cannot gain privileged access to all right hemisphere activities; second, why
those who suffer mixed mood states, such as agitated depression, exhibit
symptoms of both mania and depression simultaneously (for the hemispheric dysfunctions combine); and, third, why, although depressives
derive some benefit from cognitive therapy, it cannot cure their mood
swings; for word-based strategies may help the linguistically adept left
hemisphere reorganize some of its functions but give little aid to the
language-deficient right hemisphere.

To complicate matters even further, it is possible that the hemispheres
themselves may be divided into sections (brain quadrants), each of which
may affect the operation of the others.[28] For instance, in a study of trauma-
induced brain damage to the right hemisphere, it was found that the closer
the injury to the frontal pole, the more severe the depression, a fact which

has led to the theory that the manic-depressive syndrome reflects largely right hemisphere frontotemporal dysfunction. The two hemispheres may be involved in a reciprocal relationship whose functioning depends on the specific emotion being regulated:

> The right and left controlling systems are themselves under active reciprocal interaction through transcallosal [interhemispheric] neural inhibition. In this manner, anger, euphoria, paranoid mood is evoked when the nondominant [usually the right] hemisphere no longer controls the dominant [usually the left-hemisphere] systems, together with verbal-motor disinhibition. When on the other hand the nondominant regions are no longer under dominant control, the emotional-catastrophic reaction, dysphoric emotions of anxiety or sadness are released. When the cerebral disorganization is principally restricted to the nondominant hemisphere, the depressive phase of the manic-depressive syndrome supervenes. At a certain threshold the dominant hemisphere becomes activated, triggering the manic phase.[29]

The brain's responses are complex: the two hemispheres share a variety of neurotransmitters, and metabolic activity is altered in multiple areas in both hemispheres during episodes of mood disorder. Thus, to build a comprehensive explanatory model for manic-depressive illness, researchers will have take into consideration not only metabolic and neurohormonal changes but both interhemispheric and intrahemispheric mechanisms. The outcome of future research along these lines may well have profound significance for an integrative mind/brain model, and that in turn will surely affect how literary critics think about authors and texts in the future.

But one step at a time. For now, I argue that Ehrenzweig's three stages of creativity (and Jinny's "secret" resolution of subjective-objective perception) describe a successful interhemispheric integration of bipolar cognitive styles. The rhythmic alternation between analysis and undifferentiated perception, between depressive ordering and manic expansiveness in artistic composition (or between the "analytical ego" and the "ill" ego during a psychoanalytic session),[30] may be due to a complex job-sharing program between the two hemispheres, each responding and contributing to the other's method of coping with a perceptual problem. Thus, Ehrenzweig's structural unconscious—a region beyond awareness that represses, not because of conflicted content, but because the material is structurally incompatible with rationalistic consciousness—may not be a part of Freud's unconscious; it may actually be a *co*-conscious module that is not readily available to the ego. In Freudian terms, each hemisphere may have its own ego, the left hemisphere ego with a talent for organizing a word-based account of analyzed perceptions, the right hemisphere ego sensitive to data that defy closure, stasis, and theory. The successful integration of the two (and inclusion of other unconscious material, if required and/or related) deepens, enriches, and personalizes experience, which may explain why humankind has always found art endlessly suggestive and yet satisfying on a level often beyond words.

If the right hemisphere is co-conscious, why would its scanning be perceived as "unconscious"? When the two hemispheres are surgically separated, the left hemisphere *is convinced it knows* what stimuli or information was presented by experimenters to only the right hemisphere, although it can only be making a guess. If, for instance, the right hemisphere is told to rub the left hemisphere–controlled right elbow, the left hemisphere perceives the action and may assert, with a surprising degree of certainty, that *it* was responsible for the action and offer a reasonable explanation ("I was only scratching an itch," or "I guess I'm nervous"). The word-fluent left hemisphere implicitly and habitually denies that another conscious (but often word-deficient) center exists.[31] Connected hemispheres, of course, do share information, but this operation is seamlessly integrated: the left hemisphere is not aware that some of its data may be coming from and processed by another, well-organized conscious entity, for whom it is speaking. One of the most prominent features of left hemisphere consciousness is that it uses all data—whatever its origin and shape—as material for the fiction that a unitary experience has been reported by a unified self. Typically, the patient reports verbally that he regards his left hemisphere–controlled, right-hand actions as *his* actions, carried out by *his* ego; if left-hand behaviors defy explanation (e.g., the left hand pulls down pants the right hand is trying to pull up), they are viewed as "alien," as "not mine." This has led some researchers to conclude that the subjectively experienced self in these patients lies in the dominant, linguistically skilled hemisphere.[32] Thus, in creative individuals, the officially designated left hemisphere ego, though not privy to the details of dissociated activities operating in the nondominant hemisphere, nevertheless finds itself inexplicably benefiting from them if it can engage in the tricky business of self-relating while object-relating.

Perhaps, then, the "unthought but known" countertransference material (see p. 83, above) is "unthought" by the left hemisphere but "known" by the right hemisphere; making it intelligible to the left hemisphere (and therefore to the speaking patient) would resemble the process of classical psychoanalysis, but it would require a more sophisticated and flexible approach, for the search would be for material that might be (1) unconscious because forbidden, (2) unconscious because structurally incompatible with analytical thought, (3) co-conscious but not represented because filtered, or (4) co-conscious but not represented linguistically. In a clinical setting, items 1 and 3 would require the traditional Freudian deciphering of symbols to discover why the repressed material is not available, but 2 and 4 would be distorted by a Freudian reading imposed by left hemisphere cognitive style upon right hemisphere material. We may even find that the activity of the "alien subject," who reads the same text we do but experiences (beyond our awareness) a different response, also involves co-conscious interhemispheric activity.[33] At the very least, we may surmise that Woolf's rhythmical shuffling between manic and depressive cognitive styles permitted her to experience various left hemisphere and right hemisphere operations, giving her a sensitivity to the cognitive components of artistic creativity that went far beyond the Freudian formulations of repression and displacement so popular in her day.

In sum, the creative artist constructs a projective/introjective, conscious/unconscious, left-hemisphere analytical/right-hemisphere syncretistic view just as manic-depressives must construct an inclusive core self out of their several moody selves. Readers must do the same; they must accept Jacob as he is presented to us—a fragment, a figment of our imagination, what you will, and yet real, because we have felt him, though we cannot fully articulate why and how. *Jacob's Room* leaves us in a transitional space where we have suspended analysis but have not yet perceived the hidden order that comes when analysis and global empathy find each other. The Jacob we seek exists somewhere between the text and the reader—and between the left hemisphere and the right. That neither Jacob nor the reader achieves a moment of being does not make this an unsuccessful novel. It is, rather, an appropriate precursor to *Mrs. Dalloway* and *To the Lighthouse,* both of which also create this space between objectivity and subjectivity but, in addition, fill the void.

Jacob's Room seems to be aimed primarily at reeducating the reader to abandon assumptions about the novel as a form. In "Phases in Fiction," Woolf contends that psychological novels should free us from premature belief:

> Besides this fineness and sweetness we get another pleasure which
> comes when the mind is freed from the perpetual demand of the
> [traditional] novelist that we shall feel with his characters. By cutting
> off the responses which are called out in actual life, the novelist frees

us to take delight, *as we do when ill* or travelling, in things in themselves. We can see the strangeness of them only when habit has ceased to immerse us in them, and we stand outside watching what has no power over us one way or the other. Then we see the mind at work. (*Granite and Rainbow* 122; my italics)

Woolf frustrates our efforts to categorize this novel as one or another kind of perceptual experience or to feel confident that Jacob is real enough for us to empathize with him. We finish our reading in that semi-transparent envelope, awaiting an interhemispheric fusion that may never come. If we feel abandoned, it is because we have been freed to discover/create our own experience of the novel. If we feel a blank where Jacob should have been, it is because we have not yet joined Woolf in her creation. We have only been invited into Jacob's room; we stand where a creative reading can take place.

9 "The sane & the insane, side by side"

The Object-Relations of Self-Management in Mrs. Dalloway

I like going from one lighted room to another, such is my brain to me; lighted rooms.

(*Diary* 2: 310)

But when the self speaks to the self, who is speaking?—the entombed soul, the spirit driven in, in, in to the central catacomb; the self that took the veil and left the world.

("An Unwritten Novel," in *A Haunted House*)

In *Mrs. Dalloway,* Virginia Woolf complicates the problem of subjective and objective readings by eliminating the self-conscious narrator who so conveniently raised questions of interpretation and cognitive style in *Jacob's Room*. Instead, the reader is led by a shifting and impersonal narration that impartially verbalizes the intimate thoughts of various characters, throwing the reader off balance.[1] The descriptive style, highly ordered and rhythmic, does not change from one character to another. Thus the indirect interior monologues sound curiously alike, blending thoughts together—a provocative act since some of these thoughts are "insane." Woolf pursues James Hafley's question, "Are there not *two* interpretations of experience?"[2] She gives each its own voice, and the mixture disturbs us by revealing common mechanisms at work in psychotic and in normal thinking. Yet despite the mixture of mad and nonmad discourses, in *Mrs. Dalloway* Woolf extends Jinny Carslake's brief vision of a profound unity and expands her own sense of and control over herself in ways that anticipate effective treatments of depression by contemporary cognitive psychologists.

Soon after publishing *Jacob's Room* in 1922, Woolf began writing a short story entitled "Mrs. Dalloway in Bond Street," which quickly expanded beyond her original plans: "Mrs Dalloway has branched into a book; & I adumbrate here a study of insanity & suicide: the world seen by the sane & the insane side by side—something like that" (*Diary* 2: 207). The phrase "something like that" seems particularly apt. Initially, she had planned the novel without the psychotic Septimus, focusing exclusively on Clarissa, who was to die—or commit suicide—at her party. Second thoughts prompted her to divide sanity and insanity between two characters, but she reminded herself to keep them related anyway: "Septimus and Mrs Dalloway should be entirely dependent upon each other" (*Letters* 3: 189). Third thoughts led her to worry as to "whether the book would have been better without" Septimus and the mad scenes (*Diary* 2: 321). Woolf anticipated reader confusion "owing to the lack of connection, visible, between the two themes" (*Diary* 3: 4) and predicted that "reviewers will say that it is disjointed because of the mad scenes not connecting with the Dalloway scenes." But since such a disjunction was not "unreal" psychologically, she hoped her audience would somehow see a connection (*Diary* 2: 323).

Woolf also hesitated over the mad scenes because creating Septimus was "a very intense & ticklish business" (*Diary* 2: 310) for her: "It was a subject that I have kept cooling in my mind until I felt I could touch it without bursting into flame all over. You can't think what a raging furnace it is still to me—madness and doctors and being forced" (*Letters* 3: 180). Remembering madness involved plunging "deep in the richest strata of [her] mind" (*Diary* 2: 323), a metaphor Leonard also used to describe Virginia's sense that insanity lay just beneath the surface of sanity, like a parallel but alien universe:

> If, when she was well, any situation or argument arose which was closely connected with her breakdowns or the causes of them, there would sometimes rise to the surface of her mind traces or echoes of the nightmares and delusions of her madness, so that it seemed as if deep down in her mind she was never completely sane. (*Beginning Again* 79)

Woolf feared being too explicit about Septimus's madness, not only because readers might misunderstand or judge it self-indulgently confessional, but also because dredging up vivid, disturbing, and stressful memories of her breakdowns showed just how transparent was the dividing line between madness and sanity: "Why is life so tragic; so like a little strip of pavement over an abyss. I look down; I feel giddy; I wonder how I am ever to walk to the end. . . . And with it all how happy I am—if it weren't for my feeling that its a strip of pavement over an abyss" (*Diary* 2: 72-73).

This seemingly morbid sensation of walking on the edge of sanity is certainly not unique to Woolf. John Custance used the same image in 1952 (before any of Woolf's diaries had been published) to describe the manic-depressive's relationship to his own illness:

> Normal life and consciousness of "reality" appear to me rather like
> motion along a narrow strip of table-land at the top of a Great Divide
> separating two distinct universes from each other. On the one hand the
> slope is green and fertile, leading to a lovely landscape where love, joy
> and the infinite beauties of nature and of dreams await the traveller; on
> the other a barren, rocky declivity, where lurk endless horrors of distorted
> imagination, descends to the bottomless pit.[3]

Between the fertilizing joy and infinite beauty of mania and the bottomless
pit of depression, normality threads its narrow path, doubly vulnerable
because bipolars have no direct control over when they fall and are often
unaware that they have lost their balance. Mood shifts simply exaggerate
normal modes of perception, cognition, and feeling, so introspection, by
itself, fails to notice the growing discrepancies. Bipolars are repeatedly
deceived and risk losing their sense of themselves as distinct from their
moods. Only when living on the narrow strip of "normality" can anyone
see what self is, is not, has been, can never be.

But how to describe this sense of living out three lives to readers who
have felt only solid ground beneath them, who assume identity is a right
granted by divine law, who believe, as the Victorians did, that a "self-made"
man needed only his earnest free will to gain self-mastery? "Health,"
intones Dr. Holmes, brushing aside Septimus's symptoms, "is largely a
matter of our own control" (138). Holmes decides that there is "nothing
whatever seriously the matter with" Septimus (31), and Dr. Bradshaw
agrees: "'We all have our moments of depression,' said Sir William" (148).
The temptation to deny the reality of mental illness is strong, in readers
too, especially when a writer attempts to depict insanity as somehow
connected to sanity. Blatant, gibbering madness is a convenient, culturally
acceptable stereotype, but manic-depressive illness shades into normal
mentation, and this can be much more threatening.[4] Manic-depressives
are usually aware (and wary) of this fearful reaction in others, as one patient
(wishing to remain anonymous) expressed it in a letter to the author:

> "normal" people want to either romanticize or ghettoize insanity by
> denying any continuity between the normal self and the insane one,
> when in fact it is the continuity itself that is terrifying. Going out of
> your head . . . isn't nearly so frightening as remaining yourself while
> the universe suddenly goes nuts, as if you are trapped in a Twilight
> Zone episode or a Hitchcock movie where you suddenly realize that
> all these kind people trying to help you get well are really poisoning
> your milk. That's why the general in Dr. Strangelove was so wonderful:
> his insanity was perfectly *logical*. . . . If I had to put my acquired

wisdom in a motto I would say, "Beware of the universe when it starts making sense."[5]

Is it possible, without losing all distinction between the two, to be explicit about such a profound sense of unreality so closely connected to normal life? Or is the difference between sanity and insanity too great to bridge without destroying its frightening subtlety and power? The paradox of manic-depressive illness is that it is both familiar and strange, obvious and transparent, sane and insane, posing special formal problems for a fiction that purports to express it.

Although an omniscient narrator would seem an ideal device by which to make such connections visible, Woolf instead chose an impersonal and limited narration. Its refusal to discuss how it makes interpretations concerning what is described or overheard creates an "ambiguity of perspective" that gives "the 'hazy' effect so often ascribed to impressionist fiction as well as painting."[6] Only broad brushstrokes paint these characters' pasts. Of Septimus's childhood we know only that his mother had "lied" (127). But what lie? How was it significant? Or was it one of Septimus's delusions? We are not furnished with the objective truth of the characters' experiences, but only with an "uncertainty and ambiguity, multiplicity and mystery [that] are integral to impressionist epistemology."[7] Septimus's "betrayal" carries equal weight with Clarissa's irretrievable past, Peter's bruised memories, and Miss Kilman's spiritual conversion. Circumstances become irrelevant when events are universal. Such a technique effectively muddles characterization,[8] which explicates Woolf's reminder to herself in her diary: "Characters are to be merely views: personality must be avoided at all costs. . . . Directly you specify hair, age, &c something frivolous, or irrelevant, gets into the book" (*Diary* 2: 265). Although Peter Walsh's sexual affairs in India differentiate his life from Doris Kilman's cramped and pernicious religiosity in a London working-class slum, these circumstantial facts come to us in the form of reflections that resemble one another in style and tone.[9] The details wash out, and what is left is universal: the structure of disappointments, ecstasies, hopes, and despairs ubiquitous in human life.

To avoid creating distinguishable voices, Woolf generally eschews dialogue, preferring authorial summaries of conversations. What little action does occur serves only as a spur to further reflection:

> Almost all of the characters' thoughts in *Mrs. Dalloway* are daydreams of one kind or another. Relatively little of the inner monologues are related to or determined by the actual circumstantial context. . . .

> Because so much of the novel is given over to the relatively uninterrupted
> flow of daydreams and meditations controlled by an authorial voice,
> the book has an almost seamless quality.[10]

Daydreaming is stylized by mood. How we create and interact with our
daydreams (which can become objects in their own right, reassuring or
terrifying, exciting or depressing) serves as a model for how we relate to
others and to self. We are perpetually engaged in a complex relationship
with ourselves as objects, either through self-management or representa-
tionally, through self-objectification—or both, as when in subvocal thinking
we talk to ourselves as if we were talking to another person. Analyst
Christopher Bollas uses his own experience as an illustration:

> As I have been planning this chapter, for example, I have thought
> from the second person pronoun objectifying myself to say: "You must
> include Winnicott and Khan because much of your thinking comes from
> their work." . . . This constant objectification of the self for purposes
> of thinking is commonplace. It is also a form of object relation, as Freud
> so sagely understood when he evolved his theory of the superego to
> identify that part of the mind that speaks to us as its object. Naturally
> this intrasubjective relationship will change according to the person's
> state of mind.[11]

Peter Walsh also casts his daydreams in the second person. When he follows
an anonymous woman across Trafalgar Square, he imagines that she silently
calls to him, using "not Peter, but his private name which he called himself
in his own thoughts. 'You,' she said, only 'you'" (79). In this way Peter
flirts with himself when he feels romantically adventurous; he need not
involve the woman at all except as a transitional object embodying his own
inflated desires.[12]

Daydreams are ideal barometers of mood. Modulations of self-esteem,
an essential feature of mood swings, can be detected in our intrasubjective
transactions—how we value, and are valued by, figures in our inner dramas.
Mood itself is but a view, a slanted transaction. Seamlessly shifting from
daydream to daydream allows Woolf to express the subtlest aspect of bipolar
illness: its transparent connections with normal mentality, the ups and
downs of establishing personal value within a social context, its fluctuations,
which can obscure the point of departure from Woolf's "little pavement,"
from sanity. Each major character in the novel participates in this common
life of self-representation, comprising various aspects of Woolf's experience
of manic-depressive states. By focusing on intrasubjective relations, she

explores the parameters of her experience of bipolar illness: the egotistical precursor state (Peter), the psychotic "mixed" state (Septimus), and the euthymic state (Clarissa), which attempts to integrate the other two.

Because Woolf and her doctors believed that egotism presaged a shift from normal to ill mentation, and because she valued facing disappointments squarely, she designed Peter's daydreams to be egotistical compensation for his failures. As a youth, he had quarreled so often with Clarissa that she married his opposite, the quiet but effective Richard Dalloway. Sent down from Oxford, Peter left England, hastily wedded a woman aboard ship, formed an adulterous liaison in India, and has now returned to London to arrange, half-heartedly, for Daisy's divorce. Fifty-three years old, he is unemployed and still obsessed with the one woman he has never been able to conquer. But he daydreams of romantic adventures and future successes, entertaining elated fantasies that leave him with little patience for Clarissa's real needs and desires.

Significantly, Peter's divided style of self-representation elicits divided responses from readers. Some critics take the part of Peter's worst fears, condemning him as an "awkward outsider," a "shadowy identity," a "passive, ineffectual, and self-defeating" man who exploits his worthlessness, who resorts to self-humiliation and childishness in order to extract motherly concern from Clarissa.[13] Other critics are caught up in Peter's self-indulgent mythology of inner strength and forcefulness, and so they admonish his carnal passion and the masculine, sexual threat he presents to Clarissa's psychic autonomy, as if he personified "that repulsive brute with blood-red nostrils, human nature . . . that passionate and penetrating and soul-destroying love."[14] Both critical views replicate Peter's dealings with himself as an object as he feels alternately powerful and degraded. Of course, such identification helps readers to experience a character's mental states, but empathy is not always understanding. If we become too entangled in Peter's self-representations, we will fail to see Woolf's larger design.

In daydreams Peter lives out mildly bipolar subject-object transactions by creating idealized objects and expectations that are repeatedly destroyed. On a walk about town, Peter exhibits typical hypomanic euphoria, extolling London as a "splendid achievement," unknown butlers as "admirable," and chance girls as "evanescent"; to his appreciative eyes motorcars arrive "accurately, punctually, noiselessly, there, precisely at the right instant" (82). Casual bystanders are "capable," "punctual," "alert, robust," "wholly admirable, good fellows, to whom one would entrust one's life"

(83). A battered old woman's incoherent song sounds to Peter like a primeval, timeless, transcendent ode to love, "love which has lasted a million years" (122–23). Admitting his "susceptibility to impressions" because of "these alternations of mood; good days, bad days, for no reason whatever," he finds himself falling in love with every woman he meets— they are all "blooming," elegant, "becoming" (107)—and life itself seems "absorbing, mysterious, of infinite richness" (248). Captivated by his exaggeration of the goodness of the objects he sees, he yearns to possess them all, impelled by "three great emotions" that "bowled over him; understanding; a vast philanthropy; and . . . an irrepressible, exquisite delight; as if inside his brain by another hand strings were pulled, shutters moved, and he, having nothing to do with it," feels so "utterly free" that he pursues a young woman, a stranger,

> who, as she passed Gordon's statue, seemed, Peter Walsh thought (susceptible as he was), to shed veil after veil, until she became the very woman he had always had in mind; young, but stately; merry, but discreet; black, but enchanting. (78–79)

Once he has reassured himself that "she was not worldly, like Clarissa; not rich, like Clarissa," he can fancy himself "an adventurer, reckless . . . swift, daring . . . a romantic buccaneer." As she enters her house, he ends his fantasy abruptly: "Well, I've had my fun. . . . [T]his escapade with the girl; made up, as one makes up the better part of life, he thought— *making oneself up*" (81; my italics).

What has Peter made up, and how is it fun? He exaggerates the value of every object he sees including himself; desire and self-confidence are dilated by "moments of extraordinary exaltation. Nothing exists outside us except a state of mind, he thinks" (85). Like Melanie Klein's manic infant (and Woolf in her yellow grape), whose needs are all magically met, Peter floats buoyantly in an oceanic bliss incorporating everything around him. He is full of promise and energy—as long as the stranger does not resemble Clarissa. If the woman knew him as Clarissa does, the bubble would burst. Thus, the chase can never be completed. When he must face Clarissa's unspoken criticism, that "his whole life had been a failure" (11), he defensively idealizes her, endowing her with magical qualities: "(for in some ways no one understood him, felt with him, as Clarissa did)— their exquisite intimacy" (68). She has "that woman's gift," he decides, "of making a world of her own wherever she happened to be" (114). Peter's generalization of her value—it is not her gift alone, but all women's—

reveals the problem. Her individuality is glossed over by his exalted mood. Only in elated fantasy can a woman satisfy his desire.

In the opposite mood Peter criticizes Clarissa, for the reality of her can never live up to his fictions. The stranger he chases in Trafalgar Square is "the very woman he had always had in mind," a perfect amalgamation of antithetical qualities, but she has no identity; she mirrors back whatever he projects. Clarissa breaks the spell because she will not serve as glorifying mirror to his illusions;[15] she objectifies his self-hatred and becomes his scapegoat. Although he finds Daisy's undiscriminating adoration a bit of a bore, it is what he expects of a woman. He accuses Clarissa of coldness, of withholding the "woman's gift" that might have saved him from himself:

> For Heaven's sake, leave your knife alone! she cried to herself in
> irrepressible irritation; it was his silly unconventionality, his weakness;
> his lack of the ghost of a notion what any one else was feeling that
> annoyed her, had always annoyed her; and now at his age, how silly!
>   I know all that, Peter thought; I know what I'm up against. (69)

Peter recognizes her evaluation of him. Indeed, he cherishes it like a lover's keepsake and perpetuates the pain through a vainglorious daydreaming that has literally replaced Clarissa as a love-object. In his mind, Clarissa is responsible for the image she mirrors back to him; her failure to return his illusions and magnify his value is what has "reduced him" (121) to an ass. Like an infant who perceives disappointment in his mother's look, he reads it as lack of self-worth and fulfills her prophecy.[16]

Although his first impulse is to deny what he sees in Clarissa's look, Peter loses control of his pose as a martyr for love:

> I know all that, Peter thought; I know what I'm up against, he
> thought, running his finger along the blade of his knife, Clarissa and
> Dalloway and all the rest of them; but I'll show Clarissa—and then to
> his utter surprise, suddenly thrown by those uncontrollable forces
> thrown through the air, he burst into tears; wept; wept *without the least
> shame,* sitting on the sofa, the tears running down his cheeks.
>   And Clarissa had leant forward, taken his hand, drawn him to her,
> kissed him,—actually had felt his face on hers . . . holding his hand,
> patting his knee. (69; my italics)

Many critics find this a difficult scene, because the knife invites phallic readings, and Clarissa's refusal to respond is regarded as evidence of her frigidity and Peter's impotence. Why Peter cries is indeed connected to what he does with his knife, but the knife is not necessarily a symbol of childish insecurity about virility or an indictment of Clarissa's "mascu-linity."[17] Critics who see the knife as a sexual symbol interpret Peter's tears as a defeat, as if we were watching a scene of symbolic emasculation rather than realization. Woolf first referred to a pocketknife in her diary in 1918, when her cousin Harry Stephen paid a visit: "He still takes out an enor-mous pocket knife, & slowly half opens the blade, & shuts it" (*Diary* 1: 151). Like Peter, Harry had just returned from India "an undoubted failure," irresponsible and egotistical, feeling fully justified in dictating to others how they should behave, unaware of any contradiction between his behavior and his advice (*Diary* 1: 150, 221). Harry's blade was not phallic; it was an emblem of his egotistical blindness. What Peter loses, then, is an illusion about himself that requires the cooperation of an object: a woman, a daydream, a knife. When Clarissa interrupts the solipsistic pathway of Peter's self-generated illusions, he sees himself as she sees him. He desires her, not as a sexual partner, but as a perceptual partner.[18] His elaborate egotistical illusions about civilization and manly adventurism end in disillusionment, because he has severed the connection between self and world.

The novel's frequent use of the word *cut* suggests a deep interest in "divisive activities," in disconnections (41).[19] Clarissa's mirroring momen-tarily forces Peter to integrate what had been split. Her motherliness reassures him that integration is not equivalent to self-destruction; it is only a safer form of *dis*-illusionment, a destruction of disconnectedness. She tries to heal the cut of his knife. If Peter's object-relational style is based on Leslie Stephen's, as seems likely, then Woolf is saying that her father erred by indulging his cyclothymic moodiness, using it to induce a woman to comfort him, to act as a mirror magnifying his size. By implica-tion, Woolf here accepts the fact that Leslie was subject to moods beyond his control but objects to the games he played to trick others into dealing with his internal crises. By refusing to accede to Peter's demands, Clarissa brings him to the realization that his emotions, even the painful and depressive ones, are endurable if he will only face them. As long as moods are nonpsychotic, the individual possesses the capacity to make self-corrections based on a mirroring relationship with the external world.

Whereas Peter's cut is self-indulgent and treatable, Septimus's injury is psychotic and involuntary. Like Peter, Septimus creates illusions, endow-ing certain objects with value, but, unlike Peter, Septimus is unaware that he is manipulating objects. He cannot have "fun," because to him his fictions are real. Peter experiences mild disillusionment when his fanciful bubbles burst; he suffers, but only from insights that can benefit him if he chooses to face them. Septimus experiences his intense despair not as an emotion but as a hostile world; no therapeutic insight is possible. Woolf knew by experience that psychotic depression is not just Peter's self-loathing or neurotic denial but seems, to the sufferer, to be an active, corrosive agent loose in the world or in the self. Self-estranged, Septimus is constantly haunted by split-off pieces of himself that appear, inexplicable and strange, in trees, in dogs, in airplanes. Thus, the birds communicate a revelatory message to him alone, but their songs are sung in Greek, which he does not understand; the message originates in himself, but it cannot be reincorporated because it cannot be read. "Knowledge comes through suffering, said Mr. Whittaker" (196), Miss Kilman's minister, but this is true only if the pain can be made intelligible, can be "owned" by the self who feels it. No tears, no realization can heal Septimus's lacerated mind. For him, *integration is equivalent to self-destruction,* because it would require identifying with elements of self he can no longer recognize or understand. This is no comfortable "alien subject" whom we can accept as both different from and a part of us, that we can integrate and thereby use to profit from our expanded receptivity.[20] Septimus's alien fragments remain unreadable. No therapeutic insight is possible when the manic-depressive is severely ill or psychotic, because, under these conditions, altered beliefs—the premises by which all perception, thought, and introspection are evaluated—provide their own corroborating evidence. To see otherwise would deconstruct consciousness.

Woolf's insight here is that psychotic beliefs bear some disturbing similarities to "normal" convictions, as modern psychology now shows. Deluded patients are like normal people in at least one respect: they form theories to explain their experiences.[21] Ordinary events (e.g., stubbing a toe, hearing music in a park) are explained by theories we think are reasonable ("the uneven pavement must have tripped me," we suppose, or "someone's playing a portable tape recorder"). Anomalous experiences (feeling that our body is out of our control, hearing voices inside our head) elicit explanations too. We may conclude that our body is out of control because we are fatigued or, we may worry, perhaps we are manifesting the first signs of multiple sclerosis; the voices could conceivably be radio transmissions picked up by fillings in our teeth. If the voices admonish our behavior (and seem to know details of our personal life), we may theorize that an enemy has commandeered a local radio station and is singling us out for attack. If we believe that God talks to the faithful, we may think that the voice comes directly from him (and this interpretation would make eminent sense of depressive guilt). These are, of course, interpretations made with fairly intact reality testing: the radio station and the enemy and multiple sclerosis are real things. But if we are psychotic, and our experiences are uncanny, mystifying, or ineffable, because a biochemically altered brain mishandles perception, then any explanation that accounts for them may seem bizarre to others.

Some studies show that vivid and detailed delusions often arise from perceptions that lack detail—lines, dots, clicks, buzzes; it is the patient who unknowingly contributes definition.[22] Woolf herself relates such an episode: "One night I lay awake horrified hearing, as I imagined, an obscene old man gasping and croaking and muttering senile indecencies—it was a cat, I was told afterwards; a cat's anguished love making" (*Moments of Being* 123). Woolf replaced nonlinguistic sounds with an intelligible language, but preserved the cat's actual message. In *Mrs. Dalloway,* when a nursemaid spells out a sky-writing advertisement, Septimus experiences isolated letters as if they were already full of profundity:

> "K . . . R . . . " said the nursemaid, and Septimus heard her say "Kay Arr" close to his ear, deeply, softly, like a mellow organ, but with a roughness in her voice like a grasshopper's, which rasped his spine deliciously and sent running up into his brain waves of sound which, concussing, broke. A marvelous discovery indeed—that the human voice in certain atmospheric conditions (for one must be scientific, above all scientific) can quicken trees into life! (32)

What "Kay Arr" means is unimportant; Septimus (and Woolf) focuses on the structure of the perception, connecting it to other intensified sensations. Perception is no longer a neutral conduit for information transferral but has become the message itself.

Intrasubjective structural changes affect subject-world relations. Peter's daydreams are romances in which he is victor, but Septimus's intrasubjective transactions have become nightmares in which he is victim. In normal thinking we may talk to ourselves without speaking, using an implied *you* to mark the split in our subjectivity. In psychosis, a thought can take on an existence and a voice of its own: thinking is literally perceived as an outside event, as a voice intruding on our consciousness. The analyst Bollas's note to himself, "You must include Winnicott and Khan," could in mania be perceived as a divine command ("Thou shalt include Winnicott and Khan") or, in depression, as a verbal attack of hellish proportion

("Include Winnicott and Khan, or you will suffer eternal damnation").
Mood is experienced no longer as an inner state but as an outer reality.

What is worse, Septimus's world has coincidentally colluded with his
paranoia, objectified by military authorities (who can force one to kill
others) and by Doctors Bradshaw and Holmes (who can force one to
kill oneself through "conversion"). The First World War was a psychotic
dream come true. Because of this confabulation between inner and outer
horrors, Septimus's vividly distorted perceptions of ordinary urban life
persecute him with the power with which images of bloody conflict would
assault us. The fact that he never daydreams of the war in violent terms—
instead, civilian life takes on all the terror of battle—dramatizes the split
in his intrasubjective relations. His thoughts cannot even connect his
suffering to his personal history: "But what was his crime? He could not
remember it" (148). Septimus is *guilty of having suffered*—a common
depressive belief, one that common sense tells us should be correctable
by appeals to the patient to reconsider his premorbid actions and feelings
and to recognize that pain is not a sin. But delusional patients, in general,
do not benefit from their accumulated life experiences; their premorbid
judgments, however sane or appropriate, have diminished power against
the immediate force of an uncanny, aberrant, or bizarre belief or experience.[23] Robbed of a meaningful past, of a memorable event that might
explain his emotions, Septimus displaces his despair onto current objects—a
situation that creates further unmeaning, confusion, and terror. Horror
on a battlefield is understandable; horror in Regent's Park is inexplicable
and so doubly frightening. The individual who hallucinates under the
influence of LSD may see beatific or nightmarish visions, but can he be
judged insane if he understands their insubstantiality because he appreciates
their source? To see flames beneath the pavement and say, "That is really
the fear I deny myself; it belongs to me; it is really inside of me," is still
sanity. Septimus cannot make the same connection. In psychosis, the old
saying "seeing is believing" is just as true as "believing is seeing."

Some Freudians attribute Septimus's exaggerated reactions to intelligible
unconscious conflict, speculating that he is actually repulsed by repressed
homosexual feelings for Evans displaced onto symbolic objects.[24] Evidence
for this is scarce; much is made of phallic symbols (trees and bananas),
loaded words like "panic," "crime," and "love," and Septimus's condemnation of human nature, which is narrowly defined as sexual nature. That
homophobia should be singled out as the cause of psychosis tells more,
perhaps, about what these readers fear than what Septimus fears. Septimus's

guilt is too severe to be merely sexual or neurotic. It is not bottled up or repressed or channeled into a specific symptom, but is so active and pervasive that it seems to be an object itself, taking up space in the real world. Septimus is introduced to us as one whose eyes have "that look of apprehension in them which makes complete strangers apprehensive too" (20). He is incapable of analyzing such countertransference, and so the fear he sees in others' eyes only serves to reinforce his suspicion that something outside himself is dreadfully wrong. Faced with a traffic jam, he is terrified that

> some horror had come almost to the surface and was about to burst into flames. . . . The world wavered and quivered and threatened to burst into flames. It is I who am blocking the way, he thought. Was he not being looked at and pointed at; was he not weighted there, rooted to the pavement, for a purpose? But for what purpose? (21)

The world quivers, but it is he who is shaking. The street threatens to burst into flames, but the unintelligible horror exists inside him. In the same manner, the manic-depressive John Custance believed he saw visions in his bedsheets and shadows:

> A crumpled pillow is quite an ordinary everyday object, is it not? One looks at it and thinks no more about it? So is a washing-rag, or a towel tumbled on the floor, or the creases on the side of a bed. Yet they can suggest shapes of the utmost horror to the mind obsessed by fear. Gradually my eyes began to distinguish such shapes, until eventually, whichever way I turned, I could see nothing but devils waiting to torment me, devils which seemed infinitely more real than the material objects in which I saw them. . . .
>
> With these visions surrounding me it is not strange that the material world should seem less and less real. I felt myself to be gradually descending alive into the pit by a sort of metamorphosis of my surroundings. At times the whole universe seemed to be dissolving around me; moving cracks and fissures would appear in the walls and floors. This, incidentally, is a phenomenon which I have often noticed in the opposite state of acute mania, though it has then, of course, a totally different underlying feeling-tone.[25]

Since self and object are confused, mood-disordered patients see the world in terms of internal states (thus "cracks and fissures" cut the world into fragments when Custance himself is fragmented and cut off). Objects and events gain uncanny significance. Nothing in life is accidental for a mind that finds itself "revealed" in the physical world. Depressives often make derogatory statements about objects which are really displaced self-accusations—not through neurotic displacement (to avoid recognition) but because it is difficult for these patients to see themselves *as depressed,* to step outside the mood and perceive the discrepancies in their judgment. Instead they tend to focus on negative aspects of external objects ("life is pointless," "people dislike me," "this food is poison"). Septimus too feels that the world is worthless and degraded, that it cries out for redemption; he hears a cry for help but cannot trace it back to its origin. His suicidal impulses are likewise cut off from their source, creating a vicious circle: he feels he must die because he is depressed, but he thinks he is depressed because the world is murderously insane and wants him to die. Since objects embody his suicidal ideas, Septimus is often afraid to look too closely at them, for "real things were too exciting. He must be cautious. He would not go mad" (215). When he fears madness, he shuts his eyes (32), as if insanity too were an external state imposed upon self: "it must be the fault of the world then—that he could not feel. . . . it might be possible that the world itself is without meaning" (133).

Septimus attempts to deal with his despair by deciphering its meaning, but interpretation is problematical for an isolated mind that projects its moods upon everything it sees. Clifford Beers became convinced that objects contained some obscure symbolic quality directly relating to his inexplicable and indefinable guilt:

> The world was fast becoming to me a stage on which every human being within the range of my senses seemed to be playing a part. . . . [A]ll my senses became perverted. . . . Familiar objects had acquired a different "feel." . . . I began to see handwriting on the sheets of my bed. . . . On each fresh sheet placed over me I would soon begin to see words, sentences, and signatures, all in my own handwriting. Yet I could not decipher any of the words. . . . [W]ith an insane ingenuity I managed to connect myself with almost every crime of importance of which I had ever read.[26]

Septimus also misreads according to his mood swings. When "anxious to improve himself," he reads *Antony and Cleopatra,* which "lit in him a fire as burns only once in a lifetime" (128); when depressed, he regards Shakespeare as debased: "that boy's business of the intoxication of language—*Antony and Cleopatra*—had utterly shrivelled" (133). When manic, "beauty sprang instantly. To watch a leaf quivering in the rush of air was an exquisite joy" (104). Ordinary events assume profound, though inexpressible, significance:

> "It is time," said Rezia.
> The word "time" split its husk; poured its riches over him; and from his lips fell like shells, like shavings from a plane, without his making them, hard, white, imperishable words, and flew to attach themselves to their places in an ode to Time; an immortal ode to Time. (105)

What the word *time* means, Woolf does not say; she centers her attention solely on language as object, not signifier. It is Septimus's *relation* to language (and to himself), not his intended or unintended meaning, that illustrates her insights into the structure of manic-depressive illness. For instance, Septimus examines an advertisement in skywriting, believing that an important message has been sent to him. He finds a manic beauty implying some transcendent meaning: "So, thought Septimus, looking up, they are signalling to me. Not indeed in actual words; that is, he could not read the language yet; but it was plain enough, this beauty, this exquisite beauty" (31). Because he cannot read the message, he imposes significance indiscriminately, desperately when he is depressed, eagerly when he is manic—when in a mixed state, both simultaneously. Manic-depressives often connect their moods in this way.[27] The onset of sudden, manic fulfillment in the midst of emptying despair in a mixed state can be "explained" as having been given a "mission," an exalted purpose to oppose the hellish abyss that has opened up inside them. The structure of mood swings becomes their meaning.

For Septimus, manic dilation complements depressive hollowness. He concludes that he must be the Savior who fills the empty world—this must be why he feels he must die though he loves life. John Custance, who had been a naval intelligence officer, relates a similar manic attack that resulted in a messianic delusion. In 1938 he attended commemorative services on Armistice Sunday:

> Suddenly I seemed to see like a flash that the sacrifice of those millions of lives had not been in vain, that it was part of a great pattern, the pattern of Divine Purpose. I felt, too, an inner conviction that I had something to do with that purpose; it seemed that some sort of revelation was being made to me, though at the time I had no clear ideas about what it was. The whole aspect of the world about me

began to change, and I had the excited shivers in the spinal column and tingling of the nerves that always herald my manic phases.

That night I had a vision. . . .

. . . What I saw was the Power of Love—the name came to me at once—the Power that I knew somehow to have made all universes, past, present and to come, to be utterly infinite, an infinity of infinities, to have conquered the Power of Hate, its opposite, and thus created the sun, the stars, the moon, the planets, the earth, light, life, joy and peace, never-ending.[28]

This is a truly bipolar theory; it integrates opposing feelings read as existing in external objects—indeed, Custance believes that love and hate *created* those objects. Even when he subsequently became depressed, Custance held onto his divine vision, but in an altered, depressive form:

I was a sort of opposite of Jesus Christ. Satan's job had been to catch a man, get him to sell his soul to him completely and utterly, like Faust, and then take him down alive into the pit. That was a sort of necessary counterweight to the resurrection of Jesus and the elect. I was the man. But if I could only kill myself, it might blow up the whole Universe, but at least I would get out of eternal torture and achieve the oblivion and nothingness for which my soul craved. I did in fact make three attempts at suicide, the most serious of which was when I tore myself from my attendant and threw myself in front of a car, with my poor wife, who was visiting me, looking on.[29]

Trading one's paltry human soul, like Faust, to achieve a depth of knowledge not granted to non–manic-depressives is an uplifting rationale in mania (for it explains intensified sensations) but a damning one in depression (for it explains one's existential isolation as punishment for an unpardonable sin). Moods are given the status of real objects because they mediate our perception of the status of real objects. Since feelings become more powerful and more real than the self that feels them, there is little conviction that it is desirable or even possible to manage them.

When Septimus becomes manic, his euphoria comes like a divine message, a "purpose" that calls on him to stop the slaughter, and since he believes that unmeaning exists physically outside himself, he sees himself as a messiah who must redeem the world. Even his depressed sense of being a stranger in a strange place is transformed by mania into a benefit. He is indeed different, he realizes. He is Christ: "Besides, now that he was quite alone, condemned, deserted . . . there was a luxury in it, an isolation full of sublimity; a freedom which the attached can never know" (140). Seeing himself as "the eternal sufferer" (37), he has been uplifted and distinguished by a paranoid vision of the meaning of life: "Septimus, the lord of men," has been "called forth in advance of the mass of men to hear the truth, to learn the meaning" (101). His despair *means* something after all. Bipolar mood states are perceived as one rather than interrelated, and Septimus cannot analyze the relationship, because introspection is mediated by mood.

Septimus's role as savior collapses the space between self and daydream. The communication and the communicator are now one. Rather than revealing the true nature of Septimus's intrasubjective relationship, his messianic delusion commands belief by magically reversing his earlier relationship with the world. No longer does he feel passive, selfless, weak, a "relic straying on the edge of the world . . . who lay, like a drowned sailor, on the shore of the world" (140). As a messiah, he feels "excited" and powerful: "he knew the truth! He knew everything!" (212). His re-creation through his exalted identity makes sense of his earlier "revelations": "Men must not cut down trees. There is a God. . . . Change the world. No one kills from hatred" (35). What these statements say is not the point. They are assertions of a self against meaninglessness, a psychotic magnification of Leslie Stephen's rationalizations in his memoirs, which filled with comforting illusions the void left by his wife's death. Woolf sees that whereas illusions merely weaken self-structure, delusions destroy it, and that she has a special problem her father never had to face.

Since there is no evidence of impairment of reasoning ability in delusional patients, apart from the inference to be made from the presence of the delusions themselves, they do not readily abandon bizarre or unlikely explanations for anomalous experiences. The cognitive bias in all human beings, whether deluded or not, is toward evidence consistent with what they are feeling—contradictory evidence is usually filtered out.[30] Bradshaw and Holmes's prescription of conversion to "normal" beliefs therefore violates the psychotic mind, which is convinced that it reads its perceptions correctly.

In neither stage of his illness does Septimus ever gain insight into his perceptual problems. Even in a relatively calm period, when he notes disturbed perceptions, he accepts objective and subjective readings side by side, as if the contradictions between the two did not exist:

> He lay back in his chair, exhausted but upheld. He lay resting, waiting, before he again interpreted, with effort, with agony, to mankind. He

lay very high, on the back of the world. The earth thrilled beneath him. Red flowers grew through his flesh; their stiff leaves rustled by his head. Music began clanging against the rocks up here. It is a motor horn down in the street, he muttered; but up here it cannoned from rock to rock, divided, met in shocks of sound which rose in smooth columns (that music should be visible was a discovery) and became an anthem, an anthem twined round now by a shepherd boy's piping (That's an old man playing a penny whistle by the public-house, he muttered). . . . Now he withdraws up into the snows, and roses hang about him—the thick red roses which grow on my bedroom wall, he reminded himself. The music stopped. He has his penny, he reasoned it out, and has gone on to the next public-house. (103)

This is divergent thinking carried to an extreme, splitting attention in two. Septimus is aware of both kinds of knowledge—what he is perceiving objectively and what the perception means to him subjectively—but he is unable to connect or integrate them and so feel unified himself. He is like Woolf in "A Sketch of the Past," who sees two separate entities in a flower, but he is not able to do as she did and contribute a fictional construct to reconcile the two perceptions and so affirm his sense of self. In a way, he suffers from an extraordinary version of Keats's "negative capability"—the capacity to hold two opposing ideas in the mind, the precondition for a creative act. Only briefly can he question the basis of his delusions:

Why then rage and prophesy? Why fly scourged and outcast? Why be made to tremble and sob by the clouds? Why seek truths and deliver messages? (216)

But he finds no way to bridge these two interpretations of experience and so to integrate himself.

Such a state of double awareness is not merely a fictional device; it occurs in real patients. The brain is capable of establishing other, co-conscious modules (e.g., in fugue states, hypnotic beliefs, and multiple personality, as will be discussed in Chapter 11) to mediate experience in different ways. One inpatient, discussing his belief that he was a political prisoner and that the hospital treating him was a government prison, put it aptly: "Forty-nine percent of me knows that what I am thinking is too weird to be real."[31] Virginia Woolf's depressive grandfather, Sir James, described the same sensation as being oppressed by "an unwelcome, familiar, and yet unknown visitor"—who turned out to be himself—"as if [I] were two persons in one."[32] William Styron uses a more literary metaphor:

A phenomenon that a number of people have noted while in deep depression is the sense of being accompanied by a second self—a wraithlike observer who, not sharing the dementia of his double, is able to watch with dispassionate curiosity as his companion struggles against the oncoming disaster, or decides to embrace it. There is a theatrical quality about all this. . . . I couldn't shake off a sense of melodrama—a melodrama in which I, the victim-to-be of self murder, was both the solitary actor and lone member of the audience.[33]

Styron's double awareness is comparable to Leonard's observation that the real horror of Virginia's insanity was that three-quarters of her mind was still sane enough to suffer from the severe psychic dislocations shattering the insane quarter (*Beginning Again* 163–64). And Woolf herself noted in her diary that her melancholy was "half assumed" because she was so "self conscious" of it as an inner invention (*Diary* 1: 23).

This splitting of conviction fluctuates considerably in psychosis. A study of thirty-four schizophrenic patients found that, at the height of their disorder (before admission to the hospital), 82 percent of them were fully convinced of the reality of their delusional ideas, and only 18 percent indicated "some limited degree of doubt." After a month of hospitalization, 44 percent felt doubt, and 12 percent completely rejected their delusional beliefs as false. Significantly, although a high rate of conviction was felt by these patients at the height of their delusions, 74 percent of them had "partial perspective" even before hospitalization, an awareness that other people might view their beliefs as aberrant or implausible. Despite this split in self-awareness ("I believe, but it may be judged insane by others"), 82 percent before admission showed "very high emotional commitment (were never able to put their delusional ideas out of their minds, and/or acted overtly and publicly in accordance with the delusional belief)." These figures held roughly true for other major psychotic disorders, including manic-depressive illness.[34] In other words, a patient may suspect that his delusion is aberrant, but his belief and his emotions take an independent course from intellectual doubt. Clinically, the severity of the illness is often judged by how strongly belief takes precedence over the ability to doubt.

For Septimus, fact and delusion are equally real but unrelated, and his identity—that which makes connections in his experience, integrating self and object in a way that should vivify his sense of his own boundaries—has likewise become split, an unidentifiable thing, a transparency through which even flowers can grow. With no corrective image of itself mirrored back, the mind cannot discern what role it plays in perception. Thus when

Septimus agrees to see Sir William Bradshaw for treatment, he does so with a "melodramatic gesture" and a "complete consciousness" of its "insincerity": he does not want to be cured, because he cannot see that he is ill.[35] Woolf's insight here is that Conversion, "that Goddess whose lust is to override opposition, to stamp indelibly in the sanctuaries of others the image of herself" (154), cannot work on psychotic patients because belief operates in ways neither patients nor doctors can fathom. The origins of even "normal" beliefs elude introspection.[36] I may "know" that Columbus discovered America in 1492, but I "believe" that one person's vote counts. I may remember the particular occasion of learning the first but not when I was converted to the second, yet I do not doubt the validity of either—which is strange, because nothing specific to my personal experience supports my belief in democracy (most of my candidates for president lost). Yet I still believe. It just seems self-evident. This is always the problem with multi-layered consciousness: we are aware only of the end-product of myriad nonconscious processes. Only after much thinking is done out of sight does its conclusion become available to us, ready-made and complete (e.g., "I believe in democracy," or "I've fallen in love"), and by then it is already persuasively self-evident. Although Septimus's beliefs seem paranoid, unrealistic, or unintelligible to us, to him they are "self-evident," and so his despair should not be "penalised" (151), nor can it be argued away. No one can prove that paranoia is *always* wrong, that it is entirely without insight into the treachery of fate—especially after the British soldier's experience in the Great War. Subjectivity, Septimus's delusions seem to say, is still a virgin wood untrodden by Bradshaw's heavy boots and should be accorded some respect. But nothing is so difficult for us, for it undermines our self-accorded guarantees that our belief-forming thought processes are fundamentally different from his; that they are privileged, whereas his are not; and that they are completely under our control.

From the tortured world of Septimus Smith it is a problematical journey to Clarissa Dalloway's serene life in Westminster. Because Woolf publicly asserted the characters' doubleness, most critics feel committed to argue for a personal connection between Clarissa's privacy and Septimus's pathological isolation. *Privacy* takes on two meanings in this controversy. For some critics, it is tantamount to a neurotic frigidity, or at least a stultifying orderliness.[37] Clarissa is condemned as a latent lesbian, so afraid of intimacy and femininity that she yearns for manhood or death (a homophobia Woolf did not share).[38] She is a "frigid and withdrawn heroine . . . clinging to a thin but triumphant capacity to create illusion in defense against her fear of sexuality, her despair of barreness [*sic*]," although, curiously, both Woolf and Clarissa seem "to insist on the gallantry of this defense."[39] For other critics, Clarissa's need to be alone is a justified response to life's threats, preserving her creativity, sensitivity, dignity, and self-confidence, though she "is beleaguered by thoughts of inadequacy brought on by the intimidating power she projects onto the general masculine force operating in the world," the same authority that destroys Septimus.[40]

Clarissa's daydreams illustrate how privacy cultivates the sanity that eludes her double. As in *Jacob's Room*, we see two interactions with objects: a holding on and a letting go of self-world boundaries. Clarissa treasures all the "bits and pieces" of existence—June, leaves in St. James's Park, Peter, flowers, "the fat lady in the cab" (12), the unadorned features of daily life; but she also releases them to the past, to themselves, to their own destinies. She occupies an object-relational space between Peter's defensiveness against chaos and Septimus's helpless surrender to it. This "space" is not static but rhythmic, like the process of reading itself. Accepting life's "furious winter's rages" seems no easy task, for Clarissa's first reaction to a threat is defensive: typically, she "stiffens." We first meet her exulting in party preparations and a perfect day ("what a morning—fresh as if issued to children on a beach"); she plunges into delightful memories of the past and the young Peter; but, reminded of her bitter estrangement from him, "she stiffened a little on the kerb" (4). Big Ben warns that the "irrevocable" hour is passing, creating a heartrending sense of "suspense" (5). Feeling momentarily isolated and empty, she wonders (like Jacob's narrator) why people love life, since it "dissolves" so quickly, but she admits her love for it too, "with an absurd and faithful passion, being part of it" (6). Thinking of Hugh Whitbread (who makes her feel "a little skimpy . . . schoolgirlish" [8]) and "all his colleagues, the gentlemen of England," who enjoy political power she cannot share, "she stiffened a little" (25). Memories of Clarissa's dead parents "caught her heart, made the muscles of her throat stiff, and contracted her lips in a spasm" (63).

Most trying is the intense hatred Doris Kilman inspires in Clarissa—Kilman, who "was never in the room five minutes without making you feel her superiority, your inferiority," whose "soul rusted" with bitterness (16). Clarissa's initial reaction is a defensive countertransference. But self-analysis reveals that her hatred "undoubtedly had gathered in to itself a great deal that was not Miss Kilman; had become one of those spectres with which one battles in the night . . . dominators and tyrants"

(16–17)—not Kilman at all, but herself. Clarissa discovers a connection between the way she feels about Kilman and the way she feels about herself:

> It rasped her, though, to have stirring about in her this brutal monster! . . . this hatred, which, especially since her illness, had the power to make her feel scraped, hurt in her spine; gave her physical pain, and made all pleasure in beauty, in friendship, in being well, in being loved and making her home delightful rock, quiver, and bend as if indeed there were a monster grubbing at the roots, as if the whole panoply of content were nothing but self love! this hatred!
>
> Nonsense, nonsense! she cried to herself, pushing through the swing doors of Mulberry's the florists. (17)

Like Septimus, Clarissa visualizes her hatred as a horrible monster lurking beneath normality, but, unlike him, she detects its source. Upon Kilman is visited the denial of self-love transformed into object-hate—an insightful reaction, because Kilman does despise "women like Clarissa" who like themselves. In Doris's own daydream she wants to attack Clarissa, "overcome," "humiliate," and "unmask" her, subdue her "soul and its mockery" (189). Clarissa responds, first by hating Kilman, then by hating herself, which she can then dismiss as "nonsense!" Her ability to examine emotion and to question its source and its meaning diffuses the attack. She need not fear fear itself, as Septimus does, for she realizes that it cannot destroy the self. Self, for Clarissa, is more real than transitory emotions. Similarly, the paranoid hostility that urged Virginia to hurl vitriolic abuse at her loved ones, the hypersensitive vulnerability that made any slight or balk seem a catastrophic threat, was not the center of Woolf's being.

We see now why Hugh's elevated position in society makes Clarissa feel "skimpy" and why the childhood memory of her parents makes her feel small and unaccomplished. Clarissa stiffens when faced with attacks upon her self-confidence: implacable parents, an "important" man, a woman who holds a grudge. Self-worth and emotion are interrelated, for she finds life empty, disillusioning, or frightening as she views herself as skimpy, guilty, or weak—the typical cognitive profile of depression. The novel charts her progress in strengthening her self-image. Against a backdrop of Peter's fantasies (which deny inadequacy) and Septimus's projections (which exteriorize his fragmented self), Clarissa learns to tie together the goodness of life and the goodness of self. Not coincidentally, what Clarissa finds therapeutic is also one of the aims of cognitive psychotherapists who deal with depressed patients. Lithium or anti-depressants alleviate the biochemical defect, but patients must also learn how mood has affected their ability to evaluate self and object. Like Clarissa, they can adjust their interpretations when they differentiate self and feeling by questioning the seemingly self-evident reality of mood.[41]

Clarissa connects self-esteem to life's value in three ways. First, she organizes parties to create a moment that enhances the goodness of life. Peter discounts the value of Clarissa's parties, but as Woolf observed in 1903 in her journal, a hostess raises the spirits of her guests and of herself:

> To be socially great, I believe, is really a noble ambition—for consider what it means. You have, for a certain space of time to realise as nearly as can be, an ideal . . .—to make you something more brilliant than you are by day. This seems to me a good ideal. You come to a party meaning to give pleasure; therefore you leave your sorrows & worries at home. . . . And the Lady [who amuses you though she lost a son in the war] —you may call her heartless, but surely she does more good making the world laugh than by sitting at home & weeping over her own sorrows. (*Passionate Apprentice* 168–69)

Not coincidentally, modern-day cognitive psychotherapists assign home-work, asking depressed patients to record and examine their reactions to normally pleasurable activities.[42] Repeated positive experiences help them build a repertoire of self-enhancing object-relations. They learn how to see the good in their perceptions of world and self, or at least to establish a more memorable history of positive interpretations they can relate to when depression skews perception to the negative. If patients, comparing past happiness to present despair, can understand that a drastic shift in evaluation has occurred, they may resist acting on the mood-induced belief that suicide is the only appropriate conclusion for their worthless lives. Of course, severely depressed individuals are unable to redirect their think-ing; they conclude that their present despair *is* the truth, always has been the truth, and that their previous optimism was the illusion. Those, such as Leslie, who suffer milder forms of mood disorders can at least avoid becoming the dupe of depression, not through Peter's defensive illusions but by opening themselves up to experiences beyond the narrow focus of one particular mood state. Indeed, reading Woolf's fiction tests the ability of us all to read inclusively, to open ourselves up to the vitality and profundity of literature.

Clarissa's second therapeutic method deals mainly with the past. She reviews and reaffirms her decision not to marry Peter:

So she would still find herself arguing in St. James's Park, still making out that she had been right—and she had too—not to marry him. For in marriage a little license, a little independence there must be between people living together day in day out in the same house; which Richard gave her, and she him. . . . . But with Peter everything had to be shared; everything gone into. And it was intolerable. (10)

Some readers see her reevaluations as proof of a cowardly misjudgment on her part, her fear of sharing anything ("What is wrong with sharing?" Shirley Panken innocently asks), and so they interpret the novel's elegiac tone as a mourning for her frigid withdrawal from an ardent lover.[43] But this position ignores the cognitive function of memory in establishing identity. Reviewing past decisions can strengthen our sense of self by revealing to us the continuity of our character through time. When Clarissa reaffirms her decision, she aligns past self with present. Indeed, reliable interpretation appears to be the strongest affirmation of self in the novel. Compare Clarissa to Septimus, whose sense of himself is as mutable, fragmented, and transitory as his chaotic perceptions. Identity is not a given, an object we possess; it is the continual process of recognizing patterns (divergent though they may be) in our lives through our object-relations. Reexamination, like successful psychoanalysis, reveals who we are when we see how past connects with present. Significantly, Clarissa's rejection of Peter is based on precisely this issue of identity, for he imposes upon Clarissa his own self-serving definition of who she is: she must be everything he is not. This is the "conversion" she resists, just as Septimus resists Bradshaw's judgment that patients should adopt their doctor's smug sense of proportion.

Clarissa's third method of fostering self-esteem involves, paradoxically, anonymity. Mounting the stairs to her attic room, she thinks of herself as a nun, a child, or a virgin (45–46), undefined by the role of friend or mother or wife. Critics are fond of focusing on the emptiness of her room and its narrow bed as evidence of Clarissa's frigidity and her fear of life and death.[44] But in her essays Woolf uses the terms *virgin, emptiness, nun* to imply a liberation from confining sexual and familial roles, an anonymity that frees the woman artist from restrictive definitions imposed by cultural hegemony:

That refuge she would have sought certainly. It was the relic of the sense of *chastity* that dictated anonymity to women even so late as the nineteenth century. Currer Bell, George Eliot, George Sand, all the

> victims of inner strife as their writings prove, sought ineffectively to *veil*
> themselves by using the name of a man. . . . Anonymity runs in their
> blood. The desire to be veiled still possesses them. (*Room* 52; my italics)

Sex and self invariably become confused in the minds of readers, Woolf
argues, so nineteenth-century women writers effaced the former by publishing under male pseudonyms or as "Anon." The "chaste life," as both of
Woolf's aunts, Anne Thackeray Ritchie and Caroline Stephen, suggested,
"allows a woman her own work and her *choice* of emotional ties."[45]

Chastity fosters a life "blessed and purified" (*Mrs. Dalloway* 42), protecting, beneath the cosmetic personality presented to others, a vital central
core too vulnerable to be exposed. That core is anonymous because it is
private, chaste because it is the untouchable center of self undistorted by
emotion and mood swings. Thus, Woolf judges, "the great poet and the
lover are both representative—in some way anonymous" (*"The Moment"*
168). When Woolf criticizes her own work, it is for lacking anonymity,
for being egotistical: "The dream is too often about myself. To correct
this, & to forget one's own sharp absurd little personality, reputation
& the rest of it, one should read; see outsiders; think more; write more
logically; above all be full of work; & practise anonymity" (*Diary* 3:
168–69). She describes her preparation for writing as a retreat:

> This has been a very animated summer: a summer lived almost too
> much in public. Often down here I have entered into a sanctuary; a
> nunnery; had a religious retreat; of great agony once; & always some
> terror: so afraid one is of loneliness: of seeing to the bottom of the
> vessel. That is one of the experiences I have had here in some Augusts;
> & got then to a consciousness of what I call "reality": a thing I see
> before me; something abstract; but residing in the downs or sky; beside
> which nothing matters; in which I shall rest & continue to exist. Reality
> I call it. And I fancy sometimes this is the most necessary thing to me:
> that which I seek. (*Diary* 3: 196)

When she can sink beneath the waves of emotion, the illusory distractions of ego, the solipsism of mania, and the self-destructive despair of
depression and enter "the healing sanctuary of anonymity" (*Diary* 4: 145),
Woolf finds she can face life and coexist with it while retaining a sense
of strength and worth.

Unadorned, she achieves a state of purity she elsewhere specifically
connects to the advantages of illness:

We do not know our own souls, let alone the souls of others. Human beings do not go hand in hand the whole stretch of the way. There is a virgin forest in each; a snowfield where even the print of birds' feet is unknown. Here we go alone, and like it better so. Always to have sympathy, always to be accompanied, always to be understood would be intolerable. But in health the genial pretence must be kept up, and the effort renewed—to communicate, to civilise, to share, to cultivate the desert, to educate the native, to work together by day and by night to sport. In illness this make-believe ceases. (*"The Moment"* 14)

Illness purifies by inviting us to question the reality of one's feelings and beliefs, to clear away the clutter. A self so secret that it is not evident can feel immune to conversion, as Woolf describes in 1932:

"Immunity" I said to myself half an hour ago, lying back in my chair. Thats the state I am (or was) in. And its a holy, calm, satisfactory flawless feeling—To be immune, means to exist apart from rubs, shocks, suffering; to be beyond the range of darts; to have enough to live on without courting flattery, success; not to need to accept invitations; not to mind other people being praised; to feel This—to sit & breathe behind my screen, alone, is enough; to be strong; content; to let Nessa & D. go to Paris without envy; to feel no one's thinking of me; to feel I have done certain things & can be quiet now; to be mistress of my hours; to feel detached from all sayings about me; & claims on me; to be glad of lunching alone with Leonard; to have a [*sic*] spare time this afternoon; to read Coleridge's letters. Immunity is an exalted calm desirable state, & one I could reach much oftener than I do. (*Diary* 4: 116–17)

Both Woolf and Clarissa sink deep enough into themselves to escape the waves of emotion, the helter-skelter of distractions, the lies of egotism. Neither opts for Leslie and Julia's strategy of filling the internal emptiness with external relationships, losing themselves in busy domestic lives. Immunity requires privacy and freedom. Like Richard, Leonard tolerated that needed immunity. Neither he nor Richard sought to "convert" his wife to respond to him in any stereotyped way.[46] Such open-endedness may look inconclusive, blank, virginal. No definite principle or philosophy or personality may be uncovered when the self can be pared down to its essence. But that is an advantage. Woolf intends no prescription here: each of us must seek our own path through the virginal forest.

Woolf's most interesting insight is that such freedom to be oneself brings with it guilt. In *A Room of One's Own*, she argues that for women writers the pressures of society (in the form of neglect and scorn) combine with inner pressures: the disappointment of loving parents and the moral disapproval of society become internalized, and the daughter, unable to reconcile her artistic ambitions with her wish to be dutiful and "good," risks destroying herself (49–51). In *Mrs. Dalloway,* Clarissa feels guilty for having "failed" Richard in a way Woolf avoids specifying by using unclear and unreferenced pronouns:

> Lovely in girlhood, suddenly there came a moment—for example on the river beneath the woods at Clieveden—when, through some contraction of this cold spirit, she had failed him. And then at Constantinople, and again and again. She could see what she lacked. It was not beauty; it was not mind. It was something central which permeated; something warm which broke up surfaces and rippled the cold contact of man and woman, or of women together. For *that* she could dimly perceive. She resented it, had a scruple picked up Heaven knows where, or, as she felt, sent by Nature (who is invariably wise); yet she could not resist sometimes yielding to the charm of a woman, not a girl, of a woman confessing, as to her they often did, some scrape, some folly. And whether it was pity, or their beauty, or that she was older, or some accident—like a faint scent, or a violin next door (so strange is the power of sounds at certain moments), she did undoubtedly then feel what men felt. (46–47)

It would be tempting to assume that this failure is frigidity, but both Clarissa and Woolf tend to use sexual words to mean nonsexual things, as if they were desexualizing and liberating terms and images that are too often oversexualized and reductive. So what, exactly, is being said here? On the one hand, it appears to be a confession of frigidity and latent lesbianism; on the other, we see a deliberate, teasing ambiguity, a reluctance to specify anything beyond a "scruple," "some scrape," or "what men felt." How should we interpret the sexuality of the language? Like Clarissa herself, these words have become anonymous, veiled, their definitions escaping conventional meaning that would pin them down. Mitchell Leaska readily concludes that Clarissa failed Richard sexually in Clieveden, even though, in an odd footnote, he remarks on the illogic of the word "*fail*":

> Mrs. Woolf's use of the verb *fail* is a very curious choice in the present context, because sexually, it is the man who "fails" his partner through impotence. Even a frigid woman may refuse her man or may "fake" the act, but there is no failing him. A woman's conditioning may be such that she is unable to participate genuinely in the act of sexual

intercourse; and if so, she has failed herself. But that failure is emotional, not physical.[47]

If we assume that Clarissa's meditations are sexual because the language is vague, anonymity looks like an avoidance of sex. But Clarissa does not think she failed *herself*; she failed *Richard,* she feels guilty—just after she thinks about how much she enjoys her privacy. Her chastity, as Woolf's Aunt Anny argued, allows a woman to choose what or who will engage her emotions—be it a June day, new gloves, the old woman across the way, the evening sky over Westminster. Clarissa's love for Sally is "completely disinterested" (50); it allows her "to connect without imposing."[48] This is not the kind of love a Victorian woman was raised to think was due to her husband. If she has disappointed her husband (and there is no evidence she has), it is because she is not dependent on him, because she lacks "something central" that can be offered to another woman without fear of being expropriated. "What men felt" could be the self-confidence to feel, as Hugh Whitbread does, safe and valued and powerful in the presence of others, whether or not the interpersonal transaction is sexual.

It is significant, then, that when Peter barges into her private room shortly thereafter and criticizes Clarissa, she does not retreat. If his knife stands for his ability to believe in himself, she bears her own standard— her needle—against his intrusion:

> What an extraordinary habit that was, Clarissa thought; always playing with a knife. Always making one feel, too, frivolous; empty-minded; a mere silly chatterbox, as he used. But I too, she thought, and, taking up her needle, summoned . . . to her help the things she did; the things she liked; her husband; Elizabeth; her self, in short, which Peter hardly knew now, all to come about her and beat off the enemy.
> "Well, and what's happened to you?" she said. So before a battle begins, the horses paw the ground. . . . So Peter Walsh and Clarissa, sitting side by side on the blue sofa, challenged each other. (65–66)

Liking herself, Clarissa does not flatter Peter by becoming frivolous, empty-headed; in this way, too, she has failed him—failed to give what he expects of a woman. As before, she regrets having stood up to a man: "It was all over for her. The sheet was stretched and the bed narrow. She had gone up into the tower alone" (70). Clarissa, like the women writers Woolf admires in *A Room of One's Own,* and the Stephen daughters, still pays homage to a social convention by feeling guilty for thinking of herself.

Independence and anonymity help Clarissa face the novel's climax, Septimus's suicide. She imagines his point of view and calmly considers what it could mean:

> A thing there was that mattered; a thing, wreathed about with chatter, defaced, obscured in her own life, let drop every day in corruption, lies, chatter. This he had preserved. Death was defiance. Death was an attempt to communicate; people feeling the impossibility of reaching the centre which, mystically, evaded them; closeness drew apart; rapture faded, one was alone. There was an embrace in death. (280–81)
>
> . . . and the words came to her, Fear no more the heat of the sun . . . . She felt somehow very like him—the young man who had killed himself. She felt glad that he had done it; thrown it away . . . . He made her feel the beauty; made her feel the fun. (283–84)

Acting on his beliefs, delusional or not, Septimus throws away his life, but not himself. Septimus faces a loss of autonomy in the hands of Bradshaw and Holmes: "His state again is Clarissa's, is woman's; he becomes an object; his body is not his own. As Dr. Bradshaw approaches, Septimus literally has no room, so he hurls himself out the window to reality." His death affirms Clarissa's "sense of herself as *subject,*" not object.[49] Self must be real if it can decide to die.

Woolf's attitude toward death did change during the writing of *Mrs. Dalloway*. In 1924 she recounted her fear after an automobile accident involving her niece, Angelica Bell, who had for a few hours been thought to be near death: "What I felt was . . . that death & tragedy had once more put down his paw, after letting us run a few paces. People never get over their early impressions of death I think. I always feel pursued" (*Diary* 2: 299). But next year, after finishing *Mrs. Dalloway,* she reacted differently to the news of the death of her friend Jacques Raverat:

> Jacques died, as I say; & at once the siege of emotions began. I got the news with a party here—Clive, Bee How, Julia Strachey, Dadie. Nevertheless, I do not any longer feel inclined to doff the cap to death. I like to go out of the room talking, with an unfinished casual sentence on my lips. That is the effect it had on me—no leavetakings, no submission— but someone stepping out into the darkness. (*Diary* 3: 7)

Both Woolf and Mrs. Dalloway receive at a party the news of a sudden death—news that should inspire Clarissa's stiffening, what Woolf called her "screen making habit"[50] (what Norman Holland calls a filtering identity-theme) of automatic denial in response to the threat of loss. Instead, they let go of fear, abandoning their sense of vulnerability, of "penetrability" (to paraphrase Peter Walsh) in order to see what the event might mean. Death itself becomes personal—not Rachel's or Jacob's senseless imposition, but an experience to be integrated into a lifetime of experiences. It is a "new vision of death," Woolf notes in a November, 1926, entry to her diary, one that is "active, positive, like all the rest, exciting; & of great importance—as an experience" (*Diary* 3: 117) that can be "owned."

The form of *Mrs. Dalloway* invites the reader to experience the frustration of the manic-depressive, the one person who seems to be three but is not three. Because the manic-depressive possesses three sets of beliefs and affects, his or her identity is periodically deconstructed. Cyclical shifts blur the line between sanity and insanity by repeated crossings—paralleling *our* repeated crossings from one character's mind to another's. What haunts us about reading this novel is the suspicion that there is an unsettling connection between the sane and the insane, that from one moment to the next a mind—any mind—may not know itself or see how it has temporarily disappeared in the grip of strong anomalous or contradictory feelings it cannot control or "own." Personality then seems ephemeral, unrelated to identity. The novel only urges us to hope that identity must lie somewhere below the superficial differences—names, roles, gender, manic projections, depressive desiccations. Like Clarissa, we must learn to create "every moment afresh" (5) and to question our protective beliefs, paring ourselves down to a central essence; like Peter, we must feel the fun of fiction and run the risk of becoming foolish and egotistical; like Septimus, we must open ourselves to divergent thinking and "alien" experiences, but without losing ourselves completely. Such an inclusive view may seem impossible, but it is often the goal of great novelists, who, "by disrupting the reader's harmony with his world, in an important sense challenge the very conditions of sanity. Injuring our vanity by upsetting our order, such writers seldom tell us the 'truth' we want to hear."[51]

The design of *Mrs. Dalloway* may have been shaped in part by Leonard's approach to Virginia's illness, which was to connect it to her sanity:

> There were moments or periods during her illness, particularly in the second excited stage, when she was what could be called "raving mad" and her thoughts and speech became completely unco-ordinated, and she had no contact with reality. Except for these periods, she remained all through her illness, even when most insane, terribly sane in three-quarters of her mind. The point is that her insanity was in her premises, in her beliefs. She believed, for instance, that she was not ill, that her

symptoms were due to her own "faults"; she believed that she was hearing voices when the voices were her own imaginings; she heard the birds outside her window talking Greek; she believed that the doctors and nurses were in conspiracy against her. These beliefs were insane because they were in fact contradicted by reality. But given these beliefs as premises for conclusions and actions, all Virginia's actions and conclusions were logical and rational. (*Beginning Again* 164)

It is easy to identify Septimus's madness in this passage, but more important is Leonard's strategy: he not only describes Virginia's symptoms but argues that an underlying logic connects the sane Virginia and the insane Virginia. This is a cognitive explanation of delusions. He asserts that a core self still operates; only her beliefs have no objective basis. What Leonard gave Virginia was the sense that she was still *real,* that she survived beneath the crests and troughs, and that somehow the sane Virginia and the insane Virginia were related.

In Virginia's diaries and letters we can see Leonard's influence gradually evolving over time (though she always revises for her own purposes). In 1920, she wrote of her alternating moods when thinking about Mary Hutchinson: "L. at tea put me right: M. H. is one of the few people I dislike, I said. No: he replied: one of the many you dislike & like alternately" (*Diary* 2: 63). Not much is made of the incident, except that Leonard tries to generalize Virginia's emotions of the moment, to set them into a larger pattern. By June of 1924, she attempts self-analysis:

If I weren't so sleepy, I would write about the soul. I think its time to cancel that vow against soul description. What was I going to say? Something about the violent moods of my soul. How describe them, even with a waking mind? I think I grow more & more poetic. Perhaps I restrained it, & now, like a plant in a pot, it begins to crack the earthenware. Often I feel the different aspects of life bursting my mind asunder. . . . I mean, what's the use of facts at our time of life? Why build these careful cocoons: why not say straight out—yes, but what? (*Diary* 2: 304)

What is the soul if its moods burst asunder the pot of description? The waking mind, with its narrow focus on coherent evidence, cannot encompass the sundered fragments of madness. Woolf will not be satisfied with the careful cocoons of a tidy, coherent theory. But if work is done by total inclusion on a syncretistic, unconscious level, what can be said "straight out"? In November of 1928, acknowledging her skepticism, she gropes for what may lie beyond it:

that is my temperament, I think: to be very little persuaded of the truth of anything—what I say, what people say—always to follow, blindly instinctively with a sense of leaping over a precipice—the call of—the call of—now, if I write The Moths [*The Waves*] I must come to terms with these mystical feelings. (*Diary* 3: 203)

How can Woolf get beyond the wordless, mystical, inexpressible openness of Jinny's vision without either feeling cramped by facts or denying facts with illusory dreams? The temptation to identify self with "the waking mind" is strong, but it gives merely the illusion of substantiality:

I am so important to myself: yet of no importance to other people: like the shadow passing over the downs. I deceive myself into thinking that I am important to other people: that makes part of my extreme vividness to myself: as a matter of fact, I dont matter; & so part of my vividness is unreal; gives me a sense of illusion. (*Diary* 3: 188)

Woolf reasons that the illusion of personality camouflages one's true identity, just as her manic-depressive swings do. The first egotism of personality is a voluntary dalliance that leads to a more serious, involuntary fragmentation of the self. Anonymity gives her a protective distance from the choppy waves of mood, but it is not her final goal. Rest is welcome, but it does not answer all her questions. The most important question is: who would she be without her moods? This is a difficult problem for any manic-depressive. Can the other selves be ignored with the claim that identity lies only in the "normal" self that family and physician approve of? Most patients do ignore their other selves, because society rewards consistent behaviors: doing one's job, loving one's family, making interpretations others can understand. Consensus and practicality are strong reinforcers for "getting straight." And psychotic behavior can undoubtedly be dangerous and self-destructive. Still, it distresses some patients to dismiss the inconvenient but vivid perspectives that mood swings impose. However much Woolf felt terrorized by her hellish nightmares of persecution or her ecstatic hallucinations, she valued these unusual experiences as insights that normality restrained.

The problem here was that insight could be useful only when she was well enough to write. Neither madness nor anonymity could by itself produce art. A chaste anonymity could suspend egotism, a stoic immunity might resist the temptations of "bad" impulses, but bipolar mood swings periodically defocused conscious attention and opened Woolf to syncretistic perception which, in a return to sanity, she then creatively integrated. Just

as Clarissa must be threatened by Miss Kilman's raspy monster clawing
inside her before she can see herself afresh, Woolf valued her decenteredness
in illness as the counterweight to her revitalizing return to sanity:

> I have a great & astonishing sense . . . of my own strangeness. . . .
> Who am I, what am I, & so on: these questions are always floating
> about in me; & then I bump against some exact fact—a letter, a person,
> & come to them again with a great sense of freshness. (*Diary* 3: 62–63)

Once she descended past personality and its capacity to identify itself by
tangential qualities, Woolf achieved a sense of self that was too open, too
elemental to be defined by the answers to such limiting questions as "Who
am I?" and "What am I?" The core self existed, like other real objects, on
the level of touch in the dark, without coherent attributes or characteristics,
without the organizing ego. Dedifferentiating scanning, like the sense of
touch in the dark, ratified self's substance if the chaos inside could be
aligned with the chaos outside, with no overt specifications, no restraint
from a "careful cocoon." Self was no depressive phantom, no manic
daydream, no florid production of theory, but a thing with which she
could have a relationship—in fact, as many relationships as she cared to
imagine. Privacy paradoxically enriched her intrasubjective object-relations
because illness gave self boundless possibilities as well as containment.

Clarissa experiences the same kind of withdrawal and emergence. Having
sunk into "the depths of her heart" (281) in empathy with Septimus's
suicide, she resurfaces thrilling at an ordinary sight, the sky above
Westminster: "It held, foolish as the idea was, something of her own in
it, this country sky, this sky above Westminster. . . . It was new to her"
(282–83). Self and world are rhythmically connected and disconnected
again and again. The novel ends with her return to her party, her secret
joy inside her. Peter momentarily becomes aware of irreducible, inexplicable
feelings ("What is this terror? What is this ecstasy?" [296]), but characteristically attributes them to Clarissa's "womanly" magic (an essential
feature of *his* identity-theme) and so gains no insight. Even the novel's
narration seems to draw our attention away from Clarissa's vision by concluding, "For there she was," as if to undercut the majesty of Peter's
adoration with a deliberately subdued declarative sentence, one as unques-
tionable as it is unremarkable. Like the Westminster sky, Clarissa *is* there,
but what makes her so special cannot be shared with anyone else because it
cannot be formulized or said "straight out." Language cannot go into that
secret, untrammeled wood of self that lies beyond ego. Manic-depressives

find no words that can reliably formulate their senseless shifts of mood or systematize elusive feelings. The next mood swing will destroy any rigid schematization. One must learn to question all moods and ideas, tolerate chaos, and hope that some wordless unity exists somewhere to embrace all that one is, senseless or sensible.

Woolf accepted, however grudgingly, the fact that she could not explain the profound multiplicity of her inner life to others or expect them to give her a sense of self that could weather mood swings. In a letter to Vita Sackville-West, she complained about her isolation:

> I wish you could live in my brain for a week. It is washed with the most violent waves of emotion. What about? I dont know. It begins on waking; and I never know which—shall I be happy? Shall I be miserable[?] I grant, I keep up some mechanical activity with my hands, setting type; ordering dinner. Without this, I should brood ceaselessly. And you think it all fixed and settled. Do we then know nobody?—only our own versions of them, which, as likely as not, are emanations from ourselves? (*Letters* 3: 245)

How, unable to know herself, could she be known? The answer came in the form of a wish: if Vita could experience Virginia's inner world—without explanation—she might "know" her, or at least feel what it is like to be her. This is essentially what *Mrs. Dalloway* does. We live in a bipolar brain for a day. We experience the isolated lives of several characters who might be one character if only that underlying, anonymous yet inclusive self could be fully verbalized. The sane and the insane are paralleled but without specific connections, so that the reader is faced with the same insoluble problem Virginia wished Vita could face: how to find a center in all this multiplicity, a core beyond ego and its mood-congruent linguistic and cognitive powers, and yet one enriched by a panoply of feeling, an all-inclusive self that paradoxically exhibits both unity and difference. If such a view can be gained, it must come from the reader, who plays the part of Woolf, mothering the text, returning a gaze that mends the cut separating author and audience. But there may be no words for such a vision.

10 "It is finished"

Ambivalence Resolved, Self Restored
in To the Lighthouse

Woolf reported that she ceased to be obsessed with both her mother and her father after writing *To the Lighthouse* (1927), theorizing that she "expressed some very long felt and deeply felt emotion" which writing finally laid to rest (*Moments of Being* 81, 108; *Diary* 3: 208). There is much in this novel to evidence a critical and conscious reevaluation of her parents. Woolf was able to portray her mother as she desired rather than as Leslie's idealized angel. Although she resented (and represented) her father's exhausting dependency on Julia, her treatment of him as Mr. Ramsay is balanced by a recognition that he was as much victim as victimizer, and she subsequently began to think of him as " 'my' father, not 'father' any more" (*Diary* 3: 194). It was a reconciliation that lasted for the rest of her life; in 1941, she felt able to look at Leslie from two angles, "as a child condemning; as a woman of 58 understanding" (*Diary* 5: 281). Completing the family portrait, Woolf stepped into the story herself to offer a unifying vision: Lily Briscoe masters self-destructive disturbances in the creative process and finds autonomy.

To the *Lighthouse* extends and modifies elements from the previous novels. As in *The Voyage Out,* a motherless woman seeks answers to inexpressible questions. Lily's mood shifts, however, are not always presented sequentially, as Rachel's are, but are simultaneously set off against one another in a pattern resembling ambivalence. Although until she read Freud's definition of it in 1939 Woolf did not realize that bifurcated emotion could be called *ambivalence* (*Diary* 5: 249), she did note in 1925: "I think I might do something in To the Lighthouse, to split up emotions more completely. I think I'm working in that direction" (*Diary* 3: 38). By collapsing the temporality of mood swings (and perhaps using her experience of "mixed" states of conflicting manic and depressive feelings), she could frame the resolution of bipolar shifts more clearly as a theory of pictorial art, two masses balanced by a vertical line. Like *Jacob's Room,* *To the Lighthouse* invites readers to relinquish the wish for an objective narrative truth—by giving us not simply two irreconcilable views but seventeen subjective points of view, each provisional. This novel ventures beyond the remote attic room protecting Mrs. Dalloway's secret self; Mrs. Ramsay carries her privacy with her in the hubbub of family life. Lily's painting and Mr. Ramsay's voyage to the lighthouse celebrate the strength of self in spite of loss—as Rachel's death and Jacob's fecklessness do not. The longing for mothering, for an idyllic past and manic omnipotence to overcome depressed helplessness, is replaced by adult self-sufficiency.

Woolf explores the relationship of her bipolar illness to her childhood experiences by focusing on the connections between loss, self-esteem, and the ambiguous nature of mothering. Julia had been the emblematic focus of Virginia's illness because premorbid childhood seemed infinitely better than adult depressions, especially when a manic imagination could mine Julia's obscure depths for source material. But the euthymic Woolf was not satisfied by obsessive longing for the past, and, wisely, she knew that loss brought gain: it revealed life's "reality," the "gashes" and "cracks" in the fabric that the younger Virginia had neglected (or had been protected from) while her mother was alive. Julia's death had been an abrupt weaning, but it led to growth and creative insights whose components were illustrated (and magnified) by manic-depressive illness. Once the euthymic Woolf understood this, her own phantom memories of a "generalised" Julia (*Moments of Being* 84) lavishing perfect nurture, making babies of loved ones, no longer sufficed.

Whereas the loss of beneficial nurturing results in grief, loss of self-destructive dependency elicits an ambivalent response. An infant will miss what was supportive, but a variety of reactions—anger, fear, guilt, denial, despair—can follow the loss of what was also debilitating.[1] Leslie craved such dependency, but Woolf clearly saw the disadvantages of living in the yellow grape of illusory immunity. The deeply felt emotion she expressed and laid to rest was not one but two—a bipolar attitude toward an idealized mothering that could both cripple and delight. Thus, Mrs. Ramsay centers a conflict in the novel between the desire for perfect support and the need to be self-sufficient,[2] a conflict that parallels the manic-depressive's fundamental problem of letting go of mood-induced delusions that seem to explain the illness. Leslie could not face the destructive elements of his view of Julia's role as the inexhaustible, sacrificial family goddess upon whom everything, even her family's mental health, depended. Virginia wanted to create a more human Julia, not a target for her projections but an equal, a contemporary with whom she could have a personal relationship.

It is significant, then, that idealization lies at the heart of an old critical debate on the simple question of how to judge Mrs. Ramsay as a mother. Many readers respond to her with outright idolatry. They identify her with the "Primordial Goddess" of pagan myth, the goddess Demeter, deity of corn and abundance; compare her to the Blessed Virgin, Jesus Christ, and Eve; raise her to the level of a "Platonic ideal"; or endow her with "magical" qualities of "almost supernatural force."[3] Such an exaggeration of maternal virtues is common in childhood, but it has two drawbacks. First, it exacerbates the egoism of primary identification: the infant does not perceive the mother as a person separate from himself, and so he does not accept the mother's other interests or attachments, but perpetuates the myth that the perfect mother's whole being is supposed to be devoted to serving her child. This attitude can extend well into adulthood and become a self-fulfilling prophecy for people who become mothers and fathers themselves.[4] Second, such an inflated view of the virtues of the mother relegates the father to the role of tyrant or fool—an unfortunate position because, although in most cultures the mother establishes and symbolizes a symbiotic relationship with the infant, the father plays an equally important role, that of differentiation. The enculturated child identifies with the mother (self defined by similarities) but uses the father to perceive the self in opposition (self defined by differences).[5] Fathers integrate their children into a larger social context by denying ready retreat into total care; whereas mothers provide a reassuring sense of oneness with other human beings, fathers supply a reassuring sense of individuality. Children need to learn both kinds of object-relations.[6]

The disadvantage of this duality comes when the developing child sees the mother as symbolizing the infantile—"dependence, regression, passivity, and the lack of adaptation to reality"—and, turning from her toward the father, who "represents independence and individuation, progress, activity, and participation in the real world,"[7] arrives at the erroneous conclusion that it is—and should be—"a man's world out there." Perhaps, this explains why other critics, citing much the same evidence from *To the Lighthouse,* arrive at quite negative, even vindictive conclusions about Mrs. Ramsay's motherhood, thinking of her as a narcissist who mothers obsessively to avoid examining her own emptiness or as a tyrannical, husband-dominating, son-suffocating bitch who must die before the final resolution, spearheaded by the "heroic" Mr. Ramsay, can take place.[8]

Mr. and Mrs. Ramsay have become the victims of our cultural biases about gender and parenting. One critic considering this problem of critical response to the Ramsay marriage concludes that

> sex role stereotyping is not only criticized by *To the Lighthouse* itself, but has seeped into the reading of it. The desire to see Mrs. Ramsay as intuition, sensual perception, loving concern, and empathy, and the

desire to believe that all Mr. Ramsay is is, to quote the omniscient narrator of *Middlemarch*, "a lifeless embalmment of knowledge," leads to not really seeing what the text is saying. What the text is saying is not that "men are this way" and "women are that way" and so of course "no marriage of true minds" is possible for them, but the male mind and the female mind, when they are in action, are a good deal alike, and are both inextricably tied to emotion.[9]

What sex-role stereotyping reads into mentality is an extension of the subject-object lessons children learn from their parents. Problems arise when assigning a particular object-relational style (self/object confusion or self/object differentiation) exclusively to a specific sex. Thus, it is not surprising that the depressed Woolf would locate her manic sense of idyllic fusion and magical joy in women rather than men. Culturally prescribed notions of maternity, Virginia's early experiences, and her mood swings reinforced her impression that it was Julia who best symbolized a blissful, premorbid past when self was not burdened by its depressing sense of isolation, the limitations of "reality," as represented and enforced by males (Leslie, Gerald and George, and the Cambridge dons). But in *To the Lighthouse* this rigid mold is broken. Woolf makes here a provocative connection between sexism and manic-depressive illness, for the failure of so many readers to see Mr. and Mrs. Ramsay's inner lives has been modeled for us by Lily's bifurcated emotional response to them. Much of the evidence used to condemn the husband and eulogize the wife (or the reverse) comes from Lily's own internal monologues as she struggles with mood swings that interfere with her ability to know her own feelings about Mr. and Mrs. Ramsay. Reconciling oneself to parental figures involves seeing them as individuals, not as symbols or projections serving unacknowledged needs or cultural prescriptions. How well children wean themselves from idyllic subjectivity depends on how completely they are able to give up the mother as mythic deity, without whom paradise is forever lost, and to give back to the father his capacity for parenting. But seeing others in the fullness of their being is just the problem that the manic-depressive (or a reader of this novel) finds so difficult.

On the surface Mrs. Ramsay seems the twin of Leslie's *Mausoleum Book* Julia, the selfless fount of perfect mothering. The emotional center of a large family, hostess to her guests, nurse to her neighbors, she is "a hen, straddling her wings out in protection of a covey of little chicks" (34) that includes her husband: "If [Mr. Ramsay] put implicit faith in her, nothing should hurt him; however deep he buried himself or climbed high, not for a second should he find himself without her" (60). Even the skeptical

Lily yearns to be a dependent child leaning on Mrs. Ramsay's knee. But this idyllic dream cannot be fulfilled. Young James *is* that dependent child leaning on Mrs. Ramsay's knee, and he is neither happy nor secure. He jealously hoards his mother, whom he industriously idealizes. To him, she seems "to pour erect into the air a rain of energy, a column of spray, looking at the same time animated and alive as if all her energies were being fused into force," while his father is "like a beak of brass, barren and bare," demanding "to be taken within the circle of life, warmed and soothed, to have his senses restored to him, his barrenness made fertile" (58–59), as if his self were empty unless someone else filled it—which is precisely James's predicament. But what both James and his father want is impossible. It is true that once he is fed with this illusory reassurance, Mr. Ramsay, "like a child who drops off satisfied," believes himself "restored, renewed" (60), but Woolf makes it clear that the cost of extended mothering is great: Mrs. Ramsay worries that she has only made her husband even more dependent (62), the needy Lily is infuriated that "Mrs. Ramsay gave him what he asked too easily" (71), and James feels cheated. The more his mother looks like an angel, the more his father looks like a devil, the emptier James feels, the angrier and more isolated Lily becomes. The illusion of perfect mothering creates endless hunger.

It is important to remember that the sexual imagery here so complimentary to Mrs. Ramsay (the column of spray) and so critical of Mr. Ramsay (the brass beak), though expressed without corrective comment or bias, in the sophisticated language of an omniscient narrator, is intended to represent a small child's phallic point of view, not Woolf's. Woolf makes sure that all views in this novel are provisional. What purpose, then, can James's symbolism serve besides that of revealing his impotent narcissism? He notices that when his father has had his fill, his mother feels exhausted, empty, and turns for her own refreshment to the lighthouse. She watches it, fascinated, "hypnotised, as if it were stroking with its silver fingers some sealed vessel in her brain whose bursting would flood her with delight" (99). What has happened here? If we limit ourselves to James's narcissistic point of view, we might believe that the lighthouse symbolizes a "fantasy lover pulled up out of the unsatisfied inner world of Mrs. Ramsay's violated consciousness"[10]—but the fantasy of violation is James's, and he would most likely cast himself as the secret lover born of his mother's deepest inner life. Because both the beam and the lighthouse have a phallic shape, it is easy to penetrate no deeper than the oedipal bias of a young boy and conclude that Woolf presents us with a sexual drama—the animus fertilizing the anima, the wife assuming dominance because the husband is inadequately male. But what do these terms—*masculinity, femininity, animus, anima*—tell us that is useful? The analysis is as metaphoric as the text, and dividing up the psyche into masculine and feminine parts limits complex mental processes to narrowed sexual roles which "not only deny the flexibility of the symbols but also fail to make sense of them."[11]

But can we avoid metaphorical language here? Woolf uses this image of self as vessel in "A Sketch of the Past" to describe a moment of being in a nonsexual context: "we are sealed vessels afloat upon what it is convenient to call reality; at some moments, the sealing matter cracks; in floods reality" (*Moments of Being* 142). Absolute separation of self from object versus confusion of self with object are the two extremes of bipolar object-relations. Unlike the other characters, Mrs. Ramsay is nurtured not by the emotional dynamics of familial roles but by a perception of oneness immune to the flux of experience. Something is learned beyond what can be characterized as subjective or objective knowledge, something inexpressible, "intimacy itself, which is knowledge" (79), a fusion that is neither flooded with the manic's supercharged reality nor sealed off by the depressive's alienated self. All these elements—subject-object fusion, stroking fingers, mirroring, and feeding—replicate infant-mother transactions, and, like that infant, Mrs. Ramsay sees both the object and herself: "It was odd, she thought, how if one was alone, one leant to inanimate things; trees, streams, flowers; felt they expressed one; felt they became one; felt they knew one, in a sense were one; felt an irrational tenderness . . . as for oneself" (97–98).

Successful fusions, like successful interpretations for manic-depressives, increase the self's worth. By reconciling bipolar patterns of hoarding and surrender, Mrs. Ramsay creates, in object-relational terms, what D. W. Winnicott called "an intermediate area of *experiencing*, to which inner reality and external life both contribute . . . a resting-place for the individual engaged in the perpetual human task of keeping inner and outer reality separate yet interrelated".[12] In this "transitional space" Mrs. Ramsay feels something like the initial, seemingly magical fusion an infant experiences with its mother, while simultaneously recognizing that this subjective sense of sacred rapport is joined to the objective fact of separateness: "She looked up over her knitting and met the third stroke and it seemed to her like her own eyes meeting her own eyes, searching as she alone could search into her mind and her heart, purifying out of existence that lie, any lie" (97). The "lie" is a sudden phrase that occurs to her when feeling safe and complete: "We are in the hands of the Lord." It strikes her as insincere because she knows objectively that the world is dangerous. But it is not that simple. The "lie" is a fiction created by culture to explain away the uncanniness of the feeling, yet the *sensation* of security is real, and the stroking of the lighthouse beam occasions the "waves of pure delight" this moment of oneness produces in her.

Mrs. Ramsay is careful to accept the feeling without seeking/imposing an explanation for it that denies the possibility of randomness and loss. This nurturing moment seems to be outside her control, sponsored by "something else"—thus the temptation to attribute it to a deity. But such an explanation is as metaphorical as Septimus's delusion that his ecstasy/despair proves he is the messiah. So too would be our psycho-analytic explanation that she feels an uncanny rapport because she once again *becomes* the infant transacting with a comforting mother who magically seems to know her thoughts, wants, and needs. All our attempts to explain the "lie" are, in a sense (though not a clinical one), delusions that disguise how experience is modulated by the perceiver. The objective truth is that Mrs. Ramsay comforts herself when she fully perceives not only the object but herself in relation to the object, when neither is put into a position of dominance by mood. But the subjective truth is that the world seems *meant* to be perceived and rejoiced in—like a loving mother or a loving God. The "semi-transparent envelope" of perception cannot be fixed to delineate exactly what happens to subject and object when a moment of being occurs, and Woolf does not speculate on why such moments are provided for/available to us. She makes clear only the practical result of this prerepresentational miracle: when Mrs. Ramsay feels herself to be as real as the world, her self-confidence is restored. This balance between the subjective impression of oneness and the objective knowledge that oneness cannot exist independent of her ability to imagine it proves the self's power. No demon lover is needed to refresh Mrs. Ramsay's "violated" soul. Through Mrs. Ramsay, Woolf explores the paradoxical nature of creativity: that it both discovers and creates what is perceived.[13]

Although Woolf uses mothering as a metaphor for bipolar object-relational issues, her ruminations on how self deals with loss are not limited to Mrs. Ramsay's death. The preeminence of that loss is continuously undercut: the novel is full of losses, from the dramatic to the prosaic, and each is painful in its own way.[14] The whole middle section, "Time Passes," goes into great detail about the erosion of household goods, relegating the deaths of family members to abbreviated, parenthetical notations, re-creating a "disembodiment" that erases "human agency."[15] Woolf here follows her father's example in his *Mausoleum Book*: he only briefly mentions the deaths of Minny, Julia, and Stella, whereas he recounts nostalgically what has passed away generally—old times, old friends, happy occasions, opportunities gone forever, things never said that should have been said—evidence marshaled to justify his depressive feelings of unredeemable loss and his unquenchable need for comfort from his family. In the novel, Mr. Ramsay's anticipated loss of fame is as keenly felt as Bankes's loss of friendship, itself compared to death (35). Bankes mourns his childless widowerhood just as Mrs. Ramsay grieves because her children will grow up. Woolf reasons that at the object-relations level all losses are the same. The loss of Mrs. Ramsay is foregrounded but not absolute; it becomes an emblematic, but not definitive, event. The valuable lesson of the father—that blows to our narcissism are not cosmic disasters, for we occupy only a small space in a large world—is dramatized by a decentered death.

Unlike the novel's other characters, who are wrapped up in their personal griefs and lacks, Mrs. Ramsay contemplates loss in these object-relational terms, picturing it as "a sort of transaction [that] went on between them, in which she was on one side, and life was on another, and she was always trying to get the better of it, as it was of her" (92)—a paraphrase of Leslie's remarks about Julia's attempts to balance a "mournful account of pain and happiness" after Herbert's death.[16] Thus, Mrs. Ramsay reacts with a "spasm of irritation" when she recalls that the Swiss girl is crying because her father has just died, for it reminds her of her own unspecified loss, "some other, earlier lover" (45-46), a parallel to Julia's first husband. But Mrs. Ramsay does not lose her faith, as Julia did. She listens to the monotonous beat of the waves, hearing both an experience of good mothering (for they seem "consolingly to repeat over and over again . . . 'I am guarding you—I am your support'") and a frightening "ghostly roll of drums," remorselessly beating, threatening engulfment (27-28). She knows that loss is not contained in a particular event (as the depressive typically believes): instead, it becomes a universal context, a philosophy of life.

Woolf revises Julia freely to explore untapped potential that Virginia herself has actualized. Unlike Julia, Mrs. Ramsay does not sacrifice herself because of morbid guilt; this transaction is between equals. She accepts life's losses *as anonymous,* impersonal and undeserved, sometimes even grotesquely inhuman, and she encourages others to risk the same tragedy that overpowered Julia: "And yet she had said to all these children, You shall go through with it . . . knowing what was before them—love and ambition and being wretched alone in dreary places" (92). Mrs. Ramsay's immunity establishes an order inside the self as well as in the outer world, allowing her to see that "there is a coherence in things, a stability; something, she meant, is immune from change . . . she had the feeling she had had once to-day, already, of peace, of rest" (158). Actual losses can be endured if we feel entire ourselves. Julia could not nurse herself— she felt both deadened and dutiful, as if Herbert had taken with him that central core which gave her life—but nursing others required nothing more than a cheerful face disguising her emptiness. Mrs. Ramsay does what Julia wished she could have done: she sinks down into diffusion with the lighthouse until her self can rise up again refreshed. Virginia has given her mother another chance to realize untried strength in her character, to disarm depression. Had Julia lived, this was something she could have shared with her daughter.

Woolf recognizes that neither manic dream nor depressive nightmare is final. Like the image of Rose's dish of fruit, the perfection of which must be destroyed in order to feed the guests, the dinner scene presents loss and nurturing as equal parts of a benevolent transaction: need can never be fully satisfied, but deprivation is never total. Minta's loss of her grandmother's brooch is compensated for by the gain of a fiancé, and the marriage itself is viewed by Mrs. Ramsay, its chief proponent, as an equivocal blessing:

> This will celebrate the occasion—a curious sense rising in her, at once freakish and tender, of celebrating a festival, as if two emotions were called up in her, one profound—for what could be more serious than the love of man for woman, what more commanding, more impressive, bearing in its bosom the seeds of death; at the same time these lovers, these people entering into illusion glittering eyed, must be danced round with mockery, decorated with garlands. (151)

Implicit here is the recognition that Julia's idealized marriage was an illusion and would have fallen of its own weight. In her 1907 memoir, "Reminiscences," Woolf hints that Julia would eventually have learned that nothing is perfect and that "sorrow is our lot" even if Herbert had lived (*Moments of Being* 32)—not that love is always a mockery, but thinking of love and death as natural opposites is rigid, convergent thinking. In the same year, Woolf wrote:

happiness and sorrow are equally good, and beautiful, if you can only find the form for them, because that tickles, supplies, the sense which is above the reach of these accidents. (*Letters* 1: 310)

We judge the seamless flux of experience by bifurcated extremes (in Mr. Ramsay's terms, "A" is not "Z"), those reassuringly simple concepts such as *good* and *bad*, *happy* and *sad*, that elicit large blocks of primary emotion rather than subtler, more perceptive responses. Creating a "community of feeling" among the diners that is immune to death's threats and to love's illusions because she admits both, creating, in other words, a "form" in which happiness and sorrow are equally good and beautiful, Mrs. Ramsay embraces opposites and is thus subsequently able to reconcile Cam's fear of the boar's skull with James's desire for it. An infantile retreat into perfect mothering is not needed here.

Lily Briscoe enjoys no such immunity; she feels deeply bifurcated. Like Rachel Vinrace, Lily ranges between self-assertion and self-abasement, keeping "a feeler on her surroundings lest someone should creep up" and yet longing for communion. Alternating between confidence and despair, Lily paints by fits and starts, for it is in painting that Lily finds and defines herself. In painting her ambivalence is most evident, as a cyclic fluctuation between holding on and letting go—Leslie's old intestinal pattern— that is both defensive and self-destructive:

> It was in that moment's flight between the picture and her canvas that the demons set on her who often brought her to the verge of tears and made this passage from conception to work as dreadful as any down a dark passage for a child. Such she often felt herself—struggling against terrific odds to maintain her courage; to say: "But this is what I see; this is what I see," and so to clasp some miserable remnant of her vision to her breast which a thousand forces did their best to pluck from her. And it was then too, in that chill and windy way, as she began to paint, that there forced themselves upon her other things, her own inadequacy, her insignificance, keeping house for her father off the Brompton Road, and had much ado to control her impulse to fling herself (thank Heaven she had always resisted so far) at Mrs. Ramsay's knee and say to her—but what could one say to her? "I'm in love with you"? No, that was not true, "I'm in love with this all," waving her hand at the hedge, at the house, at the children? (32)

Lily feels forced to choose between rejecting the beloved mothering figure or becoming again a panicky, dependent child whose poor self-image undermines her ability to have a vision of her own.[17] Somewhere between resisting the manic impulse for complete, heedless fusion and fighting off the depressive dread of isolation must lie a transitional space in which one's conception survives realization—indeed, in which life invites and sponsors rapport as though with a "third voice."

But something about the Ramsays prevents Lily from forming nurturing fusions in art. The "miserable remnant" clasped to her breast is like a child's transitional object, a security blanket or a teddy bear that takes the place of the mother, in the hope that this will make weaning (and establishing independence) less traumatic. The object is invested with "manic" meaning (symbolizing the mother's magical power to sustain the infant's illusion that she and it are one and perfect) while remaining only an object (representing the "depressive" lesson from father that mother and child are separate, unmergeable entities, each imperfect). But because the goodness of this nurturing object comes from the goodness of the self that helps create its sponsorship, a child who lacks self-confidence and so harbors unresolved, ambivalent feelings toward its parents may find the transitional object embodying more conflicts than it resolves.[18] When overcome by despair, Lily produces a miserable remnant that gives less sustenance than throwing herself on the mercy of Mrs. Ramsay promises to provide, though that sustenance would come at the expense of self-esteem. Either way, Lily goes hungry.

Lily's ambivalence echoes manic-depressive fragmentation in tying self-worth to misinterpretation. Typically, she blames the Ramsays for her divided feelings: "what happened to her, especially staying with the Ramsays, was to be made to feel violently two opposite things at the same time; that's what you feel, was one; that's what I feel, was the other, and then they fought together in her mind, as now." Deeply divided about her own worth, she sees in the Ramsays her bifurcated attitude toward love's goodness: it is "so beautiful, so exciting," yet also "the stupidest, the most barbaric of human passions . . . tedious, puerile, and inhumane" (154–55). Lily fails to understand how her conflicting emotions have become confused with external realities and so condemns the Ramsays' love as a mixture of exultation and illusion, an "unreal but penetrating and exciting universe which is the world seen through the eyes of love" (73)—that is to say, a delusion. This condemnation is especially strong when she sympathizes with the wife and despises the husband: "That man, she thought, her anger rising in her, never gave; that man took. She, on the other hand, would be forced to give. Mrs Ramsay had given. Giving, giving, giving, she had died" (223). James of course shares this opinion, but when the narration portrays Mr. Ramsay from his own point of view, neither Lily's nor James's interpretation holds fast. Transactions between husband and wife, though often shaky, work toward an acceptable mutuality. To evaluate Lily's ambivalence, we must first understand the nature of the Ramsay (and the Stephen) marriage and why Lily (and Woolf) initially misjudged it.

In studies of manic-depressive families, researchers have found that bipolar illness in a parent presents both the spouse and the children with a emotional dilemma:

> The relationship between the spouses proved critical to childrearing patterns. The balance between mutuality/isolation in the husband-wife relationship was strained by the birth of successive children. Many of the spouses of patients tended to view manic or depressive episodes as willful abdications of responsibility or as manifestations of weakness of character and self-indulgence that had to be met with a firm display of power and control. The unspoken but forcefully communicated dictum to the child that mommy (or daddy) is "sick" through some fault of his or her own thrust the child on the horns of a dilemma: the "sick" parent was lovable but irresponsible, while the well parent was responsible but also to be feared. Thus a pattern was set in which caretaking roles were vague, loyalties were tenuous, and affection and approval were dependent on degree of health and responsibility.[19]

Woolf knew that her father was moody though obviously not psychotic, not "mad" as she and her family felt she was periodically (or James Kenneth was terminally). He had "bad" moments when he groaned and whined (*Moments of Being* 112), but when Leslie was flushed with good feelings, Woolf felt that

> Beautiful was he at such moments; simple and eager as a child; and exquisitely alive to all affection; exquisitely tender. We would have helped him then if we could, given him all we had, and felt it little beside his need—but the moment passed. (*Moments of Being* 46)

In "A Sketch of the Past," recounting incidents of the happy Leslie, Woolf doubts her negative assessment: "He cannot have been as severe and melancholy and morose as I make him out. . . . Undoubtedly I colour my picture too dark" (*Moments of Being* 113). But three pages later he becomes "the exacting, the violent, the histrionic, the demonstrative, the self-centered, the self pitying, the deaf, the appealing, the alternately loved and hated father."

Here is precisely the problem that families of bipolars, whether cyclothymic or manic-depressive, recurrently face. Relationships develop over time, but mood shifts occur rapidly. The sense of trust, affection, and loyalty that good days foster is ruined by the next bad day. One moment Leslie would reassure his children that Stella's coming marriage and departure was no tragedy deserving of tears, and "the moment after he was groaning to her that the blow was irreparable" (*Moments of Being* 50). Unpredictable people create confusion in intimate and important familial relationships and tend to elicit strong emotional reactions from spouses and/or children who do not understand why they are treated so inconsistently. What is worse, because cyclothymia is milder than frank manic-depressive illness, a cyclothymic's moodiness shades into those subtler shifts experienced daily by "normal" people and by the patient himself when he happens to be euthymic. It is therefore very difficult for family members, who have become accustomed to lifelong moodiness, to identify a particular behavior as a "trait" (expressing the patient's character) or a "state" (expressing a transitory mood).

It is easy to develop an intolerance for uncertainty and conclude rashly that a cyclothymic misbehaves because he chooses to, for which violation he should be held responsible, as any other family member would be. Normally, such a judgment would be made by the spouse, who is equal in authority to the patient. But rather than respond to her husband's seemingly "willful abdication" with "power and control," Julia tolerated Leslie's outbursts and his glooms. She bore the brunt of the former and nursed him until he shifted out of the latter, and so she earned pity and admiration as a martyr sacrificed upon the altar of marriage. Thus, the crucial "balance of mutuality/isolation" in the Leslie-Julia relationship was weighted toward isolation. She stoically endured abuse by contracting into herself, nursing in private her chronic grief over Herbert's death and life's injustice, to which no outrage Leslie committed could compare. After her death, it fell to her children to assume the caretaking role, and they did so with both isolation and disapproval. They became all the more judgmental because they had been raised according to a more stringent rubric that did not forgive misbehavior easily: Julia was sterner with her children than she was with her husband.

The injustice of this situation was further strained because Leslie let it be known that sharing his wife's attentions with the births of successive children caused him to feel even more neglected and vulnerable. Since the children felt they were implicated in Leslie's unhappiness, draining maternal affection he had craved for himself, perhaps feeling that he had begrudged them, they became much more sensitive to the issue of his responsibility when he became histrionic after Julia's death. Since no one then understood the biochemical mechanisms of cyclothymia, and since Leslie clearly retained his reason and sense of reality—he could not be excused as "mad"— his children saw instead a man who indulged himself in fits of temper and tried to blame it on his inherited "thin skin," the skin of the genius, which for them was the definitive mark of his vanity. It was on the grounds of vanity that his suffering could be condemned as a weakness, a moral defect. Leslie's intense "oriental gloom," Woolf claimed, was a manifestation of "his traditional pose; he was the lonely; the deserted; the old unhappy man" craving affection (106). He had a "violent temper," one

> that he could not control, and that, considering his worship of reason, his hatred of gush, of exaggeration, of all superlatives, seems inconsistent. It was due, I suppose, to the fact that he was spoilt as a child; because of his nervous delicacy, and that delicacy excused his extreme irritability. . . . [M]en of genius were naturally uncontrolled. (109)

Inconsistency—the most visible and often the most damaging effect of mood swings—implied hypocrisy, and that was unforgivable. Even his subsequent euthymic states, when he felt guilty for having abused his family during fits of depression or rage, were interpreted according to the model of the egotistical genius who indulged himself because he felt privileged to do so: "It was part of the convention," Woolf wrote, "that after these outbursts, the man of genius became 'touchingly apologetic'" (110). His sincerity was obscured by his children's sense of the injustice of his demands, especially after the deaths of Julia and Stella, when they had not been allowed to express their grief and lay it to rest. "Misery of this kind tends to concentrate itself upon an object," Virginia noted, and Leslie became a suitable target because of his dependency upon those two women, now dead, as he turned his attention to Vanessa, his "next victim" (55). He even urged Vanessa to follow Julia and Stella's example in not examining his moods critically: "When he was sad, he explained, she should be sad; when he was angry, as he was periodically when she asked him for a cheque, she should weep; instead she stood before him like a stone," which irritated him all the more. Alarmed about their safety and integrity, Vanessa and Virginia regarded him as a "tyrant of inconceivable selfishness" (56).

Ironically, they focused so much of their suspicion and hatred upon the moody Leslie that they judged less harshly the uniform George, whose behavior was in fact much more pervasively tyrannical and hurtful, combining as it did brotherly love, sexual abuse, and the reification of society's anti-feminist values. Unlike the complex and intellectual Leslie, George was merely "stupid" and "good natured" (58), and so one could forgive him. George was considered to be too simple to qualify as the hated neurotic genius of the Stephen male line, but Leslie was smart enough to have known better. Woolf admitted that she and her sister had been "simply credulous" about George's true intentions "and ready to impose our conventional heroic shape upon the tumult of his character" (58), which resulted in bedroom embraces, passionate kisses, and dictatorial orders about propriety in dress and conversation at social occasions. The "old wretch," Leslie, looked so much worse.

Woolf suspected that her hatred of her father's tyranny was to some extent undeserved, a reaction to the deaths of Julia and Stella. It was, Woolf wrote,

> like being shut up in the same cage with a wild beast. Suppose I, at fifteen, was a nervous, gibbering, little monkey, always spitting or cracking a nut and shying the shells about, and mopping and mowing, and leaping into dark corners and then swinging in rapture across the cage, he was the pacing, dangerous, morose lion; a lion who was sulky and angry and injured; and suddenly ferocious, and then very humble, and then majestic; and then lying dusty and fly pestered in a corner of the cage. (116)

Both father and daughter were moody, but they were frequently out of synch with each other. Only when their moods corresponded did she feel that she and he "were in league together. There was something we had in common" (111) that created a sense of "passionate fumbling fellowship" (137). When he shouted and swore because stout Dermod O'Brien, one of Stella's admirers, had been invited to dinner, Virginia found herself agreeing with him that Julia's hospitality was sometimes too impulsive, and "I affirmed my sympathy, felt my likeness" to her father (112).

It was a likeness that also implied difference—as every child feels when comparing himself or herself to a parent. Woolf recognized her father's predicament and sympathized even as she criticized:

> he was a man in prison, isolated. He had so ignored, or disguised his own feelings that he had no idea of what he was; and no idea of what other people were. Hence the horror and the terror of those violent displays of rage. There was something blind, animal, savage in them.
> . . . He did not realise what he did. No one could enlighten him. Yet

he suffered. Through the walls of his prison he had moments of realisation.

From it all I gathered one obstinate and enduring conception; that nothing is so much to be dreaded as egotism. Nothing so cruelly hurts the person himself; nothing so wounds those who are forced into contact with it. (146–47)

Of her mother's complicity in Leslie's tantrums Woolf was equally critical:

Too much obsessed with his health, with his pleasures, she was too willing, as I think now, to sacrifice us to him. It was thus that she left us the legacy of his dependence, which after her death became so harsh an imposition. It would have [been] better for our relationship if she had left him to fend for himself. (133)

Julia's tolerance for Leslie's inability or unwillingness to cope with his mood swings led to a destructive isolation. Protecting him against others but not against himself, Julia inadvertently allowed him to remain in his "prison," unenlightened. Mutuality might have helped him gain some autonomy; treated as an equal rather than as a child or a God, he might have become more aware (as cyclothymics and manic-depressives often are not) of the effects of his moods on himself and on others. It is the therapeutic action of mutuality in healing the cut that egotism creates between self and world that Woolf explores in *To the Lighthouse*.

Mr. Ramsay's lesson in mutuality begins immediately. The initial confrontation between husband and wife centers on a question of knowledge and mood. Mrs. Ramsay offers James a hope that tomorrow's weather will permit a sail to the lighthouse. The "good enough" mother, she reads the child's desires and offers the playful illusion that the world might grant his wish. Mr. Ramsay acts out the father's role of *dis*-illusioning his son, reminding him that the world is treacherous and life a disappointment:

He shivered; he quivered. All his vanity, all his satisfaction in his own splendour, riding fell as a thunderbolt, fierce as a hawk at the head of his men through the valley of death, had been shattered, destroyed. . . .

Not for the world would she have spoken to him, realising, from the familiar signs, his eyes averted, and some curious gathering together of his person, as if he wrapped himself about and needed privacy into which to regain his equilibrium, that he was outraged and anguished. (48–49)

Expressed in the hyperbolic terms of Tennyson's portrait of a bungled military campaign, Mr. Ramsay's feelings seem utterly ridiculous but are not. Destructive objectivity looks like "exactingness and egotism" to young

James (58), but it evidences a depressed self tortured by isolation in a "poor little world" (108) that appears mechanical, inhuman, and entropic. In a 1924 letter Woolf describes, in precisely the same terms, a sudden depression that came upon her as she was walking in the rain:

> It was a wet windy night; & as I walked back across the field I said Now I am meeting it; now the old devil has once more got his spine through the waves. (but I cannot re-capture really). And such was the strength of my feeling that I became physically rigid. Reality, so I thought, was unveiled. And there was something noble in feeling like this; tragic, not at all petty. . . . Off I rode, without much time, against such a wind; & again I had a satisfaction in being matched with powerful things, like wind & dark. I battled, had to walk; got on; drove ahead; dropped the torch; picked it up; & so on again without any lights. Saw men & women walking together; thought you're safe & happy I'm an outcast. (*Diary* 2: 270)

The despair in both cases is real enough, though the context may seem inappropriate. Woolf's mixture of poetic fantasy and prosaic reality implies that Mr. Ramsay is reacting, not to his wife's remark, but to an interior disaster related to it—"that he was a failure" (59). He feels shattered because he reads into her "little lie" a denial of his preoccupation with rationality—the depressive's typical defense against despair and a chaotic, uncaring universe—and she becomes the target for all his anger. Agitated depressives often do turn suddenly upon loved ones, but their attacks are misplaced: the real enemy gnawing at self's foundations lurks within. Ironically, though Lily's talent lies in spatializing on canvas inner worlds, she cannot sympathize with Ramsay, but wonders "why so brave a man in thought should be so timid in life; how strangely he was venerable and laughable at one and the same time" (70). Unable to detect a common denominator for them, she sees only how inappropriate his emotions are—because she is guilty of projection herself.

Mrs. Ramsay understands her husband's despair. She objects, not to the reality of his feelings, but to his method for coping with his vulnerability, which she effectively exposes:

> without replying, dazed and blinded, she bent her head as if to let the pelt of jagged hail, the drench of dirty water, bespatter her unrebuked. There was nothing to be said.
>
> He stood by her in silence. Very humbly, at length, he said that he would step over and ask the Coastguards if she liked.
>
> There was nobody whom she reverenced as she reverenced him.
>
> She was quite ready to take his word for it, she said. (51)

Her reaction is therapeutic: without replying to the content of his moody rage, she acknowledges its effect, her victimization, by bending her head—just as a psychoanalyst initially accepts his patient's transference (also an unconscious transferral of emotion from an appropriate object to an inappropriate one—usually the analyst) so that he can bring it to the patient's attention. When the patient becomes aware that he has read into his analyst feelings or ideas that really belong somewhere else, the transference stops. Mr. Ramsay is likewise touched and repentant. His wife's mirroring helps him acknowledge and correct misbehavior, even though he is still depressed; Woolf does not create a magic solution for her father's mood swings, just a practical one. Shortly afterward, when his wife enjoys a private moment with the lighthouse beam, Mr. Ramsay successfully resists the temptation to interrupt her and seek reassurance. Seeing this, she calls to him, giving him "of her own free will what she knew he would never ask" (100).

Stressing depressed spouses' needs for autonomy and self-sufficiency, Woolf has Mr. and Mrs. Ramsay accomplish their mutuality tactfully, from a distance, much like Lily and William's seaside intimacy (33–34). When walking silently in the garden, Mr. Ramsay is tempted to whine, but he becomes uncomfortable, "as if he were breaking into that solitude, that aloofness, that remoteness of hers" (103)—again, another noticeable change Woolf makes in her portrait of her father, who complained that he "required" "proofs of [Julia's] love" in specific language to dispel his "morbid" feeling of inadequacy.[20] Mr. Ramsay *does* learn to resist, because he is connected to his wife in a mirroring relationship. Like the cognitively narcissistic infant, Ramsay overcomes his "*archaic, egoistic* way of loving" when his wife denies him automatic reciprocity;[21] by making him aware that she has interests unconnected with her maternal function, she weans him from dependence and socializes him for balanced object-relations with others who will not mother him. She, in turn, gives him the same respect. When she wants to tell him that she has been reading fairy tales to James, she stops herself: "No, they could not share that; they could not say that" (104), for her husband does not believe in fairy tales. In their final moments together in the novel, they silently read books which uplift and reassure them, each in a private corner, until the time comes to retire to the bedroom.

This is a difficult moment, for the separate but equal object-relational transaction of reading texts that reflect their inner feelings must now combine into the one shared transaction of the relationship. In an unspoken dialogue, he asks to be told she loves him and she refuses, keeping her distance. But then she smiles, and from this small sign he takes his solace—and keeps his self-sufficiency—allowing her her reticence: "[T]hough she had not said a word, he knew, of course, that she loved him." Mrs. Ramsay then admits silently that he was right about the weather though wrong in his defensiveness. Enigmatically, she ends the chapter by smiling, "for she had triumphed again" (186). Remembering that Woolf has resisted painting Julia as a "chronic mourner" who resorted to motherly sacrifices in place of romantic love, we have a distinctly playful, sexually adult scene here. Mutual autonomy is preserved, first in the reading of separate texts and then in their wordless intimacy. After this scene Mr. Ramsay's insecurities and his depressive clutching of objective certainty are greatly muted: "But now, he felt, it didn't matter a damn who reached Z (if thought ran like an alphabet from A to Z). Somebody would reach it—if not he, then another" (179). Mrs. Ramsay's triumph is that of any parent whose child has grown beyond its initial dependency and any spouse whose mate has learned how to survive mood swings with dignity.

Mr. Ramsay's initial progress toward self-sufficiency explains his behavior ten years later, after his wife's death. Still moody and lonely, "he had been a little out of temper too at breakfast," and he bears down upon Lily for sympathy (225), groaning and assuming "a pose of extreme decrepitude" (227). Lily feels she is no Mrs. Ramsay, whose inner resources she idealizes because she does not believe in her own. She responds characteristically, first with a depressive self-negation and then with agitated defensiveness. She blames herself for not being able to imitate "the glow, the rhapsody, the self-surrender" of Mrs. Ramsay (224) and concludes that she is "not a woman, but a peevish, ill-tempered, dried-up old maid presumably" (226) who cannot nurture. Although tempted to fake it, to put on the "face" of the motherly nurse, Lily feels nauseated by Mr. Ramsay's effusive needs, which disregard her legitimate interests that do not include him. She wants to pull her psychic skirts up, to wall herself against intrusion. Suddenly, and accidentally, she discovers how to avoid both abject submission and cold retention. She diverts his attention from sorrow to boots, which become transitional objects shared by the two players: "They had reached, she felt, a sunny island where peace dwelt, sanity reigned and the sun for ever shone, the blessed island of good boots. Her heart warmed to him." Mr. Ramsay surprises Lily, becoming gentle and affectionate, and she responds with genuine, even filial sympathy: "Thus occupied he seemed to her a figure of infinite pathos" (230), but also one of sudden revivification, that sudden flare (when she praised his boots), that sudden recovery of vitality and interest in ordinary human things, which too passed and changed (for he was always changing, and hid nothing) into that other final phase which was new to her and had, she owned, made herself ashamed of her own irritability, when it seemed as if he had shed worries and ambitions. (233)

When he leaves her, she feels a sudden emptiness, for just as she is finally ready to sympathize, to efface herself and surrender emotional sustenance, "he no longer needed it" (231).

Lily has inadvertently duplicated Mrs. Ramsay's strategy for steering Mr. Ramsay toward mutuality and autonomy. Put in the position of the mother whose separate interests are ignored by the needy and cognitively narcissistic child, she reacts as Mrs. Ramsay did at the end of Part One. She resists surrender and encourages a neutral transaction—replicating the lesson of Mrs. Ramsay's dinner: that needs can never be fully satisfied, but deprivation is never total. To her surprise, Lily finds that Mr. Ramsay has not simply been put off; he has changed. His readiness to consider "ordinary human things" (233), in contrast to his previously fiery unworldliness ("born blind, deaf, and dumb, to the ordinary things" [107]), indicates a subtle modification within. James, "the image of stark and uncompromising severity," who frowns "at the sight of human frailty" (10) and who fantasizes on the boat trip to the lighthouse that his father will, at any moment, become self-indulgent and tyrannical (273), finds himself being praised for his seamanship and relents. Cam admires her father (308). The immunity he learned from his wife has given him the strength to resist feeding on his children in order to fill his inner emptiness. Now he can nurse others and deserve their love.

Until this moment, Lily has clearly been ambivalent about Mr. Ramsay, mothering, and art, alternately desiring Mrs. Ramsay and rejecting her, extolling her own artistic vision and ridiculing it. When she first realizes that she both admires William (a "generous, pure-hearted, heroic man!" [39]) and despises him (he is unsympathetic to dogs, spoiled by a valet, and fussy with food), Lily asks herself an important question: how is it possible to hear one's "own voice saying without prompting undeniable, everlasting, contradictory things" (40)? But she does not arrive at an answer; her thought spins until it explodes "of its own intensity" (41). Ambivalence cannot be resolved when it is dealt with in the cocoon of private thought. Lily's inner world lacks unity, and so her early attempts at painting are painful, her relationships conflicted, and her self-image that of an "old maid" who neither desires nor feels desirable (226). Love and marriage seem like frighteningly real invasions, feeding "on the treasure of the house, greedily" (261)—Mrs. Ramsay's fecund, nurturing self. Later, Lily consoles herself that she "need never marry anybody" and feels an "enormous exultation" (262), just as Rachel Vinrace feels impenetrable to assault in her hatred of Richard Dalloway. The world makes demands; Lily holds on, holds herself back, and admires William's love for Mrs. Ramsay because it makes no demands. Only under such tight security can she feel "gratitude" for "this 'rapture' . . . for nothing so solaced her, eased her of the perplexity of life, and miraculously raised its burdens" as a love that does not task self (74), a vision that does not have to be made real.

Painting, however, requires a vision that is both magical and real, and it is painful precisely because it exposes her inner vision "which a thousand forces did their best to pluck from her" (32), among them her own voice saying contradictory things. Thinking conceptually about art and relegating human relations to the realm of the insincere is safe, but it cannot put the sundered fragments back together: Lily cannot see herself until she spatializes, in the mirroring circuit of artist and canvas, her inner world. As an artist and psychoanalyst, Marion Milner, notes, the blocked artist's problem is both bipolar and circular. It is comprised

> not only of endowing the outside world with one's own dream and so giving it desirability, coming to believe that what it offers is what one wants, but also the reverse problem of coming to believe that the outside world wants what one has to give. Obviously this belief can be very precariously established; and it is impeded, not only by inner doubts about one's wish to give, doubts of the strength of one's love and constructive wishes as compared with one's hate and envy and greed, but also by actual failures of one's surroundings to need what one has to give.[22]

Lily sees the outer world as hateful and finds that it resists her painting it so long as Mr. Ramsay embodies villainy, so long as he threatens the only source of nurture and goodness in her life: the mythologized Mrs. Ramsay. She sees her inner world as hateful and unworthy so long as she fears that her feeding off the idealized mother figure diminishes both Mrs. Ramsay and herself. It is the "image of the pelican woman, feeding her brood with her own vital substance," that so depresses Lily and obscures the real Mrs. Ramsay (whose nonmaternal interests Lily cannot imagine).[23] If women's selves are meant merely to be sacrificed, how can they truly give, in marriage or in art? The creative act, in Lily's own words, is "to feel simply that's a chair, that's a table, and yet at the same time, It's a miracle, it's an ecstasy" (300). But in the presence of the Ramsays she feels either that the chair is degraded or that the miracle is tawdry, because her bipolar object-relations prevent her from having a creative relationship with exterior objects.

Lily feels stuck between asserting the goodness of her own vision against Mr. Ramsay's realism and accepting reality's goodness enough to risk contact. She struggles against rejecting reality outright and painting merely an abstract scene, but she also struggles against "her own inadequacy, her insignificance," which degrades imagination.[24] Milner argues that every artist faces the same bipolar conflict: he or she "has to reckon not only with one's hate of the external world, when it fails to live up to one's expectations, but also hate of oneself when one similarly fails."[25] When we cannot make the world desirable through our dreams (and depression interferes with this fundamental function of imagination to make perceptions of the world personally meaningful), we despise the world and ourselves. Lily seems to realize this when at last she understands her hostility toward Tansley:

> Her own idea of him was grotesque, Lily knew well, stirring the plantains with her brush. Half one's notions of other people were, after all, grotesque. They served private purposes of one's own. He did for her instead of a whipping-boy. She found herself flagellating his lean flanks when she was out of temper. (293)

Her hostility is a defensive displacement: she hates Tansley as she hates herself.

But since Lily's painting is also a product of her self-world relationship, she herself becomes *art's* whipping boy. Tansley and the world and the canvas are in concert, saying, "Women can't write, women can't paint" (130). Lily sneers at him, but when she describes her painting as the "residue of her thirty-three years, the deposit of each day's living mixed with something more secret than she had ever spoken or shown," something "immensely exciting" (81), her language reveals that what is inside, the product of the self, is both feces and vision, repulsive yet attractive, unwanted but desired. In contrast, painting mother and child "without irreverence" (82) requires an art that gives value to external things by incorporating the sense that in some uncanny way the object itself co-sponsors Lily's aesthetic understanding. Wishing for a sacred rapport is not enough; the "third voice," that unthought but known familiarity between Lily and the canvas or between Lily and the Ramsays, must be heard in the dialogue between self and object. To solve her artistic problem of balancing "the relations between the masses," Lily must refer it to her ambivalence about the Ramsays.

What, then, moves Lily out of her autistic world into the artistic? At the moment of final creation, a "wave of white" appears at the window, duplicating the shape of Mrs. Ramsay and James seen in Part One:

> "Mrs. Ramsay! Mrs. Ramsay!" [Lily] cried, feeling the old horror come back—to want and want and not to have. Could she inflict that still? And then, quietly, as if she refrained, that too became part of ordinary experience, was on a level with the chair, with the table. Mrs. Ramsay—it was part of her perfect goodness to Lily—sat there quite simply, in the chair, flicked her needles to and fro, knitted her reddish-brown stocking, cast her shadow on the step. There she sat.
>
> And as if she had something she must share, yet could hardly leave her easel, so full her mind was of what she was thinking, of what she was seeing, Lily went past Mr. Carmichael holding her brush to the edge of the lawn. Where was that boat now? And Mr. Ramsay? She wanted him. (300)

Lily initially feels the infant's narcissistic needs and its depressive helplessness to satisfy them. Yet this "horror" loses its magnitude and becomes a simple fact, like the existence of a chair—differentiated, isolated, but real. The ability of the self to survive the need, to perceive it as only one need among many, a wave that will eventually be gone, defuses the threat. Fluctuations in mood need not confuse our sense of identity if we, as someone who really exists, can question them. Once Lily feels both real and, in an uncanny way, invited to paint, Mrs. Ramsay sits there "quite simply," not a goddess but an object wishing to be painted and a feeling needing to be expressed. But where has this new strength come from? And why is Mr. Ramsay necessary to Lily's vision?

Lily's discovery of Mr. Ramsay's otherness models her ultimate discovery of the sponsorship she seeks in art—the sensation that she has been invited to paint. Ramsay's version of reality denigrates the value of artistic imagination because it denies the existence of the "third voice" that beckons subject-object fusions. For him, all objects are impersonal, silent, dead, amenable only to ordering in a linear progression from A to Z. Ironically, because he regards all subject-object relations as man-made, he can never achieve his goal of objectivity, for every idea he has must be merely imposed by himself. He cannot get beyond the subjective limitations of "R"

—Ramsay himself—which obscure and negativize the object world, creating "a world of impossible loneliness, so that he craves his wife's sympathy."[26] Because Ramsay's vision is never invited by the objects he studies but only opposes them, as a stake driven into a channel defies the waves rather than being invited to ride them, both his inner and his outer world are impoverished. Ramsay is the polar opposite of Septimus, who feels victimized by inscrutable meanings called up from objects against his consent. In psychosis, the "third voice" shrieks from all sides for total, self-annihilating fusion. Mr. Ramsay hears nothing but his own voice; he is to be pitied, not feared. Lily's anger, then, must be a reaction to what she hates in herself: the isolated ego that inhibits creativity by turning other people into objects—reducing them *with irreverence.*

The reconciliation on the island of good boots not only relieves Lily of the burden of resisting Ramsay's objectifying ego but also jolts her into considering his *otherness,* a reality that no longer conforms to her autistic dreams but demands a new dream, a new vision, to incorporate the changed object. No longer can Mr. Ramsay serve as devil, Mrs. Ramsay as goddess incarnate for "private needs." Painting makes the private public, gives it form, and so foregrounds unexamined "needs." Ten years earlier, when Tansley's egotism denied Lily's validity as an artist, she had felt "her whole being bow, like corn under a wind"; she had retreated into a private world and thought only of the abstract form of her portrait: "I must move the tree to the middle; that matters—nothing else" (130). Now she paints fluently, like a swimmer alternately dominating the curl of a wave and being carried along by it (235).

The transformation comes when she lets go of the fear that she would become the dupe of art and its bipolar rhythm:

> With a curious physical sensation, as if she were urged forward and at the same time must hold herself back, she made her first quick decisive stroke. The brush descended. It flickered brown over the white canvas; it left a running mark. A second time she did it—a third time. And so pausing and so flickering, she attained a dancing rhythmical movement, as if the pauses were one part of the rhythm and the strokes another, and all were related; and so, lightly and swiftly pausing, striking, she scored her canvas with brown running nervous lines which had no sooner settled there than they enclosed (she felt it looming out at her) a space. Down in the hollow of one wave she saw the next wave towering higher and higher above her. . . . It was an exacting form of intercourse anyhow. (235–36)

The pauses here are not merely depressive hoardings but incorporations of new material which, moment by moment, are transformed into brush strokes; the brush strokes are not only manic projections but also responses to the demands of the canvas. When Lily does suffer a block a page later, it is because she momentarily remembers Tansley reminding her that the world may not want the gift of her inner life. But she resists the temptation to act on a depressive belief and instead concentrates on the canvas ("for the mass loomed before her"). In so doing she experiences an uncanny fusion comparable to Mrs. Ramsay's with the lighthouse. Even the imagery of fecundity is the same:

> Then, as if some juice necessary for the lubrication of her faculties were spontaneously squirted, she began precariously dipping among the blues and umbers, moving her brush hither and thither, but it was now heavier and went slower, as if it had fallen in with some rhythm which was dictated to her. . . . Certainly she was losing consciousness of outer things, and her name and her personality and her appearance, and whether Mr. Carmichael was there or not, her mind kept throwing up from its depths, scenes, and names, and sayings, and memories and ideas, like a fountain spurting over that glaring, hideously difficult white space, while she modelled it with greens and blues. (237–38)

When this bipolar rhythm, co-sponsored by the canvas, is aligned with manic-depressive object-relations, boundaries dissolve and reform. Woolf's version of artistic creativity resembles Marion Milner's report of how painting made her feel "whole":

> It was the discovery that when painting something from nature there occurred, at least sometimes, a fusion into a never-before-known wholeness; not only were the object and oneself no longer felt to be separate, but neither were thought and sensation and feeling and action. . . . [T]hought was not drowned in feeling, they were somehow there together. Moreover, when this state of concentration was really achieved one was no longer aware of oneself doing it, one no longer acted from a centre to an object as remote; in fact, something quite special happened to one's sense of self.[27]

Milner feels as if the pieces of herself (thoughts, feelings, consciousness, unconsciousness) are brought together into a creative relation by her object-relations during painting. A self-other transaction shapes an intrasubjective transaction; it is as if by painting the object she has incorporated it. Lily, like Milner, experiences the pleasure of "finding a bit of the outside world . . . that was willing temporarily to fit in with one's dreams, [so that] a moment of illusion was made possible, a moment in which inner and outer seemed to coincide."[28] Out of this fusion comes an enrichment of the self, because, like Mrs. Ramsay's lighthouse, the object with which she fuses (the painting, good boots) reciprocates; it becomes desirable because it is both an object and her dream. Artistic fusion makes imagination real while still acknowledging the object's otherness, and this rhythmic integration of manic and depressive perspectives strengthens the self. The transcendence of separateness—like the unity gained in the boat by the Ramsays working together toward a common goal—replicates the experience of successful weaning. Both Lily and the remaining Ramsays carry out Mrs. Ramsay's original, promised voyage. They have survived her death.

The restoration of Mrs. Ramsay, the growth of those left behind, their new independence: all of this recapitulates and redeems her lost mothering. The body of the mother has been demystified; it is no longer seen as the only source of nurture and stability. The father has been reclaimed; he is now "her" father (*Diary* 3: 194), a contemporary whose moody misbehavior can be seen in a more forgiving light. Clinical research shows that children of mood-disordered parents often suffer from identification with the ill parent and may wish to become "magic helpers," obsessively trying to order their parent's chaotic world.[29] If Woolf's repeated explorations of variations of her parents' marriage in fiction is akin to working at being a magic helper, then in this novel she has succeeded and so has won her own release—saving, not them, but herself. Lily and Mr. Ramsay survive a second weaning by discovering sources of strength within themselves, and with self-worth come immunity and beneficial object-relations.[30]

As a prerepresentational perception, the line Lily draws down the middle of her canvas to balance two masses may symbolize the canvas itself (as a kind of meta-art), or Lily (to schematicize her psychodrama), or the "third voice" we hear when an exacting form of intercourse is suddenly replaced by an easy, joyful integration of fragments into a whole. Its possible referents do not matter; the line need only give form to the tenuous boundary between dilation and contraction, projection and introjection. Art and mood swings are tied to each other, not to the loss of the mother. Woolf's obsession with her mother ended when she realized that the absence she felt could never have been filled by Julia. Woolf no longer desired to sacrifice her autonomy for the sake of becoming a child again. Fullness came with fiction.

11 "I do not know altogether who I am"

The Plurality of Intrasubjective Life in The Waves

I think, often, I have the happiest of lives, in having
discovered stability. Now one stable moment vanquishes
chaos. But this I said in The Lighthouse.

(Diary 3: 141)

From the start, Woolf planned *The Waves* to be a difficult work. *Orlando*
had been "mere childs play" (*Diary* 3: 264), an exercise in "continuity
& narrative, & how to keep the realities at bay. But I purposely avoided
of course any other difficulty. I never got down to my depths & made
shapes square up, as I did in The Lighthouse" (*Diary* 3: 203). Now Woolf
planned to

> eliminate all waste, deadness, superfluity: to give the moment whole;
> whatever it includes. Say that the moment is a combination of
> thought; sensation; the voice of the sea. Waste, deadness, come from
> the inclusion of things that dont belong to the moment; this appalling
> narrative business of the realist: getting on from lunch to dinner: it is
> false, unreal, merely conventional. (*Diary* 3: 209)

External references were to be swept aside. What she aimed for was "an
abstract mystical eyeless book: a playpoem" (*Diary* 3: 203). Readers have
been haunted by these three adjectives, especially *eyeless,* which seems to
deny the dazzling descriptions that flood the novel. But eyes also reveal
the seer in the act of seeing, establishing reciprocal object-relations. The
infant looks into the mother's eyes both to know her and to know himself;
by her reaction he forms his first self-image. An "eyeless" novel, then, is
unresponsive; it does not accommodate itself to our needs as readers for
unity or guidance. We are treated not as audience but as eavesdroppers,
listening to voices that are not speaking to us.

   Woolf prepared herself to write an eyeless book by withdrawing from
social relations:

> I am going to enter a nunnery these next months; & let myself down
> into my mind; Bloomsbury being done with. I am going to face certain
> things. It is going to be a time of adventure & attack, rather lonely &
> painful I think. But solitude will be good for a new book. (*Diary* 3: 219)

This is quite a different voice from that of the Woolf who feared imagining Septimus's madness. The turning point had come two years earlier. On September 15, 1926, at Rodmell House, Woolf recorded a short-lived depression, which she entitled "A State of Mind":

> Woke up perhaps at 3. Oh its beginning its coming—the horror—physically like a painful wave swelling about the heart—tossing me up. I'm unhappy unhappy! Down—God, I wish I were dead. Pause. But why am I feeling this? Let me watch the wave rise. I watch. Vanessa. Children. Failure. Yes; I detect that. Failure failure. (The wave rises). Oh they laughed at my taste in green paint! Wave crashes. I wish I were dead! I've only a few years to live I hope. I cant face this horror any more—(this is the wave spreading out over me).
>
> This goes on; several times, with varieties of horror. Then, at the crisis, instead of the pain remaining intense, it becomes rather vague. I doze. I wake with a start. The wave again! The irrational pain: the sense of failure; generally some specific incident, as for example my taste in green paint, or buying a new dress, or asking Dadie for the week end, tacked on.
>
> At last I say, watching as dispassionately as I can, Now take a pull of yourself. No more of this. I reason. I take a census of happy people & unhappy. I brace myself to shove to throw to batter down. I begin to march blindly forward. I feel obstacles go down. I say it doesn't matter. Nothing matters. I become rigid & straight, & sleep again. . . . Does everyone go through this state? Why have I so little control?
> (*Diary* 3: 110–11)

Woolf's recollection here resembles Lily's experience in her struggle to paint. Both must face an irrational horror—of failure, emptiness, sterility—before they are able to "march blindly forward." Woolf survives the waves of depression that threaten to drown her by watching "as dispassionately as [she] can" what engulfs her, by questioning mood when it affects cognition and self-evaluation. She exploits the phenomenon of "double awareness" to gain perspective: one part of her watches the other part feeling depressed. To maintain such openness to pain, she tries to let go in the face of drowning, instead of holding on defensively. Lily relinquishes her hatred of Tansley and opens herself up to the liberating acceptance of chaos outside and in, excitedly, nervously, squirting paint onto the canvas. Woolf lets go of her despair and questions its validity: "Why am I feeling this?" The tactic she uses to avoid becoming the dupe of depression is to embrace more perceptions, more impressions, as creative readers are sensitive to their responses to the text. Rather than be overwhelmed by the content of mood, its message of failure, she splits her attention between the content of mood and its shape as a *wave,* a transparent deformation of the seemingly smooth surface of experience. The despair becomes "vague," less persuasive, and at last passes. By fulfilling her mother's wish to sink down completely, Woolf can rise up again refreshed. By creating another part of her self (like Alcorn and Bracher's "alien subject") to read her depression as a *different* kind of experience from the one it forcefully and narrowly presents, she can isolate despair. In effect, she exploits Leonard's schematization of her breakdowns—that she was insane in only one-quarter of her mind—by using the other three-quarters to detect, question, and survive the "mad" domain.

Woolf has learned to deal with mood swings by questioning changes in beliefs and interpretations—in effect duplicating the techniques of modern cognitive psychotherapy. Depressives can alleviate some of their distress by recognizing and correcting overly negative "automatic thoughts" that arise as a result of the depression. A number of approaches, combining cognitive and behavioral techniques, are used, including "reattribution" (reviewing the facts to show that the patient's self-blame is not deserved), "induced fantasy" (envisioning happy moments, so that despair is seen as temporary), "labeling" (focusing attention on the patient's use of negatively loaded words or phrases as self-description and encouraging more benign synonyms), and "redefining of goals" (setting reasonable goals that will reinforce self-confidence).[1] In dealing with her self-devaluation Woolf uses variations of all four methods. In reattribution, she lists her supposed failures—her childlessness, her taste in green paint—and detects the irrationality of magnifying their importance, realizing that the pain is, in reality, "vague" and inappropriately "tacked on" to specific incidents. In induced fantasy, she thinks of other people's relative states of happiness and unhappiness to resist depression's ability to seem "never-ending" and universal. In labeling, she shifts her attention away from negatively loaded words ("failure," "horror," "dead") toward phrases of active agency ("take a pull of yourself," "I brace myself to shove") to remind herself that she is not powerless. And she redefines her goals, telling herself that no failure matters so much in life that she deserves death.

Having separated self from her depressed mood, she can exert some self-control: nothing matters except what she allows to matter. Essentially, she must fight for the freedom to think outside of her mood. She cannot destroy the wave, but, conversely, it cannot destroy her unless she believes it can. Like Leslie and Mr. Ramsay, Woolf sets up reason and free will as her guides, for she knows that mood-induced emotions are untrust-worthy. She must rely on other parts of the self to counter this despair. But she is careful to avoid her father's defensive rationality; instead, she allows herself to sink when the flood of emotion is too strong, opens herself up to all experiences so that she can study them. By combining elements of both her parents' responses to moods, Woolf has, in effect, discovered a prophylactic therapy for mild and/or nonpsychotic mood swings, in which she retains some control over her thinking. Like Mr. and Mrs. Ramsay, she negotiates between moods to establish a limited sense of immunity.

Negotiating with parts of the psyche acting singly or independently led Woolf to view consciousness, not as a unity, but as a debate between psychic states or agencies. Indeed, this approach would naturally have occurred to her when, during her psychotic breakdowns, she heard these agencies as voices that damned her, exalted her, or urged her to commit "acts of folly" against her will. In 1904 she obeyed accusatory voices and threw herself out a window; later she realized that they were "only my imagination" (*Letters* 1: 142). In 1924 she heard "the voices of the dead" (*Diary* 2: 283). At Rodmell she recognized her depression for what it was: a feeling that was only a part of herself, something that she could attempt to manage. The voices were part of her, even though her breakdowns gave them a seemingly separate authority.

Woolf became conscious of the affinity between writing and madness because in both mania and creativity, words are put together with such rapidity that the ego cannot track how the operation is performed. Writing the last words of *The Waves*, Woolf experienced such "intensity & intoxi-cation that I seemed only to stumble after my own voice, or almost, after some sort of speaker (as when I was mad). I was almost afraid, remember-ing the voices that used to fly ahead" (*Diary* 4: 10). A manic-depressive has extensive experience of alien feelings and spontaneously generated scripts of elation or despair, and so Woolf was intrigued by the transparent line between her own voice and the other voices she could imagine. Engag-ing them in dialogue, detecting and contradicting them, *establishing a rela-tionship with them,* made possible the sort of integration that was mediated automatically by normality but was denied to her.

As early as October of 1926, Woolf began thinking about *The Waves* as a "dramatisation of my mood at Rodmell" (*Diary* 3: 114), of "a mind thinking" (3: 229) in all its plurality, rather than the cohesive narration of a story. She considered "Autobiography" as a title (3: 229), but then abandoned it because the specific details were not to come from *her* childhood (3: 236). Rather, she wanted to write the universalized autobiography of any mind thinking, for a "scientific" purpose rather than a biographic one:[2] to express her belief that creative thought incorporates elements of manic and depressive cognitive styles. Woolf split up intra-subjective experience into six voices delivering dramatic soliloquies, six mood-congruent points of view. They live a common life, "running homogeneously in & out, in the rhythm of the waves," sometimes sharing thoughts, images, and linguistic style (*Diary* 3: 312), but each interprets differently, according to a predominant mood that colors both their inner and outer worlds and so irrevocably separates them. The agitated Susan barricades herself against loss to compensate for her own worthlessness. For Rhoda, the helpless self begins dissolving as soon as it is born. Neville acts out his depression through self-mutilation. To Louis, life is an enemy, a beast to be fought. An exalted, iridescent world welcomes the manic Jinny, rewarding her enlivened senses with intense pleasure and gaiety. The self-conscious Bernard ruminates upon all these disparate experiences, constantly reshaping them into narratives that quickly fall apart, for nothing permanent can hold together this dynamic confederation (that "queer con-glomeration of incongruous things") of a mind at work (*Granite and Rain-bow* 19–20). Constant movement within consciousness requires more flexibility than a single voice can long provide.

Readers feel helpless in the disconnected "mind" of the novel. Like Woolf at Rodmell, we must learn to let go of the desire to find an authoritative voice; a part of us must view the chaos dispassionately, accepting the conflicting assertions of six points of view that can be neither proved nor disproved. Rhoda's suicidal despair, Jinny's promiscuous ecstasies, and Susan's agitated possessiveness—as responses to life each represents some "truth" that is valuable, though they are all provisional. Consciousness is an unspecified blend of all six; Woolf leaves it to us to decide how to read this mind (for this is what we must learn to do with our own minds). Confused and unguided, we forge ahead, buffeted and provoked by a novel written "to a rhythm not to a plot" (*Diary* 3: 316). Woolf felt that the rhythmical form was "more natural" to her than the narrative, though she admitted that its "inchoate" (*Letters* 4: 294) qualities were "completely opposed to the tradition of fiction and I am casting about all the time for some rope to throw to the reader" (*Letters* 4: 204). But she resisted tidying up too much by running "all the scenes together . . . so as to make the blood run like a torrent from end to end," achiev-ing "a saturated, unchopped, completeness; changes of scene, of mood, of person, done without spilling a drop" (*Diary* 3: 343), wresting control of the reading away from the reader, who must experience a mind's well and ill discourses without reduction.

In a letter written just after the novel was published, Woolf considered this problem of multiplicity and unity:

> Many people say that [*The Waves*] is hopelessly sad—but I didnt mean that. . . . But I did mean that in some vague way we are the same person, and not separate people. The six characters were supposed to be one. I'm getting old myself—I shall be fifty next year; and I come to feel more and more how difficult it is to collect oneself into one Virginia; even though the special Virginia in whose body I live for the moment is violently susceptible to all sorts of separate feelings. Therefore I wanted to give the sense of continuity, instead of which most people say, no you've given the sense of flowing and passing away and that nothing matters. Yet I feel things matter quite immensely. What the significance is, heaven knows I cant guess; but there is significance—that I feel overwhelmingly. (*Letters* 4: 397)

Her concern about the disconnectedness, in *Mrs. Dalloway,* of the scenes between the sane and the insane once again emerges: can continuity and *différance* be reconciled or even represented in a single text? To underscore the problem, Woolf has Bernard plainly state the problem of identity: "[I]t is not one life that I look back upon; I am not one person; I am many people; I do not altogether know who I am—Jinny, Susan, Neville, Rhoda, or Louis: or how to distinguish my life from theirs" (276). If identity somehow grows out of many voices, the reader faces the formidable task of connecting them in order to sense the collective, inclusive psyche.

On a less abstract level, *The Waves* contains several formal and stylistic devices that help convey a sense of psychic continuity:

> All the language in the book has the same remarkable sensitivity to rhythm and metaphor, the same characteristics of repetition and alliteration, even sometimes the same use of rhyme, euphony, and assonance.
>   In fact, the separate voices often draw on the same body of imagery.[3]

Unity of consciousness is further underscored by the artificiality of the dramatic-soliloquy technique. This is especially evident in the childhood scenes, where infants report their perceptions with such sophistication that the discourse becomes a litany:

> "When the smoke rises, sleep curls off the roof like a mist," said Louis.
>   "The birds sang in chorus first," said Rhoda. "Now the scullery door is unbarred. Off they fly. Off they fly like a fling of seed." (10–11)

These voices, neither spoken nor thought, are best described as "verbalized *being*,"[4] embodiments of different intrasubjective transactions that together compose consciousness.

There remains, however, a constant tension among these six voices that live such separate inner lives yet speak with a common voice. From the start, the novel focuses on how even sense perceptions of the same experience can mean quite different things:

> "I see a ring," said Bernard, "hanging above me. It quivers and hangs in a loop of light."
>
> "I see a slab of pale yellow," said Susan, "spreading away until it meets a purple stripe."
>
> "I hear a sound," said Rhoda, "cheep, chirp; cheep, chirp; going up and down."
>
> "I see a globe," said Neville, "hanging down in a drop against the enormous flanks of some hill."
>
> "I see a crimson tassel," said Jinny, "twisted with gold threads."
>
> "I hear something stamping," said Louis. "A great beast's foot is chained. It stamps, and stamps, and stamps." (9)

The characters define themselves in terms of how they see the world. Each child's perception establishes leitmotifs that are repeated throughout the novel. Bernard's ring symbolizes his quest for a language to enclose the flux of experience. Susan's slab of yellow exemplifies her tendency to see life in simplistic terms, as love or hate, possession or rejection.[5] Neville's masochism situates him as a fragile drop menaced by others. Jinny's crimson tassel with gold threads prefigures her self-indulgent life of ecstatic sensations. Seeing is the more analytical sense, fixing, immobilizing with a stare; hearing is passive, omnidirectional, and vulnerable, and only Rhoda and Louis hear their first impressions. Rhoda does not identify the source of the sound she hears, and later in life she feels persecuted by a world that also eludes her. Louis cannot see the waves crashing on the beach and worries that an angry beast is chained, reading into the perception what will be his lifelong preoccupation with order and safety. Although the voices long to share closer ties, to become one, their irreconcilable perspectives only widen the gap between them.

Even in childhood Susan's freezing possessiveness distinguishes her from Jinny and her carefree relations with others. Catching sight of Jinny kissing Louis, Susan retreats into self-hatred:

> "Now I will wrap my agony inside my pocket-handkerchief. It shall be screwed tight into a ball. I will go to the beech wood alone, before

lessons. I will not sit at a table, doing sums. I will not sit next Jinny and next Louis. I will take my anguish and lay it upon the roots under the beech trees. I will examine it and take it between my fingers. They will not find me. I shall eat nuts and peer for eggs through the brambles and my hair will be matted and I shall sleep under hedges and drink water from ditches and die there." (13–14)

Despair contracts subject-object boundaries until agony becomes more real than self, becomes a thing to be examined and hoarded. The image of herself as a hermit mythologizes Susan's plight; she identifies with her sense of isolation until it turns into something definitive, the only appropriate fate for an unloved being. Worthlessness ironically becomes valuable, because it aptly expresses her depressed identity. Everyone needs an identity that corresponds to his or her feelings, even if they are painful feelings. So depressives are stuck: their fatalism gives them the only continuity that "fits" their experiences. As a character, Susan expresses Woolf's insight into a problem most depressives and their therapists must face: why the patient sometimes clings to a self-definition so eminently painful. Attempts to explain away a patient's self-devaluations ("I'm a failure," "I'm unlovable," "the world is against me") as unreasonable or unrealistic and arguing that his/her resistance to change is an unconscious defense cannot succeed if the patient's experience and deepest feelings seem to corroborate these negative interpretations.

To fill the emptiness of her degraded self, Susan yearns to possess objects—a husband, children, the farm—and feel all the fierce maternal emotions ("I would fell down with one blow any intruder" who would harm her young, "making of my own body a hollow, a warm shelter for my child to sleep in" [172]), as if family were a treasure trove to be hoarded inside herself. Depressed, Susan feels "debased and hide-bound by the bestial and beautiful passion of maternity" (132). Motherhood has given full rein to her wish to "desire one thing only," but it is a thing that *must then become hateful*. Preparing herself to find a husband after finishing school, she knows that the gift she will bring to him, her self, is an equivocal blessing: "Something has formed, at school, in Switzerland, some hard thing. Not sighs and laughter; not circling and ingenious phrases. . . . What has formed in me I shall give him. . . . I shall be like my mother, silent in a blue apron locking up the cupboards" (98–99). Susan institutionalizes her self-contempt in marriage ("What shock can loosen my laboriously gathered, relentlessly pressed-down life?" [191]), which further suffocates her:

"Yet sometimes I am sick of natural happiness, and fruit growing, and children scattering the house with oars, guns, skulls, books won for prizes and other trophies. I am sick of the body, I am sick of my own craft, industry and cunning, of the unscrupulous ways of the mother who protects, who collects under her jealous eyes at one long table her own children, always her own." (191)

Louis speculates that "to be loved by Susan would be to be impaled by a bird's sharp beak, to be nailed to a barnyard door" (120) like an old stoat. Endlessly hungry, she devours what she possesses and feels devoured in turn. Love becomes a cancerous knot, for her degraded self-image makes hurtful objects desirable. Embracing the agony that depression deems appropriate, she lives out its self-fulfilling prophecy.

But there are different levels and kinds of depression, as Woolf well knew. In the character of Rhoda, Woolf explores such severe powerlessness and helplessness that all reality seems hostile and invasive ("Life, how I have dreaded you. . . . I have been stained by you and corrupted"). Paranoid, Rhoda fears everything: people in general ("hideous," "squalid," smelly [203]), pursuing her down endless paths in dreams (28); people at parties, "throwing faint smiles to mask their cruelty"; doors opening ("terror rushes in!"); her own friends ("A million arrows pierce me. Scorn and ridicule pierce me" [105–6]). Like Septimus, Rhoda feels cut off from a world that is degraded and dangerous because it is evaluated by a pervasive nihilism she cannot question or control. Depression can become so severe that its perspective cannot be differentiated from or detected by the individual's capacity for "normal" thinking. Self-hatred, frigidity, and paranoid delusions about a hostile world spring up as totalizing explanations, fictional variations of a fundamental, unintelligible emptiness, locating in the identifiable real world what actually remains cloaked in mood.

Rhoda's vulnerability vividly dramatizes the insubstantiality of the deeply depressed self. Objects deny her very existence. She feels excluded when she finds Miss Hudson's mathematical formulas incomprehensible: "The figures mean nothing now. Meaning has gone. . . . The world is entire, and I am outside of it, crying, 'Oh, save me, from being blown for ever outside the loop of time!'" (21–22). Meaning is found when self has the power to organize perception of outer facts so that internal schemata coincide with the structure of objects. Understanding presupposes that the world *can* be organized and that the self is real enough to create or authorize schemata that illuminate previously hidden structures which bring the world closer and include the self in their life. Unintegrable perceptions attack the depersonalized, unauthorized self:

"I am afraid of the shock of sensation that leaps upon me, because I cannot deal with it as you do—I cannot make one moment merge in the next. To me they are all violent, all separate; and if I fall under the shock of the leap of the moment you will be on me, tearing me to pieces. I have no end in view. I do not know how to run minute to minute and hour to hour, solving them by some natural force until they make the whole and indivisible mass that you call life. . . . I have no face." (130)

Without some kind of continuity to perception that makes meaning, identity seems to fall apart.

Because she lacks a sense of her self as existing, Rhoda frequently casts herself as a faceless person:

"That is my face," said Rhoda, "in the looking-glass behind Susan's shoulder—that face is my face. But I will duck behind her to hide it, for I am not here. I have no face. Other people have faces; Susan and Jinny have faces; they are here. Their world is the real world. The things they lift are heavy. They say Yes, they say No; whereas I shift and change and am seen through in a second. . . . They know what to say if spoken to. They laugh really; they get angry really; while I have to look first and do what other people do when they have done it." (43)

The self Rhoda's face represents is "not here," and so she must imitate others' reactions. She feels depersonalized and transparent—a common complaint from depressives, who seem not to have the energy to be responsive or even to recognize that a situation calls for an emotional reaction. Because Rhoda describes the real world as belonging to others, some readers assume that she lives in a mystical realm that seduces her into suicide[6]—a tempting interpretation, since other characters do tend to see Rhoda's isolation as otherworldliness. But Rhoda herself characterizes it as a too real "nothingness":

"Therefore I hate looking-glasses which show me my real face. Alone, I often fall down into nothingness. I must push my foot stealthily lest I should fall off the edge of the world into nothingness. I have to bang my hand against some hard door to call myself back to the body." (44)

Depressive nothingness is neither a visionary experience nor a mystical level of consciousness. Acknowledging the solidity of the world of her friends, Rhoda attributes exclusive value to it: their world is full; hers is empty. Only by touching something solid can she get any sense of herself as existing, and then it is only a bodily sense; it has no recuperative meaning for her spirit.

Jinny escapes the violent, unsavory universe of Susan and Rhoda. Euphoric, uninhibited, and glowing, Jinny feels no fear, no limitations. Aware, as a child, primarily of bodily sensations ("'The back of my hand burns,' said Jinny, 'but the palm is clammy and damp with dew'" [10]), as an adult she indulges in a frenetic, manic pursuit of intensified sensory perception ("Our hands touch, our bodies burst into fire" [140]). Although depression typically has a "neuterizing effect," roughly half of manic and hypomanic states have a "polarizing or enhancing effect on sexual identity." Heightened psychomotor activity combines with enhanced self-esteem and self-confidence to exaggerate sexuality.[7] Jinny sees her body "ripple" in the looking glass and feels an ecstatic power in movement—"I move, I dance; I never cease to move and to dance" (42)—though she never discovers the source of all this energy: "What moved the leaves? What moves my heart, my legs?" Expansive in mood, she kisses Louis to rejuvenate him—

> "And I dashed in here, seeing you green as a bush, like a branch, very still, Louis, with your eyes fixed. 'Is he dead?' I thought, and kissed you, with my heart jumping under my pink frock like the leaves, which go on moving, though there is nothing to move them. Now I smell geraniums; I smell earth mould. I dance. I ripple. I am thrown over you like a net of light. I lie quivering flung over you." (13)

—as if the mere touch of her magical body could create life. Since, in a manic state, wielding power seems effortless, it is no wonder that some manics believe they are conduits for God or that they are somehow plugged into the energies and purposes of Nature (consider Walt Whitman's "I Sing the Body Electric").

Woolf emphasizes the energy of Jinny's world by constant use of action verbs in descriptions of her:

> "Look, when I move my head I ripple all down my narrow body; even my thin legs ripple like a stalk in the wind. I flicker between the set face of Susan and Rhoda's vagueness; I leap like one of those flames that run between the cracks of the earth; I move, I dance; I never cease to move and to dance." (42)

Her exultation in movement affects her perceptions. Just as, to explain her boundless energy and sense of well-being, she imagines that her "blood must be bright red, whipped up, slapping against [her] ribs," so too the objects she sees are highly energized: "There is nothing staid, nothing settled in this universe. All is rippling, all is dancing; all is quickness and triumph" (46). She perceives her body as "incandescent," as if a stream is pouring through it, "a deep tide fertilising, opening the shut, forcing the tight-folded, flooding free" (57). At social occasions she is witty and grandiose, drawing men to her by the pure force of her personality, giving herself up to the "rapture" of being "much admired, my dress billowing around me" (63). Other people do not frighten her, as they do Rhoda; rather, they stimulate her dilated self-confidence and her enhanced sense of power: "They are anxious to make a good impression. I feel a thousand capacities spring up in me" (102). In mania, self and body are one and substantial:

> "The torments, the divisions of your lives have been solved for me night after night, sometimes only by the touch of a finger under the tablecloth as we sat dining—so fluid has my body become, forming even at the touch of a finger into one full drop, which fills itself, which quivers, which flashes, which falls in ecstasy." (221)

But Woolf is aware that euphoria has its drawbacks. Although Jinny glows with a physical magnetism, it is an egotistical energy that draws everything to herself. Her self-centered imagination is limited to her body:

> "Every time the door opens I cry 'More!' But my imagination is the bodies [*sic*]. I can imagine nothing beyond the circle cast by my body. My body goes before me, like a lantern down a dark lane, bringing one thing after another out of darkness into a ring of light. I dazzle you; I make you believe that this is all." (128–29)

Mania dazzles but misleads, overcoming reality testing by its sheer energy. Manics feel they have discovered profound meaning or experienced transcendental joy when in fact they have not gotten beyond the door of physical senses. Jinny's "feather-headed carelessness" (55) causes her teacher, Miss Matthews, to grumble because Jinny "cannot follow any word through its changes . . . any thought from present to past" (42). So distracted and ceaseless are her vivified perceptions that she quickly creates similes out of them, but without going beyond the sensations themselves: "My hand is like a snake's skin. My knees are pink floating islands. Your face is like an apple tree netted under" (23).

Because the manic imagination, in its sensuous exercise of self's power, makes myriad ephemeral connections, Jinny's relationships are only moments of intense, short-lived intimacy, beginning with a show of power: "I begin to feel the wish to be singled out; to be summoned, to be called away by one person who comes to find me, who is attracted towards me, who cannot keep himself from me, but comes to where I sit on my gilt chair, with my frock billowing round me like a flower" (46). The wish to be singled out is contingent upon someone else's subordination to the illusion of her power—her inflated sense of herself is ratified when a stranger finds her irresistible:

> "I am arch, gay, languid, melancholy by turns. I am rooted, but I flow. All gold, flowing that way, I say to this one, 'Come.' Rippling black, I say to that one, 'No.' One breaks off from his station under the glass cabinet. He approaches. He makes towards me. This is the most exciting moment I have ever known. I flutter. I ripple. I stream like a plant in the river, flowing this way, flowing that way, but rooted, so that he may come to me. 'Come,' I say, 'come.' Pale, with dark hair the one who is coming is melancholy, romantic. And I am arch and fluent and capricious; for he is melancholy, he is romantic. He is here; he stands at my side." (102–3)

As a child she feels fluid and unencompassable: "I do not want to be fixed, to be pinioned" (55); as an adult, she throws herself into the arms of many lovers and glories in their anonymity:

> "I do not care for anything in this world. I do not care for anybody save this man whose name I do not know. . . . This is rapture; this is relief. The bar at the back of my throat lowers itself. Words crowd and cluster and push forth one on top of another. It does not matter which. They jostle and mount on each other's shoulders. The single and the solitary mate, tumble and become many. It does not matter what I say. Crowding, like a fluttering bird, one sentence crosses the empty space between us. . . . The veils drop between us. I am admitted to the warmth and privacy of another soul." (103–4)

Anonymity and intimacy may seem to be contradictions, but, for the manic, intimacy with only one person would bog down the splendid experience of the body's energy, the mind's fertility, and the effortless capacity to cross barriers and touch others with a perfect (though, to us, superficial) sense of fusion. Sixty percent of manics exhibit increased sexual desire; some become voraciously promiscuous, succeeding because the manic personality can be an appealing and persistent wizard with words. It does not seem to matter what Jinny says: the words come easily, the moment is magic, and the veil drops.

The manic delights in physical movement, beauty, and experience for its own sake, operating, as John Custance remembers of his own manic breakdowns, purely on the pleasure principle and an uncanny sense of subject-object fusion:

> Perhaps it can best be described as a "breach in the barriers of individuality". What Professor Grensted has called, if I remember rightly, the "sense of estrangement, fencing in a narrowly limited ego" disappears altogether. The shell which surrounds the ego and so often gets harder with the years is pierced. The experience partakes of the nature of the goodfellowship produced by alcohol; it also constitutes in some degree a regression to a childish faith and confidence in the benevolence, the "akinness" of the surrounding world.[8]
>
> One of the most interesting features of this experience is the light it throws on the nature of the sexual urge in mania. This urge is almost entirely impersonal. The question of selecting an attractive girl, which normally plays a large part in sexual adventures, did not trouble me in the least. I was quite content to leave it to chance. . . . Like Whitman, I really did feel all women to be "my sisters and lovers."[9]

The burden of conscience, of the "super-ego" of Freudian theory, is enormous. In mania it is lifted as it were by magic.[10]

Forty percent of manics do not exhibit an increased sexual drive, as apparently Woolf did not (though we cannot be sure, if we consider her playfully erotic letters to Vita), but clearly she understood that mania expresses itself in enlivened senses and a dilated self that cannot make authentic, personal contact with others:

> Now my little tugging & distressing book & articles are off my mind my brain seems to fill & expand & grow physically light & peaceful. I begin to feel it filling quietly after all the wringing & squeezing it has had since we came here. And so the unconscious part now expands; & walking I notice the red corn, & the blue of the plain & an infinite number of things without naming them; because I am not thinking of any special thing. Now & again I feel my mind take shape, like a cloud with the sun on it, as some idea, plan, or image wells up, but they travel on, over the horizon, like clouds, & I wait peacefully for another to form, or nothing—it matters not which. (*Diary* 3: 248)

Since personality becomes a production, a stagey exaggeration of desire out of control, the manic cannot tell whether an object uncannily invites his responses or whether desire itself has provided the illusion of reciprocation. Acting upon such one-sided urges disperses identity and prohibits true fusion, whether sexual or aesthetic. But the lure of complete, ecstatic fulfillment dispels doubt and inspires the frenetic devotion of a lover whose beloved promises bliss that permeates body and soul, earth and stars.

Mood states are also divided up among the males in the group. Like Rhoda, Louis feels the arrows of other people's attention aimed at him ("I suffer for all humiliations") and wants to be unseen to protect himself ("my shivering, my tender, and infinitely young and unprotected soul. For I am always the youngest" [219]). Unless he is able to organize them, he is unable to tolerate the discontinuous and violent perceptions of life. When, at Hampton Court, the six reassemble to remember Percival, Louis finds "this moment of reconciliation" to be "black" and intolerably painful: "What is the solution, I ask myself, and the bridge? How can I reduce these dazzling, these dancing apparitions to one line capable of linking all in one?" (219).

But, although depressed, Louis does not retreat into nothingness; he asserts himself against those "dancing apparitions" by imposing his own brand of order on the world and on himself: "My hair is made of leaves. I am rooted to the middle of the earth. My body is a stalk. I press the stalk. A drop oozes from the hole at the mouth and slowly, thickly, grows larger and larger" (12). Here is Rhoda's isolation combined with Susan's contracted being: only by pressing can Louis's essence be squeezed out, a thick, unpalatable ooze—a potent defense, which helps him assert himself: " 'I have signed my name,' said Louis, 'already twenty times. I, and again I, and again I. Clear, firm, unequivocal, there it stands, my name. Clear-cut and unequivocal am I too' " (167). The repeated "I" underscores Louis's egotism dictating order. Although he reassures himself by accumulating and mastering knowledge ("I could know everything in the world if I wished" [20]), he also suppresses himself ("My eyes are wild; my lips tight pressed" [58]) and feels he has found safety in the numbers of students filing into chapel: "I like the orderly progress. We file in; we seat ourselves. We put off our distinctions as we enter. . . . I become a figure in the procession, a spoke in the huge wheel" (34–35).

In his position in the shipping company Louis is able to fulfill his wish to make "orderly progress" real:

> "We have laced the world together with our ships. The globe is strung
> with our lines. . . . My shoulder is to the wheel; I roll the dark before
> me, spreading commerce where there was chaos in the far parts of the
> world. If I press on, from chaos making order, I shall find myself
> where Chatham stood, and Pitt, Burke, and Sir Robert Peel. Thus I
> expunge certain stains." (200, 168)

Like Virginia's depressed grandfather, Sir James, that monster of industry who controlled himself by abstaining from any indulgence, even the pleasure of a good cigar, Louis becomes a judge with "solemn and severe convictions" (201) to establish coherence in himself. Only by opposing corrosive reality can he feel real: "I take the trees, the clouds, to be witnesses of my complete integration. I, Louis, I, who shall walk the earth these seventy years, am born entire, out of hatred, out of discord" (39). Opposition coalesces his fragmented identity and channels his agitation. If discord gave birth to him, he, like Klein's vengeful infant, turns upon his mother and tries to devour her, but his self-description is hideously negative: "Life has been a terrible affair for me. I am like some vast sucker, some glutinous, some adhesive, some insatiable mouth. I have tried to draw from the living flesh the stone lodged at the centre" (201). Louis reduces life to an ordered paste, a minimalist meaning which can be squeezed out by netting the globe, pressing his lips, regulating until all proceed into the chapel, uniform, indistinguishable. Louis silences all other voices but his own.

Howard Harper is right to describe Louis as a "superego" character, but only in the sense that he responds to self-hatred with rule, severity, and conformity.[11] Self-loathing and fear of loss of control often lead depressives to fall back upon habitual and rigid modes of thought.[12] Whereas manic cognition is expansive and elastic, depressive thinking lacks imagination and relies excessively on order and logic to oppose black despair. For a bipolar, the depressive desire for severity is not in itself moralistic in the Freudian sense (it does not result from a forbidden fantasy or wish), although, for want of a better one, patients may adopt such an "explanation" for why everything looks so bleak to them, why they feel so bad (and so Woolf has Louis offer us an inadequate reason for his pervasive sense of inferiority: that he is Australian). The feeling is compellingly real no matter what ideas are tacked onto it. Depressives think they deserve no better because mood limits their ability to mediate positive thoughts.

To underscore depression as a problem in perceptual processing, Woolf presents Neville's depression as a double bind:

> "Oppose ourselves to this illimitable chaos," said Neville, "this
> formless imbecility. Making love to a nursemaid behind a tree, that
> soldier is more admirable than all the stars. Yet sometimes one trembling
> star comes in the clear sky and makes me think the world beautiful and
> we maggots deforming even the trees with our lust." (226)

This is the depressive's version of the squinting modifier: Neville objects alternately to life's formlessness and to his own "deforming" instincts. Depression must have a vacuum, a center of emptiness or corruption, but patients vary as to where they place the source of their despair. It can be inside, outside, particularized in some other person (e.g., a disapproving lover) or relationship (e.g., parent-child), or generalized to all people and all relationships (society as victimizer, society as abusive parent). In the 1960s, when the phrase "I'm depraved on accounta I'm deprived" from *West Side Story* became a formula in popular psychology, society was blamed for all sorts of abnormal behavior, from criminality and suicide to drug abuse and anorexia. Some cases of pathology were correctly attributed to social context, but other patients were ill served when their own depressive projections were adopted by therapists.

Depression, then, can take any form the human mind can think of to represent what it is experiencing. Unlike Louis, who controls himself by controlling objects, Neville wants to be dominated, to be put into the position of object: "We are in that passive and exhausted frame of mind when we only wish to rejoin the body of our mother from whom we have been severed. All else is distasteful, forced and fatiguing" (233). He acts out his self-loathing in self-destructive object-relations, submitting to repeated severances, which he symbolizes as a knife cutting: " 'Now Biddy scrapes the fish-scales with a jagged knife on to a wooden board,' said Neville" (11). Soon Neville has a knife of his own, which he mentions often, as an expression of his own critical sharpness and his need to make distinctions ("I hate wandering and mixing things together" [19]). Upon learning that each tense in Latin means something different, he exults: "There is an order in this world; there are distinctions, there are differences in this world, upon whose verge I step" (21). The depressive is so aware of difference, of gulfs separating and fragmenting, that he sees only a world of isolated objects. Severance becomes a defining characteristic of what life means; like Susan with her knot of agony, for Neville painful severance becomes real, emblematic of value, to be hoarded as part of his identity. Thus, as an adult in love with Percival, Neville associates affection with cutting ("I need some one whose mind falls like a chopper on a block. . . . To whom can I expose the urgency of my own passion?") and with self-mutilation ("Nobody guessed the need I had to offer my being to one god; and perish, and disappear" [51–52]). The jagged knife embodies the only peace depression can promise: that of self-annihilation. Seeing Percival, Neville seeks a continuity of depressive experience by allying desire, order, and pain: "'Now,' said Neville, 'my tree flowers. My heart rises. All oppression is relieved. All impediment is removed. The reign of chaos is over. He has imposed order. Knives cut again'" (122).

When depressives like Neville identify themselves completely with their mood, they cannot love without pain, for mood shapes their worldview, their philosophy of life, and their psychological economy. Percival provides for Neville both that needed security of order and the "solidity" (122) of cruelty. Neville loves Percival's "pagan indifference," his remoteness, and his potential for giving pain: "He should have a birch and beat little boys for misdemeanours" (36). Neville craves attention, especially if it is harmful, because it fulfills his depressive expectations:

> "He despises me for being too weak to play [cricket] (yet he is always
> kind to my weakness). He despises me for not caring if they win or
> lose except that he cares. He takes my devotion; he accepts my
> tremulous, no doubt abject offering, mixed with contempt as it is for
> his mind. For he cannot read. . . . He will forget me. He will leave
> my letters lying about among guns and dogs unanswered. I shall send
> him poems and he will perhaps reply with a picture post card. But it is
> for that that I love him. . . . [M]y suffering [is] an unceasing excite-
> ment." (48, 60, 129)

It takes pain and humiliation to make Neville feel real, just as it takes order to make Louis feel real. Being "cut" by his Percival makes him love even more the wielder of the knife. His beloved's contempt *is* his returned love, just as Neville's suffering becomes the proof of loving. In keeping with depression's inversion of values, Neville feels contempt for Percival's mind, which he considers far inferior to his own. The "love" he feels reflects the value of the love object. He accepts Percival's disdain as an appropriate evaluation of Neville's debased self, but he also despises his master because Percival, as recipient of a "deformed" Neville's love, must be unworthy as well. Depression can mediate negative readings either way. Self and object despise each other. Neville condemns what life has to offer ("Let me denounce this piffling, trifling, self-satisfied world" [70]) but also welcomes life's degradation: "Come, pain, feed on me. Bury your fangs in my flesh. Tear me asunder. I sob, I sob" (152). Self-destruction is seductive when it seems to explain everything.

Compared to the other five characters, Bernard is "diffuse" as a personality, "malleable to the point of dampness."[13] He is so aware of circumstances that he becomes different men in different environments, acting various parts: "[W]hich of these people am I?" he asks. "It depends so much upon the room" (81). The plurality of his fictional "faces" defies categorization by mood. He is not, like Rhoda, afraid of life's "little deaths." With easy aplomb he considers the fattened rabbit about to be killed for Sunday dinner (234). Unlike Susan, he is curious about the world. Unlike Louis, Bernard delights in chaos and multiplicity: "[W]hat am I? There is no stability in this world. Who is to say what meaning there is in anything? Who is to foretell the flight of a word? It is a balloon that sails over tree-tops. To speak of knowledge is futile. All is experiment and adventure" (118). He does not care to lace the globe together tight until the world is uniform and safe: "[I]t is the panorama of life . . . that delights me" (242). Nor does he lacerate himself, like Neville, with fated pain. And he knows—unlike Jinny—that the body is not the "whole self." Bernard accepts all states of mind freely, even contradictory ones, as at graduation ceremonies: "We are all deeply moved; yet irreverent; yet penitent; yet anxious to get it over; yet reluctant to part" (59). Others industriously organize perceptions, but Bernard "distrust[s] neat designs of life that are drawn upon half sheets of notepaper" (238), concluding, like the narrator of *Jacob's Room,* that "life is not susceptible perhaps to the treatment we give it when we try to tell it" (267). He is that part of the mind that can stand apart and detect the shape of the wave of mood (as Woolf did at Rodmell), and so he is preoccupied with narratives—not stories about anything in particular (that exclusivity would bring the risk of drowning) but narrative in itself, as a means of giving shape to self's plurality.

Bernard is happiest when he creates a transitional space where imagination and fact combine to produce meaning—but without the requirement that it be absolute, true, or persuasive meaning. His stories do not even have endings, so flimsy and unhurried are they, mere "linked phrases in which I run together whatever happens so that instead of incoherence there is perceived a wandering thread, lightly joining one thing to another" (49). Other characters criticize his fictions as inconclusive or absurd, phrases dangling in the wind. But it is this reluctance to impose meaning or closure that makes his narratives playful, creative, life-affirming, that makes him immune to pernicious perspectives imposed by a reigning mood. Since personality is a "fictitious" order too, to impose it on reality—to order the world as a simple extension of one's personality and desires—obscures life's discontinuity and self's myriad possible forms.[14]

Bernard's earliest fiction is of Elvedon, a mythical kingdom he creates while he and Susan wander the grounds of a neighboring house. Susan has just seen Jinny kiss Louis, and she runs off clutching her knotted agony, convinced of its soul-defining truth. Bernard tells her the story of Elvedon, a secret and sacred landscape where life is only a dream and nothing is defined. He specifically describes his fiction in terms of softening the knot of hardness in Susan:

> "When I heard you cry I followed you, and saw you put down your handkerchief, screwed up, with its rage, with its hate, knotted in it. But soon that will cease. . . ."
> "I love," said Susan, "and I hate. I desire one thing only. . . ."
> "But when we sit together, close," said Bernard, "we melt into each other with phrases. We are edged with mist. We make an unsubstantial territory." (15–16)

Urging her to "sink like swimmers just touching the ground with the tips of their toes," to let go of the knowledge that this is merely a neighbor's yard and that Jinny is prettier than Susan, Bernard leads her down a secret path where she temporarily forgets her agony and sees what he can imagine: " 'I see the lady writing. I see the gardeners sweeping,' said Susan. 'If we died here, nobody would bury us' " (17). An ordinary house lodges a mystery woman and the garden offers the thrill of danger and adventure. Life proves malleable as long as she steps out of her mood and creates a fictional Susan, the "alien subject" who is capable of feeling anything—or at least of reading the same text, mental state, or self-history and seeing something new, Other, different.

But Susan cannot sustain this fictional self and the "double awareness" it can support; she slips quickly back into her desperate hoarding, identifying mood with self, assuming that how she feels must be the way she is. In contrast, Bernard supports so many fanciful selves that he becomes concerned about ever finding his real self and its own distinguishing emotions: "For I changed and changed; was Hamlet, was Shelley, was the hero, whose name I now forget, of a novel by Dostoevsky; was for a whole term, incredibly, Napoleon; but was Byron chiefly" (249). Role-playing enlarges our behavioral repertoire, for by identifying with others we discover facets of ourselves: "To be myself (I note) I need the illumination of other people's eyes, and therefore cannot be entirely sure what is my self" (116). But who is the Bernard who plays the roles? In public, he "bubbles; in private, is secretive" (76), but what that secretive self is, he cannot describe: "A man of no particular age or calling. Myself, merely" (81). Personality belongs to the "many rooms" that provide the stimulus to create "many Bernards" (260). In solitude he disappears: "When I cannot see words curling like rings of smoke round me I am in darkness—I am nothing. When I am alone I fall into lethargy" (132–33). If there is an underlying self to the many Bernards, it extends beyond language, beyond mood. We may be tempted to consider him the euthymic self, pale and transparent compared to the vivid manic and depressive alternatives, but he is more than that. He is the problem Woolf has been considering for thirty years: when "normal," she looked back upon her various moods and marveled at the difference between them. Who was the real Woolf? Obscured by moods, unavailable to introspection, resisting neat answers, can the inclusive Woolf even be approximated by language?

In summing up the novel, Bernard attempts to incorporate all these various selves. As in *To the Lighthouse,* a work of art provides the model:

> "And now I ask, 'Who am I?' I have been talking of Bernard, Neville, Jinny, Susan, Rhoda, and Louis. Am I all of them? Am I one and distinct? . . .
>
> Thus when I come to shape here at this table between my hands the story of my life and set it before you as a complete thing, I have to recall things gone far, gone deep, sunk into this life or that and become part of it; dreams, too, things surrounding me . . . shadows of people one might have been; unborn selves." (288–89)

Harper speculates that this configuration of characters is analogous to Freud's psychic triad: Neville and Jinny as the id, Louis and Rhoda the superego, Bernard and Susan the ego. Since Freud's therapeutic goal was to facilitate ego mastery over ever-increasing areas of the unconscious, Bernard should logically emerge as identity-spokesperson.[15] But the role of the authoritative word-giver cannot capture the experience of the many selves, the plurality of intrasubjective life—as Bernard himself tells us: "Whatever sentence I extract whole and entire from this cauldron is only a string of six little fish that let themselves be caught while a million others leap and sizzle. . . . Neville, Susan, Louis, Jinny, Rhoda and a thousand others. How impossible to order them rightly; to detach one separately, or to give the effect of the whole" (256). Identity is never complete, because even *unborn* selves must be embraced. Bernard is composed not merely of actual selves but of selves that must be continually created and continually integrated without conclusion. What can be *imagined* for oneself is as real as what one *feels* to be true; indeed, they often amount to the same thing. Identity is not an illusory order imposed by ego but an irreducible array of shimmering fragments: the wave, the trough, the self sinking and floating, the self as subject watching and the self as object being watched, "and a thousand others": the all-inclusive Bernard. Woolf here suggests a valuable lesson for other manic-depressives: that finding out who they are should not involve denying "ill" selves, reducing identity to the sanest, most conventional, socially conforming part of themselves. Manic and depressive selves are "ill" only if exclusively in control, just as the euthymic self can also be "ill" if it pretends that there are no irrational depths to subjectivity, that all is clean, orderly, and apparent. A sane reading of literature is not necessarily a good one if it slavishly reinforces our habitual beliefs about literature.

Although Woolf's awareness of the plurality of consciousness came through her experience of manic-depressive illness, her insight into intrasubjective life extends far beyond her particular disorder. The proliferation of self-representations, the creation of other "me's" within "myself," appears in florid forms in mental states such as fugues, multiple personality, and hypnotically induced dissociation. In multiple personalities, for instance, autonomous self-representations have no specified limit. Some patients exhibit only three personalities; Sybil Dorsett presented sixteen, two of whom were male. Each new personality emerged in response to a particular crisis or change in circumstance and took on an entirely independent existence, exhibiting distinctive traits and attitudes, buying its own clothes, establishing separate bank accounts under its own name, taking different jobs. Some were aware of each other and regarded the others as separate persons. All these subpersonalities were active concurrently, even though only one at a time determined Dorsett's behavior and subjective experience.[16]

Hypnosis also provides evidence that consciousness can be subdivided. Ernest Hilgard instructed normal individuals to create a "hidden observer" within themselves who watched unmolested while the "official ego" was hypnotized and behaved in uncharacteristic ways. He told a hypnotized student that he was deaf but then suggested that a part of his mind would remain intact to hear and remember everything that was said to him. The "deaf" personality was obediently unresponsive to verbal questions and unexpected loud noises behind his back, but Hilgard was also able to interview the hidden observer, who did hear and reacted to all that transpired. Upon awakening from his trance, the student was unable to recall having heard anything during the procedure until he was hypnotized again and the "deafness" was removed from memory. Only then did the barred auditory information, which had been fully processed, understood, and stored by the co-consciousness, become available. Hilgard concluded that "the hidden observer is in all respects like the normal observing part as found in waking. It is objective and well oriented to reality." Divided consciousness also occurs, of course, in ordinary waking life—e.g., when we indulge in fantasy while talking to others, working, or driving a car.[17]

The functional compartmentalization of consciousness, in which two concurrent streams of processing selectively feed into self-awareness, can help enrich and deepen experience. Many readers screen whatever ideas or feelings a text inspires that are incongruent with their identity-theme— the left hemisphere-dominant program of consciousness—and thus find themselves cheated of a full response to the text.[18] Christopher Bollas likewise maintains that unless a psychoanalyst is willing to become "situationally ill" by creating a generative split in his own ego—one part receptive to varying degrees of his patient's "madness," the other part simultaneously observing as a "not-ill" analyst—he will perceive only what his analytical skills and his psychoanalytical theory will allow: a one-dimensional view of the patient.[19] In both reading and psychoanalysis, "alien thoughts" create a subtle dissociation within the self: an "alien subject" who finds (or is "created" to find) these anomalous ideas compelling. If we integrate this other subject, we grow as human beings. But before growth there must first be discovery, the recognition of that dissociated subject who has read the same book but has had a different experience of it. This particular dissociated subject need not be a permanent feature of our makeup; it may be only an ongoing capacity that is "reprogrammed" each time an occasion arises that calls for divided or plural responses. Thus, each book we read invites us, in its own unique way, to co-create our experience of reading it. One blanket reading strategy is inadequate. Perhaps that is why human beings like to read fiction: it gives us the opportunity to put our multiple subroutine programming capabilities to use.

As Woolf knew by experience, such doubling occurs frequently in delusional psychotics. In hypnosis, the subject believes in imagined experiences directed by the hypnotist ("Your arms feel heavy"); in psychosis, the patient believes in his interpretation of a perception as if it were itself the perception ("My arms are being restrained by powerful magnets"). Neither subject is sufficiently aware of his own role in creating the experience and so shows less skepticism than a "normal" individual would.[20] Both may harbor a "hidden observer" or co-consciousness who doubts that the anomalous or suggested experience is real, but psychotics tend to invest a great deal of emotional commitment in their delusions, whereas hypnotized subjects rarely defend their adopted ideas with conviction and vigor: one is ill (and cannot integrate conflicting domains of consciousness); the other is only hypnotized (though "blind," he will not walk in front of speeding cars, evidence that some integration is still operating). Both demonstrate that the key to conscious awareness of reality is self-reference, which links the internal representation of a current perception with the representation of the self as the experiencer. As long as consciousness is divided into domains that cannot be integrated fully (because of psychosis or hypnotic suggestion), the "I" loses integrative control over perception, belief, and behavior.[21] Thus, because Peter Walsh is not ill, his "I" can entertain fantasies in one domain while another co-conscious "I" keeps tabs on and control over conviction and behavior (just as readers do), but Septimus's self-reference is overwhelmed by two unintegrated domains processing contradictory experiences: the "I" who sees flames beneath the pavement, and the "I" who wonders futilely why he is seeing such impossible things. A biochemically disordered brain not only mismanages sensory perception, combining fear and flames into one percept, but also disables the ability of consciousness to integrate various domains: experience, instead of being processed as a richly layered, multidimensional, and personal event, is unraveled by many hands grasping for meaning. Richness is squandered on florid and inappropriate interpretations, and the individual, cheated of the reward of finding comprehension in his or her perceptions, is impoverished.

Woolf too saw the mind as many-chambered ("I have a very clear notion which parts of my brain think" [*Letters* 1: 357]) and herself as a traveler who walked through lighted rooms, exploring. She saw her experience of overproductive mania versus debilitating depression as related to the disintegration of identity, while recognizing that even delusion demonstrated the infinite capacities of her imagination. She also realized that a creative reading and writing strengthened the integrative capacity of consciousness she needed to survive manic-depressive illness. It made her feel whole, gave her the ability to entertain all sorts of perspectives, while creating a narrative that gave a liberating form to the self that felt so many fragmented things.

If secondary-process thinking can be creatively subdivided, then our model of the psyche must become more complex than Freud had envisioned. Hilgard argues that we need to reexamine those "sudden inspirations" that seem to come out of nowhere but which yield innovative solutions or creative products. We have traditionally associated creativity with the spontaneity of fantasy-oriented primary-process thinking rather than with the more reality-oriented secondary process, an assumption that readily authorizes psychoanalytic explorations of the unconscious significance of works of art. Artists themselves (Woolf included) customarily describe their creative experiences in terms of extreme depths which bubble up to reveal new perspectives, ideas, or shapes, characters who come to life, sometimes even whole lines or stanzas of verse.[22] Energized by hypomania, Woolf conceived her plan for *To the Lighthouse* "in a great, apparently involuntary, rush" while walking around Tavistock Square:

> One thing burst into another. Blowing bubbles out of a pipe gives the feeling of the rapid crowd of ideas and scenes which blew out of my mind, so that my lips seemed syllabling of their own accord as I walked. What blew the bubbles? Why then? I have no notion. But I wrote the book very quickly. (*Moments of Being* 81)

The source of inspiration need not be unconscious simply because it is obscure or spontaneous, or because it is related to the artist's past or personal needs. A divided consciousness using parallel processing to work on two or more problems would produce similar effects, and it would explain why whole stanzas or theoretical solutions may present themselves, well-ordered, coherent, yet deeply meaningful, even though the artist felt only dimly aware (or even completely unaware) that an answer was forthcoming.

There is a provocative connection between this doubled mind and the fact that each hemisphere of the brain is capable of separate consciousness: "the subjective unity of self, of thought and of personal experience is an illusion created by the limited capacity of self-awareness systems and their need to process information sequentially" in the dominant hemisphere.[23] Woolf reached essentially the same conclusion through her experience with cyclic bipolar states, which can correspond to successive dual personalities.[24] She too saw how limited self-awareness was, how the ego sees only one facet of experience at a time and creates the illusion of unity and coherence only by filtering out dissonance (via Holland's identity-theme, discussed in chapter 3, above).

In *The Waves,* Woolf suggests that we can at least begin to know ourselves better if we constantly create new, more meaningful fictions to embrace our disparate experiences, always accepting them—and our "selves"—as provisional. When Bernard asks his existential question—"How can I proceed now, I said, without a self, weightless and visionless, through a world weightless, without illusion?" (285)—he is meeting the challenge of discovering just how shifting and insubstantial identity is. Many domains of consciousness may coexist within us, unrealized, "unborn," created when the need arises; like Jacob Flanders choosing his seat in the opera house, we find it convenient to settle upon habitual modes of thought. Bernard, however, makes the inconvenient choice. By imagining psychic fragmentation and accepting unborn selves, by recognizing that the problem of identity is always unfinished—and always unfinished theory, not substance—he creates the strength to proceed against death, the realm of true nothingness, the antithesis of consciousness and identity, the experience that cannot be narrated. Through writing, he gives voice to these debating selves, gives birth to himself, incorporating with new understanding what was actually always a part of himself. Death and madness no longer have the power to prove that identity is an empty illusion simply because it must be constructed out of fragments. If thinking is a confederation of narratives, a work of art, then Bernard can survive living for moments as Neville, Susan, Rhoda, Jinny, and Louis, each of them a wave rising and crashing. The mother's body is no longer needed to authorize identity.

Thus, *The Waves* ends a series of novels that allowed Woolf to imagine herself surviving as a manic-depressive. Fiction could not cure her biochemically based illness, but it did give her a stage on which to set characters embodying bewildering, unconnected symptoms, and this dramatization of her mental states helped her recognize not only her illness but her wellness too: the sane and the insane, side by side, plural yet one, the one Virginia Woolf.

Epilogue: Science and Subjectivity

My "story" of Virginia Woolf's manic-depressive illness ends here, but its implications do not. Her most profound insight into her disorder—that the unity of consciousness is a tidy fiction with which to build our "comfortable cocoons" of consistent identity—continues to challenge how we write histories of the mind, because it has been reinforced by recent advances in neuroscience. This intersection between literary and scientific inquiries may eventually lead us to a new model of the human psyche, one that integrates the valuable insights of psychoanalysis and neuroscience, mind and brain, Freud and Woolf. Indeed, some convergence of the "hard" and "soft" sciences must be an inevitable step if psychoanalysis is to survive through the next century. And it would be a fitting sequel to a neurobiography of Virginia Woolf (certainly more rewarding than lingering over her suicide), for she left us a legacy that extends beyond her personal tragedy. She can be more than a Freudian lesson on how *not* to cope with trauma. She stands at the crossroads where art, science, biography, and biology meet.

Woolf's "ensemble psyche" in *The Waves* lives on in Michael S. Gazzaniga's theory of the brain's "modular-type organization." Gazzaniga's famous experiments with split-brain patients have led him to conclude that the human brain is organized into "relatively independent function-ing units that work in parallel. The mind is not an indivisible whole, operating in a single way to solve all problems," but a confederation. Most of these modules, which are capable of their own actions, moods, and responses, remembering events and storing affective reactions to those events, operate in nonverbal ways apart from the conscious verbal self and so are unavailable for introspection. A sudden impulse to act, a shift in emotion or mood, may arise in one module. The "ego" of the dominant hemisphere will then evaluate that impulse and mediate it (a hallucinating patient may even "hear" this module's intent as a "voice"). If one part functions in isolation and displaces the ego's program to integrate other, counterbalancing modules, the resulting "impulsive" behavior can be catastrophic and/or psychotic.[1]

Gazzaniga's modules are not necessarily "unconscious" in the Freudian sense (although some probably are); most are "co-conscious but nonver-bal."[2] We are unaware of our multiple selves because our brain has a special program in the dominant hemisphere that Gazzaniga calls the "interpreter," a Bernard-like spokesperson who instantly makes inferences and constructs a theory, or narrative, to explain why a behavior or thought or emotion has occurred. But too often the left hemisphere strives for subjective consistency (like old Professor Sopwith twining "chaos" into a neat thread) at the expense of right hemisphere sensitivity to inconsistent data; consequently, ignored modules may act independently. Perhaps, then, manic-depressive mood shifts produce misbehaviors and chaotic self structure because they impair the usually seamless integration of these modules. They certainly heightened Woolf's sense of the mind's innate program to fight chaos with narrative order as opposed to its potential for perceptual plasticity, out of which she created a "modern" view of subjectivity. In this sense, postmodern science has finally caught up with her.

What can biology offer psychoanalytic theory besides blank opposition? Intriguing possibilities. In Chapter 8 I spoke of how each hemisphere mediates perceptions and thinking differently, contributing various styles and insights that successful interhemispheric processing integrates, and how events in the nondominant (usually right) hemisphere often go unnoticed or unacknowledged by the dominant (usually left) hemisphere, which presumes that it is the only seat of authority and knowledge. Inadequate integration may thus constitute a functional "invisible deficit." I borrow this term from neurology, where it is used to describe the inability of a patient to be aware that, due to brain injury, he is lacking a prominent feature of consciousness. If, for instance, certain visual areas of the right hemisphere are damaged by a stroke, patients will not see or attend to any object situated on their left, and they will be unaware that they are so blinded. When asked to draw the face of a clock, they will accurately recreate only the right side, with numbers 12 through 6 dutifully noted, but 7 through 11 will be missing. Oliver Sacks reports on a patient, Mrs. S., who had suffered a massive stroke in her right cerebral hemisphere and lost her ability to perceive objects on her left: when served dinner, she ate only from the right half of the plate; when applying lipstick, she covered only the right side of her mouth. She could not look left, or turn left, so she learned to turn right, in a circle, until she found what she was looking for. The object on the left (indeed, the direction "left") did not exist unless her "right looking" left hemisphere perceived it.[3] Another patient's right-hemisphere stroke damage extended into visual imagination and memory: when asked to imagine himself walking through his town square, Dr. P. listed only those buildings that would have appeared on his right side, none on his left. When asked to imagine himself walking in the opposite direction, he listed only the previously missing buildings, those that would have appeared on his right, which he had failed to remember moments before. His subjective world was exclusively right-handed.[4]

The nervous system is arranged to build a spatial map of the body and its environment. Disturbances within the system can have profound effects on the individual's sense of what constitutes his body and his mind—in effect, his identity. If a stroke impairs afferent and motor neurons, the patient may become unaware that he has an arm or leg; when it is pointed out to him, he will report that he "feels" or "believes" that it belongs to someone else, not him. One of Sacks's patients threw himself out of his hospital bed trying to rid himself of what looked like someone else's leg, "*a severed human leg,* a horrible thing" that he could only assume a prankster had surreptitiously attached to his body. He called it a "counterfeit" because it did not feel "real"—at least, *not really his.* When asked to locate his own left leg, the patient became pale and claimed that it had "disappeared." His identity no longer included a left leg.[5]

Dr. P., Mrs. S., and the young man without a leg all suffer from a psychic dissociation because of their neurological deficit. They do not know about the dead limb or the blind or numb side; indeed, they do not desire to know. It is as if the circuits that mediate particular perceptions also generate or process the specific desire to perceive them, what a Freudian would call an object-cathexis. They literally do not know what they are missing, that they are missing it, or that they might have wanted not to miss it. The desire has disappeared along with the cognitive capacity. The implications of the "invisible deficit" present psychoanalytic theorists with intriguing challenges. Is the origin of desire limited (like Freud's id) to certain areas of the mind, or is it spread across all neural networks? In what ways are desire and cognition the same thing differently perceived? Will it be possible to chart a "map of desire" in the same way we now map areas of the brain that handle sensory data from the arms or legs? Can interhemispheric integration be affected by a functional invisible deficit, a structural dissociation that does not involve a physical injury or the censorship of forbidden content responsive to introspection and psychoanalytic insight? In what way do we all suffer from invisible deficits? Brain damage is apparent to us because we compare the patient's disability to our abilities, but even we who enjoy intact brains cannot perceive or desire to perceive that we are missing something lying beyond what our brain structure allows us to think about.

In other words, the French psychoanalyst Jacques Lacan's linguistic model may not be the only way to describe the limitations of thought. Future interdisciplinary research may shift the burden of postmodern psychoanalysis from a Saussurean linguistic base of self-referential signs and signifiers to a neurological one. For cognitive science and neuroscience also suggest that we do not perceive, interpret, or "know" reality referentially but, rather, in terms of thousands of feedback loops supporting internal theoretical models that occur on both conscious and unconscious levels, and that operate binomially, amassing and organizing differentiated units (hot/cold, rough/soft, love/hate). Just as postmodern psychoanalytic theory depicts the underpinnings of thought as a chain of signifiers whose meaning exists only in relation to each other, epitomized by opposition of polar opposites, so too neural circuitry and brain structure seem to be arranged to deal with sensory information and behavior by opposing pathways—paired hemispheres, modular processing (discrete areas of the brain handling specialized tasks which must be sorted out at higher levels of functioning), feedback circuits, paired/opposed neurotransmitter systems, the splitting off of linguistic skills from visual skills.

The import of brain research throws up a kind of Lacanian bar between the left and the right hemisphere, making self-insight, or even self-awareness, a matter of interpretation, a guess or approximation based on inadequate data fed from one hemisphere to the other. The dominant hemisphere, a specialist in linguistic signifiers, may be barred from direct knowledge of the nondominant hemisphere, the signified, where a separate self—equally developed and reality-oriented—processes many important perceptions and feelings. Perhaps the Other we most struggle to know (or whose mute gaze haunts our every look) is not the unconscious part of one self but another conscious self, co-existing in our shared body, mute and unavailable to language, yet responsible for processing the visual and emotional cues which the dominant hemisphere may misunderstand, for mistranslations are inevitable between two minds that do not speak the same language.[6]

Can inadequate interhemispheric relations be the physical basis for Lacan's observation that patients' utterances and writers' texts undercut their own ostensible meaning? Does the right hemisphere make itself known by surreptitiously sliding signifiers through metonymy (a useful procedure for a hemisphere good at recognizing widely scattered details and individual words but not at generating sustained, intentional sentences of its own) and metaphor (the right hemisphere is skilled at nonlinear modes of association and converging multiple determinants rather than at forming a causal or logical chain)? What would emerge, then, is not a composed structure of meaningful elements but Lacan's discomposed discourse in which elements are substituted and recombined, leaving seemingly mute traces or absences to litter our left-hemisphere–dominated narratives. If that is the case, then the robust left hemisphere, unaware that it is speaking the unrecognized and unrecognizable "truth" of the repressed right hemisphere, might also be one source of the Imaginary Subject created in the misreading of the infantile mirror-stage, and the Subject would be a misreading not only of the Other who is its mother but of the Other who is its hemispheric psychic partner, against which it has defined itself. Doubled selves, one of whom is a mute voyeur gazing upon the other, may create the uncanny duality of all Lacanian looking (every recognition at once a finding and a failure to find, every gaze a being gazed at), in which we are perpetually caught. Does transference originate here in the relationship between these two selves, with the right hemisphere playing the Lacanian dummy, the smoothly mirroring and mute Other (like Tansley, Lily Briscoe's whipping boy), who reveals nothing but what we project upon him? Is the left hemisphere thus burdened, defeated, and frustrated by its own mastery, its too-successful subordination of the right hemisphere, because silencing Otherness only increases the power of its haunting and inscrutable gaze? If the Lacanian unconscious includes this other thinking, witnessing, and responding self, then the old phrase about being "of two minds" will someday seem ironically profound and profoundly inadequate. Biological science now offers psychoanalytic and literary scholars promising evidence that a brain/mind integration will have enormously important theoretical implications—if we open ourselves up to them.

Some psychoanalysts resist the idea of even a future convergence between psychoanalysis and the physical sciences, for they arbitrarily assume that mind is essentially nonphysical. In *Psychoanalysis: A Theory in Crisis,* Marshall Edelson tries to reassure us that psychoanalysis is unassailable by biology because it is an autonomous, "special" science that can legitimately ask its own kinds of questions of nature by focusing on a person's internal symbolic-semantic representation of an object or state of affairs and on his or her relationship with those representations without worrying whether or not the brain's structure or function can significantly affect or shape thinking.[7] Edelson argues that the mind-body split is irreducible because the problem is really a metaphysical one: no "conceivable" empirical evidence can solve it. Subjectivity establishes itself independently of the brain, following its own rules, by which mental operations create mental states and both mental and physical symptoms. But the fact that we cannot conceive of what empirical evidence would show mind-brain identity may result, not from lack of evidence, but from lack of a model that allows us to see evidence that already exists. Edelson is right to assert that we presently do not have the descriptive terms to account for our phenomenal world in relation to its mechanical underpinnings (for instance, the subjective sensation of pain is not adequately conveyed to us by the fact that it is mediated by nerve-cell firings). But this has always been the state of science before the formulation of new models: what remains to be discovered is outside the cognitive horizons of earlier workers because the very concepts operative in the characterization of new models become available only in the course of scientific discovery. The unforeseeable tends to be of special significance just because of its unpredictability.[8]

Moreover, psychoanalysis cannot reject the implications of biology simply because it is assumed by clinicians that veracity (insights gained during analysis) and efficacy (therapeutic benefit) are directly linked.[9] Analysts in the past, for instance, concluded that cold and aloof mothers caused autism in their children because they saw that mothering treatment seemed to make the disturbed child feel or act better. In fact, the child who responded to positive reinforcement remained autistic, and such a causative argument grossly oversimplified the mother's psychological profile. Most mothers of autistics are neither cold nor aloof; some of them may become so as a result of the child's chronic, deviant, and unresponsive behavior and, being so afflicted, they seek out psychotherapy in greater numbers and so become overrepresented.[10] The analyst's insight and the child's altered behavior did not reveal the origin of autism but only the nature of a parent-child relationship strained by an incurable and severe developmental disorder. The purely psychological approach (espoused, most notably, by Bruno Bettelheim) has since been replaced by the mounting evidence that autism is a neurologic disorder in which genetics plays a substantial role.[11] Research shows us that autistic patients manifest a variety of associated neurobiological findings, and a recent study has pinpointed brain tissue damage that predates mother-child interaction.[12] Blaming the parents cruelly traumatized them further; many of these families have since come forward and condemned Bettelheim and his followers for what strikes them as "parent-abuse." The lesson we must learn here is not that Freud's approach is automatically to be considered wrong but that, without benefit of neuroscience, psychoanalytic theory has no built-in mechanism to prevent it from blundering into complex situations in search of a simplistic cause-effect relationship.

Some model making mind and body parallel must be formulated, in order to correct both the excessive metaphorizing of psychoanalysis and the dehumanizing materialism of neuroscience.[13] We have a uniquely human need for meaning, and we often benefit personally and psychologically from introspective insight, but ignoring biochemistry does not liberate psychoanalysis—it merely deregulates insight until analytic explanations haplessly mimic the patient's own anomalous and subjective experiences. Psychoanalysts often criticize psychiatrists for being too interested in the form of symptoms rather than in the thematic meaning of content, but form helps to establish a correct diagnosis, whereas content cannot, as J. K. Wing argues:

> A patient may be afraid of cats, or deluded that there is a cat controlling him, or he may see a cat when no cat is physically present. He may fail to remember the name of his own pet cat. Four completely different diagnoses are suggested in spite of the fact that there is a common theme to all of these experiences.[14]

Speculating willy-nilly on the "meaning" of the cat figure (is it Woman? uncontrolled sexuality? anima? masked rage? oral aggression?) will only permit us to indulge our own fantasies and invite inappropriate treatment until we know whether the form of the symptom indicates a phobia, schizophrenia, a right hemisphere tumor, or an unconsciously determined repression. Only after a diagnosis is reached can we decide whether behavior therapy (effective against phobias), anti-psychotic drugs (for schizophrenia), surgery (for operable lesions or tumors), or psychoanalysis (if the fear results from an unconscious conflict) is called for. As the history of manic-depressive illness has amply demonstrated, it is important for both the psychoanalyst and the psychobiographer to know in which direction cause and effect are working in each particular case.

Virginia Woolf knew little about the brain, but her experiences as a manic-depressive and as a creative artist provided a natural laboratory in which to observe the subtle dynamics of consciousness—structural dynamics too universal and anonymous to be described adequately by the highly personal Freudian conflicts of melodramatic trauma and infantile needs. To understand her contribution to our postmodern views of the mind, we must update our psychological approaches to literature, integrating narrative models of psychodynamics with medical models of brain structure and data processing. Only then will it become evident how Woolf's illness and her wellness equally illuminate her value for us.

Afterword

I am a porous vessel afloat on sensation; a sensitive plate
exposed to invisible rays . . . taking the breath of these
voices in my sails and tacking this way and that through
daily life as I yield to them.

V. Woolf, *Moments of Being*

With the breath of voices in her sails, Virginia Woolf lived her life as a
journey from one great individual moment to the next. To an extraordinary degree she was able to transform from chaos into meaning her
tumultuous thoughts and feelings. She struggled to understand her "violent
moods of the soul" and her consummate skill enabled her to couple in
her writings a somewhat disconcerting distancing and acuteness of observation with her fragmented and wildly opposing perceptions.[1] Like many
other mercurial writers, she learned to absorb what such fiery, violent,
and desolate moods might teach. In their contrasts she saw different truths,
and in seeking their reconciliation she imposed a kind of order and rhythm
unique in literature.

Woolf's ability to express heightened moments of remembered intensity came in part, no doubt, from an exquisite sensitivity to the shudderings
and inconstancies of her life. Like Edward Thomas, another of melancholic
temperament, she sought always to catch the essence of such moments,
whether bitter or sweet. What she took into prose he described in poetry:

> As for myself,
> Where first I met the bitter scent is lost.
> I too, often shrivel the grey shreds,
> Sniff them and think and sniff again and try
> Once more to think what it is I am remembering,
> Always in vain. I cannot like the scent,
> Yet I would rather give up others more sweet,
> With no meaning, than this bitter one.[2]

Without question, much of Woolf's ability to describe the transience
of the natural world came from her own rapid shifts of mood and thought.
She believed unequivocally in the importance of melancholia and madness
to her imaginative powers:

As an experience, madness is terrific I can assure you, and not to be sniffed at; and in its lava I still find most of the things I write about. It shoots out of one everything shaped, final, not in mere driblets, as sanity does. And the six months—not three—that I lay in bed taught me a good deal about what is called oneself.[3]

Yet the illness that brought forth the lava also killed her. In *The Flight of the Mind* Thomas Caramagno makes a compelling, I think almost indisputable, case that Virginia Woolf suffered from manic-depressive illness. This is not a new suggestion—indeed, it has been presumed by many psychologists and psychiatrists for decades—but Caramagno presents excellent, detailed clinical descriptions of Woolf's manias, depressions, and mixed states; follows the natural course of her illness; and, especially convincing in a discussion of a genetic disease, superbly documents a family history of mood swings, psychosis, and suicide. In uncannily modern and clinical language both Virginia and Leonard Woolf described Virginia's erratic and extreme moods and behaviors. Without romanticizing manic-depressive illness, Caramagno portrays many of its fascinating and positive aspects, as well as its debilitating, withering, and ultimately killing side. He also discusses the resistance many writers have shown toward seeing Virginia Woolf as "mad," including those of a psychoanalytic bent who have read into Woolf's life and work vastly speculative interpretations and unfounded assumptions about cause and motivation.

The Flight of the Mind goes far beyond diagnosis and clinical description, however. Powerfully, through the use of her diaries, journals, and fiction, it brings to life Woolf's struggle to bring coherence to her chaotic universe. The search for meaning and control is crucial in any writer's life, but perhaps especially so in those touched by the "wings of madness."[4] That writing itself was a means of healing Woolf said herself: "I suppose that I did for myself what psycho-analysts do for their patients. I expressed some very long felt and deeply felt emotion. And in expressing it I explained it and then laid it to rest."[5]

Most important, Caramagno is able to portray the remarkably vital personality and strength of character that Virginia Woolf focused upon her work. While understanding and giving context to Woolf's despairs and insanity, at the same time he makes clear her staggering originality and power. John Ruskin, who also suffered from manic-depressive illness, wrote that the imagination

never stops at crusts or ashes, or outward images of any kind; it ploughs them all aside, and plunges into the very central fiery heart;

nothing else will content its spirituality; whatever semblances and various outward shows and phases its subjects may possess go for nothing; it gets within all fence, cuts down to the root, and drinks the very vital sap of that it deals with . . . its function and gift are the getting at the root, its nature and dignity depend on its holding things always by the heart. Take its hand from off the beating of that, and it will prophesy no longer; it looks not in the eyes, it judges not by the voice; it describes not by outward features; all that it affirms, judges, or describes, from within.[6]

Virginia Woolf described from within, and by that fact she wrote as she was.

Caramagno, by combining the perspectives of modern psychiatry with his own background in literary criticism, gives us a broad and compassionate look into Woolf's life and work. And he has the sense and sensibility to allow her to speak for herself and for the human condition:

We do not know our own souls, let alone the souls of others. Human beings do not go hand in hand the whole stretch of the way. There is a virgin forest in each; a snowfield where even the print of birds' feet is unknown. Here we go alone, and like it better so. Always to have sympathy, always to be accompanied, always to be understood would be intolerable. But in health the genial pretence must be kept up, and the effort renewed—to communicate, to civilize, to share, to cultivate the desert, to educate the native, to work together by day and by night to sport. In illness this make-believe ceases.[7]

Kay Redfield Jamison, Ph.D.
Associate Professor of Psychiatry
The Johns Hopkins University School of Medicine
November 1990

Appendix: Virginia Woolf's Mood Swing Chart (1895–1941)

The graph below charts the periodicity of Virginia Woolf's reported mood swings (as indicated in Bell's biography, Virginia's letters, her diary, or Leonard's daily "Monks House" diary) from 1895 to 1941. Each month is rated in which an episode of any duration occurred. As the chart shows, Woolf suffered from a range of levels, from mild through moderate to severe, but she also enjoyed many years of normal mood, happiness, and productivity.

When Virginia notes in her private diary that she is feeling depressed or manic, but Leonard says she is well, I give priority to Virginia's report; inner turmoil does not always translate into behavior. When Leonard notes Virginia is ill, but she denies it, I give his report priority; manic-depressives sometimes do not know when they have become ill. Pluses and minuses appearing together indicate mixed states or rapid cycling. Irritability, temper tantrums, rage, and violence are categorized as mixed states.

Severity scale:
- − 1 = mild and/or short-lived depressed mood
- − 2 = moderate depressed mood
- − 3 = severe depression (without delusions or hallucinations)
- − 4 = psychotic depression (with delusions or hallucinations)
- + 1 = hypomania (mild mania)
- + 2 = moderate mania
- + 3 = severe mania (without delusions or hallucinations)
- + 4 = psychotic mania (with delusions or hallucinations)

Year	Jan	Feb	Mar	Apr	May	June	July	Aug	Sept	Oct	Nov	Dec
					+4							
1895												
					−4							
1896												
									−4			
		+1			+1	+2	+1					
1897												
		−1			−2	−2	−1		−2	−2	−2	−2

Year	Jan	Feb	Mar	Apr	May	June	July	Aug	Sept	Oct	Nov	Dec
1898												
								+1				
1899												
1900												
			−1									
			+1	+1								
1901												
			−1	−1								
1902												
1903												
	+1	+1	+1	+4	+4	+4	+2	+1				
1904												
	−1	−1	−1	−4	−4	−4	−2	−1				
1905												
				−1								
												+1
1906												
	+1	+1										
1907												
	−1	−1										
								+2				
1908												
					−1			−1				
							+1	+1				
1909												
			+2				+3	+3	+2			
1910												
			−2			−3						
1911												
						−1						

Year	Jan	Feb	Mar	Apr	May	June	July	Aug	Sept	Oct	Nov	Dec
		+3	+2			+2						
1912												
	−1	−3	−2			−2						
	+1	+1			+1		+3	+3	+4	+4	+2	+2
1913												
	−1	−1			−1		−3	−3	−4	−4	−3	−2
	+2	+2	+1	+2	+1	+1	+1					
1914												
	−2	−1	−1	−1	−1	−1	−1					
	+1	+4	+4	+3	+3	+2						
1915												
	−1	−1			−3							
						+1	+1			+1		
1916												
			−1									
				+1			+1			+1	+1	+1
1917												
							−1				−1	−1
		+1		+1	+1				+1	+1	+1	
1918												
			−1						−1		−1	
	+2				+1	+1	+1			+1	+1	+1
1919												
	−2						−1		−2			−1
	+1	+1			+1			+1	+1			
1920												
		−1	−1	−1					−1	−1	−1	
				+1	+1	+2	+2	+1				
1921												
	−1			−2	−1	−1	−2	−1				
	+2	+2						+1				
1922												
	−2	−2				−1		−1				
		+1				+1	+1	+1		+1		
1923												
	−2	−1	−1			−1	−1	−1	−1	+1		
		+1			+1	+1			+1		+1	+1
1924												
			−1					−1				
	+1			+1	+1	+1	+1	+1	+1	+1	+1	
1925												
					−1	−1		−1		−1	−1	−1

Year	Jan	Feb	Mar	Apr	May	June	July	Aug	Sept	Oct	Nov	Dec
	+1	+1		+1	+1		+1	+1	+2	+1	+1	+1
1926												
		-1		-1	-1	-2	-2	-1	-2	-1		
			+1		+1	+1	+1	+1	+1	+1	+1	+1
1927												
		-1	-1		-1				-1	-1		
	+1	+1					+1	+1	+1	+1	+1	+1
1928												
	-1	-1	-1			-1		-1	-1			
				+1			+1	+2	+1		+1	+1
1929												
	-2		-2			-2	-1	-2	-1	-1	-1	-2
	+1		+1		+1	+1	+1	+1	+1	+1	+1	+1
1930												
	-1	-2									-1	
	+1	+1		+1	+1	+1	+1	+1	+1	+1	+1	+1
1931												
	-1	-1	-1	-2				-1	-1	-1	-1	-1
	+1	+1		+1	+1	+1	+1	+1	+1	+1	+1	
1932												
	-1		-1		-1							
	+1	+1	+1				+1	+1	+1	+1		
1933												
				-1			-1	-1		-1		
	+1					+1		+1	+1	+1	+1	
1934												
							-1	-1	-1	-1		
						+2	+1	+1	+1	+1	+1	+1
1935												
						-2	-1	-1	-1	-1	-1	-1
	+1	+1	+1					+1		+1		
1936												
	-1	-1	-2	-3	-3	-2		-1		-1	-2	
			+1	+1	+1	+1	+1	+1	+1	+1	+1	
1937												
			-2								-1	
				+1		+1	+1	+1	+1	+1		
1938												
							-1	-1			-1	-1
												+1
1939												
				-1			-1	-1			-1	

Year	Jan	Feb	Mar	Apr	May	June	July	Aug	Sept	Oct	Nov	Dec
1940	+1				+1				+1	+1	+1	
	−1		−1			−1			−1			
1941		+1										
	−1	−1	−4									

Notes

INTRODUCTION

1. Frederick K. Goodwin and Kay Redfield Jamison, *Manic-Depressive Illness* (New York: Oxford University Press, 1990), 295. All citations from this massive (938 pages) and comprehensive book will be cited as *MDI,* with the name of the author of the passage and the page number.

CHAPTER 1

1. Jamison (*MDI* 347); Feinstein (334); Slavney and McHugh (31). Feinstein adds that Woolf's case history "fulfills every criterion" for manic-depressive illness (339). Only Morizot has addressed manic-depressive illness squarely.
2. Q. Bell 1:44. On preoedipal attachment: Love (*Virginia Woolf* 212–27); Kushen (*Virginia Woolf* 2–4); Kenney and Kenney. On unconscious guilt: Lesser (50). On fiction as defense mechanism: DeSalvo (*Virginia Woolf's First Voyage* 154–59); Spilka (6); Sherman. On "moments of being": Naremore (49–55).
3. Panken (4, 13, 68–71, 36).
4. Bond (23, 43, 38–39, 68).
5. DeSalvo (*Virginia Woolf* xvi).
6. Poole (180, 130).
7. Wolf and Wolf (44); Panken (17); Kushen (*Virginia Woolf* 165); Bond (152).
8. Spector; Segal ("Psycho-analytic Approach").
9. Crews (81).
10. Revisionists: Skura; S. Marcus; C. Bollas. Feminists: Abel; J. Marcus; Waugh.
11. Noble (63).
12. C. Bell (99).
13. Q. Bell (1: 171); L. Woolf (*Letters* 169).
14. Jamison (*MDI* 733).
15. Hyman ("Concealment" 128). Katherine Cecilia Hill makes a similar argument in her dissertation, focusing on Leslie's "unreasonable anger," excessive sensitivity, and melancholic mourning as evidence that he shared some of his daughter's manic-depression. I agree with Hill that Leslie's pronounced moodiness (cyclothymia) is related, both genetically and biochemically, to Virginia's psychotic illness, but, unlike his daughter, Leslie never broke down so severely that he became incapacitated. Cyclothymics do not lose self-control through failed reality testing (i.e., delusions and hallucinations), although they can alternate between excited "highs" and blue "lows." Symptoms are comparatively muted, and the periods of elation are short-lived. Cyclothymia is related genetically to manic-depressive illness (we find more incidence of it in the families of bipolar patients than we would in the general population), and sometimes it appears as a "premorbid"

precursor of manic-depressive illness. It has not been determined positively whether cyclothymia is an independent entity or a mild form of manic-depressive illness (Keller), although current opinion favors the latter theory. I address Leslie's mood swings in more detail in the next chapter.

16. *DSM-III-R* (xxiv).
17. Goldstein (445).
18. Scull (19).
19. J. Marcus ("Virginia Woolf" 35); Trombley (137).
20. Winokur (88); Wolpert (42). The following is only a partial list of somatic disturbances and drugs associated with depressive and manic states:

	Depression	*Mania*
Infectious	Influenza	Influenza
	Viral hepatitis	Post–St. Louis type A encephalitis
	Infectious mononucleosis	Q fever
	General paresis (tertiary syphilis)	General paresis (tertiary syphilis)
	Tuberculosis	"Benign" herpes simplex
	Cirrhosis	Encephalitis
	AIDS (HIV)	AIDS (HIV)
Endocrine	Hypothyroidism	Hyperthyroidism
	Myxedema	Vitamin B-12 deficiency
	Cushing's disease	Cushing's disease
	Addison's disease	Addison's disease
Neoplastic	Occult abdominal malignancies	Various brain tumors
Collagen	Systemic lupus erythematosis	Systemic lupus erythematosis
Neurological	Multiple sclerosis	Multiple sclerosis
	Cerebral tumors	Diencephalic and third ventricular tumors
	Sleep apnea	
	Dementia	Epilepsy
	Parkinson's disease	Right hemisphere damage
	Nondominant temporal lobe lesions	Huntington's disease
Nutritional	Pernicious anemia	
	Pellagra	

	Depression	*Mania*
Drugs	Oral contraceptives	Steroids
	Reserpine	Decongestants
	Alpha-methyl-dopa	Amphetamines, hallucinogens
	Alcohol	Alcohol
	Physostigmine	Bronchodilators
	Sedative-hypnotics	Monoamine oxidase inhibitors
	Amphetamine withdrawal	
	Barbiturate or cocaine withdrawal	Thyroid hormones
		Barbiturates

(adapted from Whybrow et al. [176] and F. K. Goodwin and Jamison [*MDI* 112])

Studies by Pflug et al. have shown that mood swings are connected to higher mean bodily temperatures compared with normal states. In fact, the more severe the depression, the higher the temperature; moreover, in some patients, manic phases produced even higher oral temperatures than did depression. Perhaps this explains why Leonard kept such close track of Virginia's fevers, and why Woolf reassures herself that her "contraction" is not accompanied by a fever.

Wehr et al. consider it possible that breakdowns can be triggered or exacerbated by the physiological stresses associated with menstruation and menopause, as do Price and DiMarzio, and F. K. Goodwin (*MDI* 458). Noting that Woolf's breakdowns may have coincided with the onset of menstruation—the first occurred when she was thirteen years old, after her mother's death—and menopause (she had several smaller breakdowns in her forties), Elaine Showalter speculates that Woolf's madness expressed her shame and anxiety over her femaleness (*Literature* [268–69]). But the intense guilt and anxiety she exhibited are more likely the result of manic-depressive illness, not its cause, and the connection was probably hormonal.

21. Wehr et al. (61).
22. Pichot and Hassan.
23. Hollister (393).
24. Levy and Krueger; F. K. Goodwin (*MDI* 533–34).
25. Panken (38–39, 36).
26. DeSalvo (*Virginia Woolf* 111).
27. Trombley (115); J. Marcus ("Virginia Woolf" 33–35).
28. Bassuk (143); Skultans (14).
29. Love (*Virginia Woolf* 161); Hyman ("Concealment" 126).
30. Spilka; Wolf and Wolf; Kenney and Kenney; Panken.
31. M. J. Clark (271–75).
32. Morizot (116).

33. Showalter ("Victorian Women" 321–23).
34. Bassuk (141); Trombley (150–51).
35. Showalter ("Victorian Women" 322–23).
36. Showalter ("Victorian Women" 330).
37. Scull (24).
38. Rapp (191).
39. Goldstein (447–50); Panken (5); DeSalvo (*Virginia Woolf* 128–34); Trombley (175–82); Kushen ("Virginia Woolf" 37).
40. Panken (5); Kushen ("Virginia Woolf" 40).
41. Sprengnether; Collins et al.
42. Garrison.
43. F. K. Goodwin (*MDI* 551).
44. F. K. Goodwin and Jamison (*MDI* 635–36).
45. F. K. Goodwin (*MDI* 554).
46. Wehr et al. (66–68); Georgotas and Cancro (312–31).
47. F. K. Goodwin and Jamison (*MDI* 738).
48. Trombley (139–40).
49. On 1/10, 1/17, 1/24, 4/17, 5/15, 6/20, 7/19, and 7/22.
50. On 2/18, 2/22, 2/23, 2/24, 2/25, 2/26, 2/27, 2/28, 3/1, 3/5, 3/7, 3/9, 3/11, 3/13, 3/16, 3/17, 3/19.
51. DeSalvo (*Virginia Woolf* 211).
52. Jamison (*MDI* 223).
53. F. K. Goodwin and Jamison (*MDI* 301, 83, 774).
54. Garnett (113).
55. Noble (158).
56. Noble (152).
57. Spater and Parsons (73).
58. Jamison (*MDI* 24, 39).
59. Witzel (386, 396, 397).
60. Rogat (112); Ozick (44).
61. Louise DeSalvo (*Virginia Woolf's First Voyage* 154–59); Heine.
62. Spilka (18, 6, 8).
63. Cook.
64. J. Marcus ("Quentin's Bogey" 487–89); J. Marcus ("Tintinnabulations" 145).
65. Arieti and Bemporad (12–13); Braceland (872).
66. Arieti and Bemporad (14).
67. Goldberg (34, 37).
68. Cooper et al. (216).
69. Freud (21: 173–94).
70. Goldberg (47–49).
71. Stevens.
72. See especially Rice.
73. Gaylin (26–49, 108–53, 338–52, 154–81); Stern; Rado; Anthonisen.
74. Witzel (395).
75. Lesser (55).

76. Cade (350).

77. Fieve (211–12).

78. Fieve (11).

79. In 1987 the discovery of a second gene in an Amish family study was announced by Egeland et al., but the finding was later retracted when two more family members, who had not inherited that particular gene, subsequently developed manic-depression. Abundance is not necessarily a blessing in genetic studies. However, the Baron et al. finding of the first gene still stands.

80. Georgotas and Cancro (63–64, 410–38); Swann (36, 97); F. K. Goodwin and Roy-Byrne (82).

81. Davis and Maas (409); Jamison (*MDI* 725–27).

82. Fieve (214).

83. Georgotas and Cancro (339); F. K. Goodwin and Jamison (*MDI* 76).

84. Fieve (150); Jamison ("Psychotherapeutic Issues and Suicide Prevention" 121); Keller (22).

85. Jamison ("Psychotherapeutic Issues and Suicide Prevention" 109–10); Davis and Maas (409–18).

86. Jamison (*MDI* 725).

87. Rush et al.; Ruehlman et al.; Beck and Greenberg.

CHAPTER 2

1. Jamison (*MDI* 336).

2. Bloom and Lazerson (330).

3. Fieve (17–18).

4. F. K. Goodwin (*MDI* 135).

5. Angst.

6. F. K. Goodwin (*MDI* 138).

7. F. K. Goodwin and Jamison (*MDI* 82).

8. Secunda et al.

9. Feinstein.

10. Q. Bell (1: 165).

11. Jamison (*MDI* 189).

12. Georgotas and Cancro (155).

13. Davis and Maas (197).

14. Georgotas and Cancro (39).

15. Dain.

16. Keller (21); F. K. Goodwin (*MDI* 136–38).

17. Jamison (*MDI* 295); Akiskal et al.

18. Jamison (*MDI* 305).

19. *DSM-III-R* (214); Jamison (*MDI* 31–34).

20. Keller (25); Q. Bell (1: 24).

21. Noble (20–21, 50).

22. Kenney (284).

23. Interview with Malcolm Muggeridge, broadcast 1966; BBC transcription housed in Monks House Papers Collection, University of Sussex library.

24. Georgotas and Cancro (58); Carlson and Goodwin.
25. Whybrow et al. (10).
26. *DSM-III-R* (215).
27. Q. Bell (1: 24); Noble (147, 47).
28. Gordon (*Virginia Woolf* 180); Noble (171).
29. Gordon (*Virginia Woolf* 180).
30. F. K. Goodwin and Jamison (*MDI* 76–78).
31. Jamison (*MDI* 251).
32. Jamison (*MDI* 27).
33. Winokur et al. (65).
34. Jamison (*MDI* 262–64).
35. Custance (31–32, 34).
36. Custance (35).
37. Oltmanns and Maher (167, ix, 20, 56).
38. Winokur et al. (65–68); Tyrer and Shopsin.
39. Whybrow et al. (7).
40. Fieve (51).
41. Winokur (14).
42. Jamison (*MDI* 30, 48).
43. Q. Bell (1: 29).
44. Custance (13, 22).
45. Jamison (*MDI* 26).
46. Packer.
47. A manic-depressive responding to my *PMLA* article in a personal letter (and wishing to remain anonymous) describes her manic fictions in similar terms:

> I also loved what you had to say about the creativity of manic-depressive fictions. That is one of the strongest impressions I retain from my misadventures seven years ago. I don't know *who* put together my delusions, but whoever it was had been studying contrapuntal symbolism with Dante and the Joyce of *Finnegan's Wake*. Bits of things I'd read about in an *LA Times* headline, a dream I'd had when I was twelve, some footnote to a scholarly book, would all be woven together into a narrative that was completely convincing—not only to me, but frequently even to the other people I told my wild stories to. How could I make such things up? And of course, *I* didn't. At the high point and low point of my manic and depressive phases, the narrative would be revised so quickly and continuously that my memory felt as if it were watching a deck of cards being shuffled or one of those old trick books—where you flip the pages rapidly to produce the illusion of a moving picture—riffled through at top speed in my head. It was perfectly terrifying, because what is a self but a little organ of conscious perception and a vast memory bank? And when the memory bank goes bananas the little organ of conscious perception is simply left recording the breakdown. Your explanation helped explain something I had never understood—why I *felt* perfectly rational in one

part of my mind even when I was perfectly psychotic somewhere else. When I came to read the various medical accounts of the illness— whether by [psycho]analysts or not—they seemed so crude and silly that I wanted to shake the authors and say "That is not it at all." This, I see, is where the alliance of neuropsychiatry and the humanities can be of some use.

48. Custance (38).
49. Custance (18).
50. Q. Bell (1: 89).
51. Panken (48–50).
52. Q. Bell (1: 148–49).
53. Spater and Parsons.
54. Noble (151).
55. Gordon (*Virginia Woolf* 156).
56. Noble (16, 75, 51, 75).
57. Noble (128).
58. Noble (178).
59. Noble (109, 174, 113).
60. Jamison (*MDI* 337).
61. Custance (151).
62. Styron (37–38).
63. Winokur et al. (86–88).
64. Cornell et al.; Jamison (*MDI* 38).
65. Whybrow et al. (7).
66. See, for example, Nelson and Charney.
67. Jamison (*MDI* 267).
68. Jamison (*MDI* 40).
69. Q. Bell (1: 45).
70. Constipation: Georgotas and Cancro (71); Jamison (*MDI* 39). Nail growth: Hershman and Lieb (29). "Vegetative" symptoms: Hamilton.
71. Styron (48).
72. *DSM-III-R* (219).
73. Wolpert (42).
74. Jamison (*MDI* 36).
75. Custance (78–79).
76. Jamison (*MDI* 39).
77. Georgotas and Cancro (55).
78. Marcia K. Johnson, "Discriminating the Origin of Information," in Oltmanns and Maher (57).
79. Joseph Westermayer, "Some Cross-Cultural Aspects of Delusions," in Oltmanns and Maher (212–29).
80. Beers (32–33).
81. Q. Bell (2: 15).
82. DeSalvo (*Virginia Woolf* 254).
83. Styron (50).

84. Beers (14); Georgotas and Cancro (268–70); Jamison (*MDI* 269).
85. Jamison (*MDI* 270).
86. Whybrow et al. (9).
87. Custance (62).
88. Hamilton; Winokur (4–9).
89. Jamison (*MDI* 227–28).
90. Winokur (71).
91. Jamison ("Psychotherapeutic Issues").
92. Jamison (*MDI* 236).
93. Georgotas and Cancro (338); Jamison (*MDI* 241–42).
94. Jamison (*MDI* 39).
95. Bond (30, 36).
96. Bond (161).
97. Bond (19).
98. F. K. Goodwin (*MDI* 136).
99. Wilberforce (178); Jamison (*MDI* 213); Jamison (*MDI* 765–77). But we must consider that Clive Bell insisted Virginia did not normally drink alcohol and had to be coaxed into drinking one or half a glass of wine (111). If his report is true, then she may have drunk only during breakdowns (when she was usually sequestered from her friends and so unobserved by Clive), or she may have developed a drinking habit fairly late in life. Since, as was said above, manic-depressive relapses often increase with age, Woolf may have felt driven to resort to this form of self-medication. Then age and alcohol would have combined to increase the likelihood of a severe breakdown.
100. Winokur (9).
101. John Milton, *Paradise Lost*, ed. Scott Elledge (New York: W. W. Norton, 1975), 1: 254–55.
102. Blaney.
103. Kinsbourne (117).
104. Jamison (*MDI* 272).
105. Beers (17, 25).
106. Hamilton (5).
107. Winokur (8–9); Goodwin and Guze (15).
108. Georgotas and Cancro (68).
109. Gaylin (390–91).
110. Hamilton.
111. Gaylin (166).
112. Q. Bell (1: 162).
113. Winokur (33–34).
114. Dooley.
115. Milden.
116. Davenport et al.
117. Georgotas and Cancro (159).
118. Kraus; Jamison and Goodwin; Georgotas and Cancro (71).
119. M. J. Clark (299).

120. One patient, from K. R. Jamison's clinical files, reported asking the same questions from personal experience—and, coincidentally, anticipated my use of Woolf:

> Madness carves its own reality. It goes on and on and finally there are only others' recollections of your behavior—your bizarre, frenetic, aimless behaviors—for mania has at least some grace in partially obliterating memories. . . . Then, too, are the annoyances. . . . Credit cards revoked, bounced checks to cover, explanations due at work, apologies to make, intermittent memories of vague men (what *did* I do?), friendships gone or drained, a ruined marriage. And always, when will it happen again? Which of my feelings are real? Which of the me's is me? The wild, impulsive, chaotic, energetic, and crazy one? Or the shy, withdrawn, desperate, suicidal, doomed, and tired one? Probably a bit of both, hopefully much that is neither. Virginia Woolf, in her dives and climbs, said it all: "How far do our feelings take their colour from the dive underground? I mean, what is the reality of any feeling?" (*MDI* 18)

121. Jamison (*MDI* 732).

CHAPTER 3

1. Holland.
2. Alcorn and Bracher (342, 349 [quoting Georges Poulet]).
3. Alcorn and Bracher (342).
4. Horner.
5. Jamison (*MDI* 332–49).
6. Jamison ("Mood Disorders").
7. Andreasen (1292).
8. Jamison ("Mood Disorders").
9. Jamison (*MDI* 22).
10. Hershman and Lieb (16); Kinsbourne (124); Alcorn and Bracher.
11. Jamison (*MDI* 338).
12. Guilford.
13. Summary of Wadeson and Bunney by Jamison (*MDI* 286).
14. Jamison (*MDI* 367).
15. Jamison (*MDI* 337–38).
16. Jamison (*MDI* 364).
17. Jamison (*MDI* 366).
18. Andreasen and Glick (215).
19. Edelson (250).
20. Felman (120).
21. Roustang.
22. C. Bollas (67).

23. C. Bollas (203).
24. C. Bollas (204).
25. C. Bollas (204).
26. C. Bollas (204–6).
27. C. Bollas (2).
28. Marotti (473).
29. Manganyi (36). Ironically, Freud himself offered similar warnings to novelist Arnold Zweig in 1936 when Zweig asked Freud for permission to write a biography of him. Freud turned down the request, arguing, "Whoever undertakes to write a biography binds himself to lying, to concealment, to hypocrisy, to flummery and even to hiding his own lack of understanding, since biographical material is not to be had and if it were it could not be used. Truth is not accessible" (E. Jones [208]).
30. Spilka (16).
31. Kenney and Kenney (170).
32. Kenney and Kenney (174).
33. DeSalvo (*First Voyage* 158–59); Panken (263).
34. Jamison (*MDI* 733).
35. Jamison ("Psychotherapeutic Issues").
36. Jamison (*MDI* 733).
37. Jamison ("Psychotherapeutic Issues").
38. Jamison ("Psychotherapeutic Issues").
39. Cooper et al. (211–12).
40. Lesser (59), seconded in Panken (72).
41. Goodwin and Guze (16).
42. Panken (72).
43. Keitel (5).
44. Keitel (29, 34).
45. Keitel (48).
46. Hunter.
47. Felman (187).
48. Felman (234).
49. Felman (64).
50. Panken (2).
51. Richter (5).
52. Mepham (139).
53. Goldberg (131–33).

CHAPTER 4

1. Gershon (*MDI* 377–98).
2. Georgotas and Cancro (200–202).
3. Keller (24).
4. Whybrow et al. (46).
5. Baron et al.
6. Hodgkinson et al.; Georgotas and Cancro (41).

7. Goodwin (*MDI* 142).

8. Nurnberger et al.; Paykel (146–61); Goodwin and Guze (16).

9. Bond (75).

10. Panken (5).

11. Keller.

12. Unpublished letters by Leslie Stephen, Nov. 9, 1890, March 5, 1891; Harrison (157).

13. Harrison (243).

14. The quotations here and below concerning James's symptoms are taken from J. K. Stephen's medical records, which were made available by Dr. J. H. Henderson, medical director of St. Andrew's Hospital.

15. Jamison (*MDI* 310–11).

16. F. K. Goodwin and Jamison (*MDI* 39).

17. Derby.

18. H. Stephen (ix); Harrison (241–42).

19. Clark and Davison.

20. Goodwin (*MDI* 93–97); Georgotas and Cancro (88); Jamison (*MDI* 53); Keller (13–14); *DSM-III-R* (227); F. K. Goodwin and Jamison (*MDI* 74, 192); Georgotas and Cancro (88).

21. Maitland (23).

22. Love (*Virginia Woolf* 89).

23. Annan (15).

24. Maitland (23–24).

25. Maitland (25–26).

26. Annan (63).

27. Love (*Virginia Woolf* 150).

28. Annan (63–64).

29. L. Stephen (*Mausoleum Book* 57).

30. Love (*Virginia Woolf* 76, 90, 123).

31. Annan (50); Love (*Virginia Woolf* 113).

32. Annan (51).

33. Love (*Virginia Woolf* 144–48).

34. Love (*Virginia Woolf* 19).

35. Gordon (*Virginia Woolf* 26).

36. L. Stephen (*Mausoleum Book* 89–90).

37. Q. Bell (1: 5).

38. Annan (14).

39. C. Stephen (61–62).

40. C. Stephen (165).

41. C. Stephen (79–81, 105, 131, 128).

42. Maitland (10).

43. C. Stephen (125–27).

44. Davis and Maas (165–81); Jamison (*MDI* 38, 186).

45. L. Stephen (*Mausoleum Book* 44, 91); Annan (122).

46. Q. Bell (1: 35).

47. L. Stephen (*Mausoleum Book* 92).

48. Love (*Virginia Woolf* 161–62).
49. Jamison (*MDI* 186); Keller (25).
50. Thackeray (1: 463); Monsarrat (113).
51. Monsarrat (126).
52. Thackeray (2: 3, 23, 41; 1: 467–68, 462, 482; 2: 3; 1: 462; 2: 23; 1: 480).
53. Ray (253); Monsarrat (118).
54. Thackeray (1: 474).
55. Thackeray (2: 23).
56. Monsarrat (124, 426).
57. Goodwin (*MDI* 143).
58. L. Stephen (*Mausoleum Book* 103).
59. DeSalvo (*Virginia Woolf* 26).
60. Trombley (116).
61. Schopler and Reichler.
62. Hyman (*To the Lighthouse* 46).
63. Garnett (32).
64. Holliday.
65. Gershon (446); Georgotas and Cancro (204).
66. Morizot (77).
67. Goodwin (*MDI* 397).

CHAPTER 5

1. Keller (22).
2. Paykel (154).
3. Haynal (24).
4. L. Stephen (*Mausoleum Book* 35–37).
5. Gillespie and Steele (245).
6. Love (*Virginia Woolf* 65).
7. Love (*Virginia Woolf* 83); L. Stephen (*Mausoleum Book* 51).
8. L. Stephen (*Mausoleum Book* 52).
9. Q. Bell (1: 39).
10. Love (*Virginia Woolf* 136).
11. L. Stephen (*Mausoleum Book* 82–83).
12. Mrs. L. Stephen (*Notes from Sick Rooms* 3, 4–5).
13. L. Stephen (*Mausoleum Book* 40).
14. L. Stephen (*Mausoleum Book* 40).
15. Love (*Virginia Woolf* 101).
16. L. Stephen (*Mausoleum Book* 41).
17. L. Stephen (*Mausoleum Book* 47).
18. Jamison (*MDI* 309).
19. L. Stephen (*Mausoleum Book* 56–57).
20. Love (*Virginia Woolf* 83).
21. Maitland (287–88).
22. L. Stephen (*Social Rights and Duties* 2: 254–56).

23. Atwood (195).
24. Garnett (23).
25. Garnett (113–14).
26. Love (*Virginia Woolf* 88, 29–30).
27. L. Stephen (*Mausoleum Book* 47).
28. Love (*Virginia Woolf* 134, 87).
29. L. Stephen (*Mausoleum Book* 40).
30. Houghton Library.
31. Goodwin (*MDI* 398).
32. Love (*Virginia Woolf* 98–100).
33. Noel Annan in L. Stephen (*Mausoleum Book* xix).
34. Love (*Virginia Woolf* 128–29, 111).
35. J. Marcus ("Woolf and Her Violin" 29).
36. Love (*Virginia Woolf* 139).
37. Nancy Topping Bazin makes a similar point, arguing that Woolf associated her experiences during mania with her mother and the "feminine" side of her psyche, those of depression with her father and the "masculine" side, and that her quest for androgyny was also a quest for "equilibrium" between mania and depression. I contend that, although Woolf clearly associated a manic, oceanic bliss with childhood and the experience of mothering, she also used her mother as a model for depression, just as her father could, at various times, represent for her manic defensiveness or irritated depression. "Equilibrium," rebuilding an identifiable self-structure, is not accomplished simply by combining or reconciling masculine and feminine characteristics.
38. Pichot and Hassan; Kraus (204).
39. Custance (95, 102).
40. Paul (18–19).
41. L. Stephen (*Mausoleum Book* 12–15).
42. Boyd (81).
43. H. Ritchie (215).
44. Annan (61–65); Q. Bell (1: 11).
45. Gerin (254).
46. Boyd (78); Gerin (254).
47. Goodwin (*MDI* 453–54).
48. Gerin (219).
49. L. Stephen (*Mausoleum Book* 23–24).
50. Q. Bell (1: 19).
51. Love (*Virginia Woolf* 109).
52. Chodorow (58–59).
53. Pine (147, 155, 160, 164).
54. Kushen (*Virginia Woolf* 13).
55. Love (*Virginia Woolf* 309).
56. Q. Bell (1: 40–41).
57. Love (*Virginia Woolf* 181).
58. Trombley (109).
59. J. Marcus ("Woolf and Her Violin" 30).

CHAPTER 6

1. Klein settled in London the next year, 1926, and dominated the English school of psychoanalysis until well after the Second World War. She published several books through the Woolfs' Hogarth Press: *The Psycho-Analysis of Children* (1932), *Love, Hate and Reparation* (1937), *Contributions to Psycho-Analysis, 1921–45* (1948), *Developments in Psycho-Analysis* (1952), and *Narrative of a Child Analysis* (1961). Although Virginia Woolf did not meet Klein until 1939, she was surrounded by people who enthusiastically adopted and propagated Klein's theories (Abel 13–14).

2. Feinstein (340). For Feinstein, Woolf's breakdown at age thirteen after the death of her mother was only the culmination of a mood-disorder instability that had been developing throughout childhood (336–37). It is reasonable to speculate that an inherited neurochemical disorder is present in some form from birth, even if it cannot be fully expressed until years later. One study reported that 39 percent of the children they studied who exhibited mood swings and polydrug abuse later developed bipolar disorder (Georgotas and Cancro 45).

3. Segal (*Introduction to Klein* 68–69).

4. Gaylin (113).

5. Segal (*Introduction to Klein* 69–70).

6. Chodorow (78).

7. Segal (*Introduction to Klein* 75, 92, 82–84).

8. Dahl.

9. Hyman ("Autobiographical Present" 24).

10. Hyman ("Autobiographical Present" 24–25).

11. Hyman ("Autobiographical Present" 27–28).

12. Love (*Virginia Woolf* 181).

13. Hyman ("Autobiographical Present" 28).

14. Bond (43).

15. Custance (79).

16. Love (*Virginia Woolf* 208).

17. Q. Bell (2: 6).

18. Skura (17).

19. R. Jones (124).

20. C. Bollas (69).

21. McCaffrey (9, 121–23).

22. DeSalvo (*Virginia Woolf* 105).

23. C. Bollas (60–62).

24. C. Bollas (31–32).

25. C. Bollas (32).

26. C. Bollas (33, 39).

27. Marotti (479).

28. Gaylin (151 [Fenichel], 344–45 [Jacobson]).

29. Horner.

30. Albright (10, 12, 13–14).

CHAPTER 7

1. Woolf and Strachey (*Virginia Woolf* 56).
2. Daiches (14–16).
3. Brown (71).
4. Neurosis: DeSalvo (*Virginia Woolf*). Plotting: Rosenthal (49); Naremore (8).
5. Q. Bell (1: 42).
6. Love (*Virginia Woolf* 193).
7. Autobiographical fragment, in Gordon (*Virginia Woolf* 50).
8. Guiguet (197).
9. Lyon (112).
10. McDowell (88–91).
11. Q. Bell (2: 8).
12. Love (*Virginia Woolf* 16).
13. Naremore.
14. Atwood.
15. Schlack (*Continuing Presences* 10–11).
16. Annan (125).
17. Hobson.
18. Segal (*Introduction to Klein* 83–84).
19. Gordon ("Silent Life" 82); Dick (178).
20. Love (*Worlds* 94).
21. Schlack (*Continuing Presences* 16).
22. Leaska (18).
23. Jamison ("Psychotherapeutic Issues" 111).
24. Schlack (*Continuing Presences* 23).
25. Although unreliable as diagnostic tools, Rorschach tests do suggest that color reactivity is associated with the impulsive emotional discharges of bipolar illness and that manics attend selectively to the objective or formalistic characteristics of ink blots by associating colors, forms, and shadings in energetic and sometimes highly imaginative ways (Donnelly et al.). Sense of hearing can also be affected: acutely depressed patients suffer a six-decibel deficit in auditory sensitivity (Georgotas and Cancro 266).
26. Scherer.
27. John Rush notes that memory difficulties are common in severe depression, which interferes with recall not only of past experiences and interpretations but even of words and facts, thus complicating word-based psychotherapies. Since psychotherapists cannot assume that memory for events within the analytical session or for recent or past events is either complete or accurate, Rush advises, they should begin sessions with a review of events in previous sessions, correcting recall with audio recordings.
28. Wheare (81); Guiguet (203); Kelley (31–32); Bazin (57).
29. McDowell (84); Ruotolo (46).
30. Moody (12); Hafley (17); Pitt (146).
31. Lyon (114).

32. S. Bollas; Hyman (*To the Lighthouse*); DeSalvo (*First Voyage*); Neuman; Panken (85).
33. Leaska (38); Apter (16–17); Schlack (*Continuing Presences* 20).
34. Lee (51); Ruotolo (43); M. Bell (671); Guiguet (198).
35. Fleishman (21).
36. Leaska (33–37).
37. L. Stephen (March 4, 1870, Houghton Library).
38. Panken (79).

CHAPTER 8

1. Little.
2. Blain (131).
3. Ruotolo (73).
4. L. Stephen (*Mausoleum Book* 40).
5. Alexander (79).
6. Morgenstern.
7. Leaska (62; my italics).
8. Bennett (95–96; my italics).
9. Rosenthal (83–84).
10. Hafley (52–53).
11. Ehrenzweig (3).
12. Leaska (35).
13. Ehrenzweig (4–5).
14. Ehrenzweig (19).
15. Ehrenzweig (32).
16. Ehrenzweig (39).
17. Custance (56–57).
18. Ehrenzweig (102–3).
19. Keitel (109–10).
20. Goodwin (*MDI* 508–11).
21. Kinsbourne (103–6, 145).
22. Hoppe (229).
23. Tucker in Kinsbourne (110).
24. Goodwin (*MDI* 509).
25. Jamison (*MDI* 273).
26. Jamison (*MDI* 278).
27. Jamison (*MDI* 509).
28. Goodwin (*MDI* 523).
29. Flor-Henry (694).
30. C. Bollas.
31. Springer and Deutsch (266–67).
32. Oakley and Eames, in Oakley.
33. Alcorn and Bracher.

CHAPTER 9

1. Harper ("Mrs. Woolf" 227).
2. Hafley (52).
3. Custance (29).
4. F. K. Goodwin and Jamison (*MDI* 3).
5. Anonymous letter from a patient to the author.
6. Ferguson (250).
7. Ferguson (245).
8. Harper (*Between Language* 133–34).
9. Haring-Smith (145).
10. Naremore (80–82).
11. C. Bollas (42).
12. As Quentin Bell reports, one of Woolf's hypomanic "conversational excesses" was to "invent" highly imaginative characters for friends and strangers alike that ignored their actual personality:

> It was never easy to know what to do with the image of oneself that Virginia could fabricate. . . . The image that she created was fanciful, but the victim—the slender basis upon which she built—could have dismissed such fancies easily enough had they not been advanced with such overwhelming force; and that force arose, not from a desire to misrepresent, but from conviction. (1: 147)

13. Harper (*Between Language* 124); Leaska (96); Poresky (115).
14. Kelley (95); Rosenthal (97); Apter (62); Spilka (66).
15. Squier (280).
16. Winnicott (111–18).
17. Schlack ("Freudian Look" 50); Leaska (98); Poresky (113); S. Bollas (156).
18. Harper (*Between Language* 123).
19. McLaurin. On July 3, 1924, as she was writing *Mrs. Dalloway,* Woolf used *cutting* in this nonsexual way:

> Solid Lord Berners, who might have [been] cleft from an oak knot, had to tell stories, could not endure silence, & much preferred laughter to thought: amiable characteristics, Clive says. To me, after a time, laborious & depressing. Good prim priggish bright eyed Peter [F. L. Lucas] is a cut above that. I met him at Clive's, & he sliced English literature up very prettily, with a pocket knife. (*Diary* 2: 305)

20. Alcorn and Bracher.
21. Oltmanns and Maher (15–33).
22. Oltmanns and Maher (54, 78).
23. Oltmanns and Maher (179).
24. Henke; Leaska (108); Bazin; Schlack ("Freudian Look" 52–53).

25. Custance (72).
26. Beers (22–25).
27. Jamison (*MDI* 262–64).
28. Custance (45–46).
29. Custance (67).
30. Oltmanns and Maher (15–33, 52, 96).
31. Oltmanns and Maher (48).
32. C. Stephen (61–62).
33. Styron (64–65).
34. Harrow in Oltmanns and Maher (184–211).
35. Harper ("Mrs. Woolf" 229).
36. Oltmanns and Maher (46).
37. Page; Kreutz.
38. Schlack ("Freudian Look"); Jensen.
39. S. Bollas (143).
40. Creativity: Alexander (92, 103). Sensitivity: Apter (57). Dignity: Ames (364). Self-confidence: Poresky (102).
41. Beck and Greenberg.
42. Yost et al. (66–79); Georgotas and Cancro (517–37).
43. Panken (125); Spilka (65–67); Harper (*Language* 131); Schlack ("Freudian Look" 51).
44. Spilka (65); Rosenthal (97); Kelley (102–3); Leaska (112–14); S. Bollas (151, 156); Schlack ("Freudian Look" 49–51).
45. J. Marcus (*Virginia Woolf* 8; my italics).
46. Harper ("Mrs. Woolf" 230).
47. Leaska (92n).
48. Ruotolo (112).
49. Lyon (119).
50. Woolf described her "screen making" in response to two hikers she and Leonard saw on a bicycle trip to Ripe:

> Two resolute, sunburnt, dusty girls, in jerseys & short skirts, with packs on their backs, city clerks, or secretaries, tramping along the road in the hot sunshine at Ripe. My instinct at once throws up a screen, which condemns them: I think them in every way angular, awkward & self-assertive. But all this is a great mistake. These screens shut me out. Have no screens, for screens are made out of our own integument; & get at the thing itself, which has nothing whatever in common with a screen. The screen making habit, though, is so universal, that probably it preserves our sanity. If we had not this device for shutting people off from our sympathies, we might, perhaps, dissolve utterly. Separateness would be impossible. But the screens are in the excess; not the sympathy. (*Diary* 3: 104)

51. Ruotolo (101), paraphrasing Woolf's *A Room of One's Own*.

CHAPTER 10

1. Chodorow (59–70).
2. Rose.
3. Blotner (547); Hafley (80); Moody (42); Love (*Worlds* 162).
4. Chodorow (81).
5. Chodorow (71).
6. Chodorow (86–87).
7. Chodorow (82).
8. E. Wolf and I. Wolf (39); Pederson; Proudfit.
9. Lilienfeld (12).
10. Pratt (428).
11. Apter (91).
12. Winnicott (2).
13. Squier (275).
14. Corsa (116).
15. Lidoff (46).
16. L. Stephen (*Mausoleum Book* 83).
17. Rose (211).
18. Winnicott (88–93).
19. Mayo et al. (*MDI* 313).
20. L. Stephen (*Mausoleum Book* 90).
21. Chodorow (62; italics in original).
22. Milner (133).
23. Rose (202).
24. Lilienfeld (21).
25. Milner (89).
26. Apter (76).
27. Milner (142).
28. Milner (119).
29. Jamison (*MDI* 314).
30. Consequently, I disagree with Ellen Bayuk Rosenman's conclusion that in Virginia's mind Julia remained an "idealized figure as if no other understanding of her had intervened since childhood" (8). Woolf did doubt the "absolute, infantile desires" of preoedipal bliss. Rosenman employs Chodorow's argument on how the child's early subject-object relations establish gender identification, but traces Woolf's art as an attempt to recapture her mother from death. Since "the 'centre' of the unifying maternal presence becomes a 'centre of complete emptiness' with her death" (16), art is both a substitute gratification and a failure because it can never attain its object. I think Woolf was not only aware of all this but thought beyond these terms. The unattainable object is intrasubjective completion, an immobilization of self Woolf neither desired nor thought desirable.

CHAPTER 11

1. Beck and Greenberg.
2. Gordon (*Virginia Woolf* 233).

3. Naremore (158).
4. Richter (129; italics in original).
5. Kelley (149).
6. Harper (*Between Language* 221–22).
7. Jamison (*MDI* 292).
8. Custance (37).
9. Custance (49).
10. Custance (49–50).
11. Harper (*Between Language* 246).
12. Whybrow et al. (9).
13. Richardson (699); Gordon (*Virginia Woolf* 222).
14. Webb.
15. Harper (*Between Language* 246).
16. Oakley (233).
17. Hilgard (233, 185).
18. Holland.
19. C. Bollas (204).
20. Oltmanns and Maher (82).
21. Oltmanns and Maher (78–81).
22. Hilgard (195).
23. Oakley (247).
24. Hilgard (25).

EPILOGUE

1. Gazzaniga (4, 74, 124).
2. Gazzaniga (117).
3. Sacks (77–78).
4. Sacks (15).
5. Sacks (55–57; italics in original).
6. Gazzaniga and LeDoux; Marks.
7. Edelson (122–56).
8. Rescher.
9. Grunbaum.
10. Eagle.
11. Smalley et al.
12. Volkmar and Cohen; Courchesne.
13. Churchland.
14. Wing (31).

AFTERWORD

1. Virginia Woolf, *The Diary of Virginia Woolf,* ed. Anne Olivier Bell and Andrew McNeillie, 5 vols. (New York: Harcourt, 1976–84), vol. 2, 304.
2. Edward Thomas, "Old Man," in *The Collected Poems of Edward Thomas,* ed. and introduction by R. George Thomas (Oxford: Oxford University Press, 1978), 19–20.

3. Virginia Woolf, *The Letters of Virginia Woolf,* ed. Nigel Nicholson and Joanne Trautmann, 6 vols. (New York: Harcourt, 1975–80), vol. 4, 180.

4. From Baudelaire's *Journals,* quoted in W. H. Auden, *The Enchafed Flood* (London: Faber and Faber, 1951), 45.

5. Virginia Woolf, *Moments of Being: Unpublished Autobiographical Writings.* 2d. ed. Jeanne Schulkind (New York: Harcourt Brace Jovanovich, 1948), 81.

6. John Ruskin, *Modern Painters,* ed. and abridged by David Barrie (New York: Alfred A. Knopf, 1987), vol. 2, part 3, 256.

7. Virginia Woolf, *"The Moment" and Other Essays* (New York: Harcourt, 1948), 14.

Works Cited

Abel, Elizabeth. *Virginia Woolf and the Fictions of Psychoanalysis*. Chicago: University of Chicago Press, 1989.

Akiskal, Hagop Souren, Robert M. A. Hirschfeld, and Boghos I. Yerevanian. "The Relationship of Personality to Affective Disorders: A Critical Review." *Archives of General Psychiatry* 40 (1983): 801–10.

Albright, Daniel. "Virginia Woolf as Autobiographer." *Kenyon Review* 6 (1984): 1–17.

Alcorn, Marshall W., Jr., and Mark Bracher. "Literature, Psychoanalysis, and the Re-Formation of the Self: A New Direction for Reader-Response Theory." *PMLA* 100 (1985): 342–54.

Alexander, Jean. *The Venture of Form in the Novels of Virginia Woolf*. Port Washington, N.Y.: Kennikat Press, 1974.

Ames, Kenneth J. "Elements of Mock-Heroic in Virginia Woolf's *Mrs. Dalloway*." *Modern Fiction Studies* 18 (1972–73): 363–74.

Andreasen, Nancy C. "Creativity and Mental Illness: Prevalence Rates in Writers and Their First-Degree Relatives." *American Journal of Psychiatry* 144 (1987): 1288–92.

Andreasen, Nancy C., and Ira D. Glick. "Bipolar Affective Disorder and Creativity: Implications and Clinical Management." *Comprehensive Psychiatry* 29 (3) (1988): 207–17.

Angst, J. "The Course of Affective Disorders: II. Typology of Bipolar Manic-Depressive Illness." *Archiv für Psychiatrie und Nervenkrankheiten* 226 (1978): 65–73.

Annan, Noel. *Leslie Stephen: The Godless Victorian*. New York: Random House, 1984.

Anthonisen, N. L. "Aggression and Anxiety in the Determination and Nature of Manic Attacks." *Archives of Neurology and Psychiatry* 38 (1937): 71–89.

Apter, T. E. *Virginia Woolf: A Study of Her Novels*. New York: New York University Press, 1979.

Arieti, Silvano, and Jules Bemporad. *Severe and Mild Depression: The Psychotherapeutic Approach*. New York: Basic Books, 1978.

Atwood, George E. "The Protective Function of Depressive States." *American Journal of Psychoanalysis* 37 (1977): 193–99.

Baron, Miron, et al. "Genetic Linkage Between X-Chromosome Markers and Bipolar Affective Illness." *Nature* 326 (1987): 289–92.

Bassuk, Ellen L. "The Rest Cure: Repetition or Resolution of Victorian Women's Conflicts?" In *The Female Body in Western Culture: Contemporary Perspectives,* ed. Susan Rubin Suleiman, 139–51. Cambridge, Mass.: Harvard University Press, 1986.

Bazin, Nancy Topping. *Virginia Woolf and the Androgynous Vision*. New Brunswick, N.J.: Rutgers University Press, 1973.

Beck, Aaron T., and Ruth L. Greenberg. "Cognitive Therapy in the Treatment of Depression." In *Foundations of Cognitive Therapy: Theoretical Methods and Practical Applications,* ed. Nicholas Hoffman and trans. Elizabeth Lachman, 155–77. New York: Plenum Press, 1984.

Beers, Clifford. *A Mind That Found Itself, an Autobiography: Clifford Whittingham Beers*. 1907; rpt. Pittsburgh: University of Pittsburg Press, 1981.

Bell, Clive. *Old Friends: Personal Recollections*. London: Chatto and Windus, 1956.

Bell, Millicent. "Portrait of the Artist as a Young Woman." *Virginia Quarterly Review* 52 (1976): 670–86.

Bell, Quentin. *Virginia Woolf: A Biography*. 2 vols. New York: Harcourt Brace Jovanovich, 1972.

Bennett, Joan. *Virginia Woolf: Her Art as a Novelist*. 1945. 2d ed. Cambridge: Cambridge University Press, 1975.

Blain, Virginia. "Narrative Voice and the Female Perspective in Virginia Woolf's Early Novels." 115–36. *See* Clements and Grundy.

Blaney, P. "Affect and Memory: A Review." *Psychological Bulletin* 99 (1986): 229–46.

Bloom, Floyd E., and Arlyne Lazerson. *Brain, Mind, and Behavior*. 2d ed. New York: W. H. Freeman, 1988.

Blotner, Joseph L. "Mythic Patterns in *To the Lighthouse*." *PMLA* 71 (1956): 547–62.

Bollas, Christopher. *The Shadow of the Object: Psychoanalysis of the Unthought Known*. New York: Columbia University Press, 1987.

Bollas, Sara Flanders. "The Narrow Bridge of Art: A Psychoanalytic Study of Virginia Woolf's First Four Novels." Ph.D. diss. State University of New York at Buffalo, 1976.

Bond, Alma Halbert. *Who Killed Virginia Woolf? A Psychobiography*. New York: Human Sciences Press, 1989.

Boyd, Elizabeth French. *Bloomsbury Heritage: Their Mothers and Their Aunts*. New York: Taplinger, 1976.

Braceland, Francis J. "Kraepelin: His System and His Influence." *American Journal of Psychiatry* 113 (1957): 871–76.

Brown, Carole O. "The Art of the Novel: Virginia Woolf's *The Voyage Out*." *Virginia Woolf Quarterly* 3 (1977): 67–84.

Cade, John F. "Lithium Salts in the Treatment of Psychotic Excitement." *Medical Journal of Australia* 36 (2) (1949): 349–52.

Caramagno, Thomas C. "Manic-Depressive Psychosis and Critical Approaches to Virginia Woolf's Life and Work." *PMLA* 103 (1988): 10–23.

———. "Neuroscience and Psychoanalysis: The Mind/Brain Connection in Biographical Studies of Woolf, Dostoevsky and Mishima." In *Biography, East and West*, ed. Carol Ramelb, 206–14. Honolulu: University of Hawaii Press, 1988.

———. "Science and Subjectivity: Toward a Psychobiological Literary Criticism." *Kennesaw Review* 2 (1) (1988): 23–31.

Carlson, Gebrielle A., and Frederick K. Goodwin. "The Stages of Mania: A Longitudinal Analysis of the Manic Episode." *Archives of General Psychiatry* 28 (1973): 221–28.

Chodorow, Nancy. *The Reproduction of Mothering: Psychoanalysis and the Sociology of Gender*. Berkeley and Los Angeles: University of California Press, 1978.

Churchland, Patricia Smith. *Neurophilosophy: Toward a Unified Science of the Mind-Brain*. Cambridge, Mass.: MIT Press, 1986.

Clark, A. F., and K. Davison. "Mania Following Head Injury: A Report of Two Cases and a Review of the Literature." *British Journal of Psychiatry* 150 (1987): 841–44.

Clark, Michael J. "The Rejection of Psychological Approaches to Mental Disorder in Late Nineteenth-Century British Psychiatry." 271–312. *See* Scull.

Clements, Patricia, and Isobel Grundy, eds. *Virginia Woolf: New Critical Essays.* New York: Vision and Barnes and Noble, 1983.

Collins, Jerre, J. Ray Green, Mary Lydon, Mark Sachner, and Eleanor Honig Skoller. "Questioning the Unconscious: The Dora Archive." In *In Dora's Case: Freud—Hysteria—Feminism,* ed. Charles Bernheimer and Claire Kahane, 243–53. New York: Columbia University Press, 1985.

Cook, Blanche Wiesen. "'Women Alone Stir My Imagination': Lesbianism and the Cultural Tradition." *Signs: Journal of Women in Culture and Society* 4 (1979): 718–39.

Cooper, Arnold M., Otto F. Kernberg, and Ethel Spector Person, eds. *Psychoanalysis: Toward the Second Century.* New Haven: Yale University Press, 1989.

Cornell, Dewey G., Ronald Suarez, and Stanley Berent. "Psychomotor Retardation in Melancholic and Nonmelancholic Depression: Cognitive and Motor Components." *Journal of Abnormal Psychology* 93 (1984): 150–57.

Corsa, Helen Storm. "*To the Lighthouse:* Death, Mourning, and Transfiguration." *Literature and Psychology* 21 (1971): 115–31.

Courchesne, Eric. "Neuroanatomical Systems Involved in Infantile Autism: The Implications of Cerebellar Abnormalities." In *Autism: Nature, Diagnosis and Treatment,* ed. Geraldine Dawson, 119–43. New York: Guilford, 1989.

Crews, Frederick. *Out of My System: Psychoanalysis, Ideology, and Critical Method.* New York: Oxford University Press, 1975.

Custance, John. *Wisdom, Madness and Folly: The Philosophy of a Lunatic.* London: Victor Gollancz, 1951.

Dahl, Christopher C. "Virginia Woolf's *Moments of Being* and Autobiographical Tradition in the Stephen Family." *Journal of Modern Literature* 10 (1983): 175–96.

Daiches, David. *Virginia Woolf.* Norfolk, Conn.: New Directions, 1942.

Dain, Norman. *Clifford Beers: Advocate for the Insane.* Pittsburgh: University of Pittsburg Press, 1980.

Davenport, Yolanda B., et al. "Manic-Depressive Illness: Psychodynamic Features of Multigenerational Families." *American Journal of Orthopsychiatry* 49 (1979): 24–35.

Davis, John M., and James W. Maas, eds. *The Affective Disorders.* Washington, D.C.: American Psychiatric Press, 1983.

Derby, Irving M. "Manic-Depressive 'Exhaustion' Deaths." *Psychiatric Quarterly* 7 (1933): 436–49.

DeSalvo, Louise A. *Virginia Woolf: The Impact of Childhood Sexual Abuse on Her Life and Work.* Boston: Beacon Press, 1989.

———. *Virginia Woolf's First Voyage: A Novel in the Making.* Totowa, N.J.: Rowman and Littlefield, 1980.

Dick, Susan. "The Tunneling Process: Some Aspects of Virginia Woolf's Use of Memory and the Past." 176–99. *See* Clements and Grundy.

Dinnage, Rosemary. "Psycho-Mom." *New York Review* (8 May 1986): 15–18.

Donnelly, Edward F., Dennis L. Murphy, and Winfield H. Scott. "Perception and Cognition in Patients with Bipolar and Unipolar Depressive Disorders: A Study in Rorschach Responding." *Archives of General Psychiatry* 32 (1975): 1128–32.

Dooley, Lucile. "Analysis of a Case of Manic-Depressive Psychosis Showing Well-Marked Regressive Stages." *Psychoanalytic Review* 5 (1918): 1–46.

DSM-III-R (Diagnostic and Statistical Manual of Mental Disorders). 3d ed., rev. Washington, D.C.: American Psychiatric Association, 1987.

Eagle, M. "Psychoanalytic Interpretations: Veridicality and Therapeutic Effectiveness." *Nous* 14 (1980): 405–25.

Edel, Leon. "Transference: The Biographer's Dilemma." *Biography* 7 (1984): 283–91.

Edelson, Marshall. *Psychoanalysis: A Theory in Crisis*. Chicago: University of Chicago Press, 1988.

Egeland, Janice A., et al. "Bipolar Affective Disorders Linked to DNA Markers on Chromosome 11." *Nature* 325 (1987): 783–87.

Ehrenzweig, Anton. *The Hidden Order of Art: A Study in the Psychology of Artistic Imagination*. Berkeley and Los Angeles: University of California Press, 1967.

Feinstein, Sherman C. "Why They Were Afraid of Virginia Woolf: Perspectives on Juvenile Manic-Depressive Illness." In *Adolescent Psychiatry: Developmental and Clinical Studies*, Annals of the American Society for Adolescent Psychiatry, ed. Sherman C. Feinstein et al., vol. 8: 332–43. Chicago: University of Chicago Press, 1980.

Felman, Shoshana. *Writing and Madness: Literature/Philosophy/Psychoanalysis*. Trans. Martha Noel Evans, Shoshana Felman, and Brian Massumi. Ithaca, N.Y.: Cornell University Press, 1985.

Ferguson, Suzanne. "The Face in the Mirror: Authorial Presence in the Multiple Vision of Third-Person Impressionist Narrative." *Criticism* 21 (1979): 230–50.

Fieve, Ronald R. *Moodswing: The Third Revolution in Psychiatry*. New York: Bantam, 1975.

Fleishman, Avrom. *Virginia Woolf: A Critical Reading*. Baltimore: Johns Hopkins University Press, 1975.

Flor-Henry, P. "On Certain Aspects of the Localization of the Cerebral Systems Regulating and Determining Emotion." *Biological Psychiatry* 14 (1979): 677–98.

Freud, Sigmund. *The Standard Edition of the Complete Psychological Works of Sigmund Freud*. 24 vols., trans. and ed. James Strachey. London: Hogarth Press, 1953–74.

Garner, Shirley Nelson, Claire Kahane, and Madelon Sprengnether, eds. *The (M)other Tongue: Essays in Feminist Psychoanalytic Interpretation*. Ithaca, N.Y.: Cornell University Press, 1985.

Garnett, Angelica. *Deceived with Kindness: A Bloomsbury Childhood*. New York: Harcourt Brace Jovanovich, 1985.

Garrison, Dee. "Karen Horney and Feminism." *Signs: Journal of Women in Culture and Society* 6 (1981): 672–91.

Gaylin, Willard, ed. *The Meaning of Despair: Psychoanalytic Contributions to the Understanding of Depression*. New York: Science House, 1968.

Gazzaniga, Michael S. *The Social Brain: Discovering the Networks of the Mind*. New York: Basic Books, 1985.

Gazzaniga, Michael S., and Joseph E. LeDoux. *The Integrated Mind*. New York: Plenum Press, 1978.

Georgotas, Anastasios, and Robert Cancro, eds. *Depression and Mania*. New York: Elsevier, 1988.

Gerin, Winifred. *Anne Thackeray Ritchie: A Biography*. New York: Oxford University Press, 1983.

Gershon, Elliot S. "The Genetics of Affective Disorders." *Psychiatry Update: American Psychiatric Association Annual Review* 2 (1983): 434–57.

Gillespie, Diane F., and Elizabeth Steele, eds. *Julia Duckworth Stephen: Stories for Children, Essays for Adults*. Syracuse, N.Y.: Syracuse University Press, 1987.

Ginsberg, Elaine K., and Laura Moss Gottlieb, eds. *Virginia Woolf: Centennial Essays*. Troy, N.Y.: Whitson, 1983.

Goldberg, Steven E. *Two Patterns of Rationality in Freud's Writings*. Tuscaloosa: University of Alabama Press, 1988.

Goldstein, Jan Ellen. "The Woolfs' Response to Freud: Water-Spiders, Singing Canaries, and the Second Apple." *Psychoanalytic Quarterly* 43 (1974): 438–76.

Goodwin, Donald W., and Samuel B. Guze. *Psychiatric Disorders*. 3d ed. New York: Oxford University Press, 1984.

Goodwin, Frederick K., and Kay Redfield Jamison. *Manic-Depressive Illness*. New York: Oxford University Press, 1990.

Goodwin, Frederick K., and Peter Roy-Byrne. "Treatment of Bipolar Disorders." *Psychiatry Update: American Psychiatric Association Annual Review* 6 (1987): 81–107.

Gordon, Lyndall. "Our Silent Life: Virginia Woolf and T. S. Eliot." 77–95. *See* Clements and Grundy.

——. *Virginia Woolf: A Writer's Life*. Oxford: Oxford University Press, 1984.

Grunbaum, Adolf. *The Foundations of Psychoanalysis: A Philosophical Critique*. Berkeley and Los Angeles: University of California Press, 1984.

Guiguet, Jean. *Virginia Woolf and Her Works*. Trans. Jean Stewart. First ed. 1965. Reprinted New York: Harcourt Brace Jovanovich, 1976.

Guilford, J. P. "Traits of Creativity." In *Creativity and Its Cultivation*, ed. H. H. Anderson, 142–61. New York: Harper and Row, 1959.

Hafley, James. *The Glass Roof: Virginia Woolf as Novelist*. Berkeley and Los Angeles: University of California Press, 1954.

Hamilton, Max. "Symptoms and Assessment of Depression." 3–11. *See* Paykel.

Haring-Smith, Tori. "Private and Public Consciousness in *Mrs. Dalloway* and *To the Lighthouse*." 143–67. *See* Ginsberg and Gottlieb.

Harper, Howard. *Between Language and Silence: The Novels of Virginia Woolf*. Baton Rouge: Louisiana State University Press, 1982.

——. "Mrs. Woolf and Mrs. Dalloway." In *The Classic British Novel*, ed. Howard M. Harper, Jr., and Charles Edge, 220–39. Athens, Ga.: University of Georgia Press, 1972.

Harrison, Michael. *Clarence: The Life of H.R.H. the Duke of Clarence and Avondale (1864–1892)*. London: W. H. Allen, 1972.

Haynal, André. *Depression and Creativity*. 1976. New York: International Universities Press, 1985.

Heine, Elizabeth. "The Earlier *Voyage Out*: Virginia Woolf's First Novel." *Bulletin of Research in the Humanities* 82 (1979): 294–316.

Henke, Suzette A. "Virginia Woolf's Septimus Smith: An Analysis of 'Paraphrenia' and the Schizophrenic Use of Language." *Literature and Psychology* 31 (4) (1985): 13–23.

Hershman, D. Jablow, and Julian Lieb. *The Key to Genius: Manic-Depression and the Creative Life*. Buffalo, N.Y.: Prometheus Press, 1988.

Hilgard, Ernest R. *Divided Consciousness: Multiple Controls in Human Thought and Action*. Rev. ed. New York: John Wiley and Sons, 1986.

Hill, Katherine Cecilia. "Virginia Woolf and Leslie Stephen: A Study in Mentoring and Literary Criticism." Ph.D. diss. Columbia University, 1979.

Hobson, J. Allan. *The Dreaming Brain*. New York: Basic Books, 1988.

Hodgkinson, Stephen, et al. "Molecular Genetic Evidence for Heterogeneity in Manic Depression." *Nature* 325 (1987): 805–6.

Holland, Norman N. "Unity Identity Text Self." *PMLA* 90 (1975): 813–22.

Holliday, Robin. "A Different Kind of Inheritance." *Scientific American* 260 (6) (1989): 60–73.

Hollister, Leo E. "Treating Depressed Patients with Medical Problems." 393–408. *See* Davis and Maas.

Hoppe, Klaus D. "Split Brains and Psychoanalysis." *Psychoanalytic Quarterly* 46 (1977): 220–44.

Horner, Althea J. "Object Relations, the Self, and the Therapeutic Matrix." *Contemporary Psychoanalysis* 16 (1980): 186–203.

Hunter, Dianne. "Hysteria, Psychoanalysis, and Feminism: The Case of Anna O." 89–115. *See* Garner, Kahane, and Sprengnether.

Hyman, Virginia. "The Autobiographical Present in 'A Sketch of the Past.'" *Psychoanalytic Review* 70 (1983): 24–32.

——. "Concealment and Disclosure in Sir Leslie Stephen's *Mausoleum Book*." *Biography* 3 (1980): 121–31.

——. *To The Lighthouse and Beyond: Transformations in the Narratives of Virginia Woolf*. New York: Peter Lang, 1988.

Jamison, Kay Redfield. "Mood Disorders and Patterns of Creativity in British Writers and Artists." *Psychiatry* 52 (2) (1989): 125–34.

——. "Psychotherapeutic Issues and Suicide Prevention in the Treatment of Bipolar Disorders." *Psychiatry Update: American Psychiatric Association Annual Review* 6 (1987): 108–24.

Jamison, Kay Redfield, and F. K. Goodwin. "Psychotherapeutic Issues in Bipolar Illness." *Psychiatry Update: American Psychiatric Association Annual Review* 2 (1983): 319–45.

Jensen, Emily. "Clarissa Dalloway's Respectable Suicide." 162–79. *See* J. Marcus, ed., *Virginia Woolf*.

Jones, Ernest. *The Life and Work of Sigmund Freud*. Volume 3: *The Last Phase, 1919–1939*. New York: Basic Books, 1957.

Jones, Richard M. *The New Psychology of Dreaming*. New York: Penguin, 1970.

Keitel, Evelyne. *Reading Psychosis: Readers, Texts and Psychoanalysis*. Trans. Anthea Bell. New York: Basil Blackwell, 1989.

Keller, Martin B. "Differential Diagnosis, Natural Course, and Epidemiology of Bipolar Disorders." *Psychiatry Update: American Psychiatric Association Annual Review* 6 (1987): 10–31.

Kelley, Alice van Buren. *The Novels of Virginia Woolf: Fact and Vision*. Chicago: University of Chicago Press, 1973.

Kenney, Susan M. "Two Endings: Virginia Woolf's Suicide and *Between the Acts*." *University of Toronto Quarterly* 44 (1975): 265–89.

Kenney, Susan M., and Edwin J. Kenney, Jr. "Virginia Woolf and the Art of Madness." *Massachusetts Review* 23 (1982): 161–85.

Kinsbourne, Marcel, ed. *Cerebral Hemisphere Function in Depression*. Washington, D.C.: American Psychiatric Press, 1988.

Kraus, A. "Identity and Psychosis of the Manic-Depressive." In *Phenomenology and Psychiatry*, ed. A. J. J. de Koning and F. A. Jenner, 201–16. London: Academic Press, 1982.

Kreutz, Irving. "Mr. Bennett and Mrs. Woolf." *Modern Fiction Studies* 8 (1962–63): 103–15.

Kushen, Betty. "Virginia Woolf and 'Dr Freud.'" *Literature and Psychology* 35 (1, 2) (1989): 37–45.

———. *Virginia Woolf and the Nature of Communion*. West Orange, N.J.: Raynor Press, 1985.

Leaska, Mitchell A. *The Novels of Virginia Woolf: From Beginning to End*. New York: John Jay, 1977.

Lee, Hermione. *The Novels of Virginia Woolf*. London: Methuen, 1977.

Lesser, Simon O. "Creativity Versus Death." *University of Hartford Studies in Literature* 10 (1978): 49–69.

Levy, Elinor M., and Richard Krueger. "Depression and the Immune System." In *Affective Disorders*, ed. Frederic Flach, 186–98. New York: W. W. Norton, 1988.

Lidoff, Joan. "Virginia Woolf's Feminine Sentence: The Mother-Daughter World of *To the Lighthouse*." *Literature and Psychology* 32 (3) (1986): 43–58.

Lilienfeld, Jane. "Fountain of Ink, Fountain of Joy: The Psychological Influence of Leslie Stephen on Virginia Woolf as Fictionalized in *To the Lighthouse*." Paper presented to the English Section, Modern Languages Association Convention, San Francisco, 1979.

Little, Judy. "*Jacob's Room* as Comedy: Woolf's Parodic *Bildungsroman*." 105–24. *See* J. Marcus, ed., *New Feminist Essays*.

Love, Jean O. "Portraying and Explaining Lives: The Case of Virginia Woolf." *Michigan Quarterly Review* 23 (1984): 529–42.

———. *Virginia Woolf: Sources of Madness and Art*. Berkeley and Los Angeles: University of California Press, 1977.

———. *Worlds in Consciousness: Mythopoetic Thought in the Novels of Virginia Woolf*. Berkeley and Los Angeles: University of California Press, 1970.

Lowell, James Russell. *Complete Poetical Works*. Boston: Houghton Mifflin, 1924.

Lundholm, Helge. *The Manic-Depressive Psychosis*. Durham, N.C.: Duke University Press, 1931.

Lyon, George Ella. "Virginia Woolf and the Problem of the Body." 111–26. *See* Ginsberg and Gottlieb.

McCaffrey, Phillip. *Freud and Dora: The Artful Dream*. New Brunswick, N.J.: Rutgers University Press, 1984.

McDowell, Frederick P. W. "'Surely Order Did Prevail': Virginia Woolf and *The Voyage Out*." In *Virginia Woolf: Revaluation and Continuity,* ed. Ralph Freedman, 73–96. Berkeley and Los Angeles: University of California Press, 1980.

McLaurin, Allen. *Virginia Woolf: The Echoes Enslaved*. Cambridge: Cambridge University Press, 1973.

Maitland, Frederic William. *The Life and Letters of Leslie Stephen*. London: Duckworth, 1906.

Manganyi, Noel Chabani. "Psychobiography and the Truth of the Subject." *Biography* 6 (1983): 34–52.

Marcus, Jane. "Quentin's Bogey." *Critical Inquiry* 11 (1985): 486–97.

———. "Tintinnabulations." *Marxist Perspectives* 2 (1979–80): 144–67.

———. "Virginia Woolf and Her Violin: Mothering, Madness and Music." 27–49. *See* Ginsberg and Gottlieb.

Marcus, Jane, ed. *New Feminist Essays on Virginia Woolf*. Lincoln: University of Nebraska Press, 1981.

———. *Virginia Woolf: A Feminist Slant*. Lincoln: University of Nebraska Press, 1983.

Marcus, Steven. "Freud and Dora: Story, History, Case History." 56–91. *See* Collins et al.

Marks, Charles E. *Commissurotomy, Consciousness and Unity of Mind*. Montgomery, Vt.: Bradford, 1980.

Marotti, Arthur F. "Countertransference, the Communication Process, and the Dimensions of Psychoanalytic Criticism." *Critical Inquiry* 4 (1978): 471–89.

Mepham, John. "Mourning and Modernism." 137–56. *See* Clements and Grundy.

Milden, Randy S. "Affective Disorders and Narcissistic Vulnerability." *American Journal of Psychoanalysis* 44 (1984): 345–53.

Milner, Marion (Joanna Field). *On Not Being Able to Paint*. London: Heineman, 1957.

Monsarrat, Ann. *An Uneasy Victorian: Thackeray the Man, 1811–1863*. New York: Dodd, Mead, 1980.

Moody, A. D. *Virginia Woolf*. Edinburgh: Oliver and Boyd, 1963.

Morgenstern, Barry. "The Self-Conscious Narrator in *Jacob's Room*." *Modern Fiction Studies* 18 (1972–73): 351–61.

Morizot, Carol Ann. *Just This Side of Madness: Creativity and the Drive to Create*. Houston: Harold House, 1978.

Naremore, James. *The World Without a Self: Virginia Woolf and the Novel*. New Haven: Yale University Press, 1973.

Nelson, J. Craig, and Dennis S. Charney. "The Symptoms of Major Depressive Illness." *American Journal of Psychiatry* 138 (1981): 1–13.

Neuman, Shirley. "*Heart of Darkness,* Virginia Woolf and the Spectre of Domination." 57–76. *See* Clements and Grundy.

Noble, Joan Russell, ed. *Recollections of Virginia Woolf*. New York: William Morrow, 1972.

Nurnberger, John I., et al. "A Risk Factor Strategy for Investigating Affective Illness." *Biological Psychiatry* 18 (1983): 903–9.

Oakley, David A., ed. *Brain and Mind*. New York: Methuen, 1985.

Oltmanns, Thomas F., and Brendan A. Maher. *Delusional Beliefs*. New York: John Wiley and Sons, 1988.

Ozick, Cynthia. "Mrs. Virginia Woolf." *Commentary* 56 (2) (1973): 33–44.

Packer, Barbara L. "Mania and Depression from the Writer's Point of View: The Case of William Cowper." In *Proceedings of the International Conference on Literature and Psychology*, 223–28. Lisbon, Portugal: Instituto Superior de Psicologia Aplicada, 1991.

Page, Alex. "A Dangerous Day: Mrs. Dalloway Discovers Her Double." *Modern Fiction Studies* 7 (1961–62): 115–24.

Panken, Shirley. *Virginia Woolf and the "Lust of Creation": A Psychoanalytic Exploration*. Albany: State University of New York Press, 1987.

Paul, Janis M. *The Victorian Heritage of Virginia Woolf: The External World in Her Novels*. Norman, Okla.: Pilgrim, 1987.

Paykel, E. S., ed. *Handbook of Affective Disorders*. New York: Guilford, 1982.

Pederson, Glenn. "Vision in *To the Lighthouse*." *PMLA* 73 (1958): 585–600.

Pflug, B., A. Johnsson, and A. Tveito Ekse. "Manic-Depressive States and Daily Temperature." *Acta Psychiatrica Scandinavica* 63 (1981): 277–89.

Pichot, P., and J. Hassan. "Masked Depression and Depressive Equivalents—Problems of Definition and Diagnosis." In *Masked Depression*, ed. P. Kielholz, 61–76. Bern: Hans Huber, 1973.

Pine, Fred. "The Experience of Self: Aspects of Its Formation, Expansion, and Vulnerability." In *The Psychoanalytic Study of the Child*, ed. Albert J. Solnit et al., vol. 37: 143–67. New Haven: Yale University Press, 1982.

Pitt, Rosemary. "The Exploration of Self in Conrad's *Heart of Darkness* and Woolf's *The Voyage Out*." *Conradiana* 10 (1978): 141–54.

Poole, Roger. *The Unknown Virginia Woolf*. New York: Cambridge University Press, 1978.

Poresky, Louise A. *The Elusive Self: Psyche and Spirit in Virginia Woolf's Novels*. Newark, N.J.: University of Delaware Press, 1981.

Pratt, Annis. "Sexual Imagery in *To the Lighthouse*: A New Feminist Approach." *Modern Fiction Studies* 18 (1972–73): 417–32.

Price, William A., and Lynn DiMarzio. "Premenstrual Tension Syndrome in Rapid-Cycling Bipolar Affective Disorder." *Journal of Clinical Psychiatry* 47 (8) (1986): 415–17.

Proudfit, Sharon Wood. "Lily Briscoe's Painting: A Key to Personal Relationships in 'To the Lighthouse.'" *Criticism* 13 (1971): 26–39.

Rado, Sandor. "Psychodynamics of Depression from the Etiologic Point of View." *Psychosomatic Medicine* 13 (1951): 51–55.

Rapp, Dean. "The Reception of Freud by the British Press: General Interest and Literary Magazines, 1920–1925." *Journal of the History of the Behavioral Sciences* 24 (1988): 191–201.

Ray, Gordon N. *Thackeray: The Uses of Adversity (1811–1846)*. New York: McGraw-Hill, 1955.

Rescher, Nicholas. "The Unpredictability of Future Science." In *Physics, Philosophy, and Psychoanalysis: Essays in Honor of Adolf Grunbaum*, ed. R. S. Cohen and L. Laudan, 153–68. Boston: D. Reidel, 1983.

Rice, James L. *Dostoyevsky and the Healing Art: An Essay in Literary and Medical History*. Ann Arbor: Ardis, 1985.

Richardson, Robert O. "Point of View in Virginia Woolf's *The Waves*." *Texas Studies in Language and Literature* 14 (1972–73): 691–709.

Richter, Harvena. *Virginia Woolf: The Inward Voyage*. Princeton, N.J.: Princeton University Press, 1970.

Ritchie, Anne Thackeray. *Toilers and Spinsters and Other Essays*. London: Smith, Elder, 1874.

Ritchie, Hester, ed. *Letters of Anne Thackeray Ritchie*. London: John Murray, 1924.

Rogat, Ellen Hawkes. "The Virgin in the Bell Biography." *Twentieth Century Literature* 20 (1974): 96–113.

Rose, Phyllis. "Mrs. Ramsay and Mrs. Woolf." *Women's Studies* 1 (1973): 199–216.

Rosenman, Ellen Bayuk. *The Invisible Presence: Virginia Woolf and the Mother-Daughter Relationship*. Baton Rouge: Louisiana State University Press, 1986.

Rosenthal, Michael. *Virginia Woolf*. New York: Columbia University Press, 1979.

Roustang, François. "How Do You Make a Paranoiac Laugh?" *MLN* 102 (1987): 707–18.

Ruehlman, Linda S., Stephen G. West, and Robert J. Pasahow. "Depression and Evaluative Schema." *Journal of Personality* 53 (1985): 46–91.

Ruotolo, Lucio P. *The Interrupted Moment: A View of Virginia Woolf's Novels*. Stanford: Stanford University Press, 1986.

Rush, A. John. "Psychotherapy of the Affective Psychoses." *American Journal of Psychoanalysis* 40 (1980): 99–123.

Rush, A. John, et al. "Comparison of the Effects of Cognitive Therapy and Pharmacotherapy on Hopelessness and Self-Concept." *American Journal of Psychiatry* 139 (1982): 862–66.

Sacks, Oliver. *The Man Who Mistook His Wife for a Hat and Other Clinical Tales*. New York: Harper and Row, 1987.

Scherer, Klaus R. "Vocal Assessment of Affective Disorders." In *Depression and Expressive Behavior*, ed. Jack D. Maser, 57–82. Hillsdale, N.J.: Lawrence Erlbaum Associates, 1987.

Schlack, Beverly Ann. *Continuing Presences: Virginia Woolf's Use of Literary Allusion*. University Park, Penn.: Pennsylvania State University Press, 1979.

——. "A Freudian Look at Mrs. Dalloway." *Literature and Psychology* 23 (1973): 49–58.

Schopler, Eric, and Robert J. Reichler. "How Well Do Parents Understand Their Own Psychotic Child?" *Journal of Autism and Childhood Schizophrenia* 2 (1972): 387–400.

Scull, Andrew, ed. *Madhouses, Mad-Doctors, and Madmen: The Social History of Psychiatry in the Victorian Era*. Philadelphia: University of Pennsylvania Press, 1981.

Secunda, Steven K., et al. "Mixed Mania: Diagnosis and Treatment." In *Mania: New Research and Treatment*, ed. Alan C. Swann, 79–94. Washington, D.C.: American Psychiatric Press, 1986.

Segal, Hanna. *Introduction to the Work of Melanie Klein*. New York: Basic Books, 1973.

——. "A Psycho-analytic Approach to Aesthetics." *International Journal of Psycho-Analysis* 33 (1952): 196–207.

Sherman, Murray H. "Psychosensory Images from Virginia Woolf's 'A Sketch of the Past.'" *Psychoanalytic Review* 70 (1983): 33–39.

Showalter, Elaine. *A Literature of Their Own: British Women Novelists from Bronte to Lessing.* Princeton, N.J.: Princeton University Press, 1977.

——. "Victorian Women and Insanity." 313–36. *See* Scull.

Skultans, Vieda. *Madness and Morals: Ideas on Insanity in the Nineteenth Century.* London: Routledge and Kegan Paul, 1975.

Skura, Meredith Anne. *The Literary Use of the Psychoanalytic Process.* New Haven: Yale University Press, 1981.

Slavney, Phillip R., and Paul R. McHugh. *Psychiatric Polarities: Methodology and Practice.* Baltimore: Johns Hopkins University Press, 1987.

Smalley, Susan, Robert F. Asarnow, and M. Anne Spence. "Autism and Genetics: A Decade of Research." *Archives of General Psychiatry* 45 (1988): 953–61.

Spater, George, and Ian Parsons. *A Marriage of True Minds: An Intimate Portrait of Leonard and Virginia Woolf.* New York: Harcourt Brace Jovanovich, 1977.

Spector, Jack J. "Freud and Nineteenth Century Aesthetic Thought." *Book Forum* 1 (1975): 263–74.

Spilka, Mark. *Virginia Woolf's Quarrel with Grieving.* Lincoln: University of Nebraska Press, 1980.

Sprengnether, Madelon. "Enforcing Oedipus: Freud and Dora." 51–71. *See* Garner, Kahane, and Sprengnether.

Springer, Sally P., and Georg Deutsch. *Left Brain, Right Brain.* Rev. ed. New York: W. H. Freeman, 1985.

Squier, Susan. "Mirroring and Mothering: Reflections on the Mirror Encounter Metaphor in Virginia Woolf's Works." *Twentieth Century Literature* 27 (1981): 272–88.

Stephen, Caroline Emelia. *Sir James Stephen—Letters with Biographical Notes.* Eastgate, Gloucestershire: John Bellows, 1906.

Stephen, Herbert. Introduction to *Lapsus Calami and Other Verses,* by James Kenneth Stephen. Cambridge, Eng.: Macmillan and Bowes, 1896.

Stephen, Leslie. *Sir Leslie Stephen's Mausoleum Book.* Introduction by Alan Bell. Oxford: Clarendon, 1977.

——. *Social Rights and Duties.* 2 vols. London: Swan Sonnenschein, 1896.

Stephen, Mrs. Leslie. *Notes from Sick Rooms.* Orono, Me.: Puckerbush, 1980.

Stern, Edward S. "The Psychopathology of Manic-Depressive Disorder and Involutional Melancholia." *British Medical Journal* 20 (1944): 20–32.

Stevens, Janice R. "Psychiatric Aspects of Epilepsy." *Journal of Clinical Psychiatry* 49 (4) (1988): 49–57.

Styron, William. *Darkness Visible: A Memoir of Madness.* New York: Random House, 1990.

Swann, Alan C., ed. *Mania: New Research and Treatment.* Washington, D.C. American Psychiatric Press, 1986.

Thackeray, William Makepeace. *The Letters and Private Papers of William Makepeace Thackeray.* 4 vols. Cambridge, Mass.: Harvard University Press, 1945.

Trombley, Stephen. *All That Summer She Was Mad: Virginia Woolf—Female Victim of Male Medicine.* New York: Continuum, 1982.

Tyrer, Stephen, and Baron Shopsin. "Symptoms and Assessment of Mania." 12–23. *See* Paykel.

Volkmar, Fred R., and Donald J. Cohen. "Neurobiologic Aspects of Autism." *New England Journal of Medicine* 318 (1988): 1390–92.

Wadeson, Harriet S., and William E. Bunney, Jr. "Manic-Depressive Art: A Systematic Study of Differences in a 48-Hour Cyclic Patient." *Journal of Nervous and Mental Disorders* 150 (1970): 215–31.

Waugh, Patricia. *Feminine Fictions: Revisiting the Postmodern.* New York: Routledge, 1989.

Webb, Igor. "'Things in Themselves': Virginia Woolf's *The Waves.*" *Modern Fiction Studies* 17 (1971–72): 570–73.

Wehr, Thomas A., David A. Sack, Norman E. Rosenthal, and Frederick K. Goodwin. "Sleep and Biological Rhythms in Bipolar Illness." *Psychiatry Update: American Psychiatric Association Annual Review* 6 (1987): 61–80.

Wheare, Jane. *Virginia Woolf: Dramatic Novelist.* London: Macmillan, 1989.

Whybrow, Peter C., Hagop S. Akiskal, and William T. McKinney, Jr. *Mood Disorders: Toward a New Psychobiology.* New York: Plenum Press, 1984.

Wilberforce, Octavia. *Octavia Wilberforce: The Autobiography of a Pioneer Woman Doctor.* Ed. Pat Jalland. London: Cassell, 1989.

Wing, J. K. *Reasoning about Madness.* New York: Oxford University Press, 1978.

Winnicott, D. W. *Playing and Reality.* New York: Basic Books, 1971.

Winokur, George. *Depression: The Facts.* Oxford: Oxford University Press, 1981.

Winokur, George, Paula J. Clayton, and Theodore Reich. *Manic-Depressive Illness.* St. Louis: C. V. Mosby, 1969.

Witzel, August E. "Regression in Manic-Depressive Reactions." *Psychiatric Quarterly* 7 (1933): 386–400.

Wolf, Ernest S., and Ina Wolf. "We Perished, Each Alone: A Psychoanalytic Commentary on Virginia Woolf's *To the Lighthouse.*" *International Review of Psycho-Analysis* 6 (1979): 37–47.

Wolpert, Edward A., ed. *Manic-Depressive Illness: History of a Syndrome.* New York: International University Press, 1977.

Woolf, Leonard. *Beginning Again: An Autobiography of the Years 1911 to 1918.* New York: Harcourt Brace Jovanovich, 1964.

———. *Downhill All the Way: An Autobiography of the Years 1919 to 1939.* New York: Harcourt Brace Jovanovich, 1967.

———. *Letters of Leonard Woolf.* Ed. Frederic Spotts. New York: Harcourt Brace Jovanovich, 1989.

Woolf, Leonard, and James Strachey, eds. *Virginia Woolf and Lytton Strachey: Letters.* London: Hogarth and Chatto and Windus, 1969.

———. Monks House Papers. Unpublished manuscripts, University of Sussex Library.

Woolf, Virginia. *The Captain's Death Bed and Other Essays.* New York: Harcourt Brace Jovanovich, 1950.

———. *The Common Reader.* New York: Harcourt Brace Jovanovich, 1953.

———. *Contemporary Writers.* New York: Harcourt Brace Jovanovich, 1976.

———. *The Diary of Virginia Woolf.* Ed. Anne Olivier Bell and Andrew McNeillie. 5 vols. New York: Harcourt Brace Jovanovich, 1976–84.

———. *Granite and Rainbow*. New York: Harcourt Brace Jovanovich, 1958.

———. *Jacob's Room and The Waves*. New York: Harcourt Brace Jovanovich, 1959.

———. *The Letters of Virginia Woolf*. Ed. Nigel Nicolson and Joanne Trautmann. 6 vols. New York: Harcourt Brace Jovanovich, 1975–80.

———. *"The Moment" and Other Essays*. New York: Harcourt Brace Jovanovich, 1948.

———. *Moments of Being: Unpublished Autobiographical Writings*. 2d ed. Ed. Jeanne Schulkind. New York: Harcourt Brace Jovanovich, 1985.

———. *Mrs. Dalloway*. New York: Harcourt Brace Jovanovich, 1953.

———. *A Passionate Apprentice: The Early Journals, 1897–1909*. Ed. Mitchell A. Leaska. San Diego: Harcourt Brace Jovanovich, 1991.

———. "Phases of Fiction." In V. Woolf, *Granite and Rainbow*.

———. *A Room of One's Own*. New York: Harcourt Brace Jovanovich, 1957.

———. *To the Lighthouse*. New York: Harcourt Brace Jovanovich, 1955.

———. *The Voyage Out*. New York: Harcourt Brace Jovanovich, 1948.

———. *The Waves*. New York: Harcourt Brace Jovanovich, 1978.

Yost, Elizabeth, Larry E. Beutler, M. Anne Corbishley, and James R. Allender. *Group Cognitive Therapy: A Treatment Approach for Depressed Older Adults*. New York: Pergamon Press, 1986.

Index

Abbreviations: J. K. (James Kenneth Stephen); mdi (manic-depressive illness); VW (Virginia Woolf)

Abel, Elizabeth, 313n.10, 326n.1
Abraham, Karl, 18, 24, 29
Akiskal, Hagop, 317.n.17
Albee, Edward, 87
Albright, Daniel, 154–55
Alcohol and drug use, and mdi, 12, 20–21, 62, 314–15n.20, 320n.99
Alcorn, Marshall W., Jr., 76, 78, 92, 272, 328n.33 (Ch. 8), 329n.20
Alexander, Jean, 328n.5, 330n.40
Allbutt, Thomas C., 71
Ames, Kenneth, 330n.40
Andreasen, Nancy, 321nn.7,18
Angst, J., 317n.5
Annan, Noel, 323nn.23,26,28, 31,32,38,45, 325nn.33,44, 327n.16
Anorexia, and mdi, 13, 24, 54, 56–57
Anthonisen, N. L., 316n.73
Apter, T. E., 328n.33 (Ch. 7), 329n.14, 330n.40, 331nn.11,26
Arieti, Silvano, 316nn.65,66
Assortative mating, 122
Atwood, George, 325n.23, 327n.14
Autism, 27, 108, 111, 301

Bagenal, Barbara, 23, 40
Baron, Miron, 317n.79, 322n.5
Bassuk, Ellen, 315n.28, 316n.34

Bazin, Nancy, 325n.37, 327n.28, 329n.24
Beck, Aaron, 317n.87, 330n.41, 331n.1 (Ch. 11)
Beers, Clifford, 37, 42, 55–57, 63, 223
Bell, Clive, 10, 98, 320n.99, 329n.19
Bell, Julian, 160
Bell, Millicent, 328n.34
Bell, Quentin: on Anne's hypomania, 325n.44; Freudian bias of, 6, 25, 85, 326n.17; on Sir James's depression, 323n.37; on Julia's death, 116, 131–32; on Laura's disorder, 323n.46; on Stella, 327n.5; on Stephen family rationalism, 128–29; on Thoby's death, 98; on VW's "amazing courage," 327n.11; on VW's marriage, 99; on VW's symptoms, 36, 39, 48, 53, 56, 313n.13, 318nn.27,43, 319n.50, 320n.112, 329n.12
Bennett, Arnold, 197
Bennett, Joan, 198
Berlioz, Hector, 53
Bettelheim, Bruno, 301
Blain, Virginia, 187
Blaney, P., 320n.102
Bloom, Floyd, 317n.2
Blotner, Joseph, 331n.3

349

Bollas, Christopher, 313n.10; on countertransference, 83–84, 148–51, 321n.22, 328n.30; on dream structure, 326n.20; on intrasubjective relations, 214, 292

Bollas, Sara: Freudian bias of, 328n.32 (Ch. 7), 329n.17, 330nn.39,44

Bond, Alma: Freudian bias of, 7, 59–61, 99, 141–42, 313n.7

Bowen, Elizabeth, 39

Boyd, Elizabeth, 325nn.42,46

Braceland, Francis, 316n.65

Brown, Carole, 327n.3

Cade, John, 30

Carlson, Gebrielle, 318n.24

Chodorow, Nancy, 129–30, 326n.6, 330nn.1,4,5–7,21,30 (Ch. 10)

Churchland, Patricia, 332n.13 (Epilogue)

Clark, A. F., 323n.19

Clark, Michael, 71, 315n.31, 320n.119

Collins, Jerre, 316n.41

The Common Reader (Woolf): on modern fiction, 94, 198, 200

Conduct disorder, 36, 108–9

Consciousness and brain structure: brain quadrants and, 205–6; double awareness and, 214, 220–21, 227–29, 289, 291–94; fugue states, 227, 291; Gazzaniga's modular theory of, 296–97; and hemispheric cognitive style, 203–8, 294, 297–300; and hypnotically-induced dissociations, 227, 291–92; invisible deficits and Lacanian psychoanalytic theory, 297–300; mind/brain nexus, 2, 8, 57, 64, 114, 296–302; multiple personality, 227, 291; split brain studies, 203–4, 207, 296–97; "unity" of consciousness, 4, 273–75, 289–302

Contemporary Writers (Woolf): and Jacob's nonbeing, 193

Cook, Blanche, 144, 316n.63

Cooper, Arnold, 316n.68, 322n.39

Cornell, Dewey, 319n.64

Corsa, Helen, 331n.14

Countertransference: definition of, 82–84; examples of, in Woolf's writings, 84–85, 222, 230–1; and hemispheric style, 207–8; as hindrance to psychobiography and psychotherapy, 83–91; as "identity theme" in reading strategies, 75–76; in reading Woolf, 95–97, 141, 170; in Woolf's theory of mirroring, 140–52. *See also* Transference

Courchesne, Eric, 332n.12 (Epilogue)

Cowper, William, 45, 77

Crews, Frederick, 9

Custance, John: cognitive shifts of, 124–25; description of normality by, 211–12; depressive symptoms of, 58, 142, 222; manic visions and delusions of, 42–43, 45–48, 50, 54, 202, 224–25; manic hypersexuality of, 282–83

Cyclothymia: and mdi, 11, 111–13, 218–19, 255–56, 311; and normal mood swings, 33, 72, 163, 212–14, 256; symptoms of, 103, 124, 256. *See also* Manic-depressive illness

Dahl, Christopher C., 326n.8
Daiches, David, 327n.2
Dain, Norman, 317n.15
Davenport, Yolanda, 320n.116
Davis, John, 317nn.81,85,13, 323n.44
Defoe, Daniel, 199, 202
Depressive states, 51–68; anhedonic depression, 116–18, 120; agitated depression, 125, 165–66, 260; cognitive impairment in, 52, 57–58, 63, 67, 69, 75, 79, 124–25, 222–23, 233, 252–53, 260, 278, 285, 325; emotional responses in, 29, 52, 54, 58, 62–65, 89–90, 142; hallucinations and delusions associated with, 34, 54–58, 60–64, 212–13, 219–23, 224–26; infantile depression, 134–37; physical manifestations of, 13, 52–54, 57–58, 66, 102, 109, 124, 144, 280; treatment of, 31–32, 89; types of, 8, 52–53, 65. *See also* Suicide; Manic-depressive illness
Derby, Irving, 323n.17
DeSalvo, Louise: on anorexia, 56–57; on fiction as disguise, 25, 327n.4; Freudian bias of, 7–8, 14, 147–48, 181, 316n.39; on Laura's disorder, 110; on suicide, 87; on VW's sedation, 21
Dick, Susan, 327n.19
Dickinson, Violet, 15, 25, 144, 162
Donnelly, Edward F., 327n.25
Dooley, Lucile, 320n.114

DSM-III-R: on genetics of mdi, 103; on limitations of neurosis, 11–12; on mania, 39–40; on sleep disturbances, 53
Duckworth, George: genes of, 112; tyranny of, 133, 247, 257–58
Duckworth, Gerald: genes of, 112; molestation of VW by, 14, 143–48, 152, 158, 167; tyranny of, 133, 247
Duckworth, Herbert: family myth of, 115–18, 122, 129, 141, 158–59, 251–52; genes of, 112
Duckworth, Julia. *See* Stephen, Julia
Duckworth, Stella: death of, 149, 158–61, 163, 257–58; genes of, 112; pursued by J. K., 101; selflessness of, 15–16; as victim of projections, 172–73, 179, 183

Eagle, M., 332n.10 (Epilogue)
Edel, Leon, 84
Edelson, Marshall, 81, 300–301
Egeland, Janice A., 317n.79
Egotism: and mdi, 10–11, 46, 50, 72, 143, 215, 241, 259
Ehrenzweig, Anton, 200–204, 206–8
Epilepsy, 27–28, 110

Feinstein, Sherman C., 313n.1 (Ch. 1), 317n.9, 326n.2
Felman, Shoshana, 82, 322nn.48,49
Fenichel, Otto, 135, 152–53
Ferguson, Suzanne, 329nn.6,7
Fiction: danger of "egotistical order" in, 185–86; fictionality

Fiction (continued)
of biographical studies,
81–83, 90, 196–97, 322n.29;
"hidden order" in, 200; integration of manic-depressive
cognition in, 70, 75–96,
135–37, 152, 239, 268–69;
and interhemispheric integration, 206; necessary ambiguity
of, 94; restores self-esteem for
VW, 148–152, 250;
subjective-objective com-
ponents of, 45; Woolf's
theory of, 79–80, 90–96,
136–37, 196
Fieve, Ronald R., 317nn.77,78,
82,84, 318n.40
Fleishman, Avrom, 328n.35
Flor-Henry, P., 328n.29
Freud, Sigmund: analytic
method of, 27–29, 60–61,
144–46, 167, 300–301;
attitudes toward art, 9, 136;
Dora's case, 18–19, 84,
144–46; "Mourning and
Melancholia," 17, 29;
popularity of, 18, 26–27;
principle of psychic determinism, 81; sexism of, 18–19
Freudianism: and diagnosis of
neurosis, 11, 25–26, 31,
65–66, 98, 114; misapplica-
tions of, 14, 27, 29–30, 111,
301–2; as paranoia, 82;
reductionism of, 2, 9, 24,
47–48, 84, 95, 170;
resistance to neuroscience in,
6–8, 26–27; sexism and, 25,
38, 84
Freudian view of manic-depressive
illness: cure rates, 30; on
mania as escape wish, 29,

141–42; on mdi's "encoded
symptoms," 7, 26–28, 39,
47–48, 55–57, 60–65,
81–82, 84, 115, 130–31,
135, 149, 179, 223, 304; on
mdi as "regressive," 24, 115;
on mdi as unreconciled conflicts, 60, 99; moralism of,
80, 87, 89; on reduction of
bipolarity, 61; on vicious
superego, 64
Freudian views of Virginia
Woolf and her fiction: 1–2,
6–9, 18; as containing encoded symptoms, 39, 47–48,
56–57, 62–64, 130; as defensive, 25, 138–40, 179,
229–30, 277; on The Voyage
Out, 170–71, 179, 181–83;
on Jacob's Room, 197–98,
201, 205–8; on Moments of
Being, 138–42, 144–49; on
Mrs. Dalloway, 217–18,
221–22, 229–30, 233,
236–37; on To the Lighthouse,
246, 248–49; on The Waves,
285, 290; view of VW as
regressive, 86–87, 141–42; on
VW's traumas, 6–8, 59–61,
130–33, 143–48
Fry, Roger, 92, 137
Furse, Charles, 160

Garland, Madge, 40, 49
Garnett, Angelica (née Bell), 22,
111, 120–21, 238
Garnett, David, 49
Garrison, Dee, 316n.42
Gaylin, Willard, 64–65,
316n.73, 326nn.4,28
Gazzaniga, Michael, 296–97,
332n.6 (Epilogue)

Georgotas, Anastasio: on age of mdi onset, 317nn.12,14, 326n.2; on anti-manic drugs, 317n.80; on depressive symptoms, 319nn.70,77, 320nn.84,108, 327n.25; on etiologies of depression, 317n.83; on genetics of mdi, 322n.2, 324n.65; on insomnia, 316n.46; on related disorders, 322n.6, 323n.20; on suicide, 232, 318n.24, 320nn.93,118, 330n.42

Gerin, Winifred, 325nn.45, 46,48

Gershon, Elliot, 322n.1, 324n.65

Gillespie, Diane, 324n.5

Goldberg, Steven, 316nn.67,70, 322n.53

Goldstein, Jan, 314n.17, 316n.39

Goodwin, Donald, 320n.107, 322n.41, 323n.8

Goodwin, Frederick: on anti-manic drugs, 317n.83; on associated infections, 315n.24; on brain structure and mdi, 328nn.20,24,28; on cognitive impairment, 318n.30, 320n.118; on constipation, 323n.16; on cyclothymia, 323n.20; on euthymic state, 313n.1 (Intro.), 329n.4; on family support of patients, 316n.53, 325n.31; on genetics of mdi, 324n.67; on manic paranoia, 318n.24; on mood cycles, 317nn.4,6,7,16, 320n.98; on sleep therapy, 316nn.43–45; on triggering mechanisms, 314–15n.20, 323n.7, 324n.57, 325n.47

Gordon, Lyndall, 48–49, 318nn.28,29, 323n.35, 327nn.7,19, 331n.2 (Ch. 11), 332n.13 (Ch. 11)

Granite and Rainbow (Woolf): on art and health, 73–74; on discordant art, 199–200, 202, 208–9, 274

Grant, Duncan, 39

Grunbaum, Adolf, 332n.9 (Epilogue)

Guiguet, Jean, 327nn.8,28, 328n.34

Guilford, J. P., 321n.12

Hafley, James, 199, 210, 327n.30, 328n.10

Hamilton, Max, 319n.70, 320nn.88,106,110

Haring-Smith, Tori, 329n.9

Harper, Howard, 329nn.1,8,13,18, 330nn.35,46, 332nn.6,11 (Ch. 11), 15

Harrison, Michael, 323nn.13,18

Harrow, Martin, 330n.34

Haynal, Andre, 324n.3

Heine, Elizabeth, 25

Henke, Suzette, 329n.24

Hershman, D. Jablow, 321n.10

Hilgard, Ernest, 291–92, 293–94

Hill, Katherine, 313n.15

Hills, Jack, 149, 159

Hills, Margaret, 160–61, 183

Hobson, J. Allan, 327n.17

Hodgkinson, Stephen, 322n.6

Holland, Norman, 75–76, 85, 238, 332n.18

Holliday, Robin, 324n.64

Hollister, Leo, 315n.23

Hopkins, Gerard Manley, 77, 93

Hoppe, Klaus, 328n.22
Horner, Althea, 321n.4,
  326n.29
Horney, Karen, 19
Hunter, Dianne, 322n.46
Hyman, Virginia: 313n.15,
  315n.29, 324n.62; Freudian
  bias of, 138–40, 154,
  328n.32 (Ch. 7)
Hypochondria, and mdi: 11,
  13, 57, 124

Introspection, limitations of,
  47–48, 54–57, 62–63,
  81–82, 205–8, 223, 229,
  299–302
Isherwood, Christopher, 49

Jacob's Room (Woolf): 98, 156,
  183, 185–210; and agitated
  depression, 188–90; and
  anhedonic depression,
  189–90; and depressive cognition, 191–92, 195; depressive
  imagery in, 188–93; hypomanic imagery in, 193–94;
  interhemispheric processing
  in, 203–8; interpretive
  strategies of, 195–200, 230,
  244, 288, 297; syncretistic
  vision in, 200–204, 206–8

Jacobson, Edith, 60, 152
Jamison, Kay Redfield: on body
  weight, 316n.58; on creativity
  and mdi, 80, 321nn.5,6,8,9,11,
  13–16; on episode cycles,
  317nn.7,11,17,18; on
  cyclothymia, 323n.20; definition of mdi by, 317n.1; on
  depression, 319nn.64,67,74,
  76, 320nn.84,85,89,104,118,

323n.16; diagnosis of VW by,
  313n.1 (Ch. 1); on drugs and
  mdi, 314–15n.20, 316n.52,
  318n.45; on euthymic state,
  313n.1 (Intro.), 317nn.17,18,
  321n.120, 329n.4; on family
  issues, 313n.14, 316n.53,
  324n.18, 331n.29; on interhemispheric processing,
  328nn.25–27; on mania, 50,
  317n.19, 318nn.31,32,34,
  323n.15, 332n.7 (Ch. 11); on
  mixed states, 53, 318n.42; on
  misdiagnoses, 317n.11,
  324n.49; on psychotherapy,
  87–88, 317nn.81,84–86,
  327n.23; on sleep therapy,
  316nn.44,47; on suicide,
  320nn.89,91,92,94,99
Jensen, Emily, 330n.38
Johnson, Marcia, 319n.78
Jones, Richard, 326n.19

Keitel, Evelyne, 91–92, 328n.19
Keller, Martin: on common
  misdiagnoses, 324nn.49,1; on
  cyclothymia, 323n.2; on
  genetics of mdi, 322n.3,
  323n.11; on mania, 317n.20;
  on mixed states, 317n.16; on
  neurosis and mdi, 317n.84,
  324n.1
Kelley, Alice van Buren,
  327n.28, 329n.14, 330n.44,
  332n.5 (Ch. 11)
Kenney, Susan, Freudian bias of,
  39, 86–87, 313n.2, 315n.30
Kinsbourne, Marcel, 320n.103,
  321n.10, 328n.21
Klein, Melanie, 134–36, 149,
  202–3, 326n.1
Kraus, A., 320n.118, 325n.38

Kraepelin, Emil, 13, 26, 28, 34–35, 90
Kreutz, Irving, 330n.37
Kushen, Betty, Freudian bias of, 313nn.2,7, 316nn.39,40, 325n.54

Lacan, Jacques, 299–300
Lamb, Walter, 10
Leaska, Mitchell: counter-transference of, 170; Freudian bias of, 181–82, 329nn.13, 17,24,44; reading strategy of, 197–98, 201, 236–37
Lee, Hermione, 328n.34
Lehmann, Rosamond, 10
Lesser, Simon, Freudian bias of, 89–90, 313n.2, 316n.75
Levy, Elinor, 315n.24
Lidoff, Joan, 331n.15
Lilienfeld, Jane, 331nn.9,24
Little, Judy, 328n.1 (Ch. 8)
Love, Jean: on meaning of *Euphrosyne*, 327n.20; Freudian bias of, 313n.2; on Gerald's abuse of VW, 144; on Julia's death, 325nn.55,57; on Julia's grief, 324nn.6,7,20; on Laura's disorder, 324n.48; on Leslie's games, 325nn.26, 28,32,34, 326n.12; on Leslie's moods, 323nn.22,27,30,33,34; on mothering, 331n.3; on Dr. Savage, 315n.29; on Stella's death, 327n.6; on VW's losses, 327n.12; on VW's weaning, 325n.51
Lowell, James Russell, 97
Lowell, Robert, 81
Lundholm, Helge, 11
Lyon, George, 327nn.9,31, 330n.49

McCaffrey, Phillip, 145–46, 150
McDowell, Frederick, 327nn.10,29
Maitland, Frederic, 323nn.21,24,25,42
McLaurin, Allen, 329n.19
Manganyi, Noel, 84
Manic-defense, infantile: Klein's theory of, 134–37, 216, 285
Manic-depressive illness, biological factors in, 39; association with bodily rhythms/disorders, 10–11, 13–14, 19, 21, 24, 33, 61–62, 66, 98, 102–3, 110, 115, 126, 314–15n.20; genetic factors in, 26, 30, 97–98, 101, 103, 111–13, 317n.79; and hemispheric impairment, 204–6; and immune function, 14
Manic-depressive illness, and creativity: 76–80, 95, 203, 264–65
Manic-depressive illness, and other psychiatric disorders: 10–11, 26, 36, 108–9
Manic-depressive illness, symptoms of: course and onset, 35–37, 44, 134, 326n.2; double awareness of, 42, 107, 227–29, 292–93; euthymic state, 2, 60–61, 68–69, 72, 114, 192, 211–12, 241; and family issues, 21–23, 54, 62–63, 105–6, 118, 122, 255–59; identity problems, 68–69, 72, 80, 239; mixed states, 35–36, 44, 53, 205; self-structure, 32, 33, 37, 114, 293, 318n.47, 321n.120

Manic-depressive illness, treatment of: 1, 13, 19–21, 26,
28–32, 103, 154, 231–32, 272
Manic states: 39–51; cognitive
impairment in, 41–42,
46–47, 51, 63, 69, 75,
78–79, 124–25, 202,
222–23, 227; and creativity,
30, 33, 40–44, 50, 76–77,
283; and delusions, 40,
42–43, 45–47, 50–51, 55,
221, 224, 229; and hallucinations, 39, 42, 175, and
hypersexuality, 54, 101, 142,
280, 282–83; and hyper-
thyroidism, 312; and
hypomania, 40, 78–79; and
impulsivity, 24, 40–41, 51,
62–63, 126; "manic death,"
102; and rage, 39, 44; and
suicide, 40
Mansfield, Katherine, 73–74
Marcus, Jane, 25, 133, 313n.10,
314n.19, 315n.27, 325n.35
Marcus, Steven, 84, 313n.10
Marks, Charles, 332n.6 (Epilogue)
Marotti, Arthur, 322n.28,
326n.27
Mayer, Louie, 22
Menstruation, and mdi, 13,
16–17, 20, 313
Mental retardation, 108, 110
Mepham, John, 322n.52
Meredith, George, 166
Milden, Randy, 320n.115
Milner, Marion (Joanna Field),
264–69
Milton, John, 63, 87
Mitchell, S. Weir, 12, 14,
16–17, 133
"The Moment" and Other Essays
(Woolf): and Anne Ritchie's
style, 127; on assets of illness,

93, 156, 234–35, 305; on
psychobiography, 85
Moments of Being (Woolf):
bipolar identity in, 63;
epiphanal perceptions in, 51,
227, 249; on J. K.'s madness,
101; on Julia's character,
116–20, 129, 252; on Julia's
death, 131–32, 183; and
Laura's disorder, 108; on
Leslie's moods, 105, 255–57;
"A Sketch of the Past,"
136–55, 196, 227; on Stella's
character, 159–60, 172–73;
and therapeutic acts, 96,
244–45; on Vanessa's
character, 158–59; and VW's
hallucination, 220; and VW's
hypomania, 294, 303–4
Monsarrat, Ann, 324nn.50,51,
53,56
Moody, A. D., 327n.30, 331n.3
Morgenstern, Barry, 328n.6
Morizot, Carol, 313n.1 (Ch.1),
315n.32, 324n.66
Mrs. Dalloway (Woolf): 210–43;
bird imagery in, 47; Bradshaw
(character) in, 122, 198;
depressive cognition in, 221,
232–33, 271–72; depressive
passivity in, 226; depiction of
double awareness in, 226–28,
293; and effect of mdi on
self-structure, 226–29, 231,
275; immunity in, 38, 150,
232–38, 244–45, 251–53;
loss in, 183, 208; mirroring
and interpretation in, 218,
228–29, 249–50; paranoia in,
223, 229, 267; projections in,
216–18; psychotic features in,
219–21, 224, 293; suicide in,
223, 232

Muggeridge, Malcolm, 317n.23

Naremore, James, Freudian bias
of, 164, 313n.2, 327n.4,
329n.10, 332n.3 (Ch. 11)
Nelson, J. Craig, 319n.66
Neuman, Shirley, 328n.32
(Ch. 7)
Neurasthenia, definition of,
11–12
Nicolson, Nigel, 49
Night and Day (Woolf): and
Anne Ritchie's expansiveness,
127; flatness of, 8, 44, 72
Noble, Joan, 313n.11,
316nn.55,56, 317n.21,
318n.27, 319nn.54,56–59
Norton, Charles Eliot, 119,
121, 183
Nurnberger, John, 323n.8

Oakley, David, 328n.32 (Ch. 8),
332nn.16,23
Oltmanns, Thomas, 318n.37,
319n.78,79, 329nn.21–23,
330nn.30,31,34,36,
332nn.20,21
Orlando (Woolf), 270
Ozick, Cynthia, 316n.60

Packer, Barbara, 318n.46
Page, Alex, 330n.37
Panken, Shirley: Freudian bias
of, 6–7, 89–90, 99; decoding
method of, 47–48, 93, 179,
181, 183, 233; on VW's
morbidity, 313n.7, 316nn.39,
40; on psychosomatic
criticism, 14, 87, 315n.30
Partridge, Ralph, 144, 167
A Passionate Apprentice (Woolf):
and Adrian's depression, 111;

and "the flight of the mind,"
93; on Stephen family, 128;
on value of sociability, 232
Paul, Janis, 325n.40
Paykel, E. S., 323n.8, 324n.2
Pederson, Glenn, 331n.8 (Ch. 10)
Pflug, B., 314–15n.20
Pichot, P., 315n.22, 325n.38
Pine, Fred, 325n.53
Pitt, Rosemary, 327n.30
Poole, Roger, 313n.6
Poresky, Louise, 329nn.13,17,
330n.40
Poulet, Georges, 76
Pratt, Annis, 331n.10
Price, William, 314–15n.20
Proudfit, Sharon, 331n.8 (Ch. 10)

Rado, Sandor, 123, 316n.73
Rapp, Dean, 316n.38
Raverat, Jacques, 238
Ray, Gordon, 324n.53
Read, Herbert, 91
Reader-response theory: and
countertransference, 83–89;
and filtering of "alien"
thoughts, 69, 76, 78, 83–86,
91–93, 219, 272, 289, 292;
and reader's role, 198–99,
230, 275, 291
Rescher, Nicholas, 332n.8
(Epilogue)
Rice, James, 316n.72
Richardson, Robert, 332n.13
(Ch. 11)
Richter, Harvena, 322n.51,
332n.4 (Ch. 11)
Ritchie, Anne Thackeray: 75,
125–29, 133, 136, 234, 237;
hypomanic features of,
125–26, 196
Rogat, Ellen Hawkes, 316n.60

A Room of One's Own (Woolf), 233–37
Rorschach tests, 327n.25
Rose, Phyllis, 331nn.2,17,23 (Ch. 10)
Rosenman, Ellen, 331n.30
Rosenthal, Michael, 327n.4, 328n.9, 329n.14, 330n.44
Rothschild, Barbara, 48
Roustang, François, 321n.21
Ruehlman, Linda, 317n.87
Ruotolo, Lucio, 328nn.34,3, 330nn.48,51
Rush, A. John, 317n.87, 327n.27
Ruskin, John, 304–5

Sacks, Oliver, 297–98
Sackville-West, Vita, 10, 20, 25, 37, 60, 144, 243
Sainsbury, Dr., 71
Savage, George, 11–20, 23–25, 38, 71, 101, 110, 133
Scherer, Klaus, 327n.26
Schizophrenia, 26, 36, 43, 108
Schlack, Beverly, 327nn.15,21, 24; Freudian bias of, 328n.33, 329nn.17,24, 330nn.38,43,44
Schopler, Eric, 324n.61
Schou, Mogens, 30
Scull, Andrew, 314n.18, 316n.37
Secunda, Steven, 317n.8
Segal, Hanna, 313n.8, 326nn.3,5,7, 327n.18
Sherman, Murray, 313n.2
Showalter, Elaine, 314–15n.20, 316nn.33,35,36
Skultans, Vieda, 315n.28
Skura, Meredith, 313n.10, 326n.18

Slavney, Phillip, 313n.1 (Ch. 1)
Smalley, Susan, 332n.11 (Epilogue)
Smyth, Ethel, 25, 39–41, 84–85
Spater, George, 316n.57, 319n.53
Spector, Jack, 313n.8
Spilka, Mark, Freudian bias of, 25, 86, 313n.2, 315n.30, 329n.14, 330n.44
Sprengnether, Madelon, 316n.41
Springer, Sally, 328n.31
Squier, Susan, 329n.15, 331n.13
Stephen, Adrian, 15, 18, 111, 134
Stephen, Harry, 218
Stephen, Herbert, 101–2
Stephen, Sir James, 52, 106–7, 112, 142–43, 146–47, 227, 285
Stephen, James Kenneth (J. K.), 101–3
Stephen, Jane (née Venn), 103–4, 112, 121
Stephen, Julia (Duckworth): death of, 6, 9, 14, 25, 34, 46–47, 60–61, 63, 67, 81, 86, 90, 131–32, 153, 158–59, 163, 183; depression of, 115–24, 187, 189, 196, 235, 272; genes of, 111–13; inadequate mothering of VW by, 7, 59, 129–31; marriage to Leslie, 106, 136, 139, 256–59; as Mrs. Ramsay, 246–47, 251–52, 262, 269; *Notes From Sick Rooms*, 117; as victim, 15–16, 96; VW's memories of, 140–41
Stephen, Katharine, 110
Stephen, Laura, 14, 107–111
Stephen, Leslie: cyclothymia of, 11, 98, 103–7, 121, 124–29,

Stephen, Leslie *(continued)* 136, 165–66, 175, 186, 194, 196, 202, 204, 253, 255–59, 272–73; and maladaptive response to cyclothymia, 14, 72, 104–5, 121–25, 131–33, 158, 183, 188, 218, 232, 235, 251, 255–60; symptoms of cyclothymia, compared to VW's mdi, 226, 311; genes of, 99, 101, 112–13; as Laura's father, 107–11; marriage to Julia, 115–24, 131–32, 139, 141, 245; *Leslie Stephen's Mausoleum Book,* 104, 106, 108–10, 115–18, 121–22, 125, 127, 132, 186, 189, 244, 247, 251, 261; *Social Rights and Duties,* 119–20; unpublished letters, 101, 121, 183; as villain, 47, 110–11, 247

Stephen, Thoby, 60, 98, 111, 149, 162–63, 195

Stephen, Vanessa: 47, 110, 160; character of, 120, 158, 173, 257; depressions of, 111; view of VW's character, 162; VW's feelings about, 15, 53, 59–60

Stern, Edward, 316n.73

Stevens, Janice, 316n.71

Strachey, Alix, 49

Strachey, Lytton, 24, 156

Styron, William, 52–53, 57, 227–28

Suicide: and age, 61; and alcohol, 62; incidence of, 58–59; in mania, 40; masked suicide, 59; seasonal suicides, 61; symbolic value of, 8, 9, 59, 87

Swann, Alan, 317n.80

Thackeray, Harriet ("Minny"), 109–10

Thackeray, Isabella, 109–10

Thackeray, William Makepeace, 109–10

Thomas, Edward, 303

Three Guineas (Woolf), 38

Thyroid disorders, 126, 312

To the Lighthouse (Woolf), 244–69; and agitated depression, 260, 264; ambivalence in, 254–56, 264–69; and bipolar art, 95–96, 253–54, 270–73, 290; and depressive cognition, 136, 266–67; and depressive depersonalization, 250–51; and distorted perceptions, 245–48, 260–61; double awareness in, 266; family issues in, 256–59; hypomania in, 44; and immunity, 183–84, 208, 251–52, 262–63; mothering in, 245–47; narcissistic perceptions in, 51, 248–49; mirroring in, 260–61; self-structure in, 37–38

Transference: 31–32, 146, 148, 152–54

Trick, K. L. K., 102

Trombley, Stephen, 314n.19, 315n.27, 316nn.34,39,48, 324n.60, 325n.58

Tucker, Don, 328n.23

Tyrer, Stephen, 318n.38

Victorian attitudes toward madness: common diagnostic confusions, 108, 110; Lunacy Act of 1890, 16; moralism of, 14–15, 24–25, 212; and diagnosis of neurasthenia, 12, 17, 20; sexism of, 14–17, 38

Volkmar, Fred, 332n.12
(Epilogue)
The Voyage Out (Woolf):
156–86; advantages of depression depicted in, 165–70;
agitated depression in, 167,
264; delirium in, 177–80;
depressive cognition in, 25,
72, 95, 176, 178; manic
perceptions in, 173–76;
mood shifts in, 244, 253;
mood without cause in,
169–70; paranoia in, 165–66,
178–79; passivity in, 164;
Rachel versus Jacob in,
190–91; rapid mood shifts in,
171–73, 173–76; and sexual
abuse, 158, 178–79

Waterlow, Sydney, 68
Waugh, Patricia, 313n.10
The Waves (Woolf), 270–95;
and agitated depression,
276–78, 284–85; and
anhedonic depression, 67,
278–79; depressive cognition
in, 285, 285–87, 288–89;
depressive depersonalization
in, 279; depressive masochism
in, 286; double awareness in,
289; and effect of mdi on
self-structure, 289–90; and
ensemble psyche, 296–97;
and Julia's death, 132, 154;
and manic state, 280–84; and
syncretistic inclusion, 241
Webb, Igor, 332n.14
(Ch. 11)
Wehr, Thomas, 314–15n.20,
315n.21, 316n.46
Westermayer, Joseph, 319n.79
Wheare, Jane, 327n.28

Whybrow, Peter, 314–15n.20,
318nn.25,39, 319n.65,
320n.86, 322n.4, 332n.12
(Ch. 11)
Wilberforce, Octavia, 320n.99
Wing, J. K., 302
Winnicott, D. W., 76, 149,
152, 249, 329n.16, 331n.18
Winokur, George, 58–59,
314n.20, 318nn.33,38,41,
319n.63, 320nn.100,107,113
Witzel, August, 316nn.59,74
Wolf, Ernest, 9, 15, 313n.7,
315n.30, 331n.8 (Ch. 10)
Wolpert, Edward, 314n.20
Woolf, Leonard: on Adrian's
depressions, 111; Beginning
Again, on VW's symptoms,
12, 17–18, 34, 46, on VW's
sanity, 37, on VW's guilt,
64, 178, 211, 228, on theory
of VW's insanity, 239–40; on
double awareness, 178, 211,
228, 239; Downhill All the
Way, 20; as possible factor in
VW's suicide, 59; Monks
House Papers, on VW's
sedatives, 20–21, 306–10;
collection of mood swing data
by, 306–10; as object of
VW's paranoia, 50; observations of Virginia's symptoms
by, 10, 12, 15, 17–18, 34,
36, 39, 71, 239, 272; as
VW's husband, 150, 158,
235; as VW's nurse, 12,
19–24, 124
Woolf, Virginia, aesthetics of:
on modern fiction, 91–96,
187, 199–200, 202; sense of
a "modern" self, 73, 151,
297; theory of a "moment of

Woolf, Virginia *(continued)*
being," 50–51, 158, its
critical-creative components,
70, its manic and depressive
components, 136–37, 155,
208, 230–35, 241–43, 249,
the "fun" of, 148, 218, 242,
269, uncanny "third voice"
in, 150–51, 250, 254,
265–67, 269, 283; open-
ended symbolism, 95–96,
149, 168, 235; and syn-
cretistic vision, 200–203,
206–8, 242; therapeutic value
of, 151–52, 155

Woolf, Virginia, attitudes of:
ambivalence, 244; projection,
196, 216–18, 245, 246–47,
260, 265; toward psycho-
analysis, 18–19, 24, 80, 96;
and reading strategies, 69–73,
117, 208–9, 238–39, 328

Woolf, Virginia, coping with
loss: 115, 122, 245; euthymic
personality, 10, 36, 37, 56,
73, 90, 124, 245

Woolf, Virginia, and depressive
states: 34; advantages of, 67–70,
90; agitated depression, 53;
anhedonic depression, 66–67;
cognition in, 57–58, 67,
125–28, 271–72; and creativity,
66–67; depersonalization,
15–16, 65, 67, 146–48;
Freudian views of, 6–7, 29,
86–87, 89–90, 130–31; guilt,
14, 34, 56–57; paranoia, 56,
64; physical symptoms, 11–13,
52–53, 65–67, 73, 271; and
sexual abuse, 7–8, 14, 47,
56–57; and suicide, 6, 16,
34, 59–62, 149

Woolf, Virginia, differentiating
moods of: distinct mood
shifts, 65–66, 73, 240–43,
271; double awareness of
moods, 271–73; mixed states,
35–37, 44, 46, 53, 244;
Leonard's observations of,
17–18, 34, 36, 211; triggering mechanisms of, 11–13,
20–22, 63, 66, 98–99, 318,
324; Virginia's observations
of, 10, 35, 37–38, 50, 71

Woolf, Virginia, and effects of
mdi on her life: achieving
immunity, 271–73; and
eroticism, 25, 144, 283; and
feminism, 15–16, 38, 67; and
hidden core, 37–38, 68–74,
208, 240–42; perception of
multiple selves, 273, 290; and
object-relations, 129–37,
142–48, 150–51; self-blame,
10, 15, 50, 72, 143, 241,
258–60; self-structure,
34, 212–13, 275; sensitivity
to egotism in art, 185–86,
202

Woolf, Virginia, manic states:
39–51; assets of hypomania,
44, 46, 48–50, 79; cognitive
impairment in, 34, 41, 44,
70, 78; hallucinations in, 34,
46, 47, 273; heightened
perceptions in, 46, 78; and
hypersexuality, 283; im-
pulsivity in, 40, 327; and
hypomanic imagery, 140–41;
and manic invention, 78,
186; paranoia/irritability in,
34, 39, 40, 47, 49, 50;
manic speech in, 34, 46;
volubility in, 48–49

Woolf, Virginia, physical symptoms: 11–14, 20, 22–23, 65–66; and rest cure, 12, 19–24, on mixed blessings of, 16, 133

Yost, Elizabeth, 232

Zweig, Arnold, 322n.29

Compositor: Execustaff
Text: 10/13 Galliard
Display: Galliard
Printer and Binder: Edwards Brothers